COMIC BOOK ★NOT FOR CHILDREN★

FANTAGRAPHICS BOOKS (SEATTLE, WA)

DRAWN MARCH 2005 → AUGUST 2007

• THREE PARTS — TAKE BREAKS FROM READING BETWEEN THEM. •

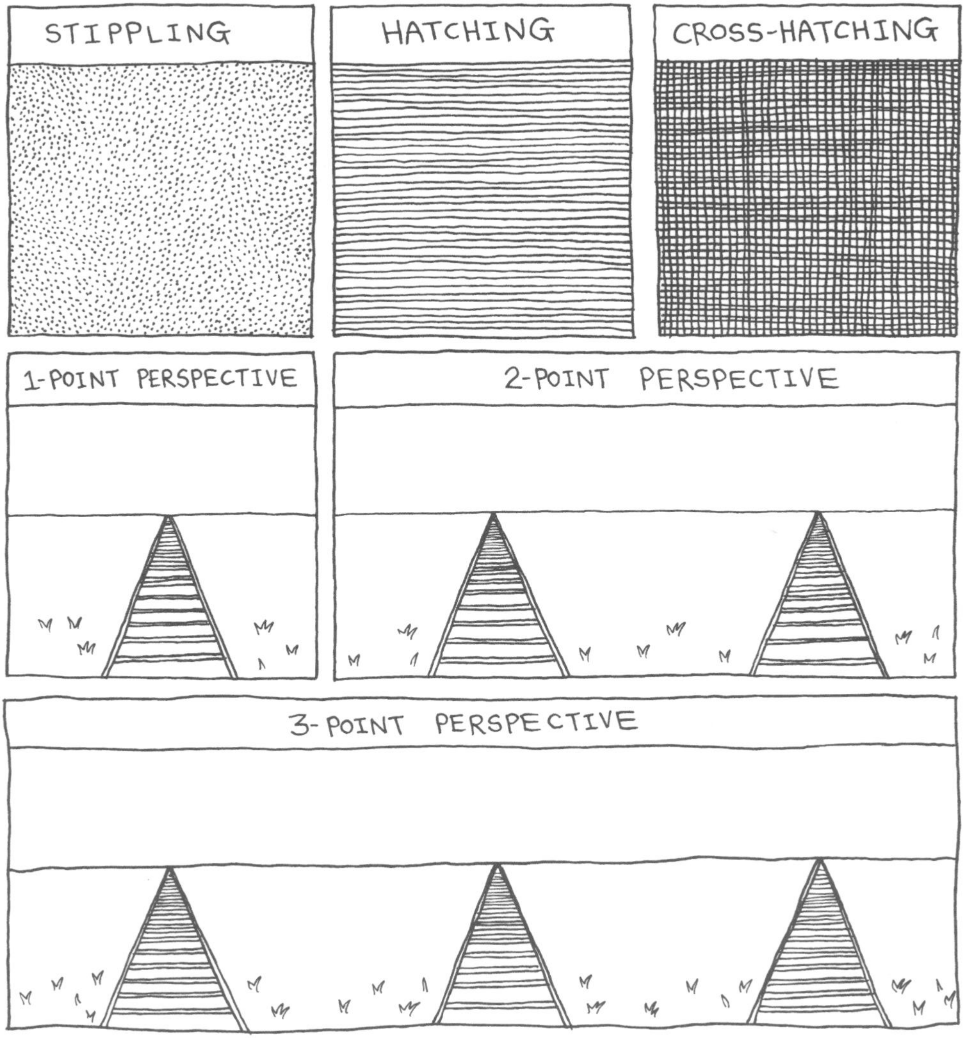

EDITED BY GARY GROTH. DESIGNED BY JACOB COVEY. PUBLISHED BY GARY GROTH.

FANTAGRAPHICS BOOKS INC. 7563 LAKE CITY WAY NE, SEATTLE, WA 98115
WWW.FANTAGRAPHICS.COM

ISBN: 978-1-56097-915-9

PRINTED IN KOREA THROUGH PRINT VISION.

Part One

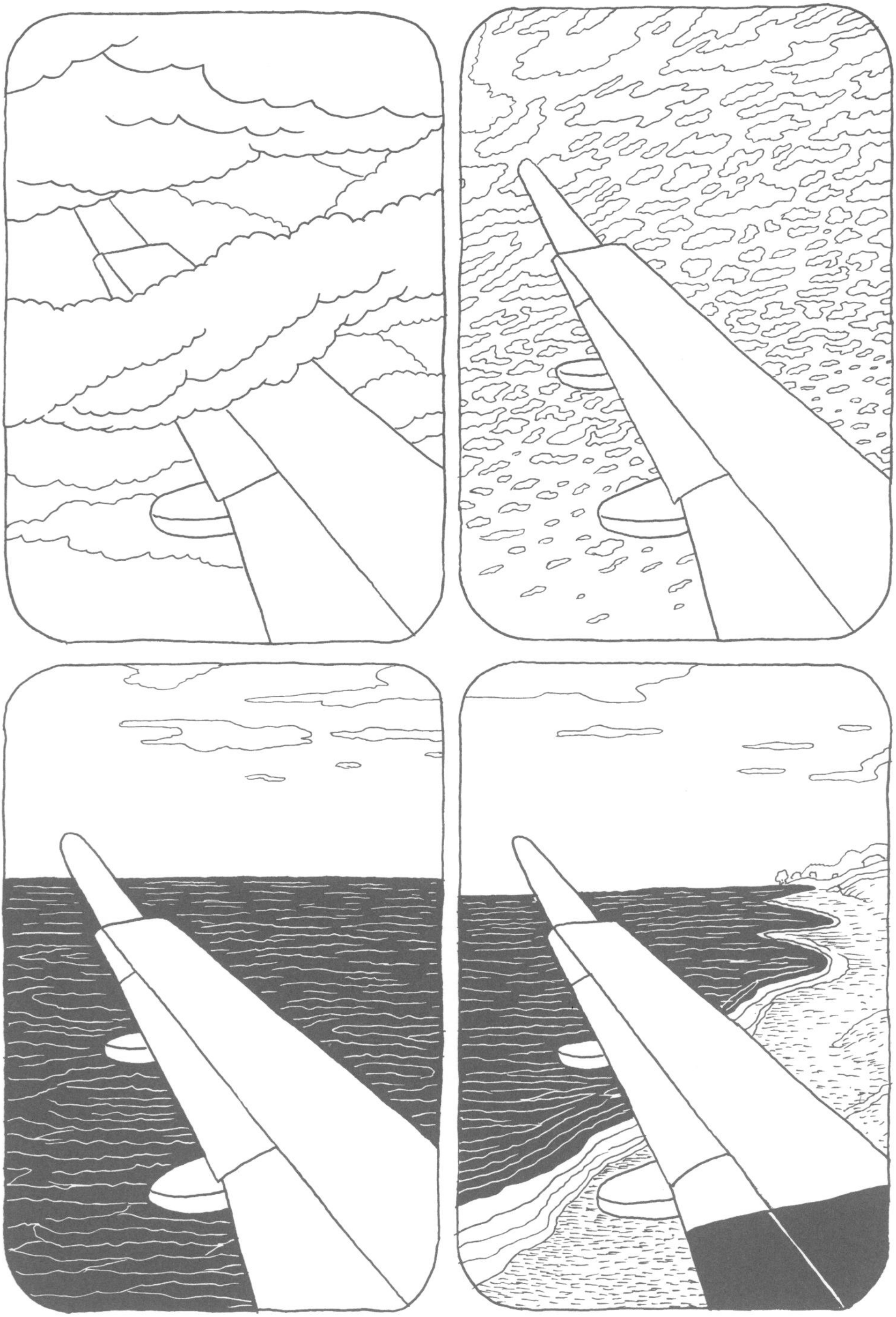

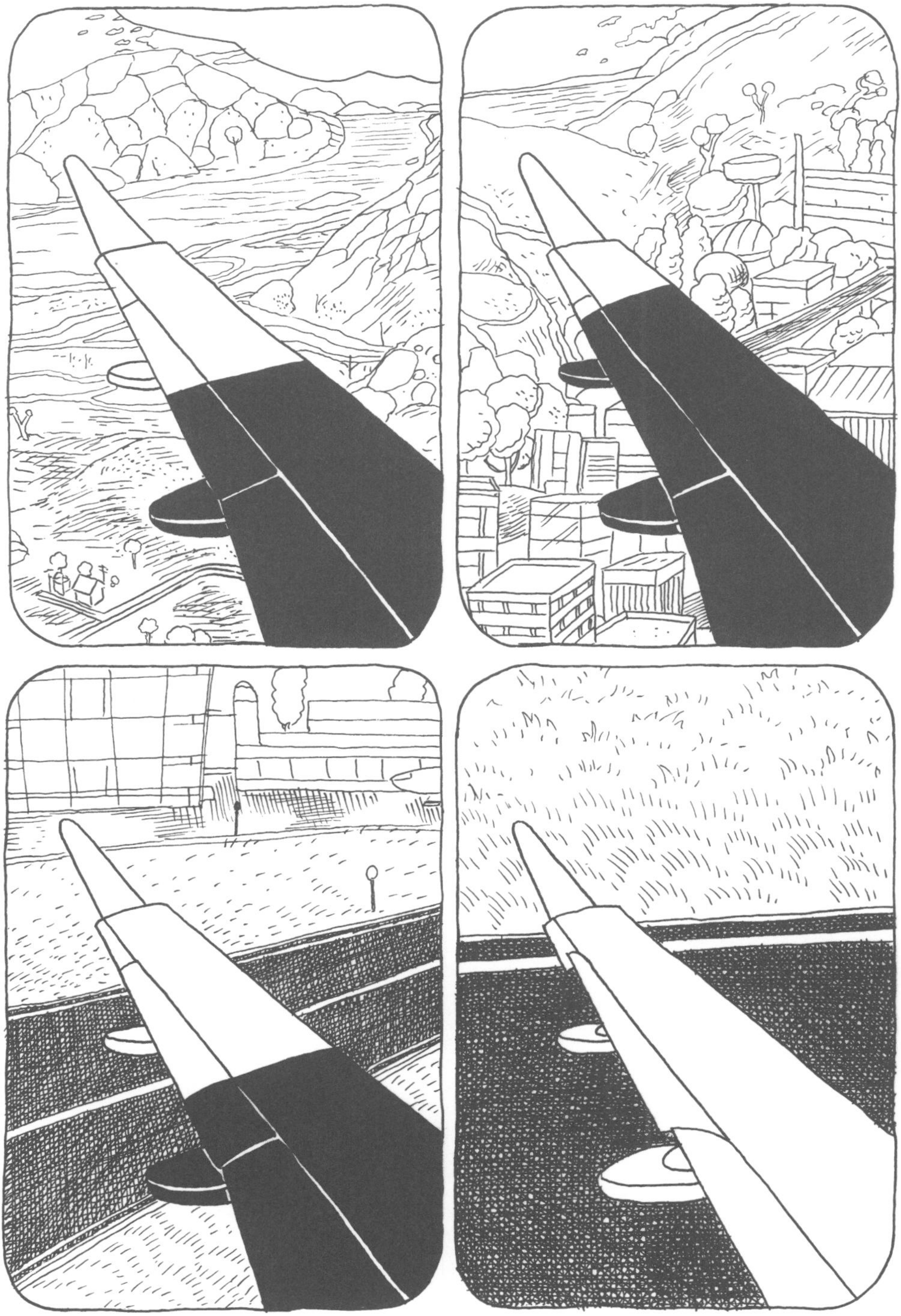

There are many
types of sand.

The cloud of sand when it's poured out of a shoe.

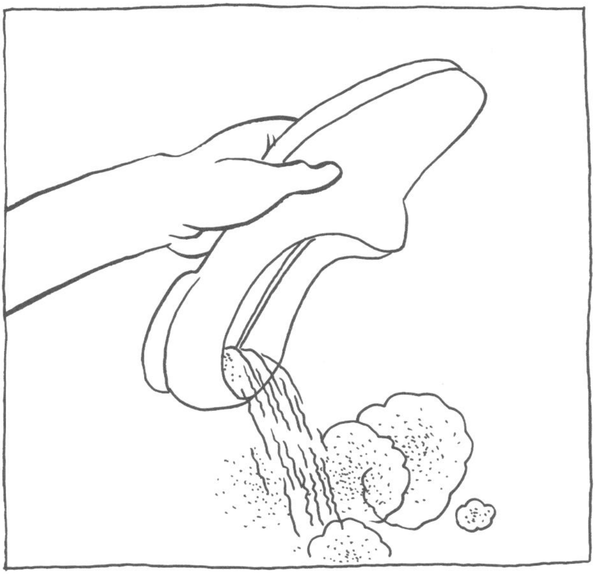

Spotty sand stuck to a naked back.

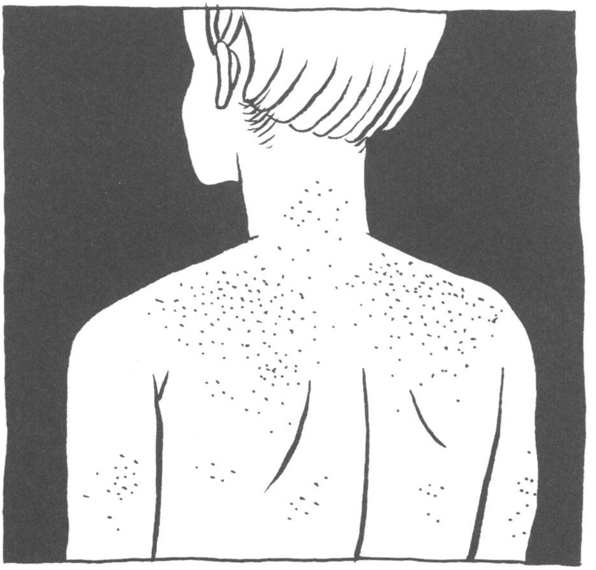

Hard sand.

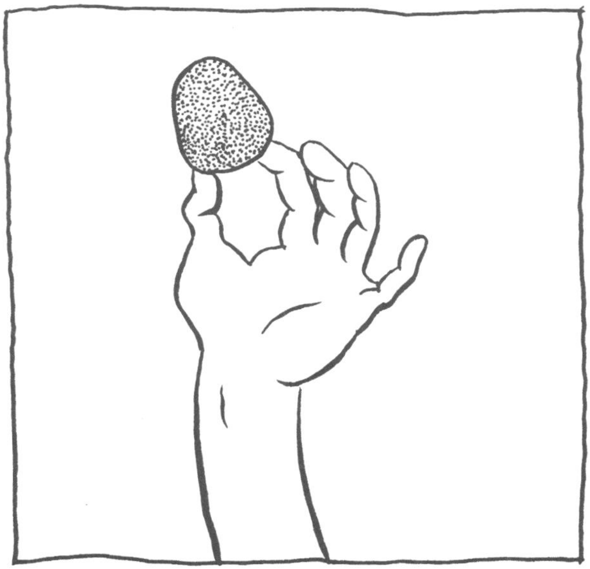

Cracked sand when you apply pressure with your heel.

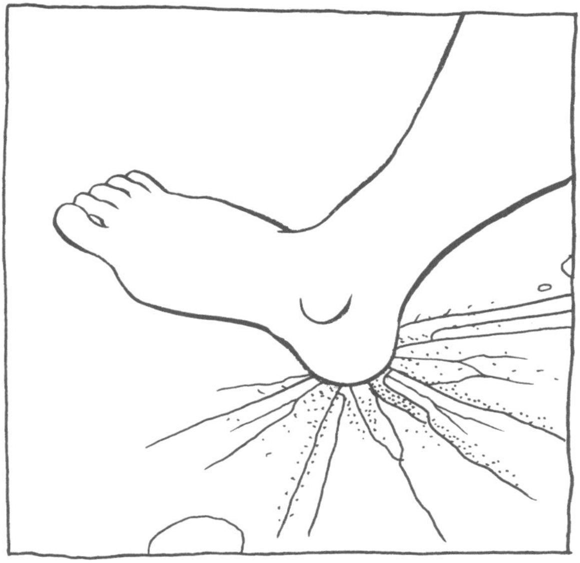

Pee on sand: it suddenly goes dark.

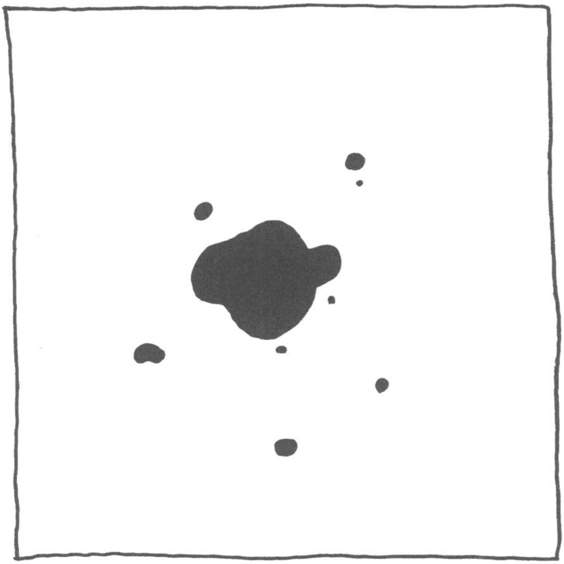

Sand sifted out of a bathing suit.

Mud sand.

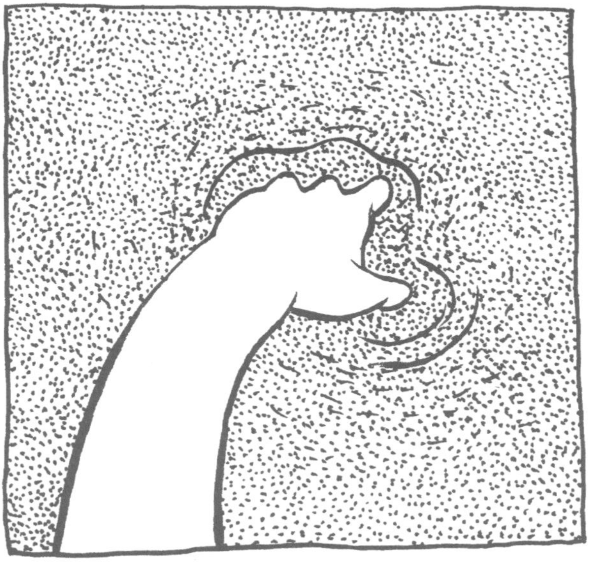

LOONY
LOONY

There are many
types of the Loony family.

The Loony Monarchy

Vehicle Diagram

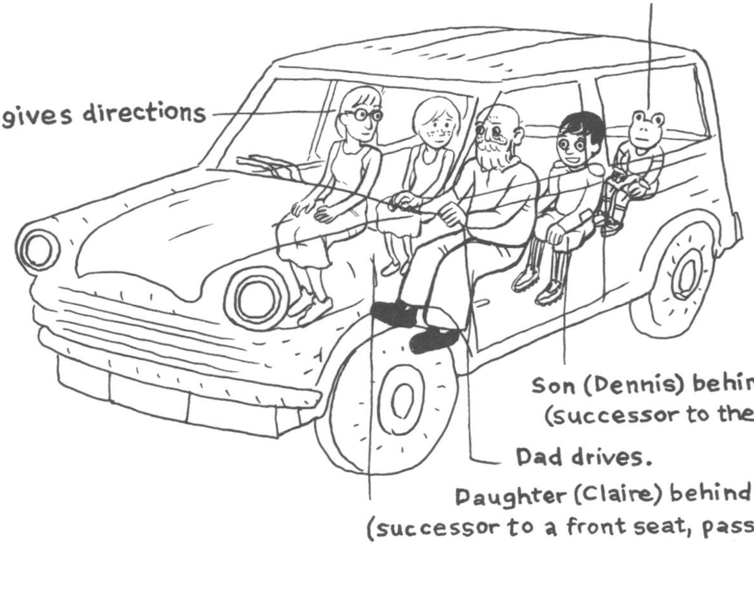

WA
DENNIS IS KICKING ME!
AAAA
NUH-UH!
LIAR!
QUIET DOWN BACK THERE!
Remember: If anything happens to your dad or me, it's just going to be the three of you.
You'll only have each-other.

King's opinion overrides Queen's.

Dennis may date whoever he likes.

Claire's dates must first be introduced to the family.

Claire may go to parties, but only if accompanied by Dennis.

Later, Peter does not date.

Eskimo Loonys

The Loonys that keep themselves warm in the cold.

Is something wrong?
SHUT
KISS
OH
KISS
THUMP
ha.
KISS
THUMP
THUMP
THUMP

Fish Bowl Loonys

The Loonys that believe nothing exists outside of the family. Everything in the real world is a reflection of themselves.

Father Loony gets a promotion at work and he brings home a cake to his family, believing they are somehow responsible for the raise.

A week later Father Loony loses the job and Mother Loony is responsible.

Civil War Loonys

Restaurant Loonys

In which Mother and Father Loony own and operate the restaurant, and their children receive what they order.

Black-Hole Loonys

In the Blackhole Loonys, each member is a floating entity separate from any other member. It is a non-family.

These are just a small sampling of the thousands of millions of different Loonys. The actual Loony family is a combination of all these types.

A pie chart would look like this:

A dense cross-section with each type given equal space/value.

Our story, The Bottomless Belly-Button, begins with a slight alteration of the family graph:

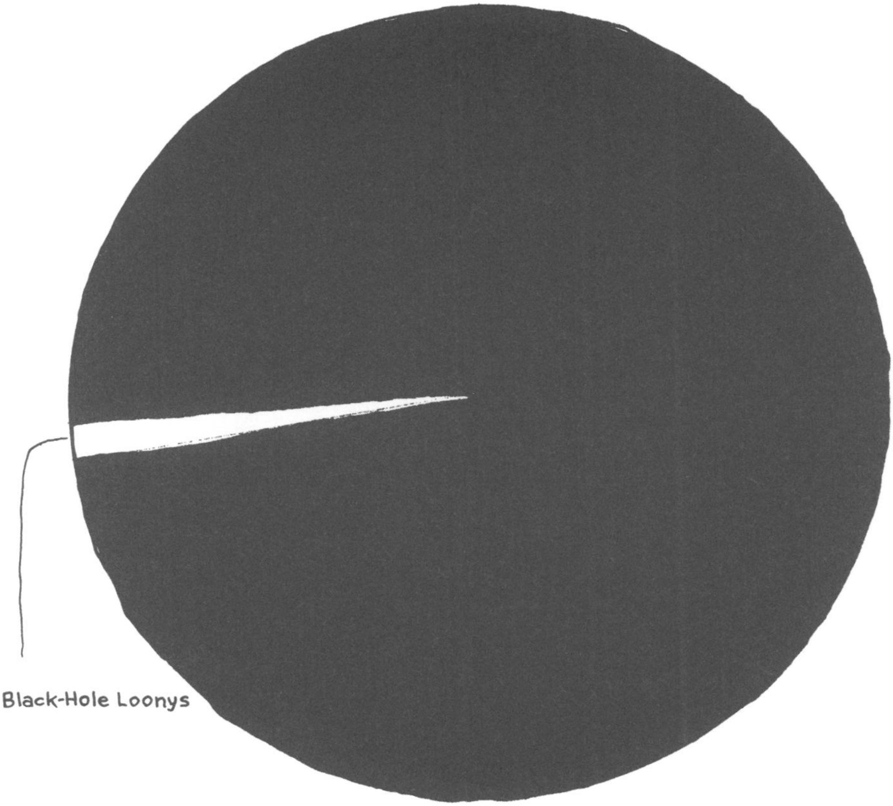

when -after forty years of marriage- Mother and Father Loony announce their divorce.

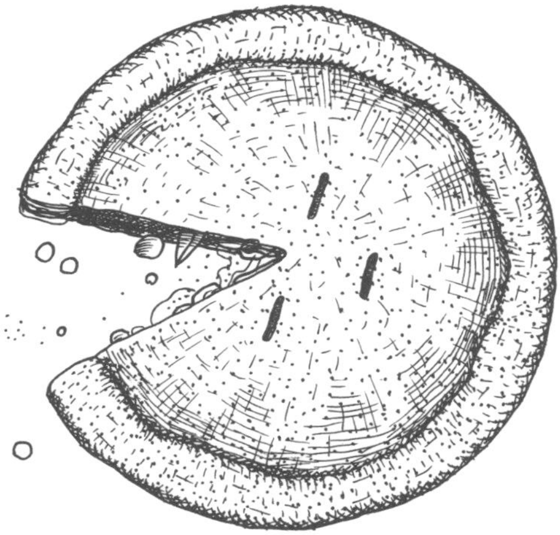

Sunlight makes dust in air visible.
CHEW CHEW
So...

I cleaned up your rooms.
You can put whatever you like in the closets.
So is this, like, our last official dinner together?
What do you mean?
Jill, last time I saw you, you were this big.
Yeah, she used to be a cutie.
Thanks for coming down. I hope everyone had safe flights.
I know this might seem strange.
YEAH. WELL, it's shocking really.
Could you pass that?

It's so nice to finally meet Alex.
ha.
Look at everyone. Everyone's all grown up now.
I'm so proud.
YAWN
CHEW CHEW

What do you think, Aki?
um.
I say do whatcha gotta do, ya'know; Divorce is cool in my book. I mean, I love Dennis and everything, but when ya gotta-
I mean about the food. Dennis tells me you're quite the chef at home.
Oh.
Yeah, it's good.
Have any advice? A critique would-
She likes it, ma.
I'm just trying to improve myself.

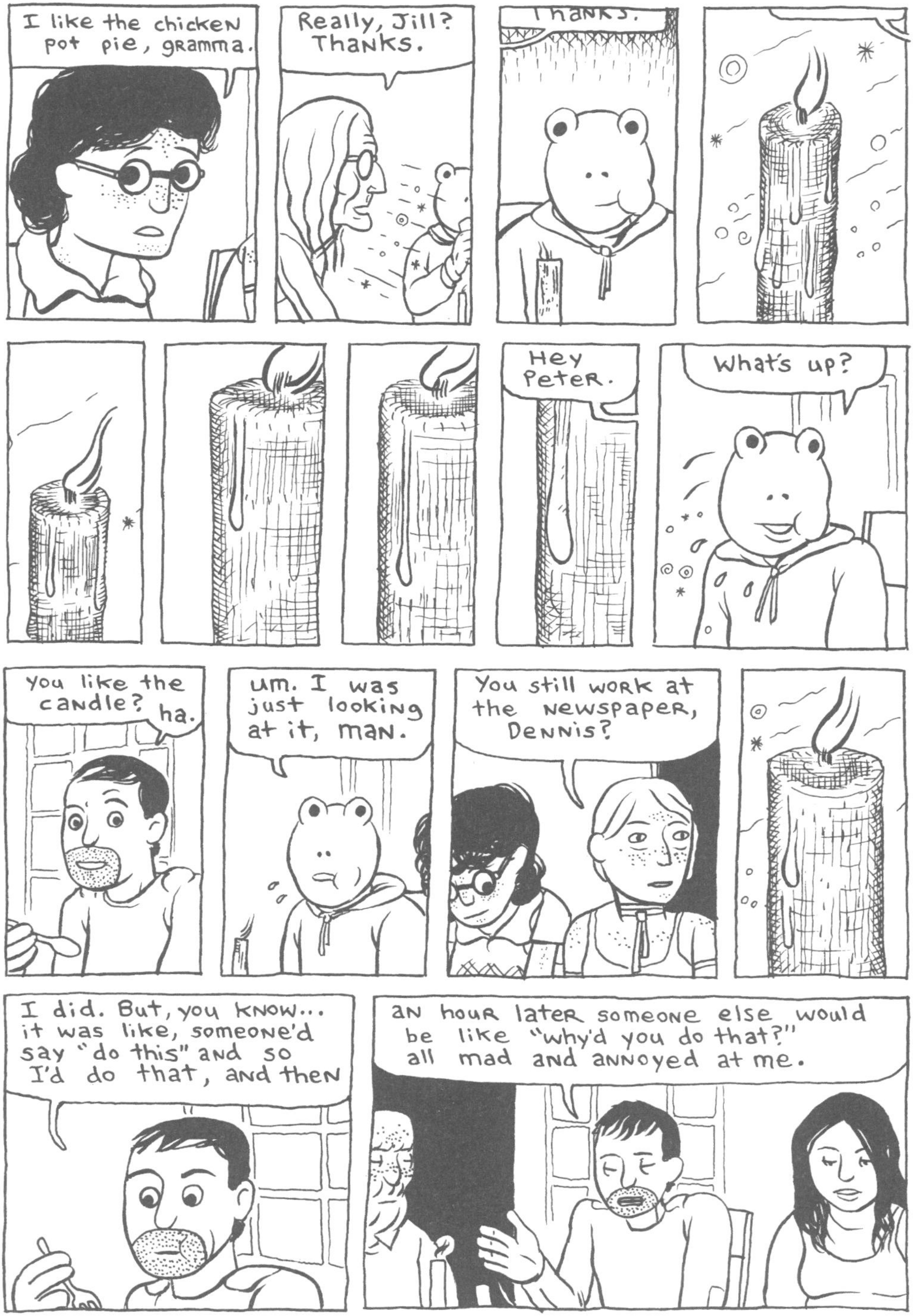
I like the chicken pot pie, gramma.
Really, Jill? Thanks.
Thanks.
Hey Peter.
What's up?
You like the candle? ha.
um. I was just looking at it, man.
You still work at the newspaper, Dennis?
I did. But, you know... it was like, someone'd say "do this" and so I'd do that, and then
an hour later someone else would be like "why'd you do that?" all mad and annoyed at me.

So I was like "screw this" and I quit.
Ha Ha Ha
It is kinda funny.
Ha Ha
Ha Ha Ha
What's funny?
Ha Ha
Just the way you said it.
SHRUG
Ha Ha Ha
Ha Ha
Ha- choke
~choke~ Ha
choke choke
Jill? sweetie?
coff
ahem.
you okay?
cof cof
PAT PAT
WAAAAAAAAAAAA
coff coff
Oh, Alex.
AAAAAAA
Jeez. Babies are so EMOTIONAL.
WAAAAAAAAAAA
coff coff

Oh, Alex, baby.
WAAAAAAA
coff coff
AAAAAAAAAA
Breathe.
AAAAAAA
shhhh...
Alex.
AAAAAAAAAA
Breathe, Jill.
caf
Oh, honey.
AAAAAAAAAA
caf caf
maybe get a cup of water.
coff coff
Shhh...
cof
I'm okay.
AAAAAAAAAAAAAA
I-
Do you want me to take Alex outside?
Breathe.
AAAAAAA
CHEW
Breathe, Jill.
DRINK this.
AAAAAAAA
cof
Shhh, Alex.
So, do you two have a justification OR anything?
AAAAAAAA
Shhh...
Breath Jill, I
AAAAAAA
caf
um.
What do you mean, Dennis?
AAAAAAAAAAAAAA
Hey, there. DRINK this.
coff
AAAAAA
Shhhh...
I mean it's pretty weird to be married forty years and then, like, suddenly announce a divorce, don't you think?
AAAAAAA
shhh...
Breathe, Easy.

coff
AAAAAAAAAAAAAAAAAAAAAA
Shhhhh
Don't you think that's strange?!
hey. Jill.
Alex.
hey, I-
AAAAAAA
caff caff
AAAAAAAAA AAA
FWOOSH!
Ah!
AAAAAH.
caf.
PSSS
Well, we're just not in love anymore.

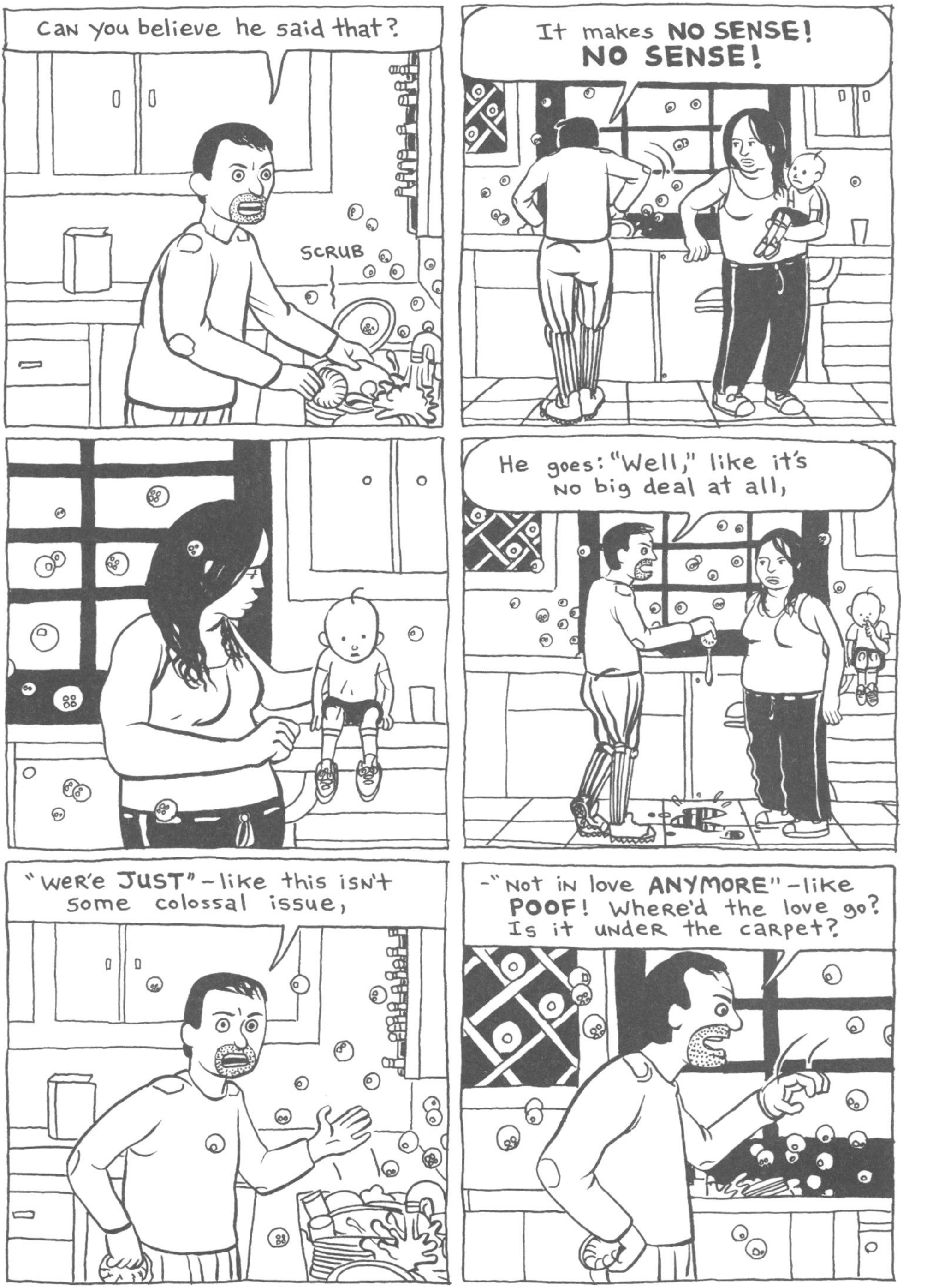

Can you believe he said that?
SCRUB
It makes NO SENSE! NO SENSE!
He goes: "Well," like it's no big deal at all,
"We're JUST"-like this isn't some colossal issue,
-"Not in love ANYMORE"-like POOF! Where'd the love go? Is it under the carpet?

Ha.
Ha.
DENNIS.
POP!
I'M SERIOUS!
Ha.
POP!
It is kinda strange, right? But I guess ya have to move on.
move on to what? To DEATH? They're not going to find someone new.
SHUT

YOU DON'T THINK THAT'S FUCKED-UP?
... I mean... I dunno...
Jill! Since when were you so BLEAK?
I'm just saying...
TWIX
TWIX
TWIX
TIC TACS
FILM MAKING
SHUFFLE

They're YOUR parents. Ask Claire to psycho-analyze them.
Claire wouldn't understand.
SCRUB
OH. my. GOD.

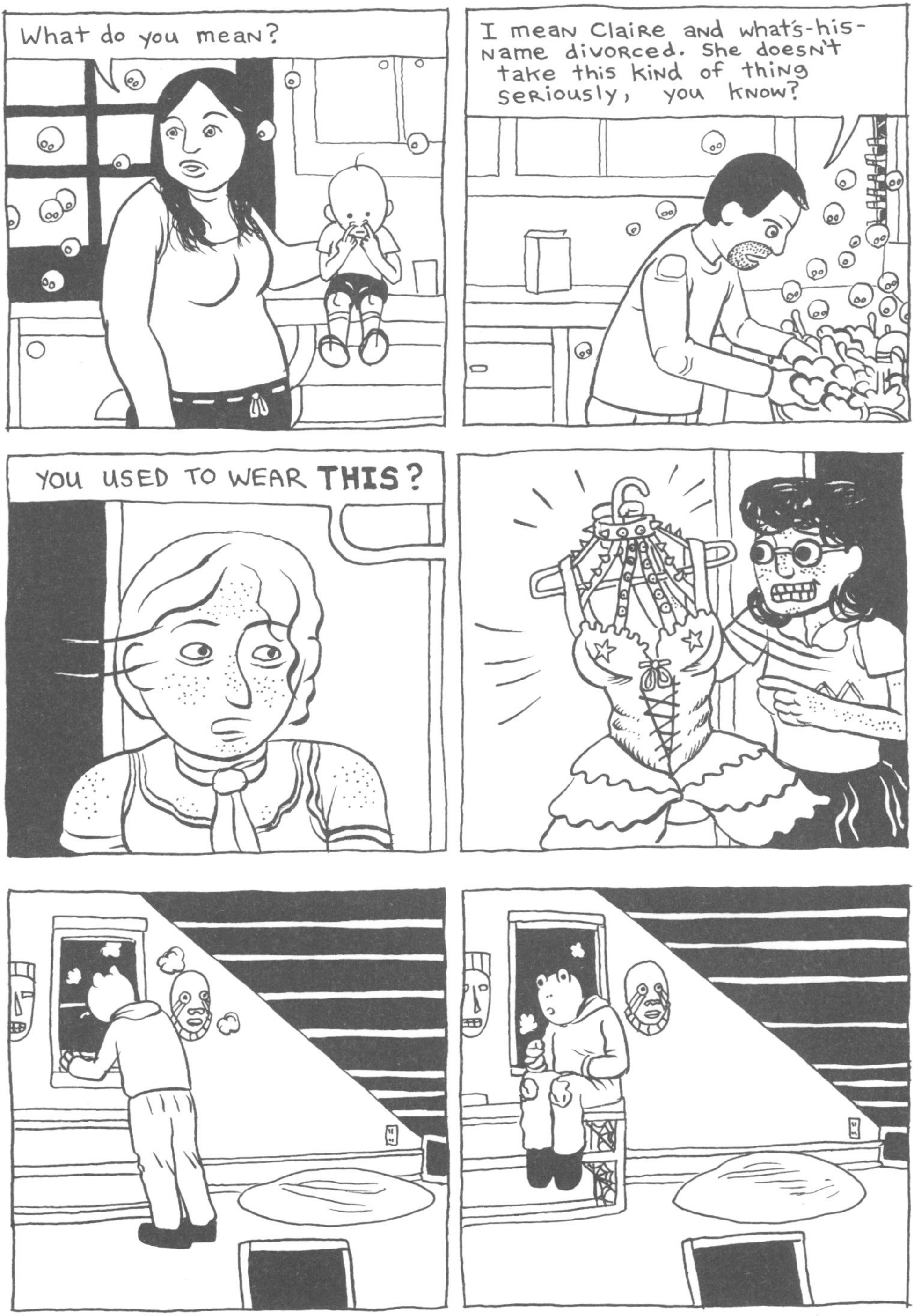

What do you mean?
I mean Claire and what's-his-name divorced. She doesn't take this kind of thing seriously, you know?
YOU USED TO WEAR THIS?

and- I mean- you were adopted so-
WHOA. WHOA.
You're upset and saying things you don't mean. I'm leaving now because I'm a responsible person.
Put that away! The dust will make you sneeze!
SNATCH!
Ha Ha Ha
SHUFFLE SHUFFLE
Ha Ha Ha Ha

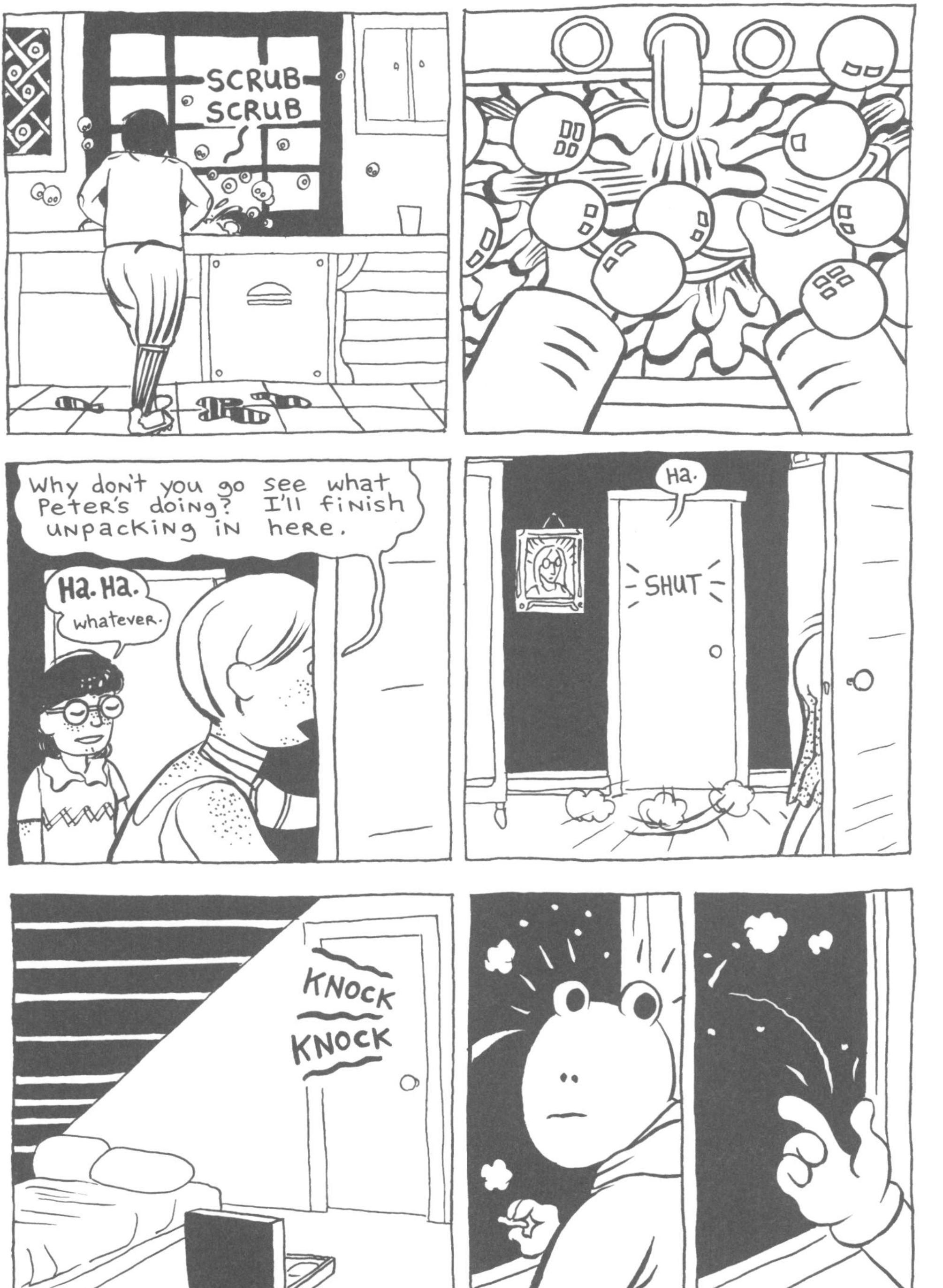
SCRUB
SCRUB
Why don't you go see what Peter's doing? I'll finish unpacking in here.
Ha. Ha.
whatever.
Ha.
SHUT
KNOCK
KNOCK

FAN
What's up?
Just unpacking.
Yeah, right. It smells funny in here.
Did you fart?
What's that?
my old bean-bag chair.

WHEEZE
How'd you feel after Claire and your dad divorced?
um.
I DUNNO.
What?
Huh?

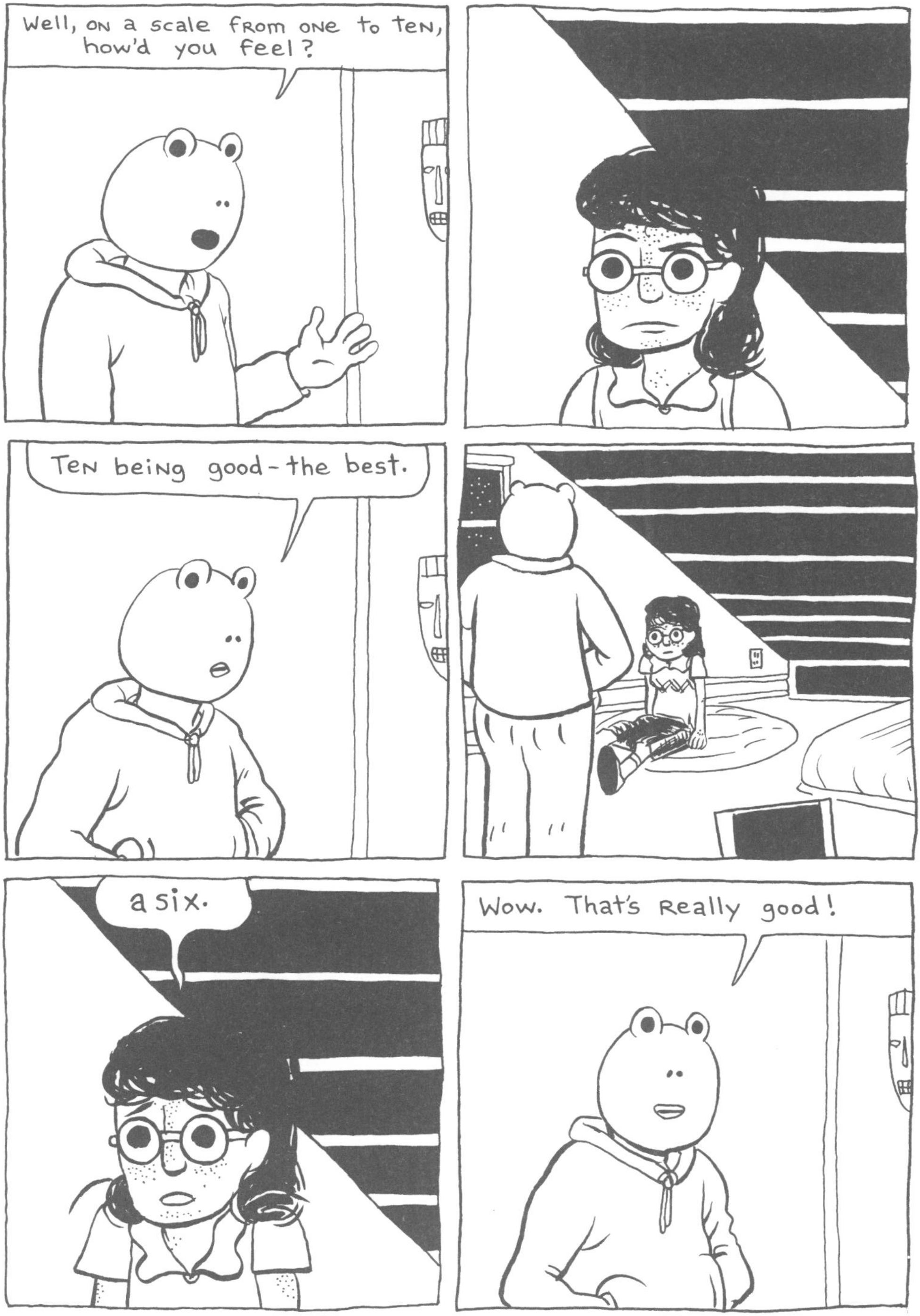
Well, on a scale from one to ten, how'd you feel?
Ten being good - the best.
a six.
Wow. That's really good!

KISS
KISS
KISS

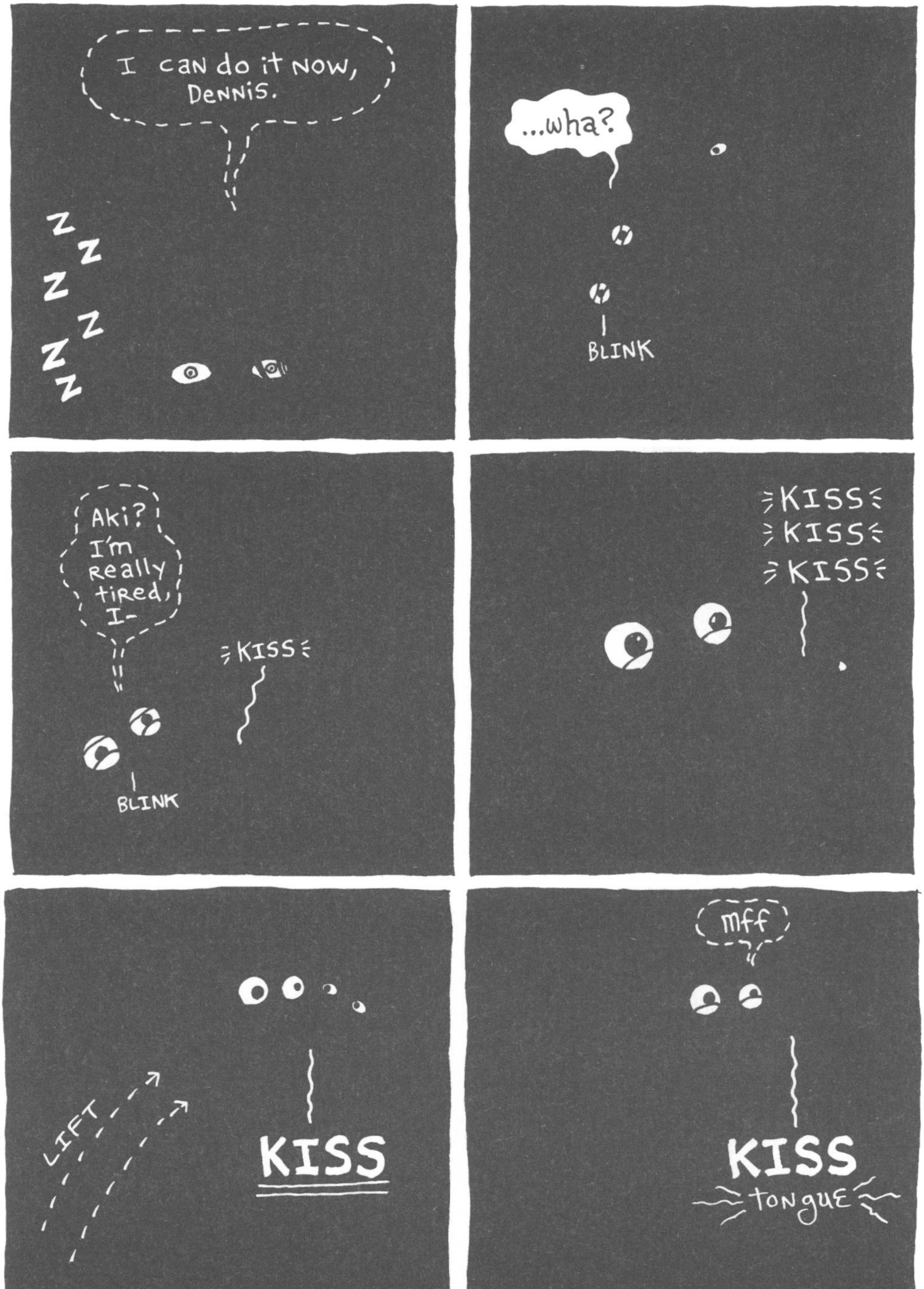
I can do it now, Dennis.
Z Z Z Z Z Z
...wha?
BLINK
Aki? I'm really tired, I-
KISS
BLINK
KISS
KISS
KISS
LIFT
KISS
mff
KISS
tongue

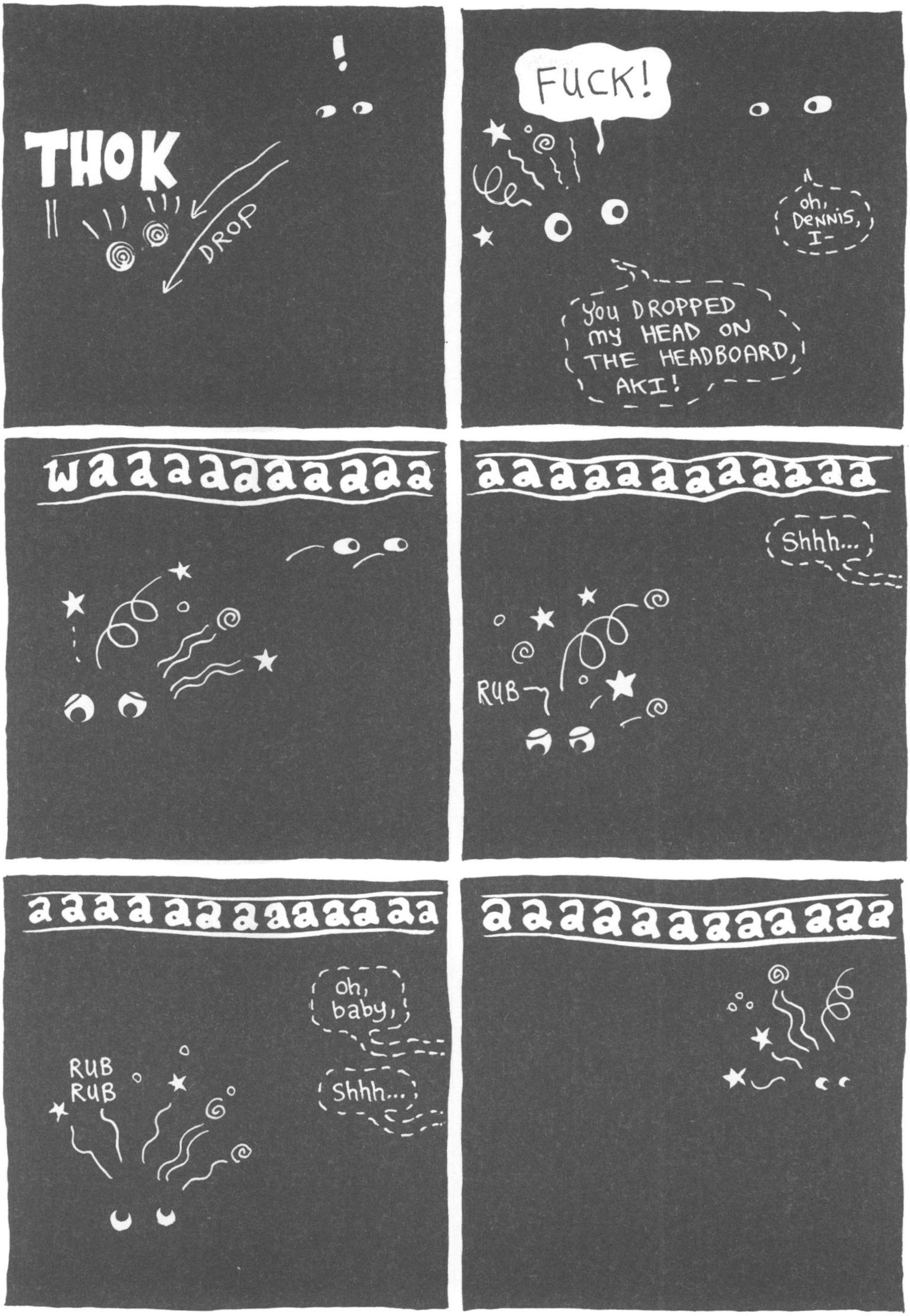
!
THOK
DROP
FUCK!
oh, DENNIS, I-
You DROPPED my HEAD ON THE HEADBOARD, AKI!
waaaaaaaaaaa
aaaaaaaaaaaaaa
Shhh...
RUB
aaaaaaaaaaaaaa
oh, baby,
Shhh...
RUB RUB
aaaaaaaaaaaaaa

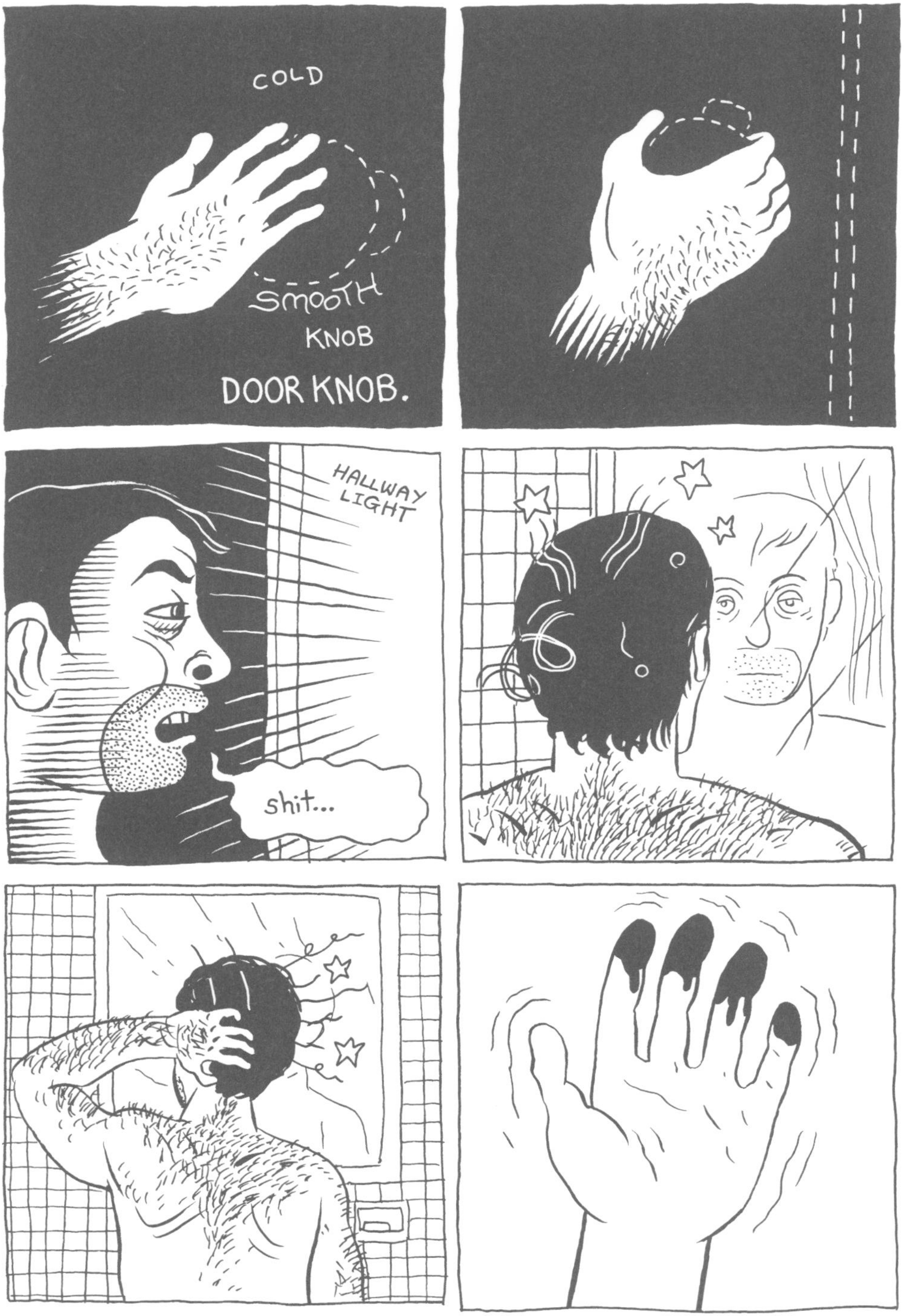
COLD
SMOOTH
KNOB
DOOR KNOB.
HALLWAY LIGHT
shit...

The sand swept off of a deck.

ORANGE DAWN
BLUE WALL
SWEEP
≷CLICK≷-EST CELEBRITY NEWS: HOLLYWOOD HEART-THROB CHAD BONES HAS ANNOUNCED HIS ENGAGEMENT TO MOVIE STAR BRYCE GIVENS.
THEY'VE BEEN SEEN DATING SINCE LAST FALL.
SLURP
BONES: "I'M SO HAPPY WITH BRYCE. IT WAS LOVE AT FIRST SIGHT. I'D LOVE TO WORK WITH HER IN THE FUTURE."
SWEEP

BRYCE: "WE WANT TO HAVE CHILDREN, BUT WE HAVE TO FOCUS ON OUR CAREERS FOR THE NEXT COUPLE OF YEARS, YA' KNOW?"
SWEEP
SWEEP
BONES' LATEST FILM, "GREY MOON", OPENS THIS FRIDAY IN THEATERS NATIONWIDE.
SWEEP
BONES PLAYS A YOUNG, COCKY SINGLE MAN OUT ON THE PROWL. HE AND HIS FRIEND, PLAYED BY CARL HAMM, PICK UP TWO SINGLE WOMEN AT A CAFE AND HIT THE CLUBS.
SWEEP
IT'S BEING WIDELY PRAISED FOR WITTY DIALOG, SEXY DANCE SCENES, BIG HEART, AND LUCIDO'S CHARISMATIC CAMERA DIRECTION.
"GREY MOON" OPENS THIS FRIDAY. BRING A DATE.
IN OTHER NEWS: HURRICANE—

I'm going for a RUN.
mmm
PRickly
mm
STRETCH
STRETCH

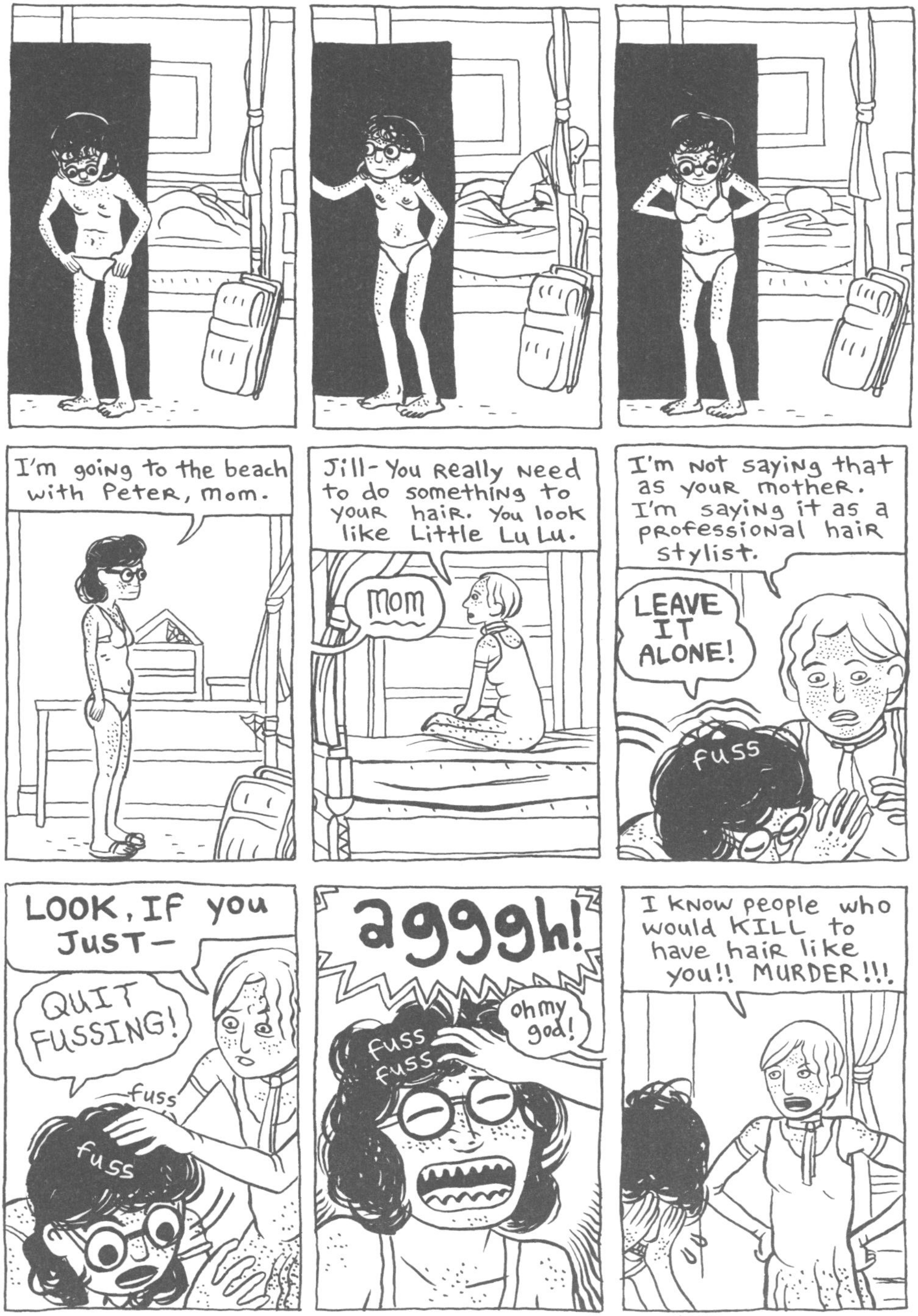
I'm going to the beach with Peter, mom.
Jill- You really need to do something to your hair. You look like Little Lu Lu.
mom
I'm not saying that as your mother. I'm saying it as a professional hair stylist.
LEAVE IT ALONE!
fuss
LOOK, IF you JUST-
QUIT FUSSING!
fuss
fuss
aggggh!
fuss fuss
oh my god!
I know people who would KILL to have hair like you!! MURDER!!!

LOOK, I'M GOING.
sigh
And P.S.: That painting is super-creepy.
That's of your granma when she was young.
OH.
seeya.

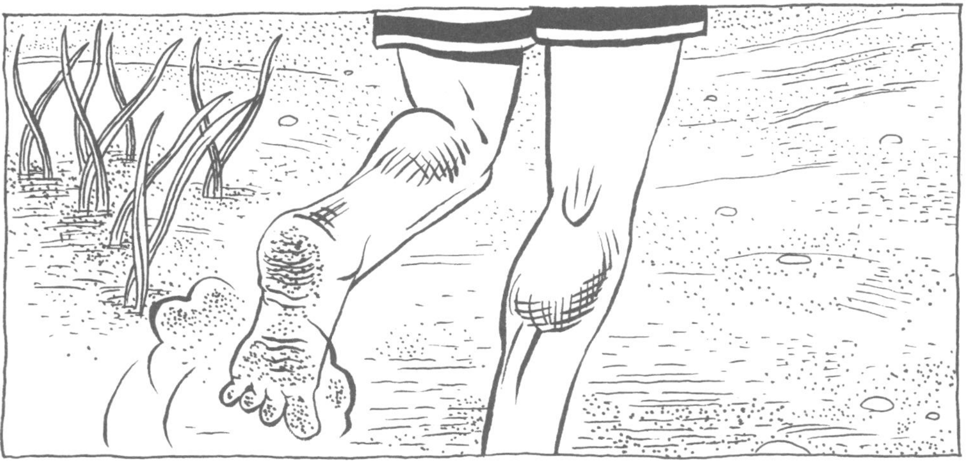

pant
PANT
PANT
pant
pant
PANT
pant

shhhhhhhhhh
shhhhhhhh
shhhhhhhhhhhh
shhhhhhhhhhh
TURN
STEAM
STEAM
STEAM
STEAM

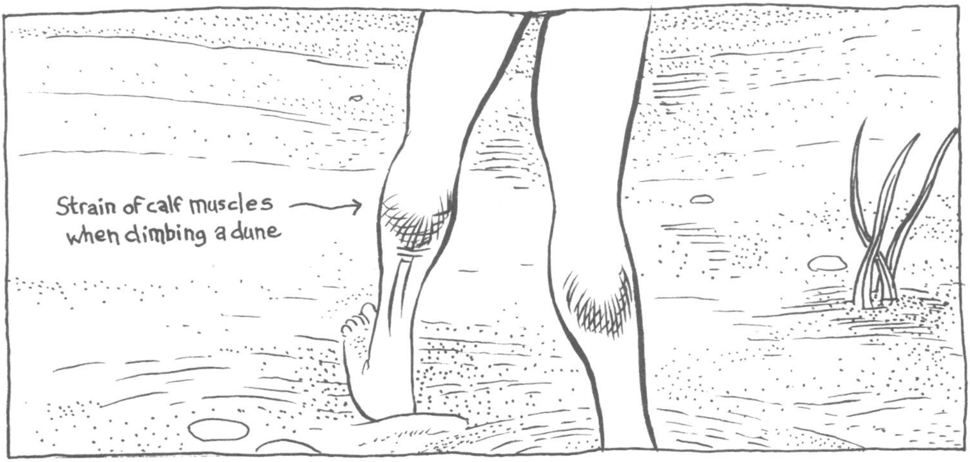
Strain of calf muscles
when climbing a dune

Hazy mist.
OCEAN SOUNDS

ha.
TAG! YOU'RE IT!
ha.
ha

ha ha

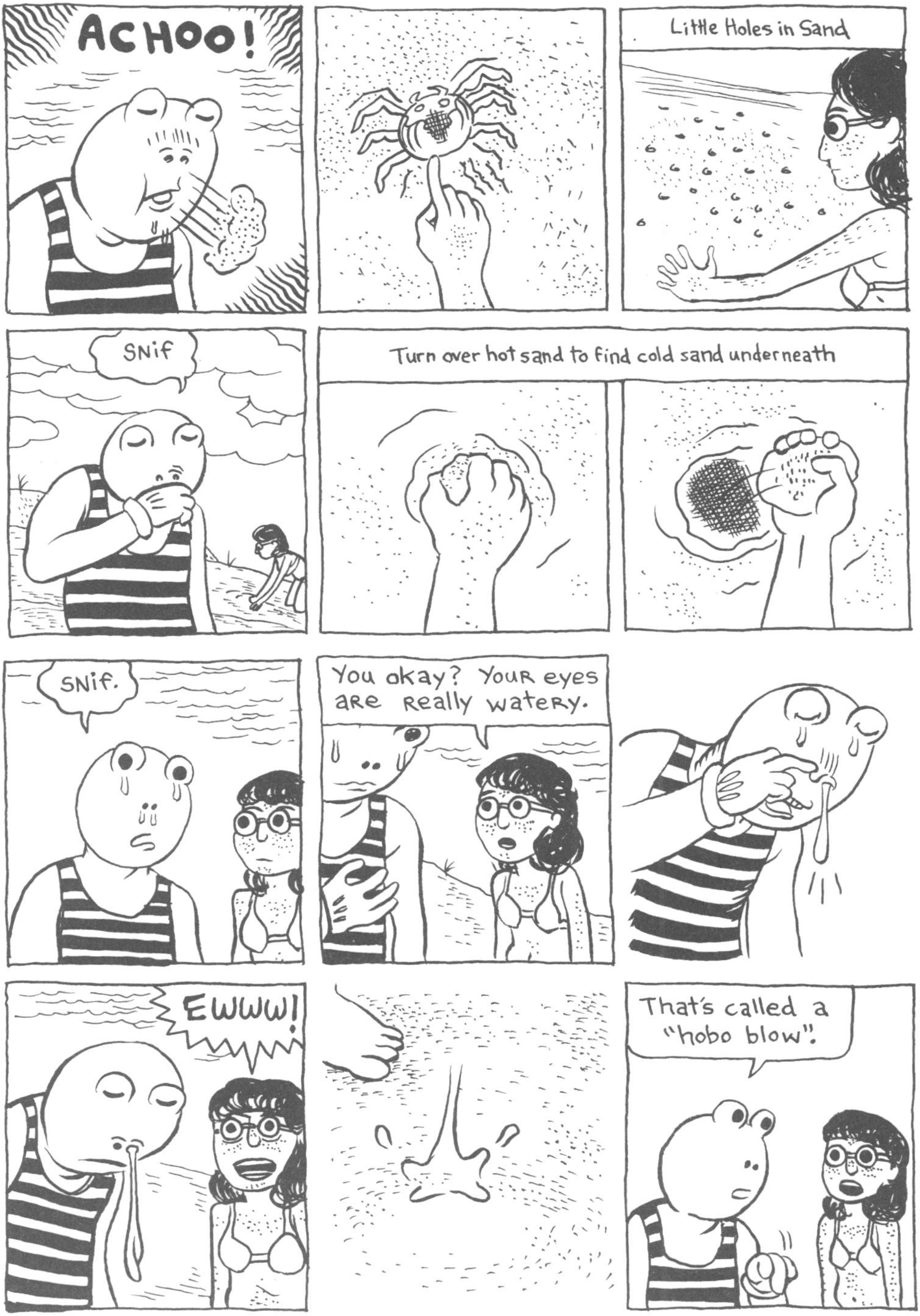
ACHOO!
Little Holes in Sand
SNif
Turn over hot sand to find cold sand underneath
SNif.
You okay? Your eyes are really watery.
EWWW!
That's called a "hobo blow".

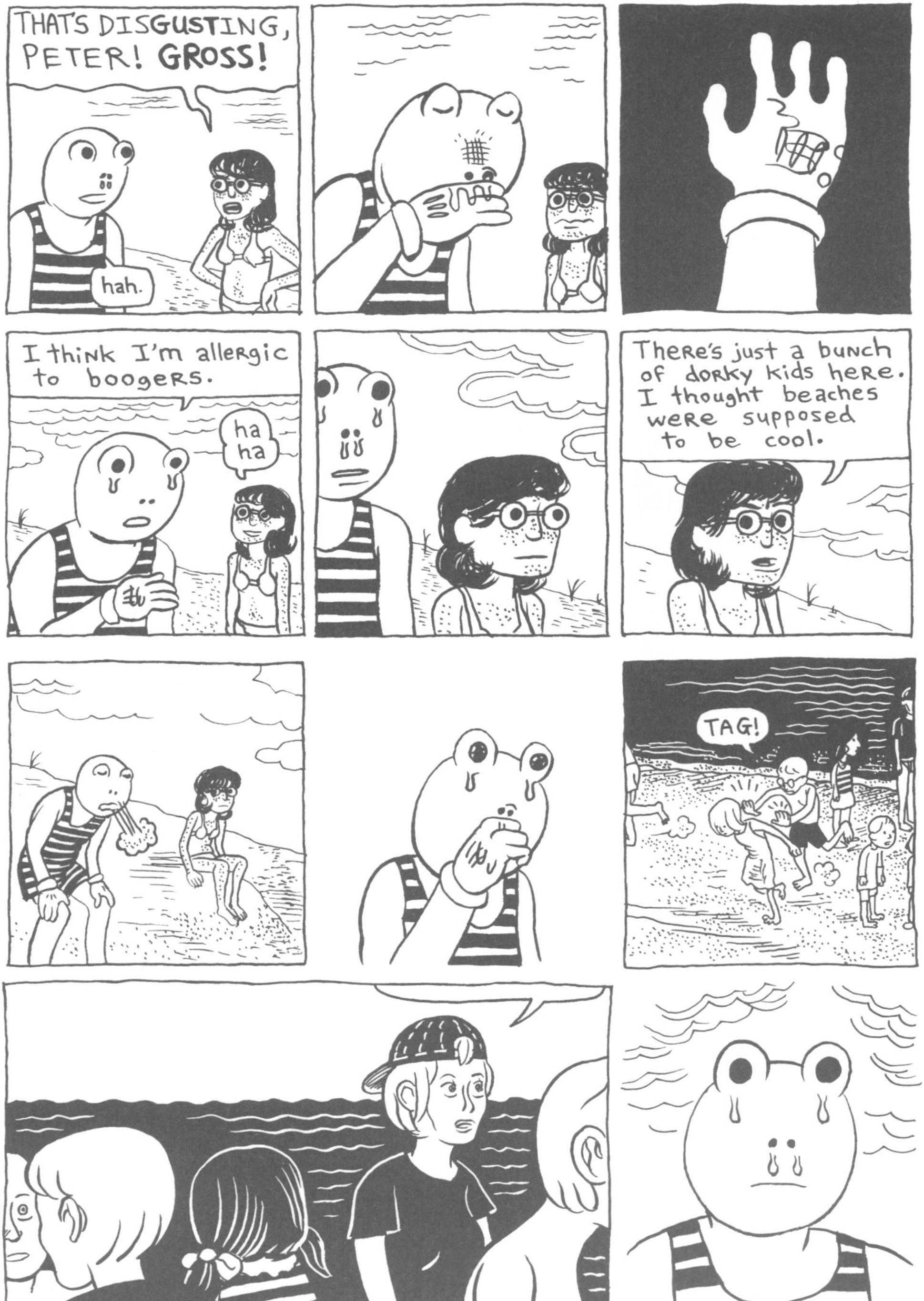
THAT'S DISGUSTING, PETER! GROSS!
hah.
I think I'm allergic to boogers.
ha ha
There's just a bunch of dorky kids here. I thought beaches were supposed to be cool.
TAG!

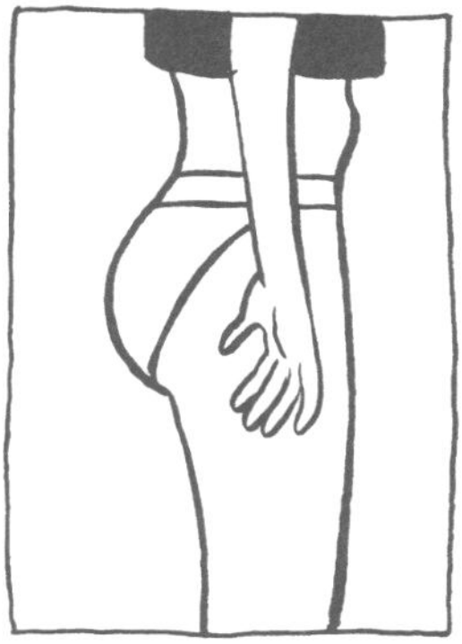

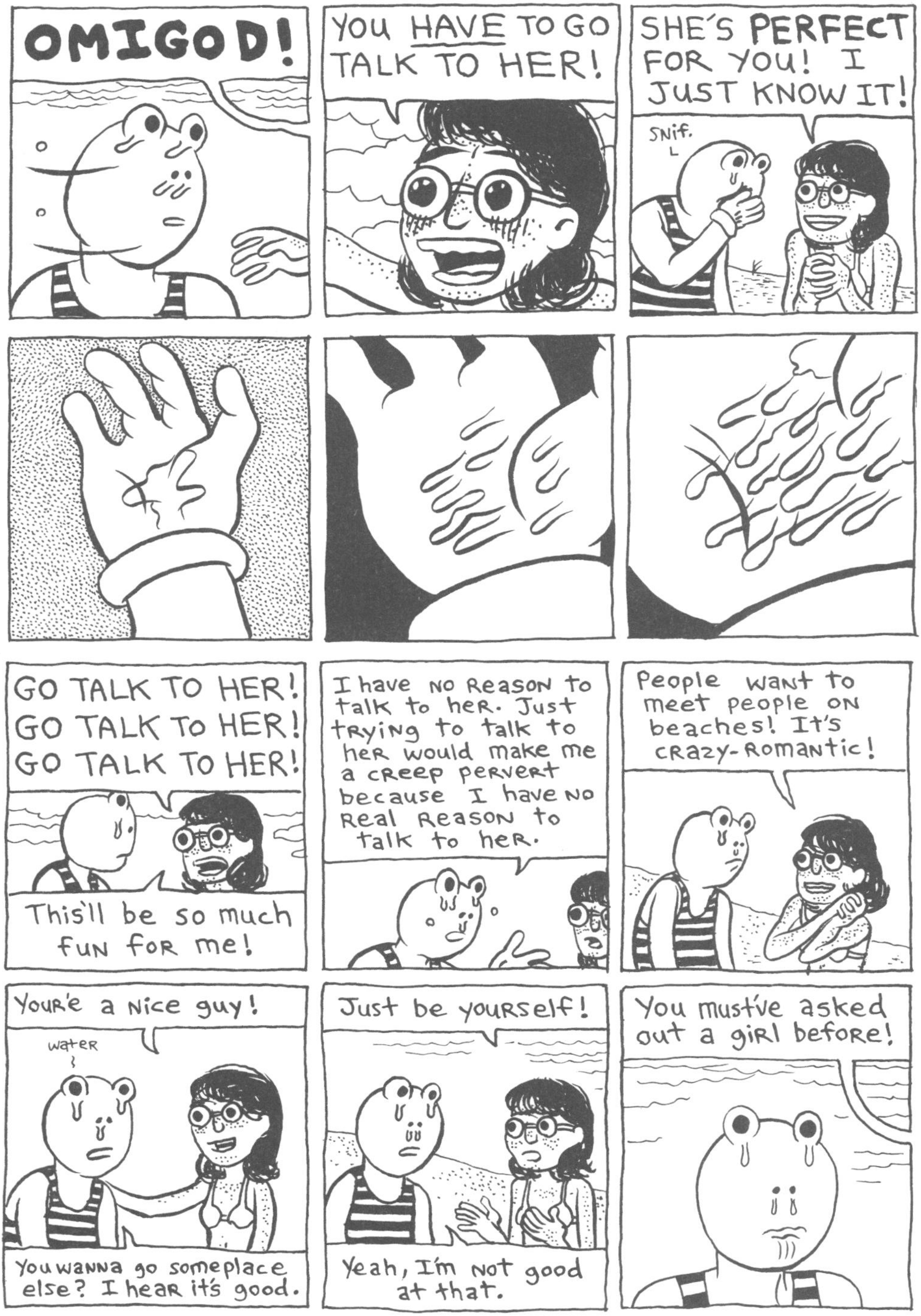
OMIGOD!
YOU HAVE TO GO TALK TO HER!
SHE'S PERFECT FOR YOU! I JUST KNOW IT!
SNIF.
GO TALK TO HER! GO TALK TO HER! GO TALK TO HER!
This'll be so much fun for me!
I have no reason to talk to her. Just trying to talk to her would make me a creep pervert because I have no real reason to talk to her.
People want to meet people on beaches! It's crazy-romantic!
Your'e a nice guy!
water
You wanna go someplace else? I hear it's good.
Just be yourself!
Yeah, I'm not good at that.
You must've asked out a girl before!

Dear Peter,

I'm officially back together with Tom. He's a great guy. I'm truly sorry we didn't work out, but it was only 1 date & I think you're blowing this out of proportion. I don't mean to stress the point, but you keep asking/insisting on a "Top 3 Reasons We Didn't Work Out." So here they are & I'm only giving you these @ your request. I would never intentionally hurt your feelings. (IN NO ORDER)

1. No attraction.
2. No common interests.
3. Don't talk about yourself so much. Dates are supposed 2B fun - not mondo depressing.

Please stop writing, calling, & finding opportunities to "bump into me" in town.

Sincerely, Mary

P.S. I'm not accusing you of this, but my dad told me he saw you & I don't know why he would make this up - Did you really drive over 2 my house, sit there for an hour, kick over the snowman in the front lawn & drive away? You don't have to answer. It doesn't matter.

Be confident.
Don't get snot on her.
Leave me alone.
Are you going to just watch her prance out of your life?
She's not in my life!
But I would love to watch her prance.
YOU'RE IMPOSSIBLE!
I'm sure she's just waiting to meet someone like you!
Well, I'm glad you're an optimist.
pfff.
I'm not sunshine, but you have to be an optimist in some circumstances!
Tell her you're a famous movie director! Girls love that stuff.
Seriously!
I dunno.

INDEPENDENT FILM FESTIVAL REVIEW

Peter Loony's sorry contribution to the festival was the insufferably dull "One Night", possibly meant as an homage to Andrew Lucido's films, but in fact establishing a new standard for the designation "hack work."

The story involves a young man played by Mr. Loony, who lucks into an unbearably trite "cute meet" with the attractive Samantha Waters at a bar. While they date, the audience suffers faux arty montages, forgettable chatter and awkward camera work. It all climaxes with a thud as Mr. Loony's character confronts the woman's handsome ex-boyfriend during a unseasonable snow storm. (We never get a hint as to why she chose Mr. Loony's character over the regal ex-boyfriend.)

Mr. Loony writes dialog like he's never talked to a living soul and stages romance scenes like his only source is the soapiest of daytime dramas.

The sterling Karl Campbell almost redeems the movie, playing the charming ex. Unfortunately, Karl's wit and natural camera presence could hardly sustain such a dreadful short film.

Stars: (no stars) out of four.

seriously, Peter!
Let's drop this.
You don't want to die alone, do you?
Jill.
fuck.
Look, she's a stranger. You don't have anything to lose.

KNIT

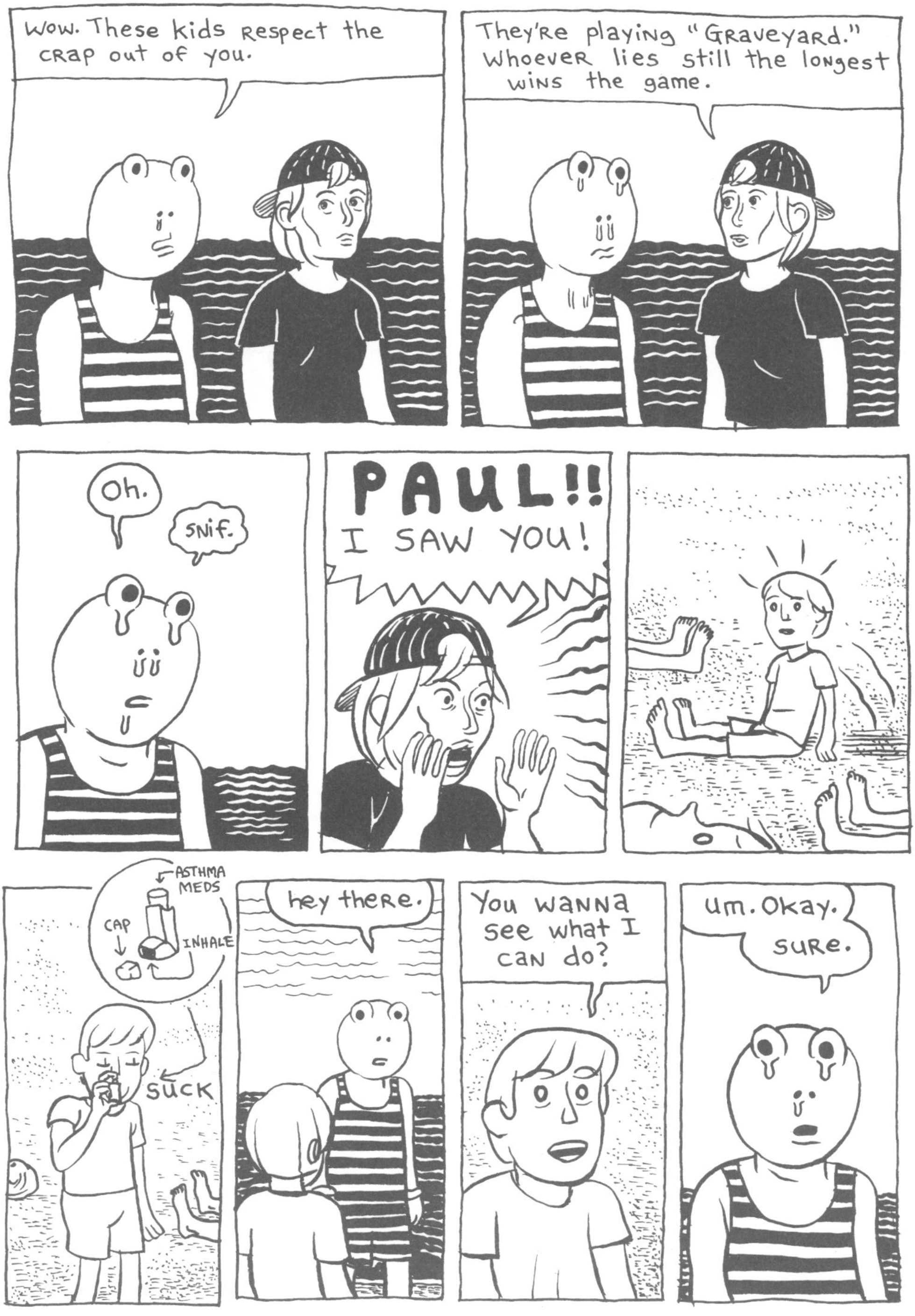
Wow. These kids respect the crap out of you.
They're playing "Graveyard." Whoever lies still the longest wins the game.
Oh.
SNif.
PAUL!! I SAW YOU!
ASTHMA MEDS
CAP
INHALE
SUCK
hey there.
You wanna see what I can do?
um. Okay. sure.

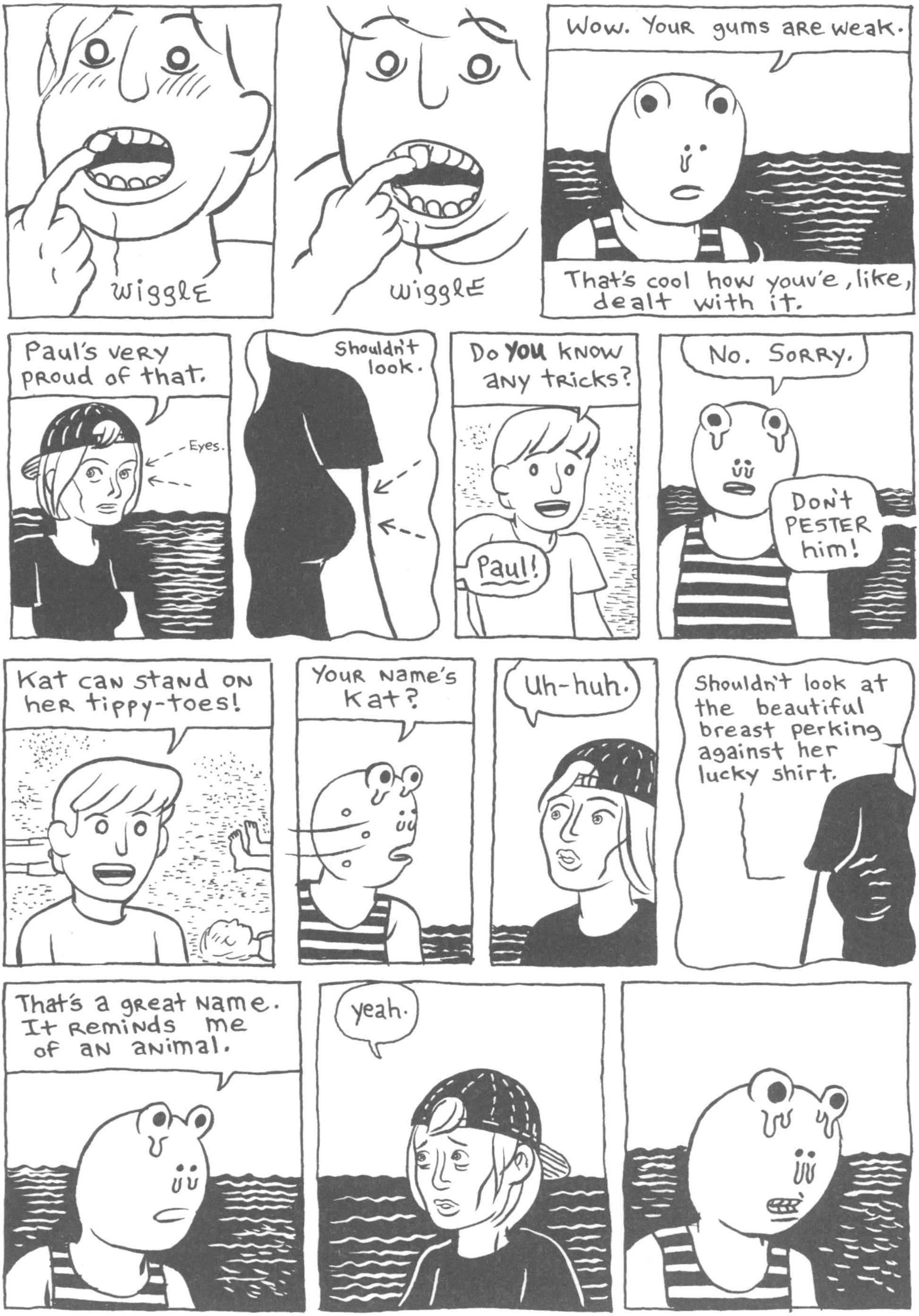

WiggLE
WiggLE
Wow. Your gums are weak.
That's cool how youv'e, like, dealt with it.
Paul's very proud of that.
Eyes.
Shouldn't look.
Do YOU know any tricks?
Paul!
No. Sorry.
Don't PESTER him!
Kat can stand on her tippy-toes!
Your name's Kat?
Uh-huh.
Shouldn't look at the beautiful breast perking against her lucky shirt.
That's a great name. It reminds me of an animal.
yeah.

My name's Peter and I like your bathing suit.
Oh, thanks.
Um, nice to meet you, Peter.
SUCK
SARA MOVED!
Okay see you later I gotta go.
oh. bye.
SARA MOVED!
SARA MOVED!
SARA MOVED!

JILL?
Hello?
Jill? where are you?
Here! I buried myself!

ha ha

You got her phone number, right?
It's hard for me to talk to a cute girl and breathe at the same time.

You're never going to see her again.

My back hurts.
When'd you decide to get the divorce?
I dunno. A week ago, I guess.
When we called you.
yeah.
STRETCH
CRACK
Well was it consensual?

Um, yeah. I mean-
yeah.
My back really hurts.
How long have you been talking about it?
I mean, we TALKED about it some. Where's Claire?
Her and Aki went to see the new Chad Bones movie.
Well, how'd you bring it up?
Who brought it up?

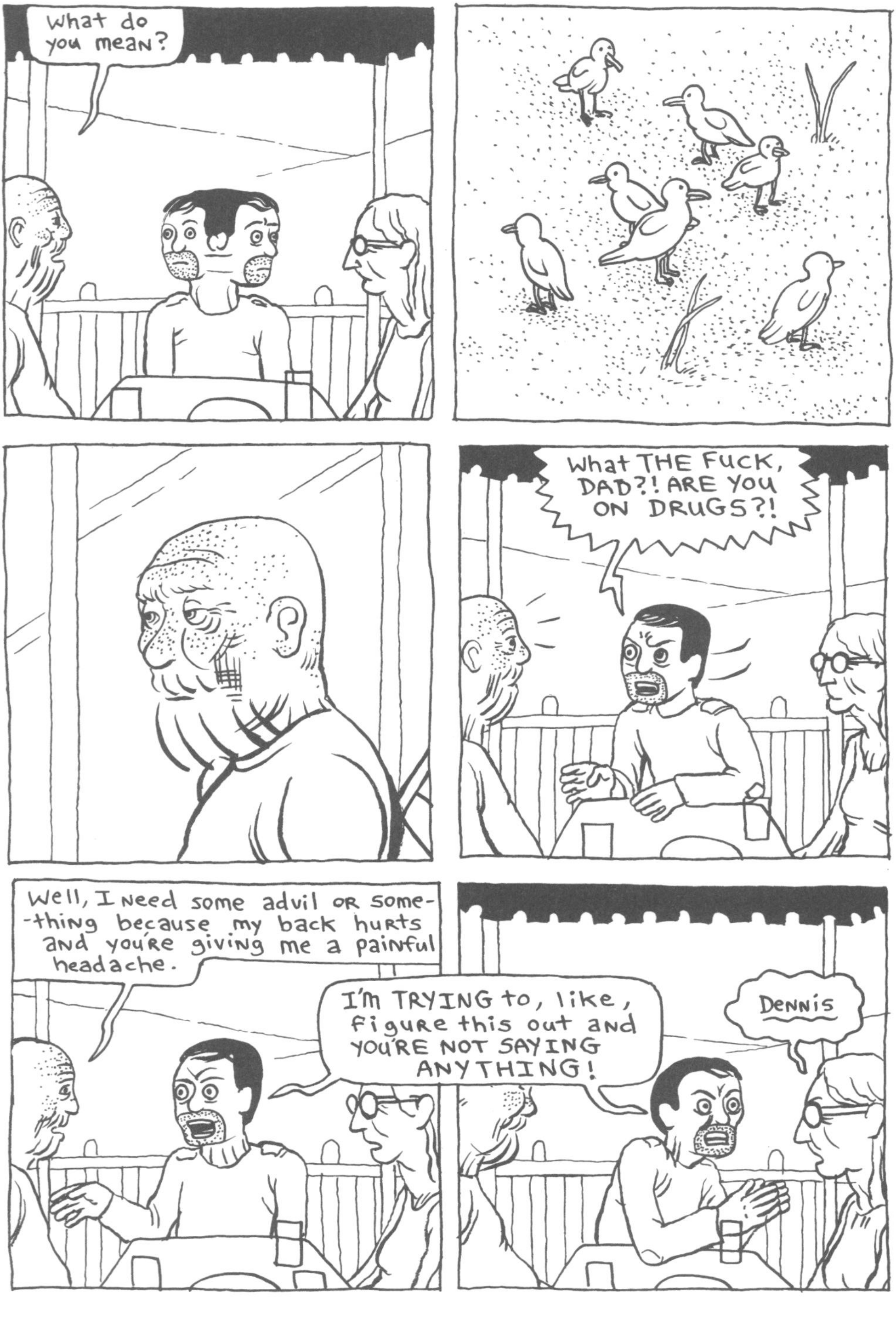
What do you mean?
What THE FUCK, DAD?! ARE YOU ON DRUGS?!
Well, I need some advil or some-thing because my back hurts and you're giving me a painful headache.
I'M TRYING to, like, figure this out and YOU'RE NOT SAYING ANYTHING!
DENNIS

I'm talking to you, aren't I?
What do you want me to say, huh?
I don't get it. I don't get it.
FUCK, DAD! I SHOULDN'T HAVE TO FEEL BAD ASKING YOU A QUESTION, YOU KNOW?!
Dennis.
My back hurts, I'm gonna go lie down and take a nap.
SLIDE

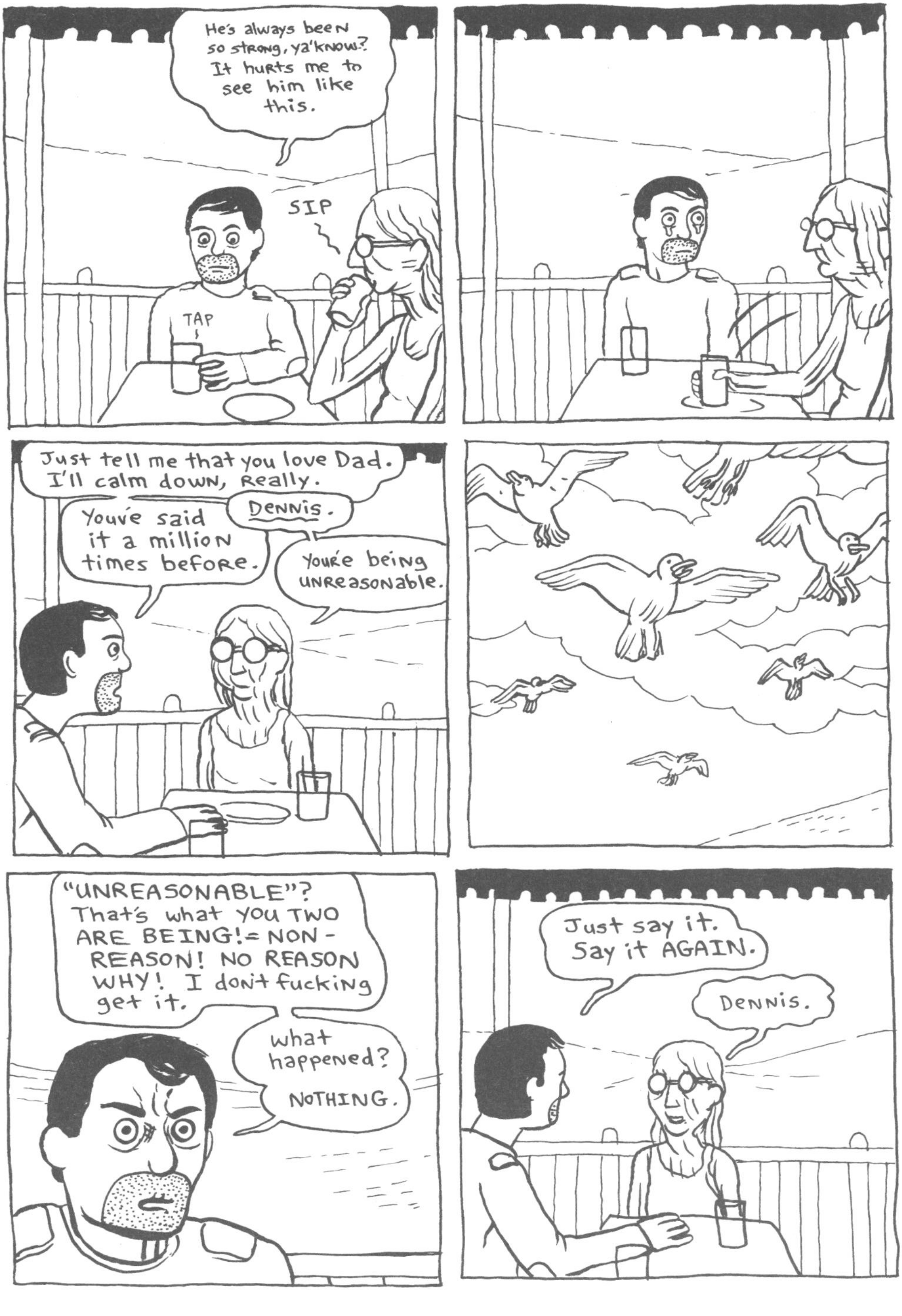
He's always been so strong, ya'know? It hurts me to see him like this.
SIP
TAP
Just tell me that you love Dad. I'll calm down, really.
DENNIS.
You've said it a million times before.
You're being unreasonable.
"UNREASONABLE"? That's what YOU TWO ARE BEING! = NON-REASON! NO REASON WHY! I don't fucking get it.
what happened?
NOTHING.
Just say it. Say it AGAIN.
DENNIS.

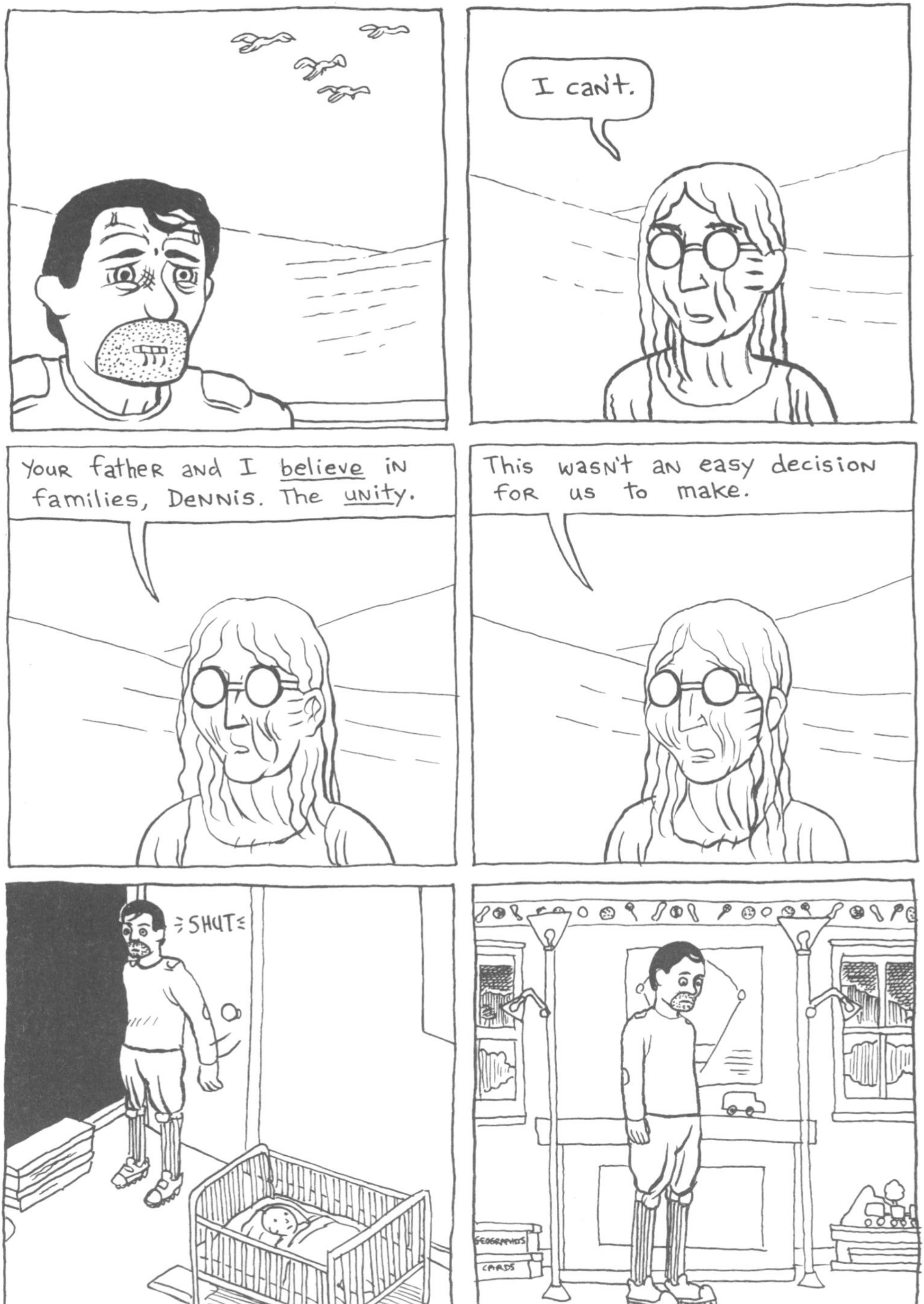
I can't.
Your father and I believe in families, Dennis. The unity.
This wasn't an easy decision for us to make.
SHUT
CARDS

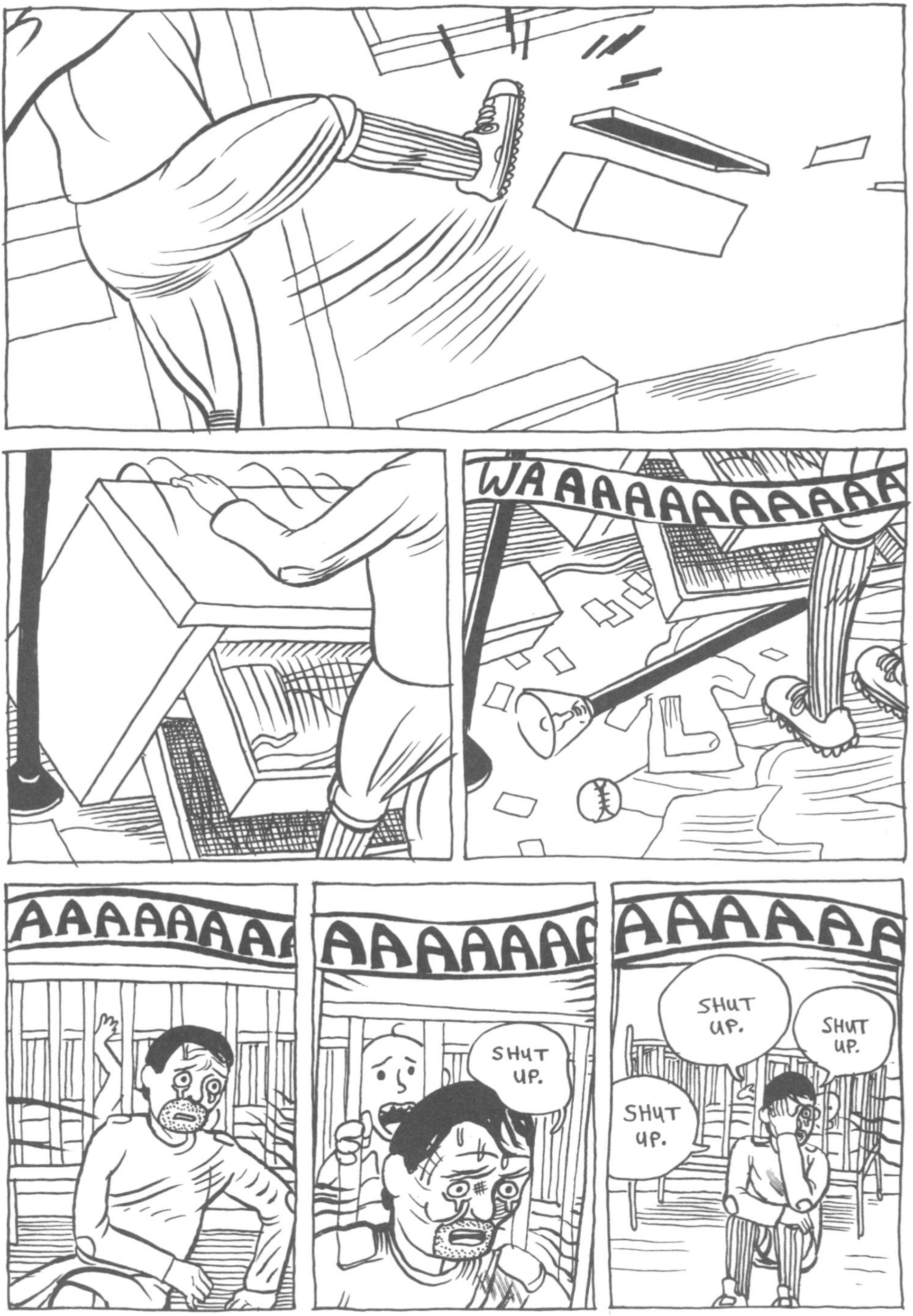
WAAAAAAAAAAA
AAAAAAAA
AAAAAAA
AAAAAA
SHUT UP.
SHUT UP.
SHUT UP.
SHUT UP.

Did you hear that Chad Bones is engaged to Bryce Givens?
Oh, Really?
How come movie stars never go out with Regular people?
Too cool, I guess.
I don't feel like seeing a movie. Why don't we stroll the city? -get something to eat?
Okay.

RED

RED
GREEN

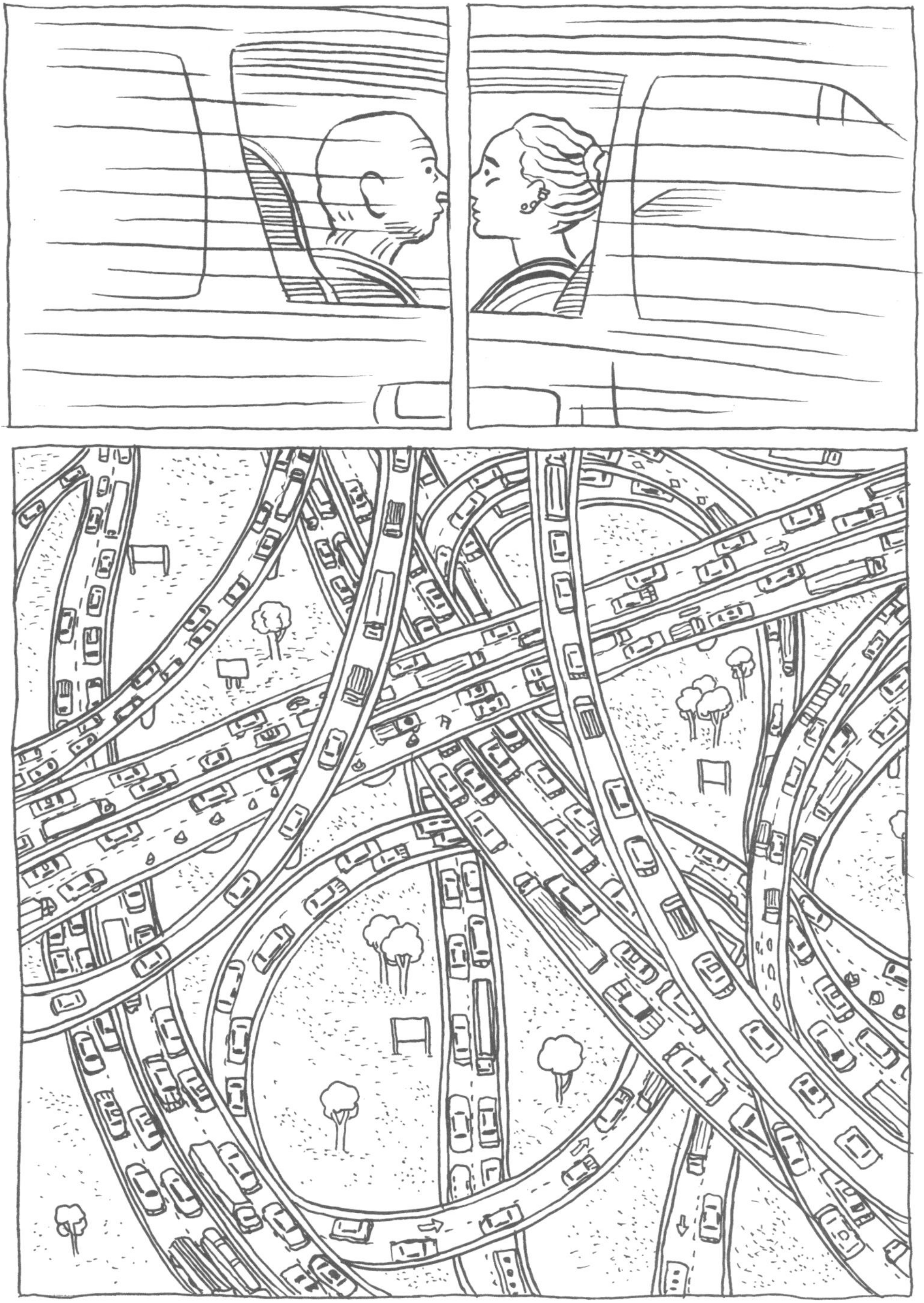

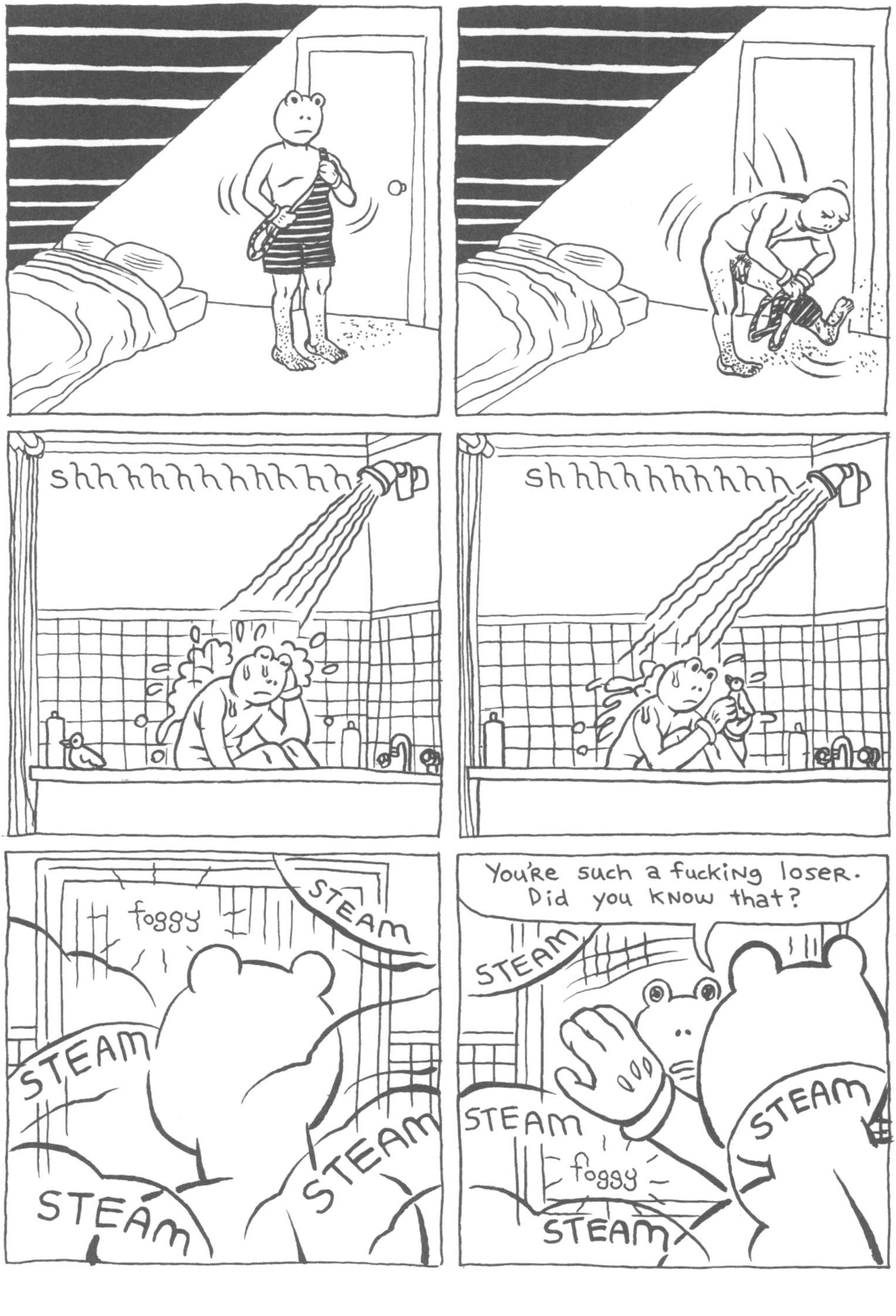

shhhhhhhhhhhh
shhhhhhhhhhh
foggy
STEAM
STEAM
STEAM
STEAM
You're such a fucking loser. Did you know that?
STEAM
STEAM
STEAM
foggy
STEAM

CLICK
hot newz
Bryce Givens let us visit her latest photo session for "Hot Thing" magazine.
She poses in a stunning bathing suit against the glimmering tidal waves.

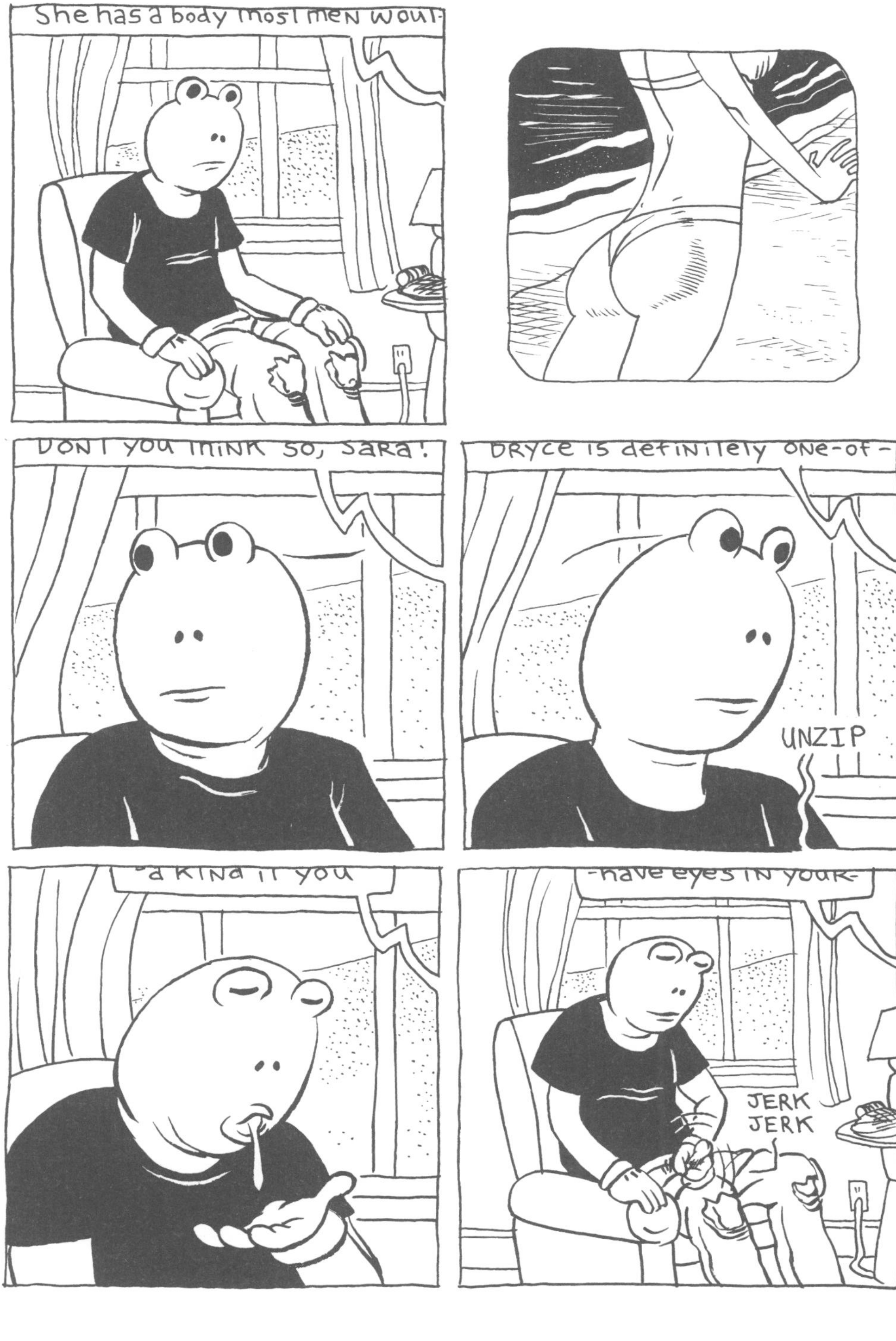
She has a body most men woul-
Don't you think so, Sara?
Bryce is definitely one-of-
UNZIP
-a kind if you
-have eyes in your-
JERK
JERK

SPURT
WIPE WIPE

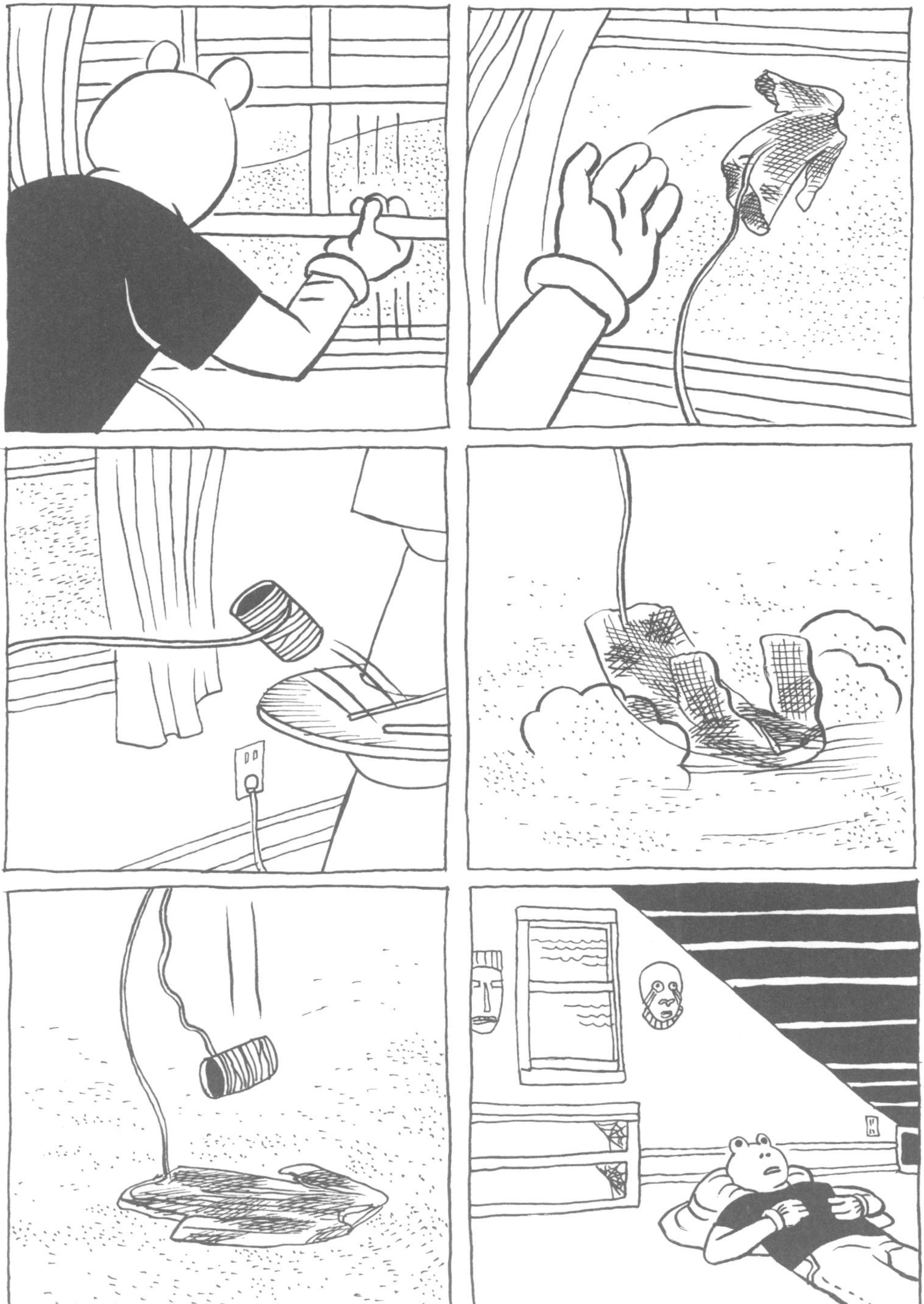

-just cuz my grandparents are getting divorced.
Yeah, it's totally boring.
Who cares? Right?
I'll take a bus and meet you there, 'kay?
Um.
Three hours.
See ya.

24

Can I sit there?
Sure.
Your'e going home?
No. I'm visiting a friend who lives in the city.
So you live by the ocean? That must be nice.
Well, I'm staying with my mom there. My whole family is there now.

A family reunion?
Sort of. My grandparents are getting divorced.
They've been married for, like, forty years. It's weird. My uncle is freaking-out about it.
How do you feel about it?
I dunno.
I barely, like, know them. Forty years is a long time, though. I've only gone out with a guy for a month, but he was a douche bag.
Oh.
I guess it's sad. But it's also kinda cool, right? Like: "It's not over yet!" But it'll prob--ably be over soon. My grampa can barely walk.
Any way, It sucks to be stuck here for a whole week.
You'd rather be with friends?

Yeah. My mom's a total tight-ass. She nags me about everything.
Uncle Peter's cool, but he's the depressed type, you know? I don't GET people like that. You can't be happy if you're totally depressed all the time. That's what I think, anyway.
Meanwhile all my friends back home are going camping and having a great time.
Sucks.
Have you ever gone camping?
No. I hate bugs, ya know.
So you're more of an indoor person.
Well,
I like beaches and, like, dunes, outdoor pools, and my grand parent's deck, I-um.
"grandparents"- are they still called "grandparents" if they're divorced?
Yes.

Yeah, I guess that makes sense.
Anyway, I like outdoor things, just not annoying, ugly bugs.
I understand that.
Outdoor pools don't get bugs?
My friend's one doesn't.
They have an outdoor spa too.
Her family's really rich and have lots of neat stuff.
You wish your family was like that?
Sure. I'm not gonna pull a "Being rich ruins you" thing. I'd love to have a lot of money.
How'd you spend it?
I'd get a motorcycle with a pony painted on the side.

You know, you're one of the nicest people I've ever met.
(HAH)
Really?
But you don't know anything about me.
24

Hey!
Do you have two bucks?
um.
Yeah.
Sure.

COME IN

NER
menu
I hope Jill's okay. She's meeting a friend in the city, I think.
She's fine, Claire. She's a teenager now. You were a teenager too.
Yeah.
Well, not really. I married Carl, junior year, and had Jill.
So, what? You want a beer?
No.
I'm getting you a beer.
WAITER?!!

My name's Tony and I'll be your server today.
Two pints of whatever's cheapest.
You need to loosen-up.
Beer makes me sick.
in my stomach.
ha. ha.
DINK
This is to Ma and Pa's futures.
The second and last divorce in your life.
WAITER!! ANOTHER!!
"last"? You think I'm going to die soon?
"Tony"
You gotta milk-mustache, only it's beer.

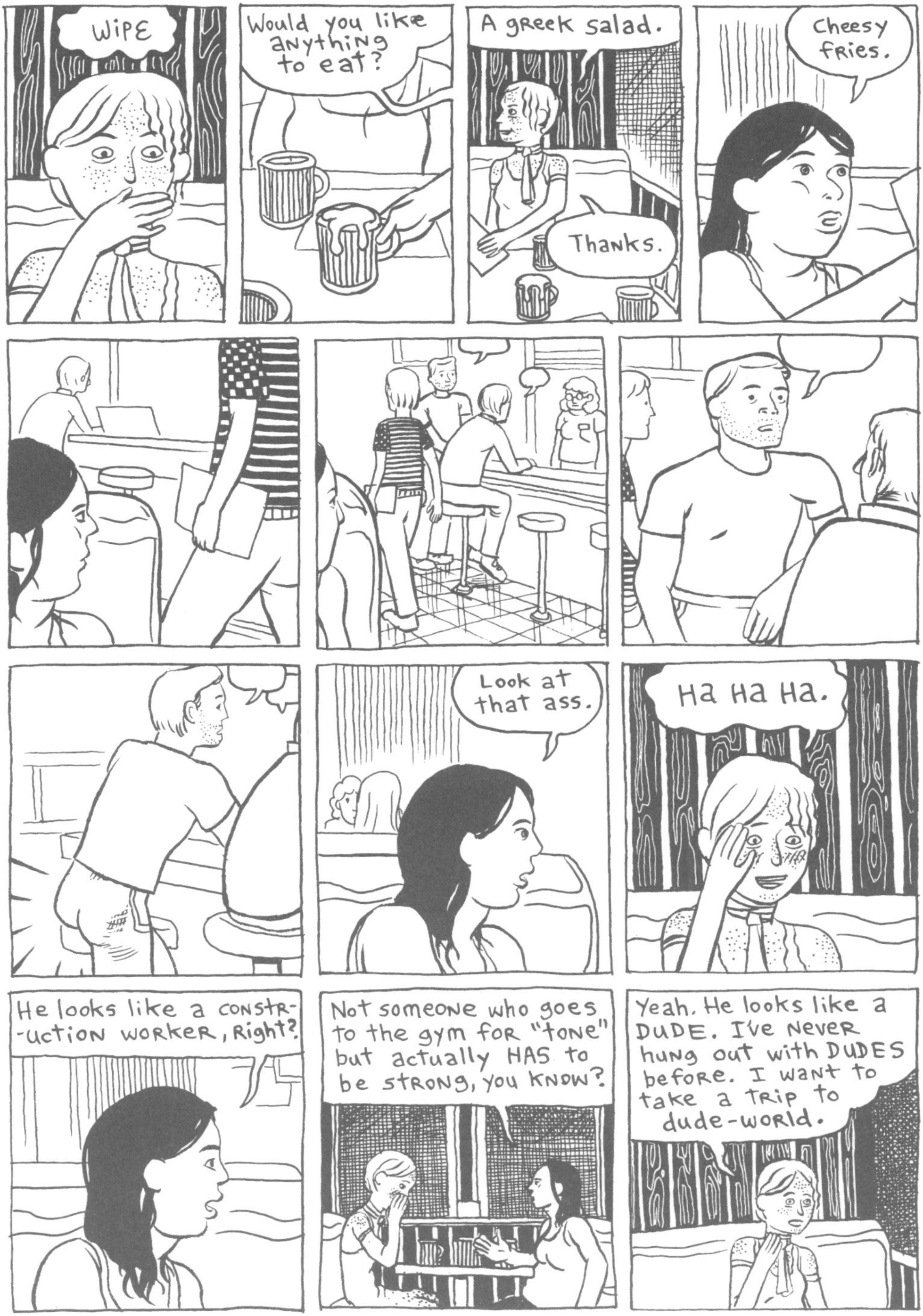
WIPE
Would you like anything to eat?
A greek salad.
Thanks.
Cheesy fries.
Look at that ass.
Ha Ha Ha.
He looks like a constr-
-uction worker, Right?
Not someone who goes to the gym for "tone" but actually HAS to be strong, you know?
Yeah. He looks like a DUDE. I've never hung out with DUDES before. I want to take a trip to dude-world.

Ha.
Ha.
Sports and all that.
I want to be a CHICK.
Carl was an arteest and he, like, existed in his own lil' world. You can't be with someone so self-involved. It's painful.
He'd get mood swings when he was creatively "stumped".
It was like being married to a girl.
Ha.
Ha.
Ha.
but the "arteest" has it's appeal, Right? I mean you LOVED him.
We were just obsessed with each-other.
Sip
Well, go up to the bar and talk to the dude, chick.
No, I can't.
So, you're "Chick"-en.

C'MON.
No.
You're a single woman.
I'm a single mother.
-Jill's all grown-up now.
What?
are you KIDDING?!
Look, I'm married, have a kid- The rest of my life is booked.
You're free.
Men are always free. It's not like now men take care of kids. Now we have jobs AND take care of kids.
I've heard that speech before, Aki.
I'm just saying: Enjoy yourself. You've earned it.
MUNCH MUNCH
look.
wait.

We're gonna go with him and a friend to a club.
WHAT?!
WAITER!! CHECK!!

SIP
SHUT
Hey, SORRY I'm late.
S'okay.
Ha
Ha Ha Ha Ha Ha Ha Ha Ha Ha Ha Ha Ha
Ha Ha
Ha
Ha
Ha
WOW.
Ha. Yeah.
Look at You.
Look at You.

What's up, girl? Love your hair.
Really? It gets frizzy.
That's a neat back-pack. It looks like you made it.
You look so much older now. You got, like, a growth spurt.
You look like you're twenty or something. You don't look 16.
Thanks.
What's up with you?
SCOOT
I haven't seen you since, like, we were freshman.
-You still going out with Andy?

ha. Well.
"Well" what?
Andy and I talked about it.
and we're breaking up on this Sunday.
omigod.
wait.
What does that mean?

We're, like, giving ourselves a tapering-off week.
He means so much to me. I love him, you know, and it blows to go out with someone for two years and then it ends in just one day.
So we're saying it'll end on Sunday and we can see it coming. Taper off.
huh.
Who's idea was that?

Mine. He was uncool with it at first but then we had this big talk and now he's totally cool with it.
ha ha.
Okay.
like-
Are you still sleeping with him? Do you kiss?
Well, YEAH.
We're still going-out with each-other.
O.K.

Do you want to go over to his place? He has beer there.
um.
Why do you always wanna talk in coffee places, Jill? Beer is the new coffee.
SHUT
COME IN
This city fucking blows.

LOUD MUSIC
CAN I GET FOUR OF THOSE!
DON'T SCREAM AT ME!
WHAT?!
I CAN'T HEAR YOU!
LOUD MUSIC
YOUR'E A GOOD DANCER!
HERE! TAKE ONE!
LOOK!
swallow

swallow
WHAT IS IT?
DO YOU FEEL IT YET?!
I DUNNO! I'VE NEVER REALLY DONE THIS KIND OF THING BEFORE!
DO YOU FEEL IT NOW?!
I'M NOT SURE!
IT'S GONNA KICK-IN! DO YOU FEEL IT?!
WHAT'S IT SUPPOSED TO FEEL LIKE?!
IT'S GONNA KICK-IN SOON! DO YOU FEEL IT NOW?!
I DON'T KNOW!
HAS IT KICKED-IN?!
YEAH

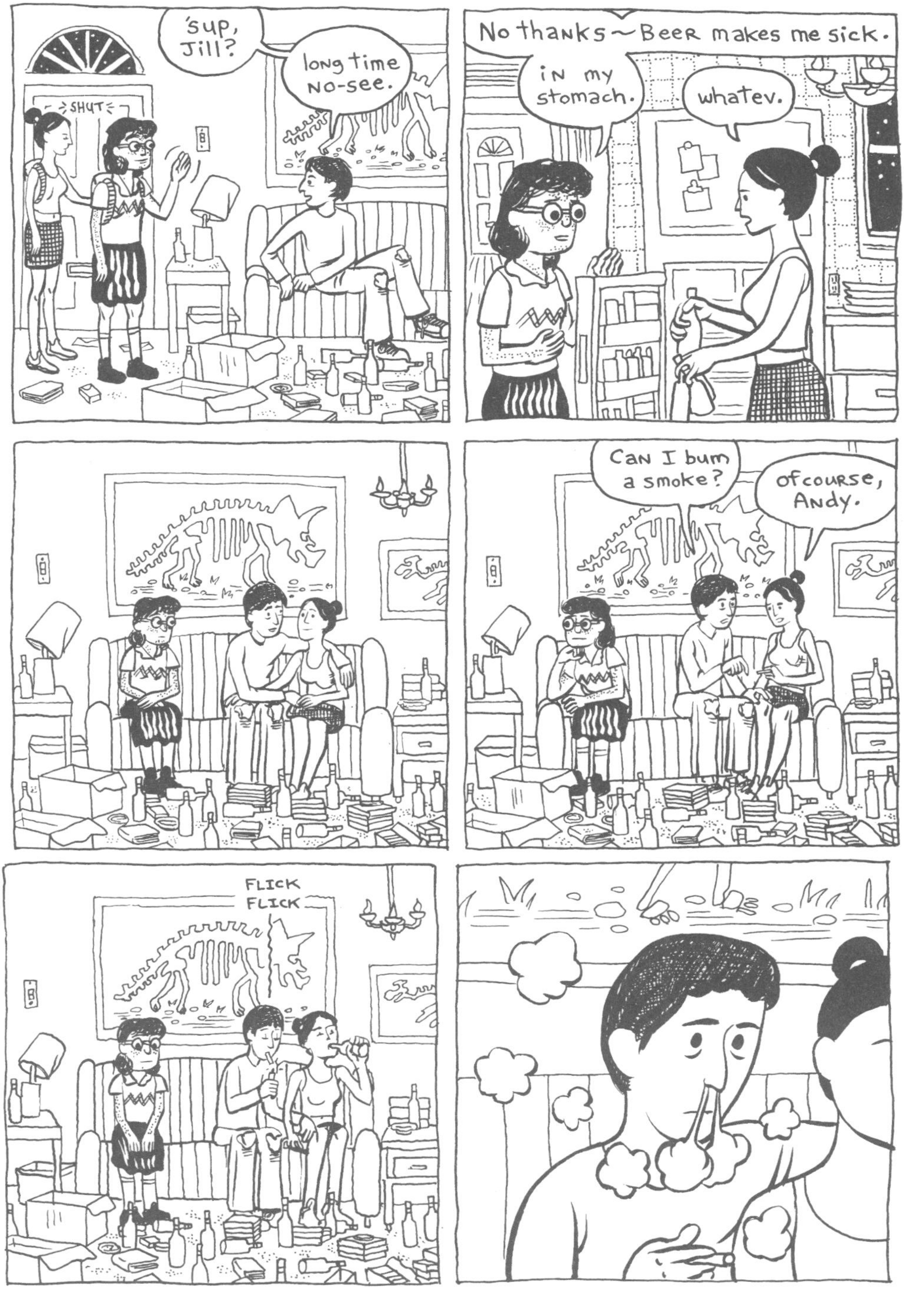
SHUT
'sup, Jill?
long time No-see.
No thanks~Beer makes me sick.
in my stomach.
whatev.
Can I bum a smoke?
of course, Andy.
FLICK
FLICK

I'm outta smokes. I'm gonna go to the store.
I'll be back in, like, five minutes.

Be safe.
I love you.
Hey. Listen to this song. I really dig it.
SHUT
So, what's up, Andy?
Well, y'know.

I like your hair. It's kinda, like, frizzy now.
Yeah, I guess so.
ha.
I always thought you were cute.
um.
Thanks.
-Sorry if that sounded weird.
(hah) No, No No.

You like this song?
S'okay.
SHRUG
I think it's beautiful. Sublime.
ha
Take off your glasses.
Why?
I'm curious.

ha.
ha.
What?
Do ya got freckles on your eyelids?

What're you doing?
huh?
I'm just going with the flow. That's, like, my philosophy.
You're going out with my friend.
You don't like me? You think I'm full of shit, right?
No, No. Andy.
You don't want to.
fine.

I dunno. I think YOU should think about it, you know?
(hah)
I mean, if you want to and I want to, what's to think about? Thoughts just get in the way of FEELINGS.
You're drunk.
Ha. No, No. Just listen to your feelings.
SLAM!
WHAT THE FUCK?!
drop

SHUT
LOUD MUSIC
SHIT STINK
TAMPON
LOUD MUS
SHIT STINK
What's up?
LOUD MUSIC
TOXIC SHOCK SYNDROME??

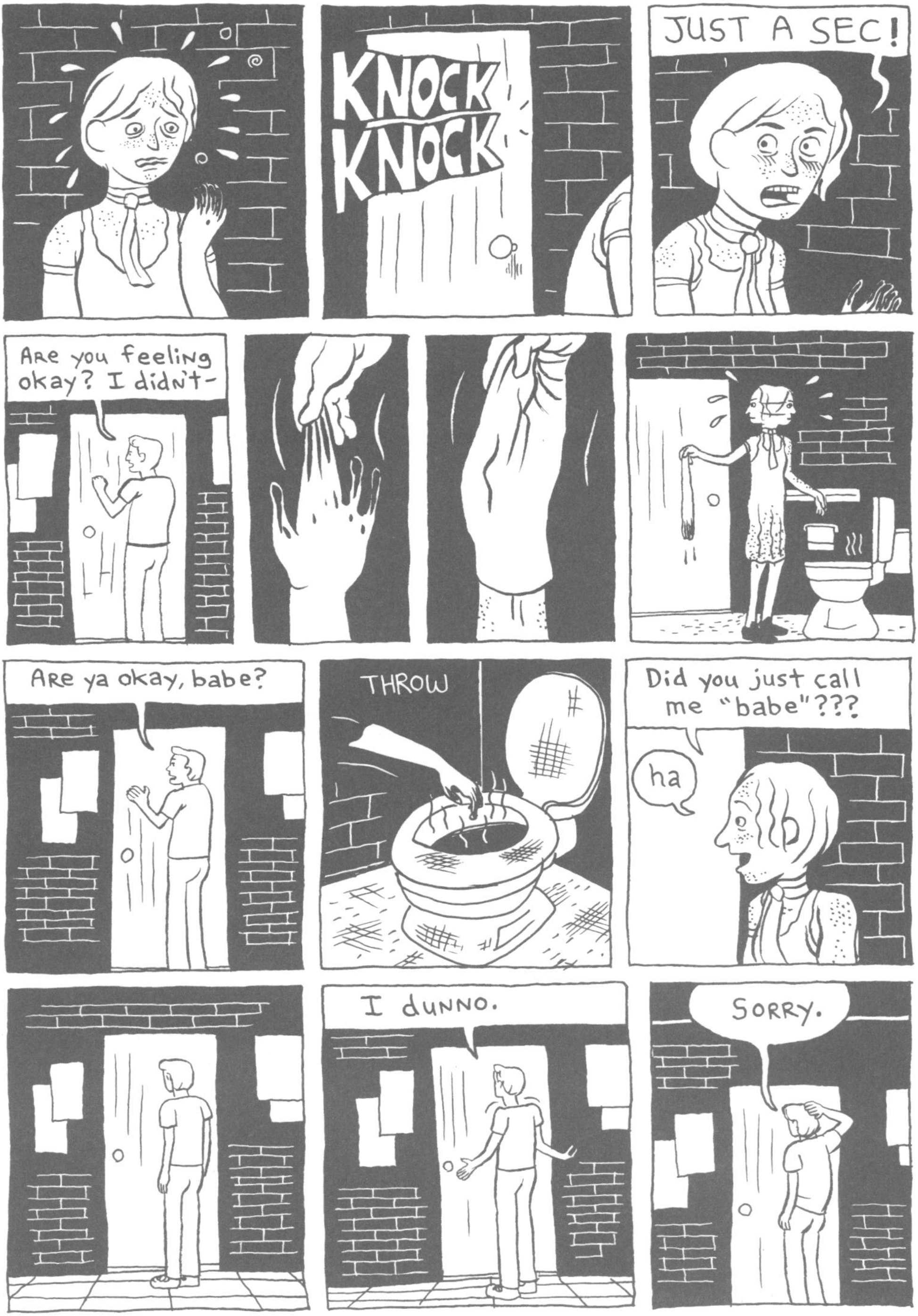
KNOCK KNOCK
JUST A SEC!
Are you feeling okay? I didn't-
Are ya okay, babe?
THROW
Did you just call me "babe"???
ha
I dunno.
SORRY.

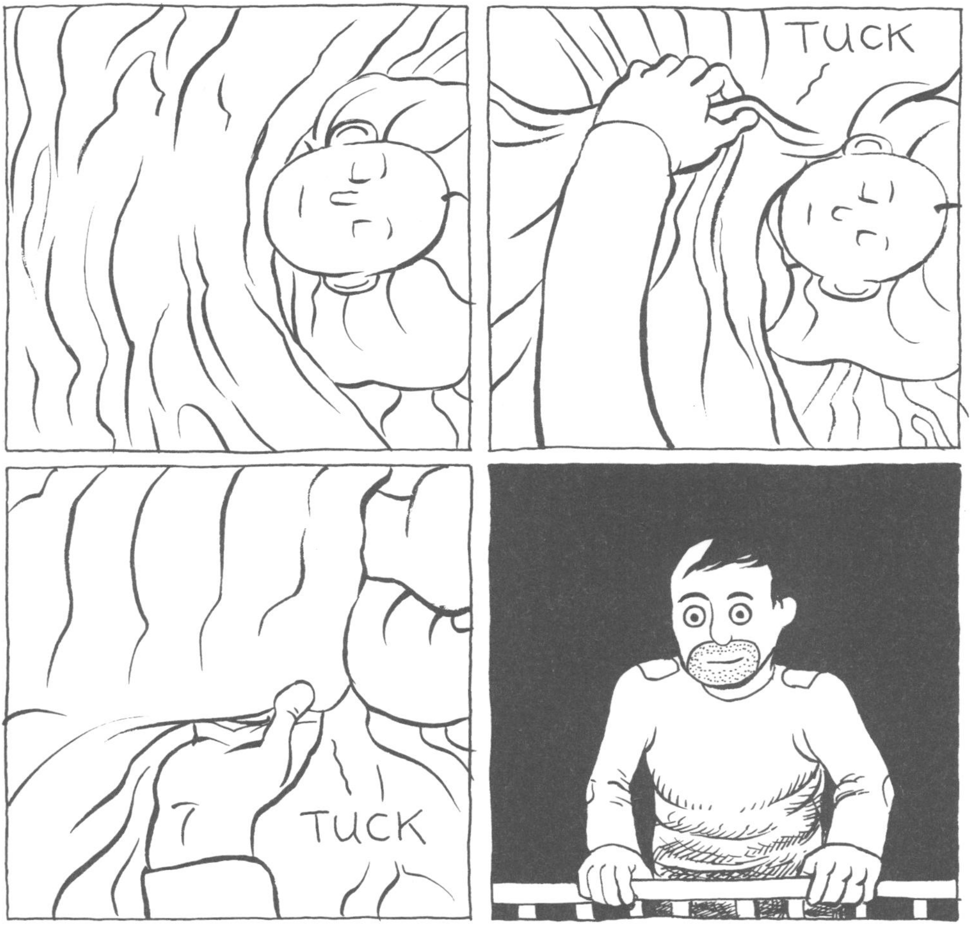
TUCK
TUCK

KNOCK KNOCK
What's up, Petey?
Whoa. You're SUDDENLY interested in talking to me?

You seem like a really interesting person.
Whoa. Whoa.
CHILL THE FUCK OUT.
Ha Ha Ha Ha Ha Ha
You trying to embarass me??
You're embarassing yourself, man.
I KNOW WHO YOU ARE! You were here, like, a year ago and hooked up with my friend a-
SHUT UP
That wasn't me! You're just a drunk creep.
I KNOW who you are. Fuck you.
SPIT

You're a fat piggy.
SOK
SOK
SOK
WACK
SOK
Let me just get my friend and then I'll leave, O.K.?
FUCK! HE *KICKED* ME!
SHUT
HEY!
Wher'd you go?
Dude?

Smack
Smack
baby baby
SMACK
Smack
SNif
I-
DON'T TALK TO ME!
YOU'RE A DICK
HEY, IT'S NOT-
um
YOU'RE NOT BET
DON'T TOUCH ME!
SLAM

FUCK-
I- I-
CALM DOWN!
baby
I JUST CAN'T EVEN FUCKING BELIEVE YOU! I THOUGHT-
BUT WHAT THE FUCK DO YOU EVEN CARE?
WITH JILL?! ~SHE LOOKS LIKE A MAN! A DOOFY, CURLY~HAIRED MAN!
BUT WHAT DOES IT EVEN MATTER TO YOU, HUH?
FUCK YOU~ "WHAT DOES"-
I'M JUST SAYING-

SURGEON GENERAL
SWIPE
SLAM
FLICK
FLICK
-SUCK
PUFF
PUFF

SUCK
caf
coff
coff
coff
SPIT

Ha
Ha Ha Ha Ha Ha Ha Ha Ha Ha Ha Ha Ha
Ha
Ha
Limp
dINK
FUCK, that prick really fucked-up my leg. God, people are such garbage.
Were you KISSING that guy?

Yeesh, No! That guy was ass-ugly!
ha
SHAKE
Are you going to tell Dennis about it?
Fuck, Claire!
Dennis freaks-out about stuff like that!
You okay?
I'm fine.
heh
BEEP BEEP
DROP
BEEP
BEEP
CLICK
WUZZUP?!

um.
Is this mom?
HUK! HUK!
ahem.
yes, Dear?
I'm outside the theater on Grace.
Can you come pick me up?

The End

How was the movie?
Good.
Ha Ha
we didn't-
oh, SHIT
I should drive. Pull over.

SHUT
SHUT
You okay?
Claire?
Ha!
HA! Ha!
You puke A LOT FOR a SKINNY gal!
I LOOK LIKE A MAN.

SHUT
I'm all good.
Did you have a good time with your friend?
S'okay.
That's great. I'm glad someone had a good time.

ha ha
UNFASTEN
FASTEN
WHAT is your PROBLEM?
my glove thingie.
I tried to flush it down the pooper, I think.
ha ha ha!
I feel so sick.
We'll be home soon and you can get some medicine.

Ha!
UNFASTEN
FASTEN
CUT IT OUT!
THAT'S DANGEROUS!
HUK! HUK!
God! ACT YOUR AGE! This really isn't like you!
YOU DON'T KNOW ME!
Ha
Ha Ha HA Ha
Ha!
GRUMBLE
GRUMBLE

OOHHHH
oooh
You NEVER drink! You are so RETARDED.
AKI WAS DRINKING TOO!
Ha Ha
Pfff.... whatever.
"Pfff"
"WHATEVER"

TAP
TAP

PHOTO ALBUM
ALBUM

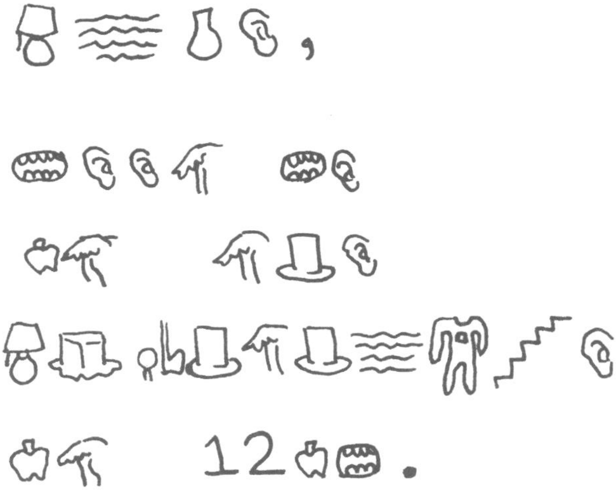
12

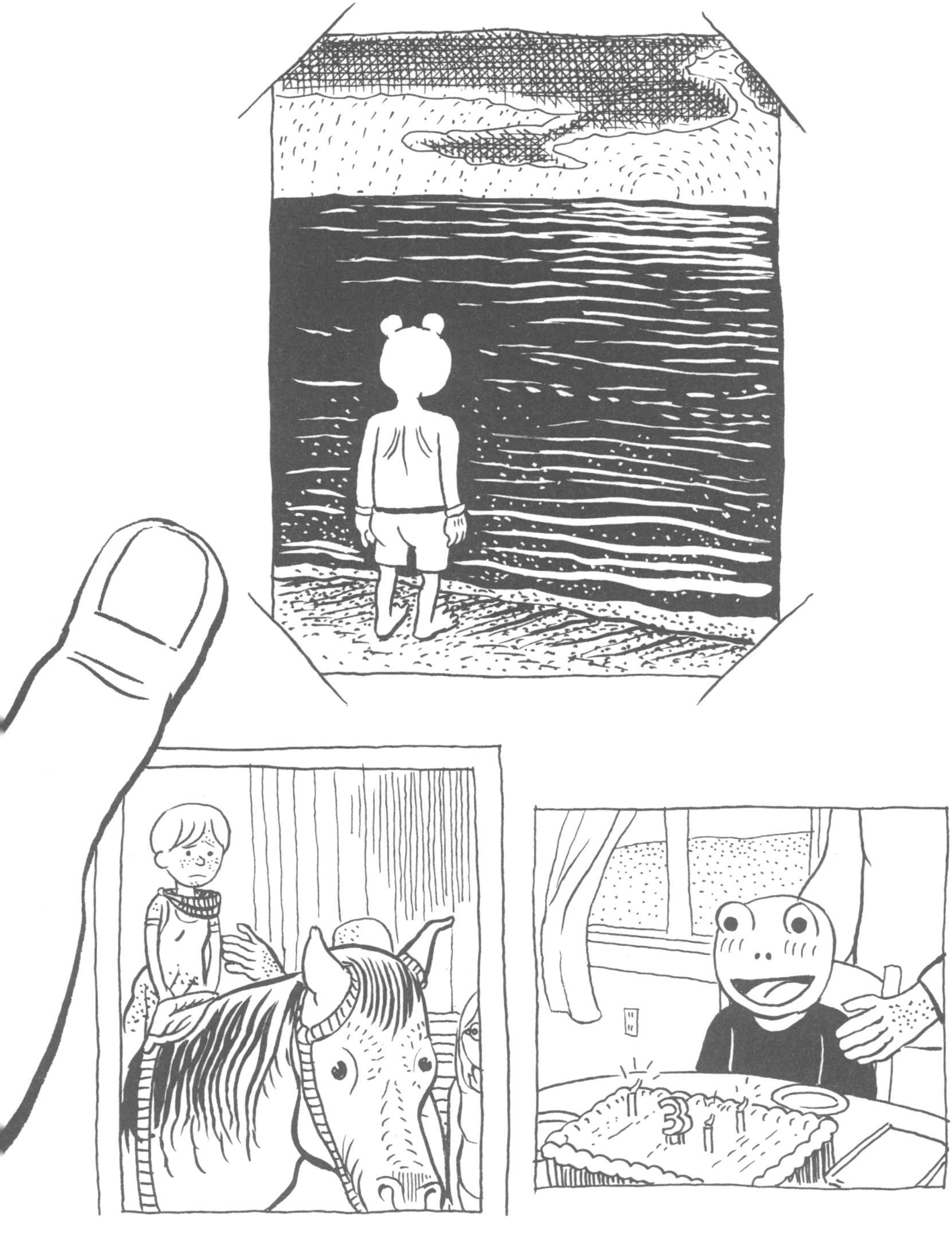

Peter's drawing of
"Mommy and Daddy,"
(age 3)

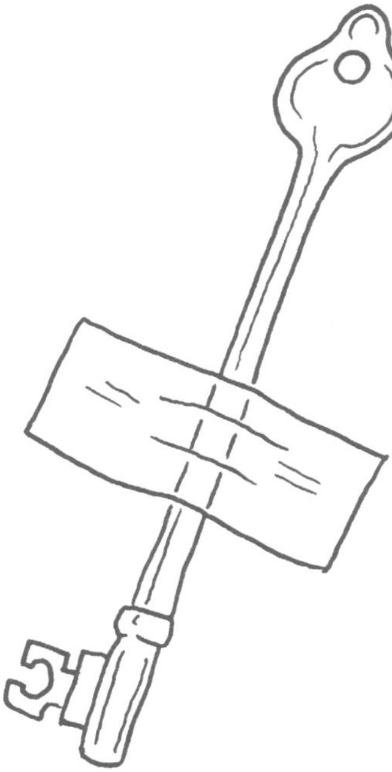

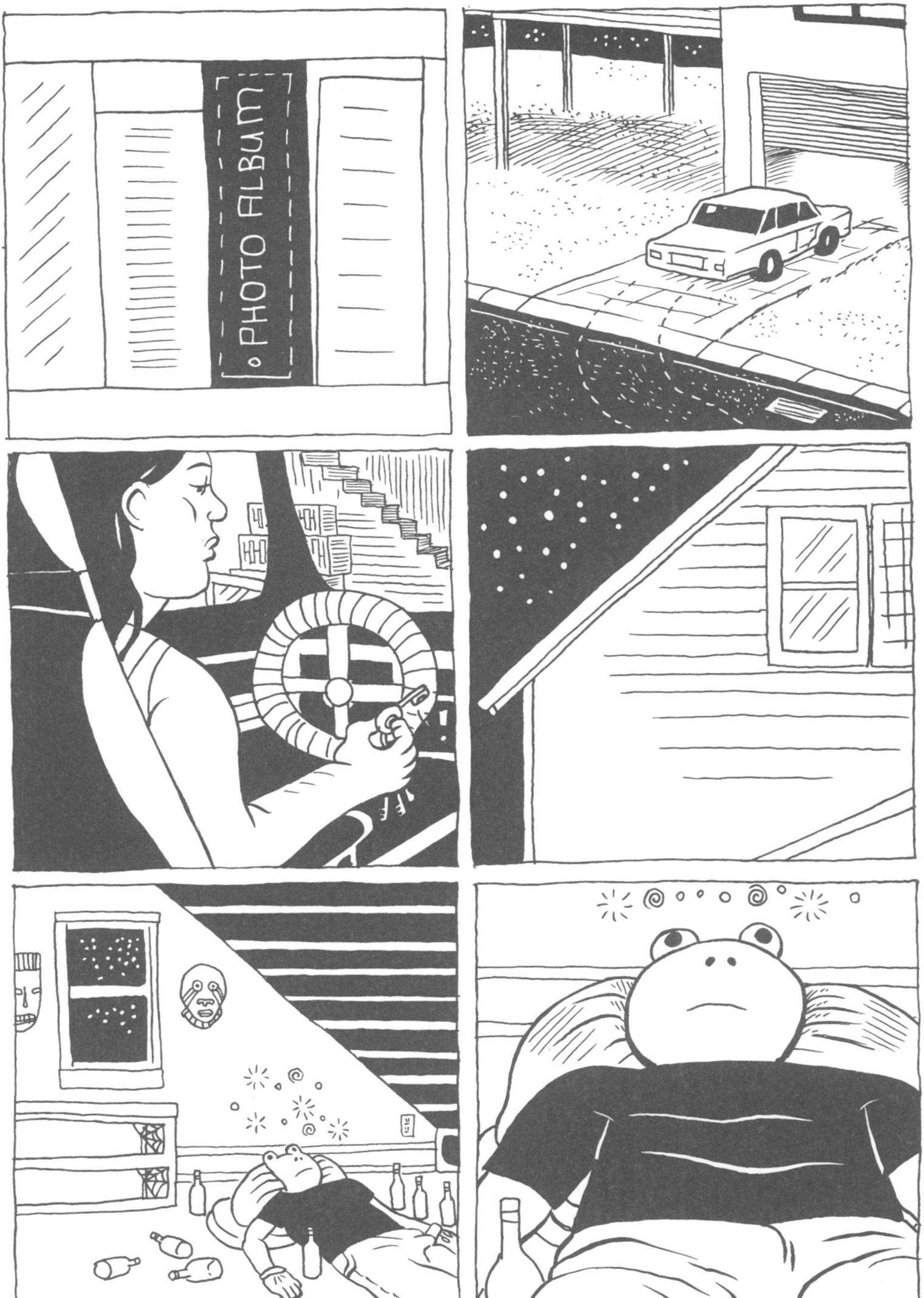
PHOTO ALBUM

WAKING DREAM

I'M JUST LIKE YOU, ONLY I DON'T SMOKE OR DRINK. I GO TO THE GYM INSTEAD.
I HAVE A BEAUTIFUL GIRLFRIEND.
ALSO, I AM NOT LONELY OR MISERABLE. I AM BETTER THAN YOU IN EVERY WAY.

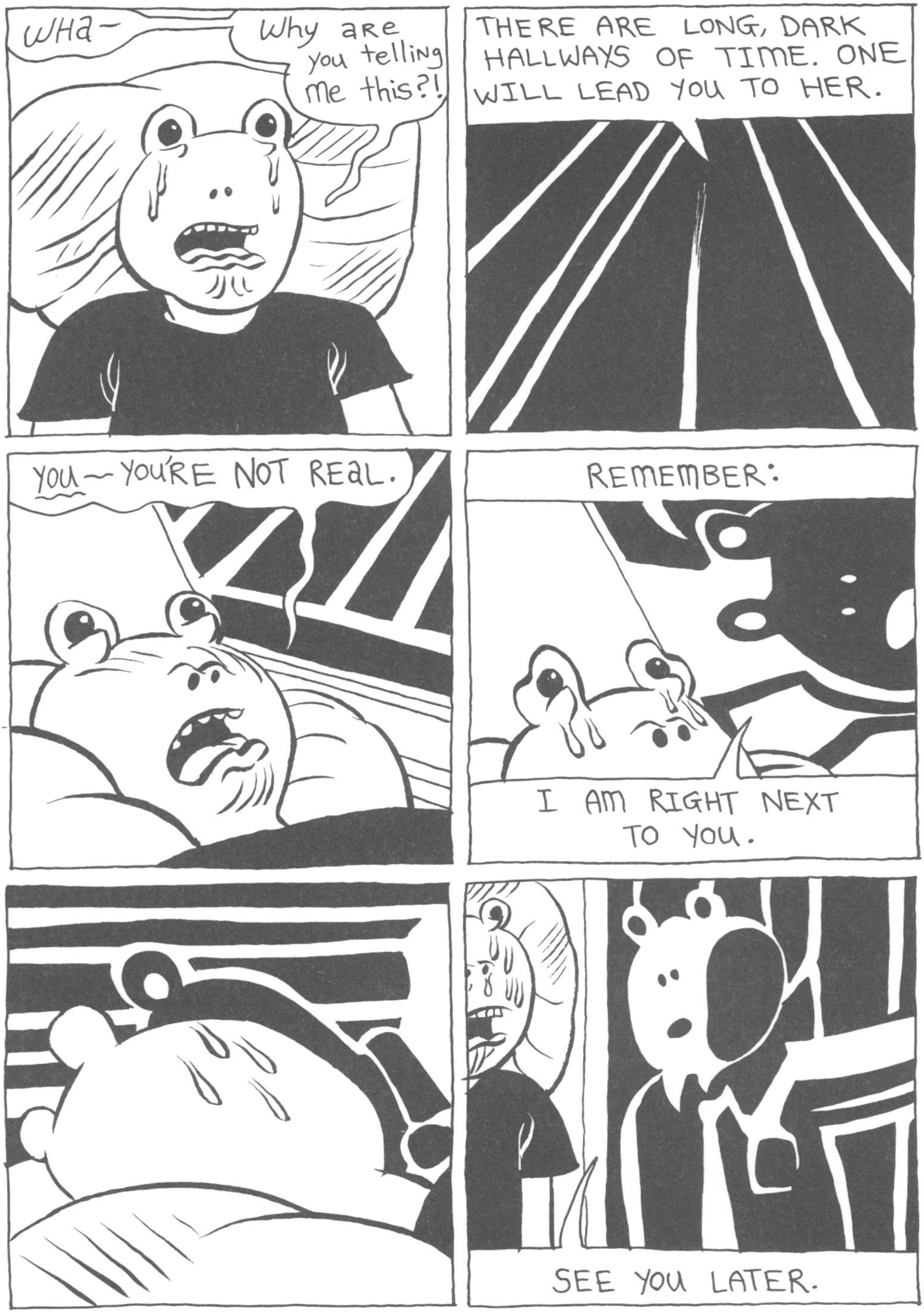
WHA–
Why are you telling me this?!
THERE ARE LONG, DARK HALLWAYS OF TIME. ONE WILL LEAD YOU TO HER.
YOU– YOU'RE NOT REAL.
REMEMBER:
I AM RIGHT NEXT TO YOU.
SEE YOU LATER.

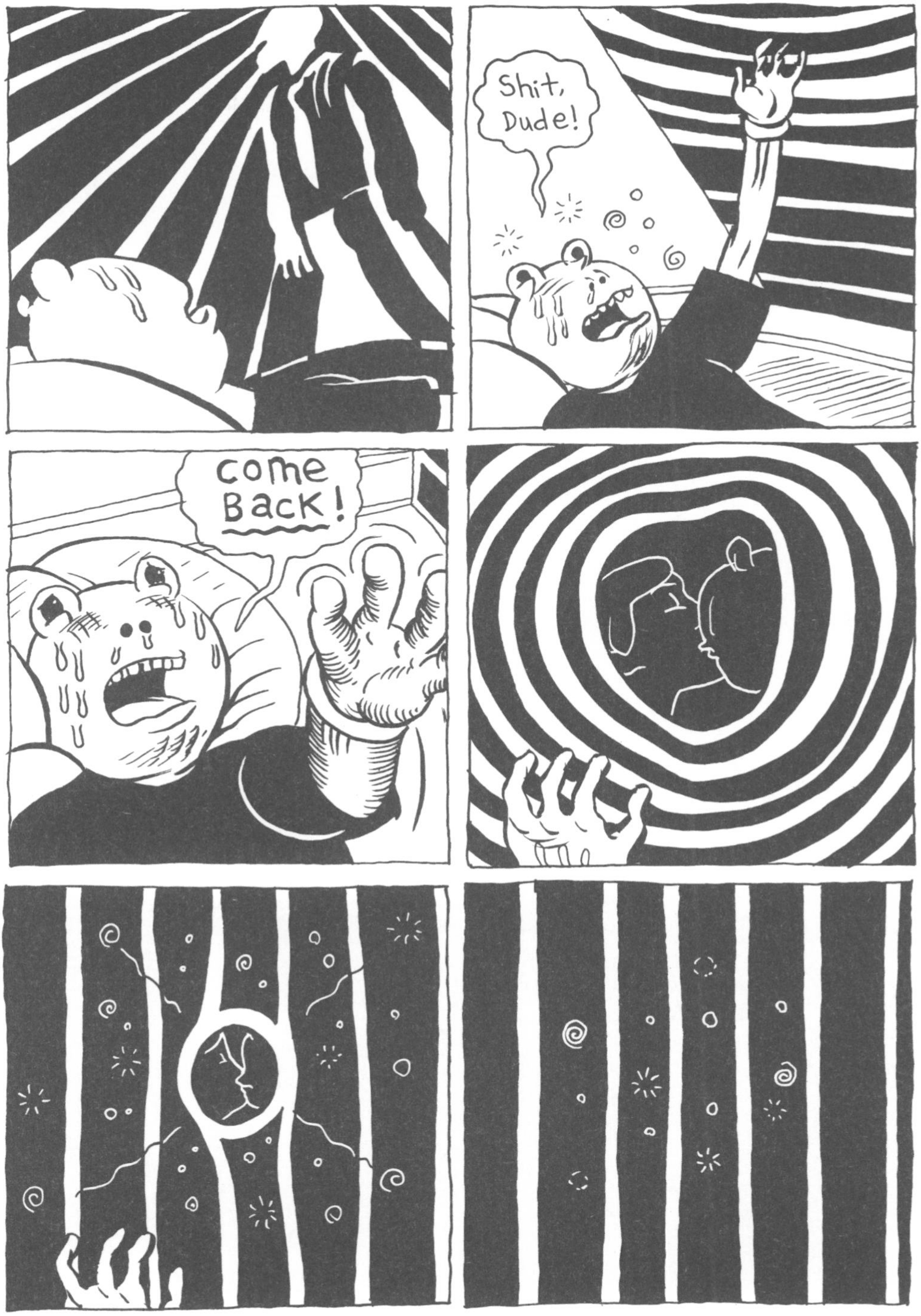
Shit, Dude!
Come Back!

GRUMBLE
BLINK BLINK

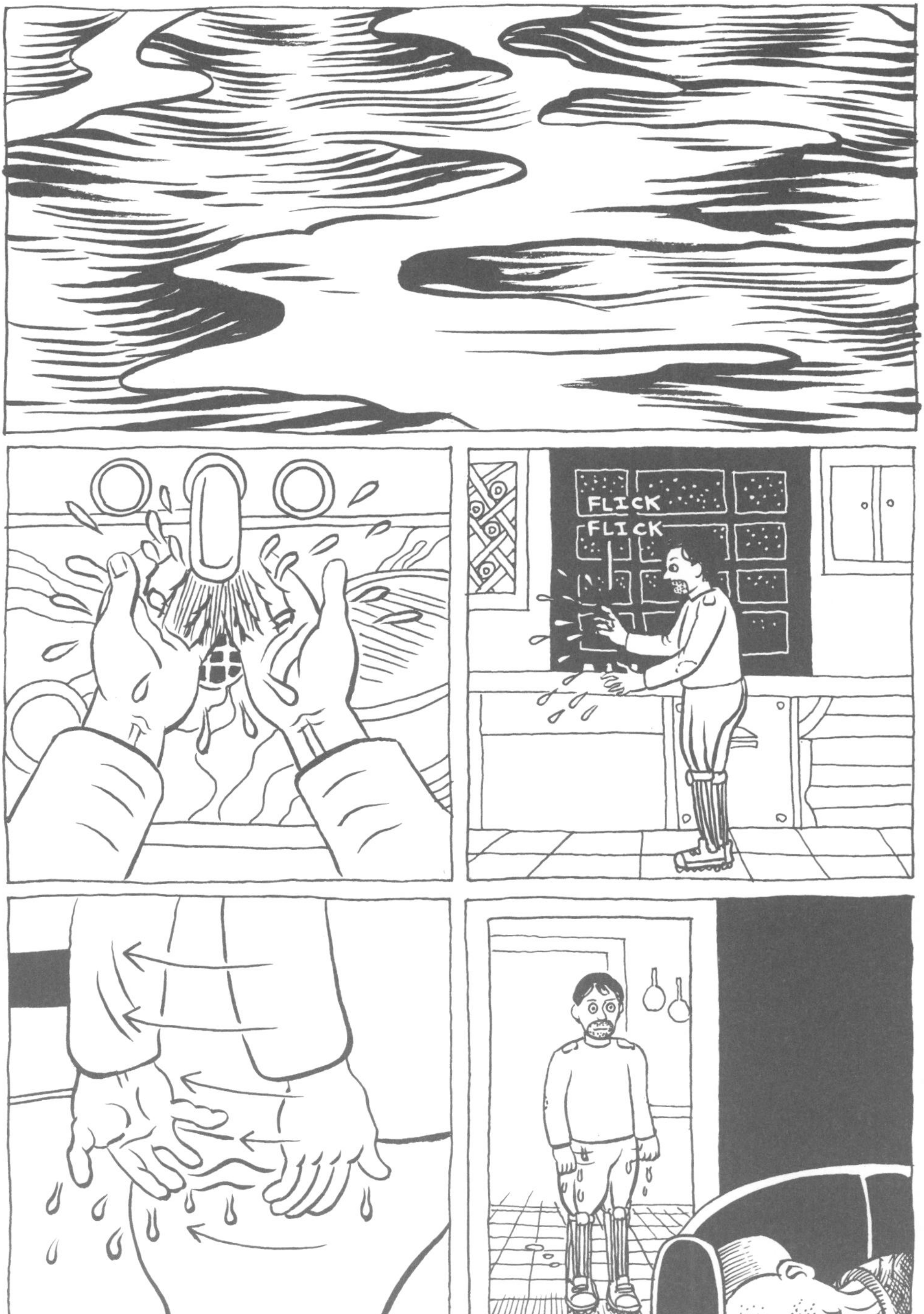
FLICK
FLICK

What're you doing down here, dad?
SHRUG
Well,
I'm tired.
Here.
Let me carry you to bed.

DENNIS.
DON'T.
I sleep on the couch.
That's not good for your back, Dad.
No wonder you ache.
ha.

Sleep in your bedroom.
Your mother has that bed.
We ARE getting divorced, DENNIS.

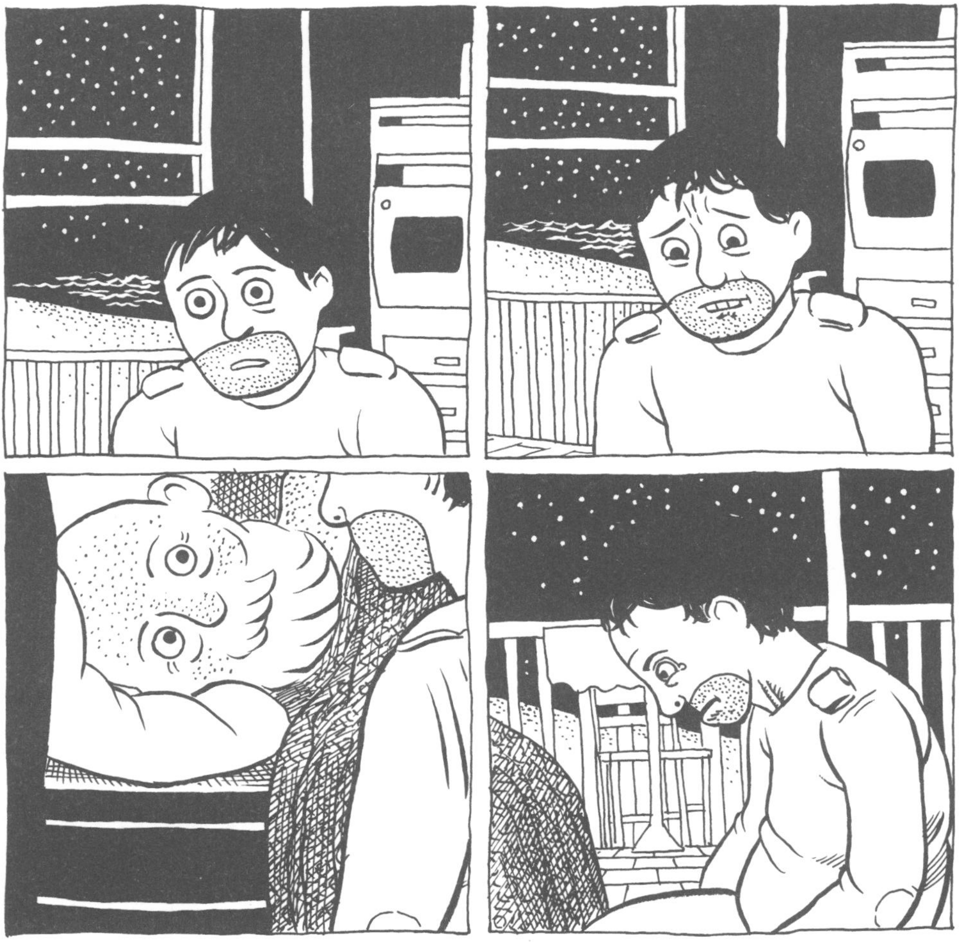

DENNIS.
SNIF
GRIT
DON'T CRY.

ZZZZ
ZZZ
ZZZ

Goodnight.
Goodnight.

LOON

Hey.

Hey.

You're up late.

So are you.

Ha. Ha.
I guess SO.
Come iN.

COLD
COLD

ha ha.

It feels Nice, Right?

Uh-huh.

It was hard to go in. But now it's nice. Really nice.

Here.
I found this.

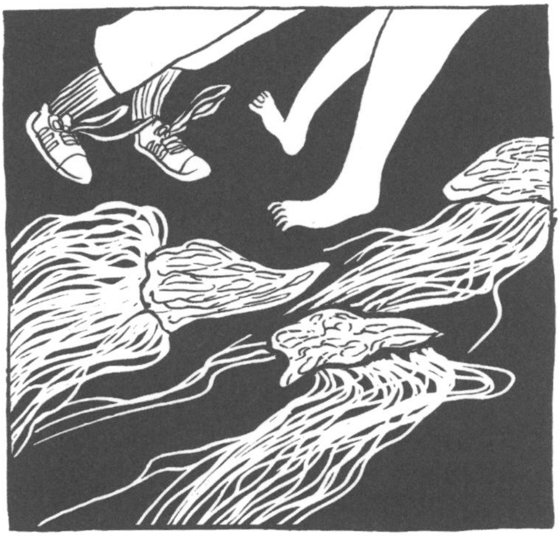

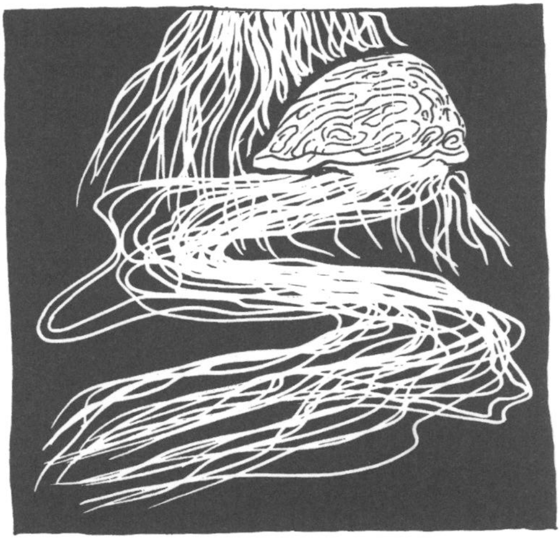

End of Part One

Part Two

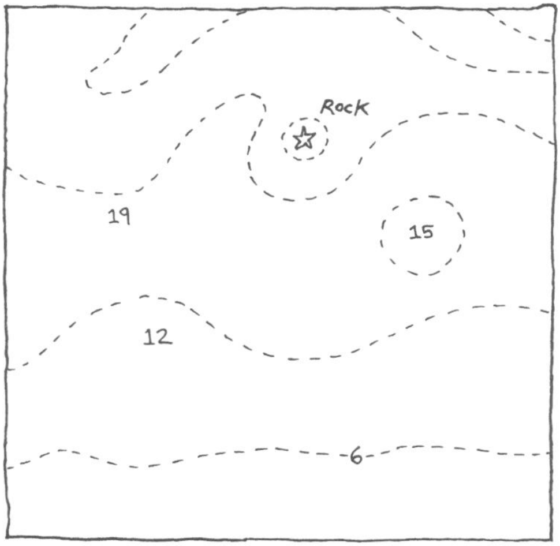
Rock
19
15
12
6

BEACH

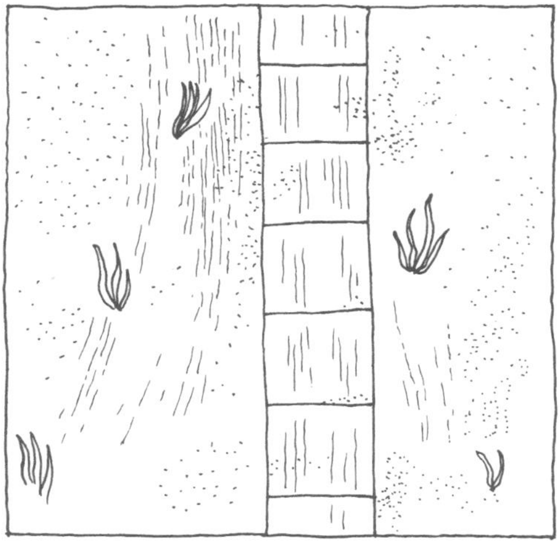

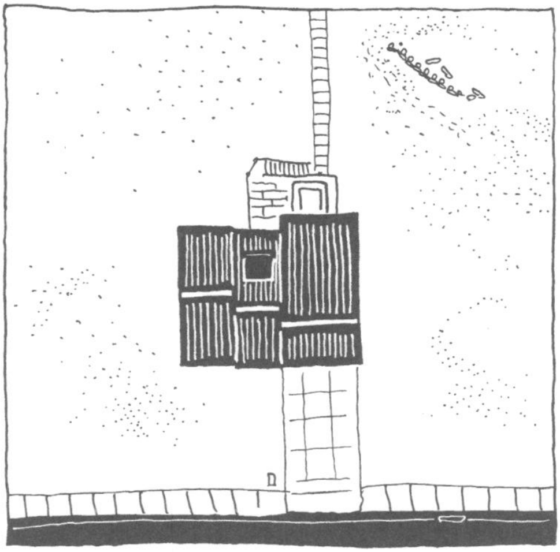

First Floor:

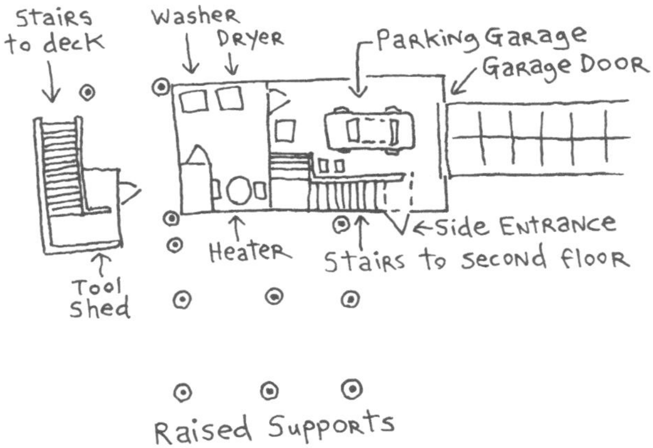

Second Floor:

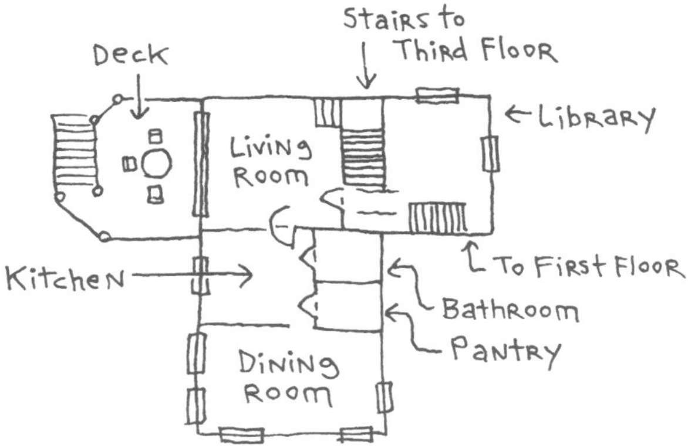

Third Floor:

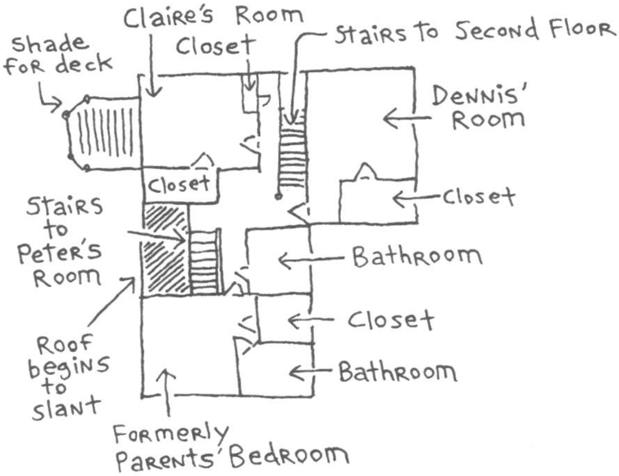

Fourth Floor (Peter's Room):

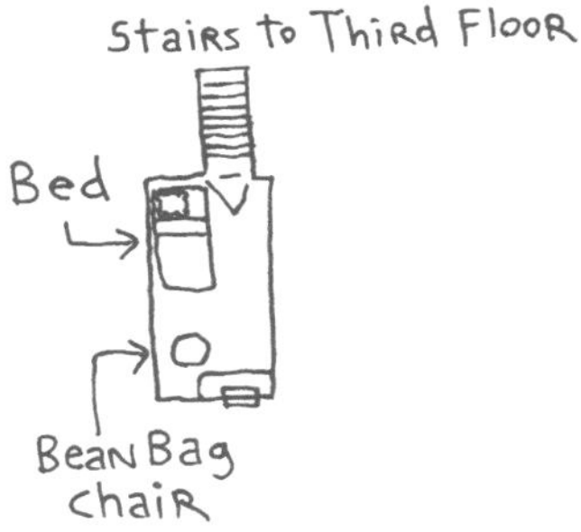

Claire's Room:

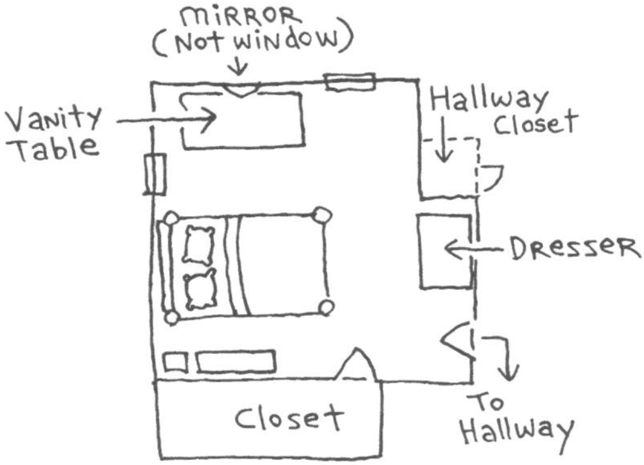

Dennis' Room:

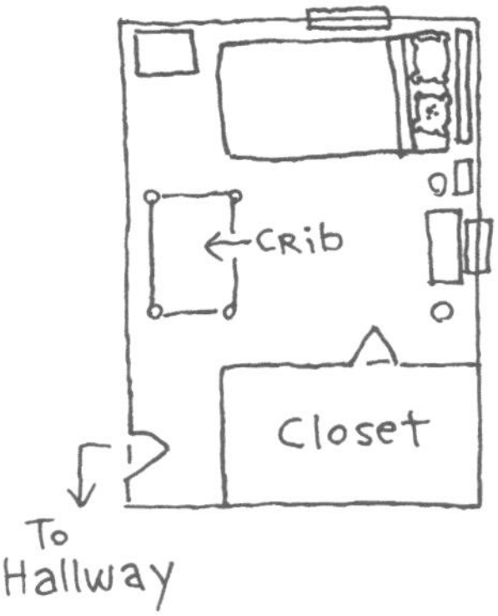

Formerly Parents' Room (Now Mom's Room):

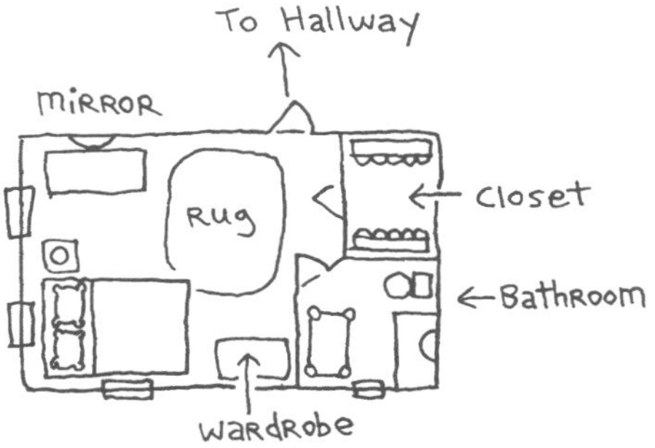

Hallway Bathroom:

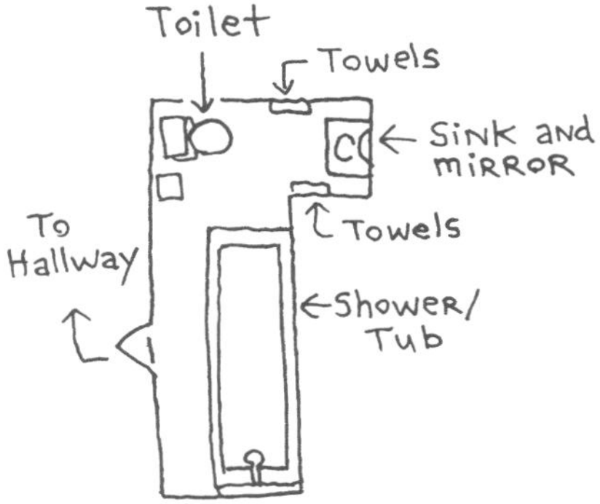

Living Room:

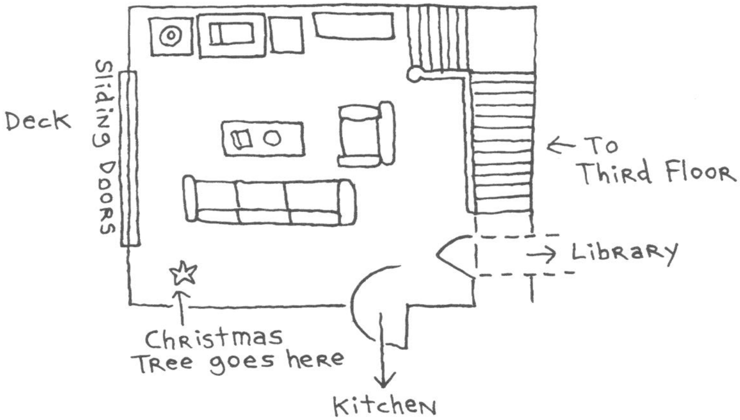

Kitchen:

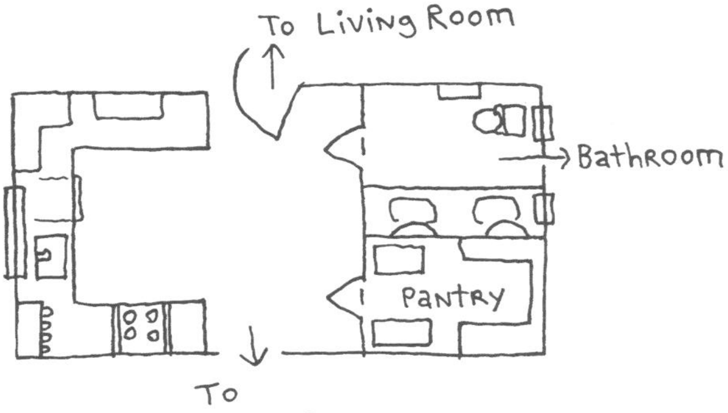

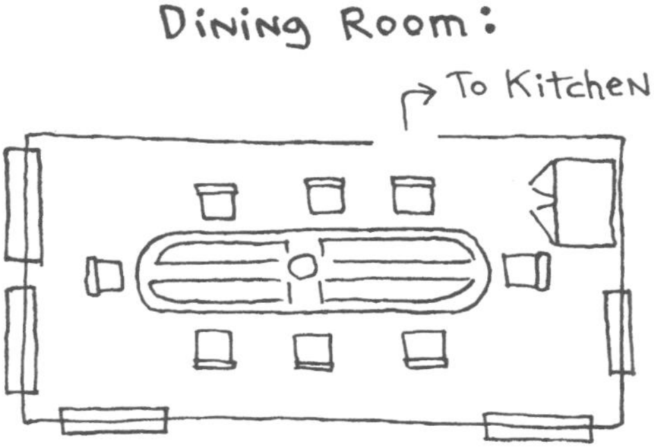
Dining Room:
To Kitchen

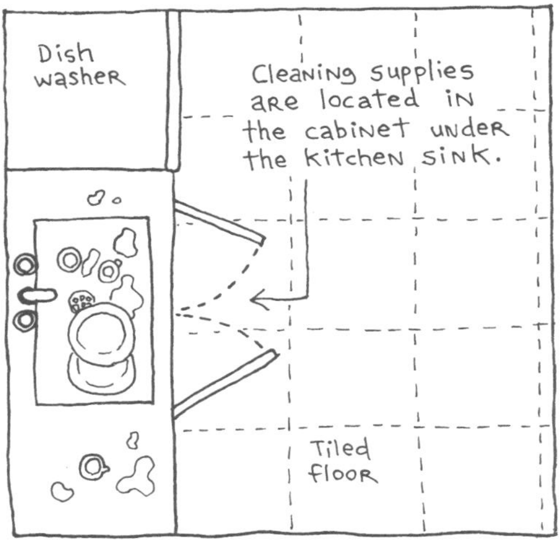
Dish washer
Cleaning supplies are located in the cabinet under the kitchen sink.
Tiled floor

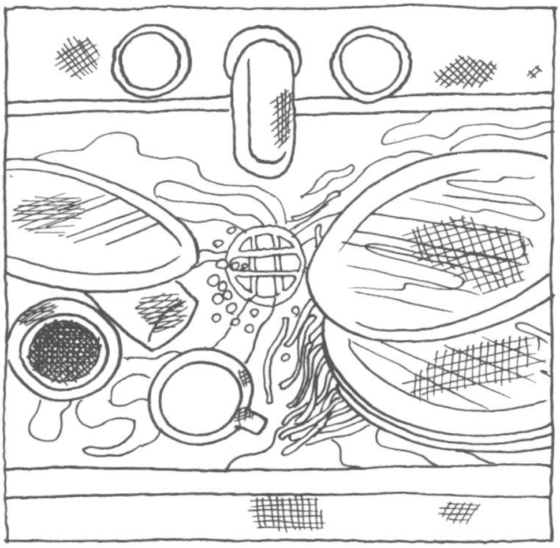

SUCK

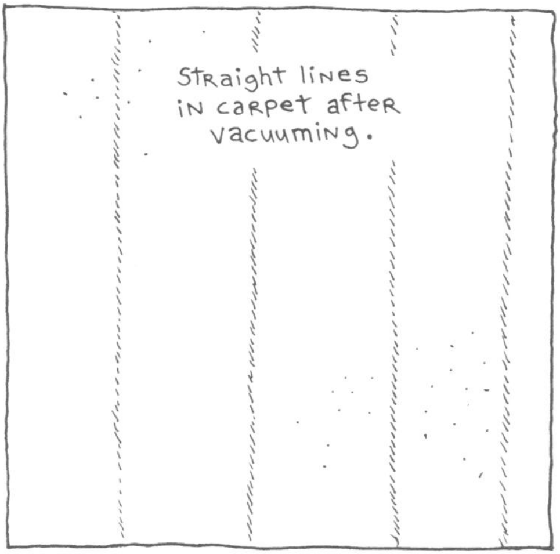
Straight lines
in carpet after
vacuuming.

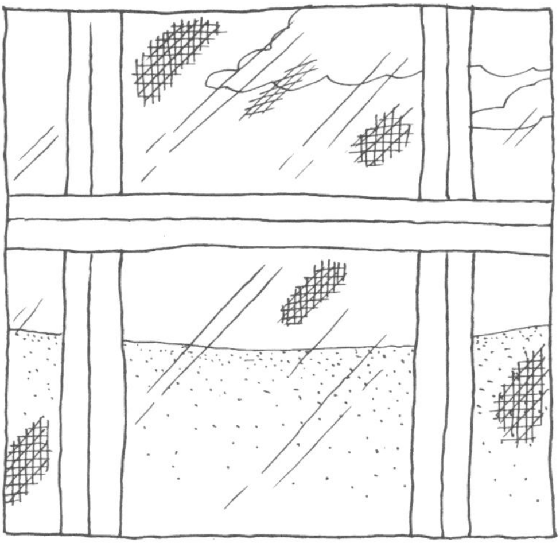

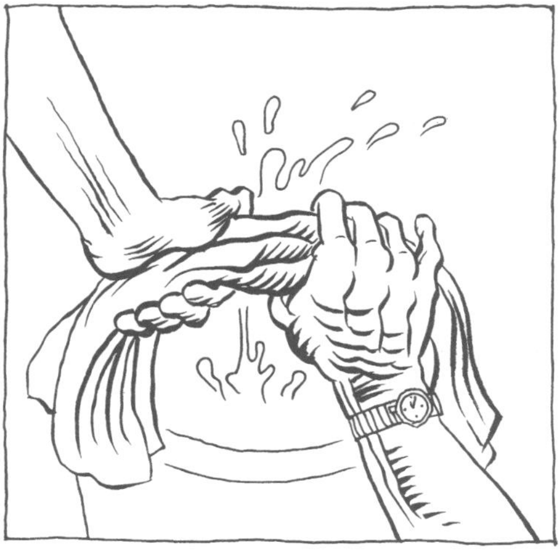

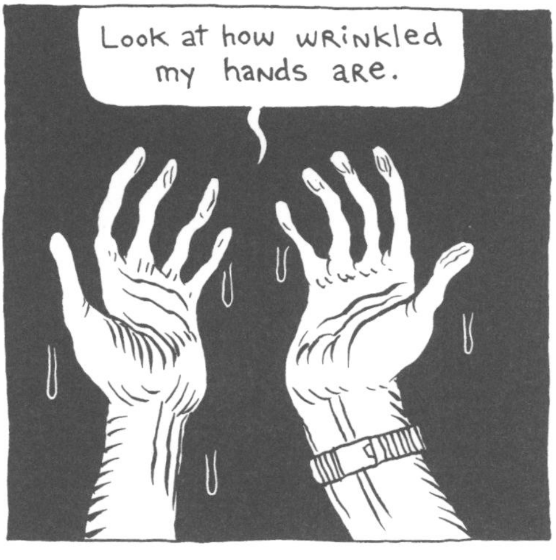
Look at how wrinkled my hands are.

Yeah, grammy.
You're old.

Oh. Look at what time it is.

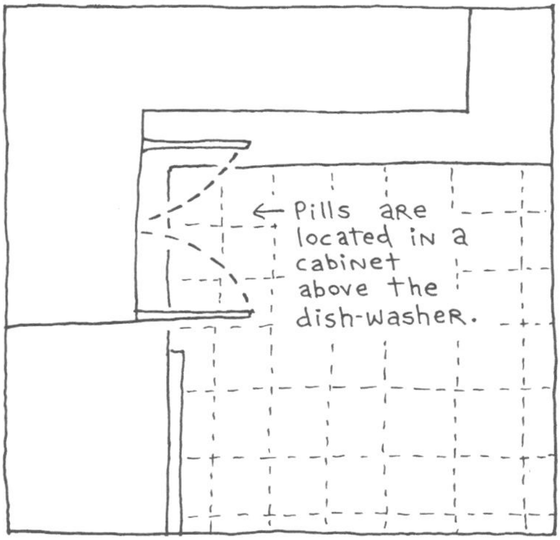
Pills are located in a cabinet above the dish-washer.

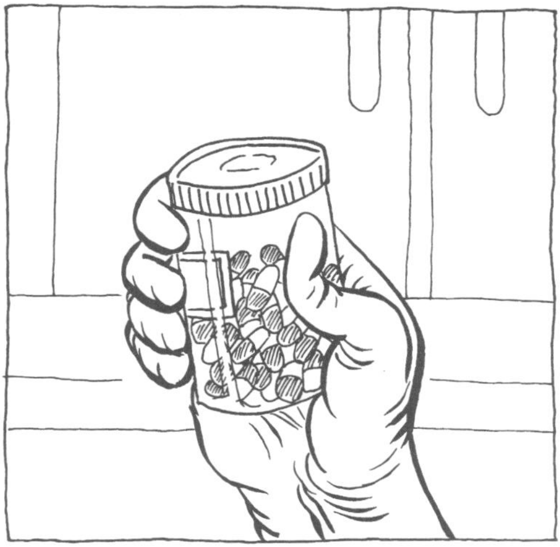

Here you go.

God damn it.

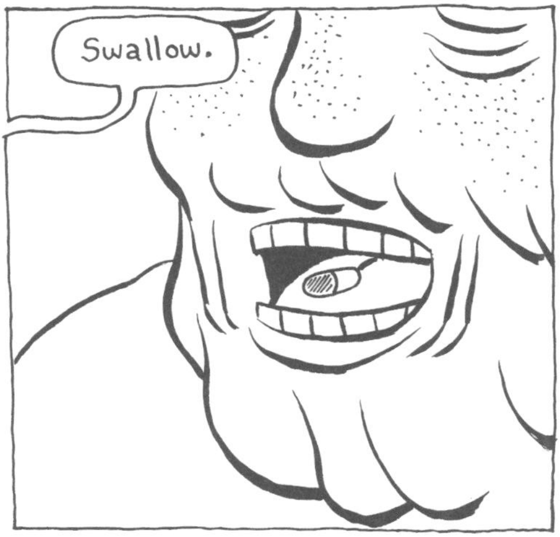
Swallow.

yawn

I hung out with that girl Kat last night.
NO FUCKIN' WAY! I told you! I knew you two would hit it off! You're a fucking PLAYER, Peter!
I-I'm not a "player," I just—
YOU'RE A FUCKIN' PLAYER!
Peter hooked up with a hot chick last night!
Is that good?

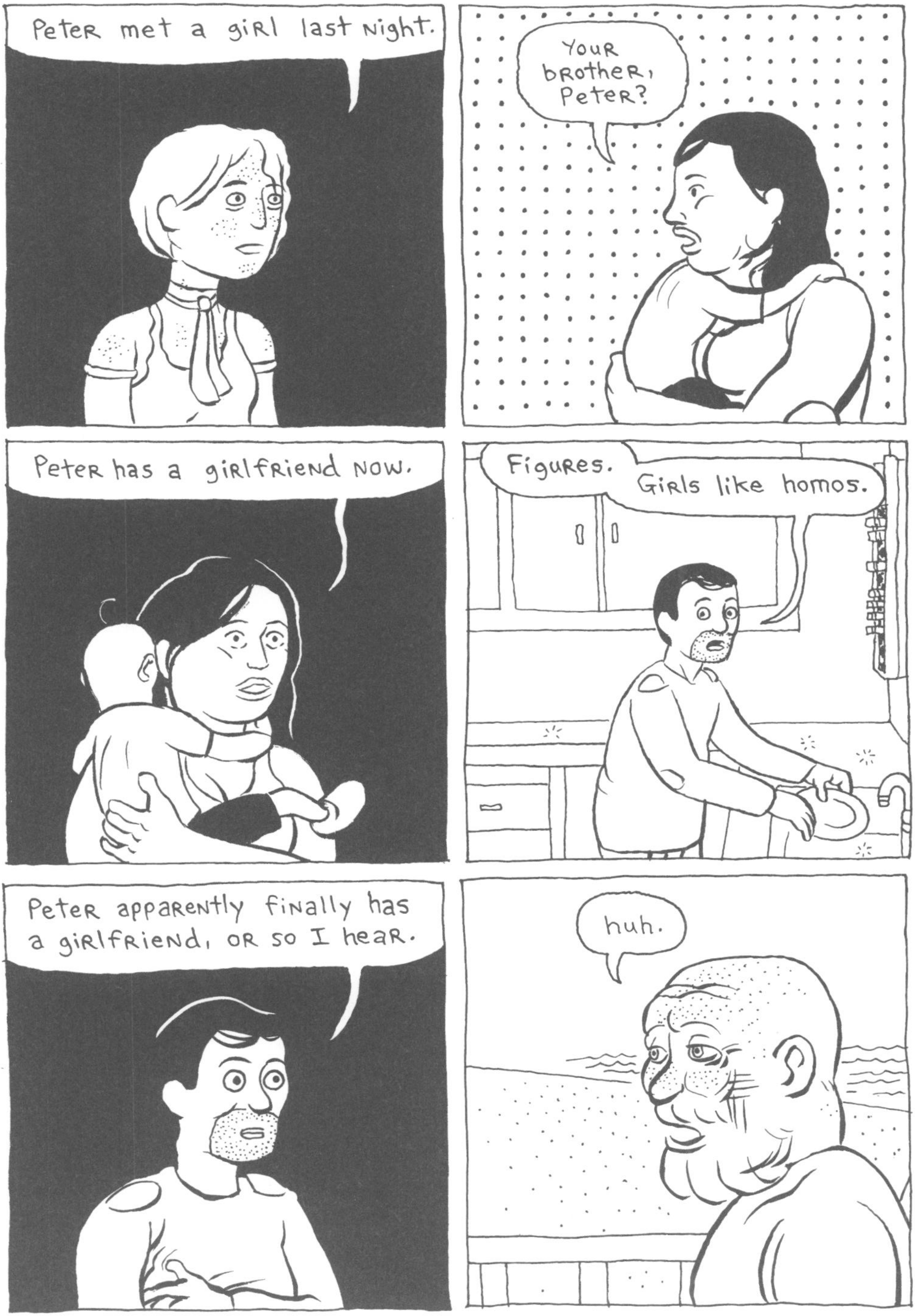
Peter met a girl last night.
Your brother, Peter?
Peter has a girlfriend now.
Figures.
Girls like homos.
Peter apparently finally has a girlfriend, or so I hear.
huh.

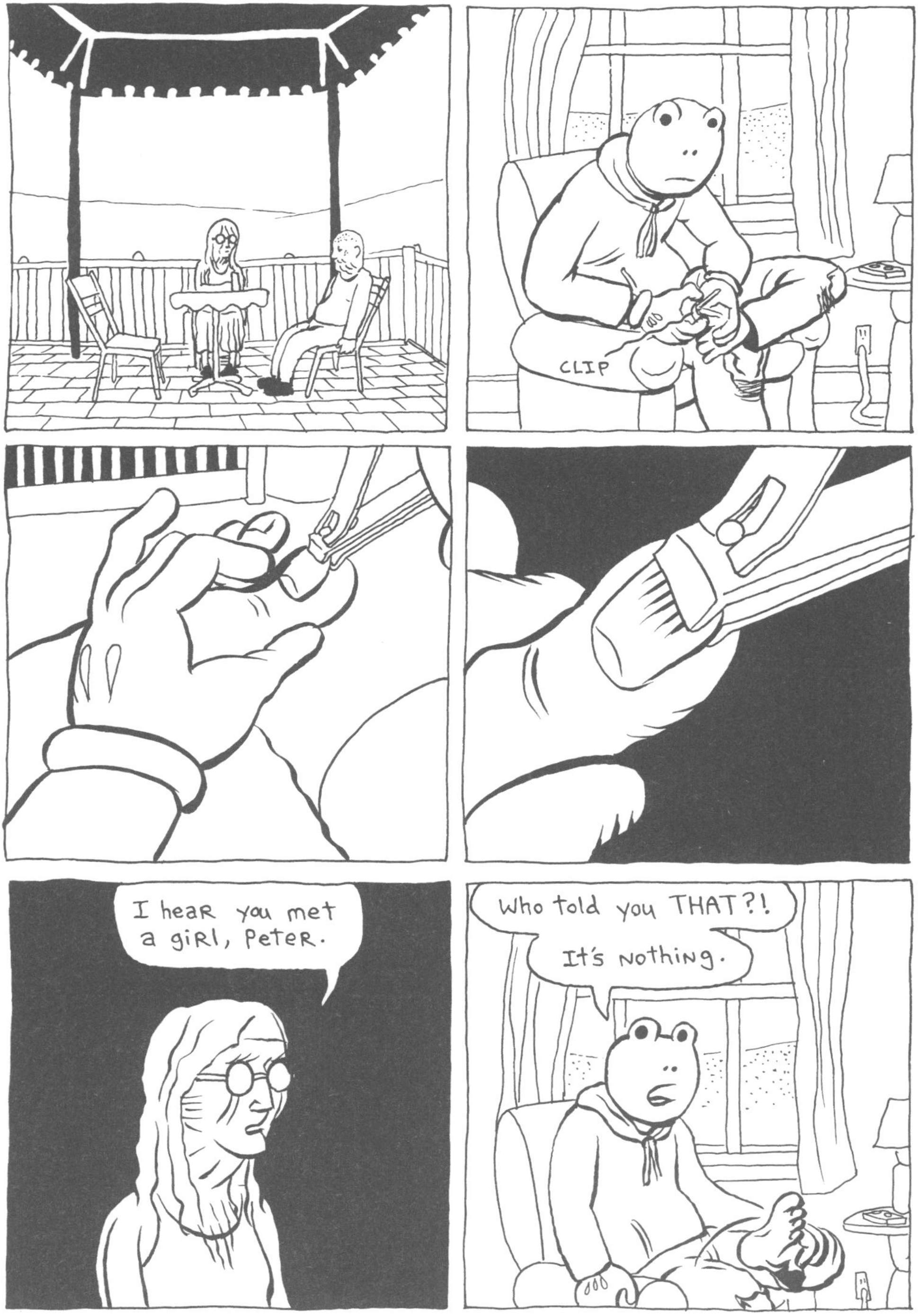
CLIP
I hear you met a girl, PETER.
Who told you THAT?!
It's nothing.

It's not gonna go anywhere.
I think it's great, Peter. You came to visit us; maybe you're supposed to meet someone here.
God gives us signals. Presents, too, sometimes. You have to see them, though. You have to WORK for them.
Oh. Right.
The other day I was knitting something, and today I found what I was knitting thrown outside, covered in sand.
Oh?
SQUEEZE

God gave me a signal. My heart wasn't in it. I was knitting just to distract myself from thinking about things. It wasn't healthy.
So God told me that I should stop distracting myself, you see? It was a message.
wiggle
Maybe God is giving you a message, Peter. Right?
uh-huh.
NODDING
Well, Ma, we were just hanging out, you know? It's no big deal, really.
You were with her at night.
Being with someone at night is different than being with them during the day.

Stairs.
Staerz.
Fence.
Fens.
Grass.
Grass.
Dune.
Doon.
Sand.
Sand.
Ocean.
Oshun.
Waves.
Wavz.

Splash.
Splass!
SPLASH
STUMBLE
SIT.
You're a cutie pie, Alex. Did you know that? You are.
I feel so OLD around you.
Ha Ha Ha.
I love you. I love you. I love you.
Look at you. I love you.
You're beautiful, Alex.
You're my beautiful little boy.

SPIN
OPEN
CLICK
PSSHT
BURRITO

TEAR
BUBBLE
Do you have any memories of Mom and Dad arguing? or fighting?
Anything like that?

Because I don't remember anything like that.
Soak
Sure.
There was a Christmas. I was, I think, ten years old maybe.
I remember I got a wind-up bird from Santa.
Dad called Mom into the kitchen.
I remember them screaming, fighting in the kitchen.
Dad slammed the door, and I was just sitting on the other side,
hearing them, like, screaming and thumping against the door.
that's bullshit.

CLICK
SUCK
But I remember it perfectly clear.
I don't remember it that way.
I don't think Dad was even at the house that Christmas.
pfft. Where would he have been?
I dunno. Business trip? Maybe he was having an affair.
Ha Ha Ha. NO WAY! I would know about something like that!
O.K.
ROLLS EYES
ROLLS EYES
Who knows, Dennis? Dad doesn't talk much.
SHRUG
Not to you, he doesn't.

I remember that exact Christmas.
They were being really flirty then.
Dad called Mom into the kitchen and they were making-out against the door.
You two were just too young to know about those kind of things.
Besides, Peter, Dad would NEVER have an affair.
He has a moral core, you know?
Once we saw a movie about an unfaithful husband and he went on a big rant about it.
Yeah. I don't think he would do that either.
Everyone's always looking for someone better.
SHUT UP! That's such a "YOU" thing to say, Peter. God.
CLICK
VRRRRR
I don't know. I'm not saying he did. But that's an easy explanation.
RRRRRR

RRRRRRRRRR
There is no easy explanation because it makes NO SENSE! NO SENSE!
DENNIS
RRR RRRRR
WHY AM I THE ONLY ONE CONCERNED ABOUT THIS?!
RRRRRR
Doesn't this upset you?
RRRR
Dennis, you know: It's THEIR, like, business. We're grown-up now.
Yeah- We're not kids. Be glad it's happening now. Rather than before.
RR RRRR
NO. No. NO. NO.
RR
I'm ENVIOUS of kids with divorcing parents. They get pampered- sent to counselors.
RR RR
It's OKAY for them to be upset. It's accepted. Hell, it's ENCOURAGED.
RRR R
But I CAN'T be upset about this?!!
RRR R
I just get weird stares? People saying I'm OVERREACTING?
RR RRRRR
RRR
CLICK
Don't you see how fucked-up that is?

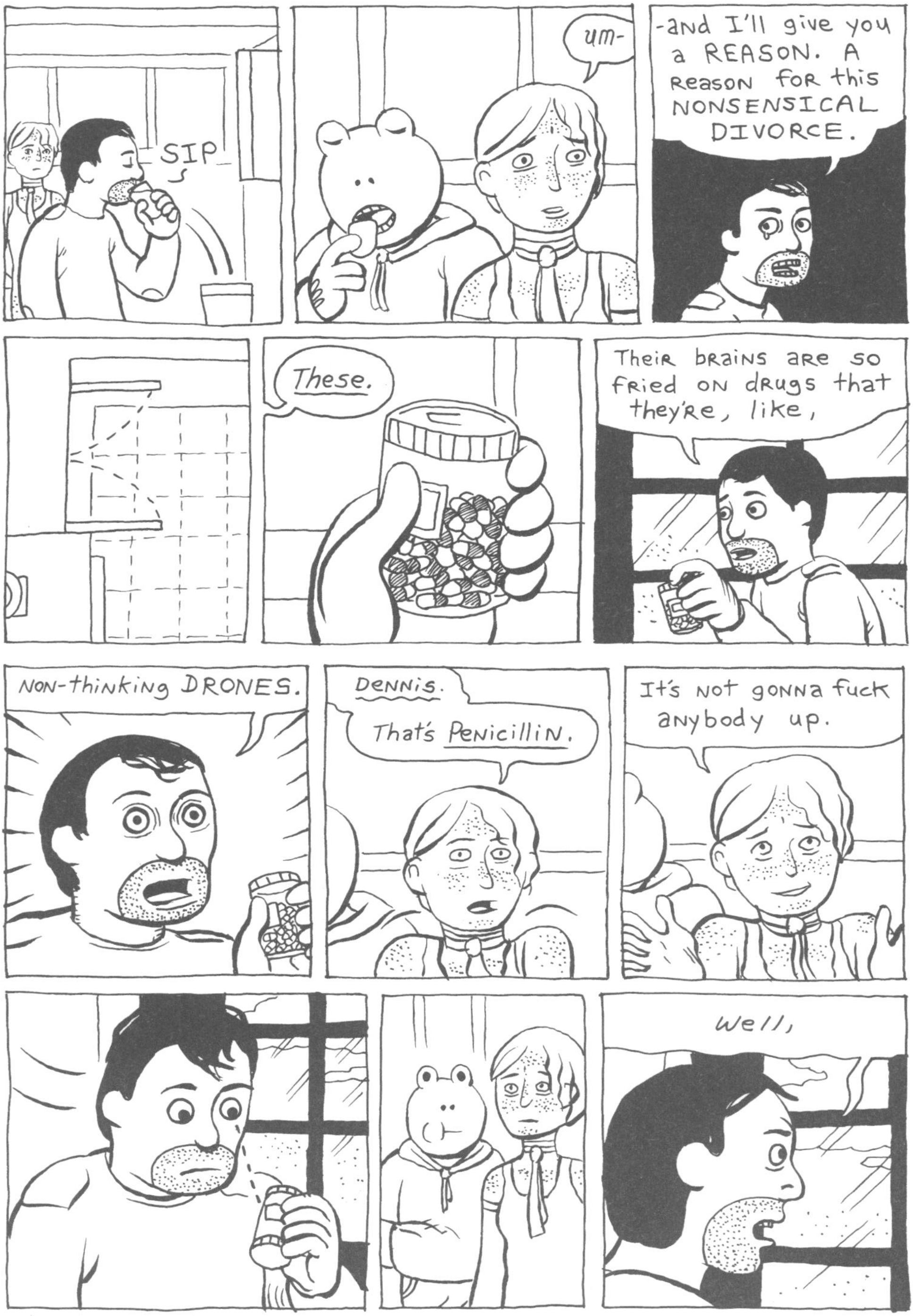
SIP
um-
-and I'll give you a REASON. A Reason for this NONSENSICAL DIVORCE.
These.
Their brains are so fried on drugs that they're, like,
NON-thinking DRONES.
DENNIS.
That's Penicillin.
It's not gonna fuck anybody up.
Well,

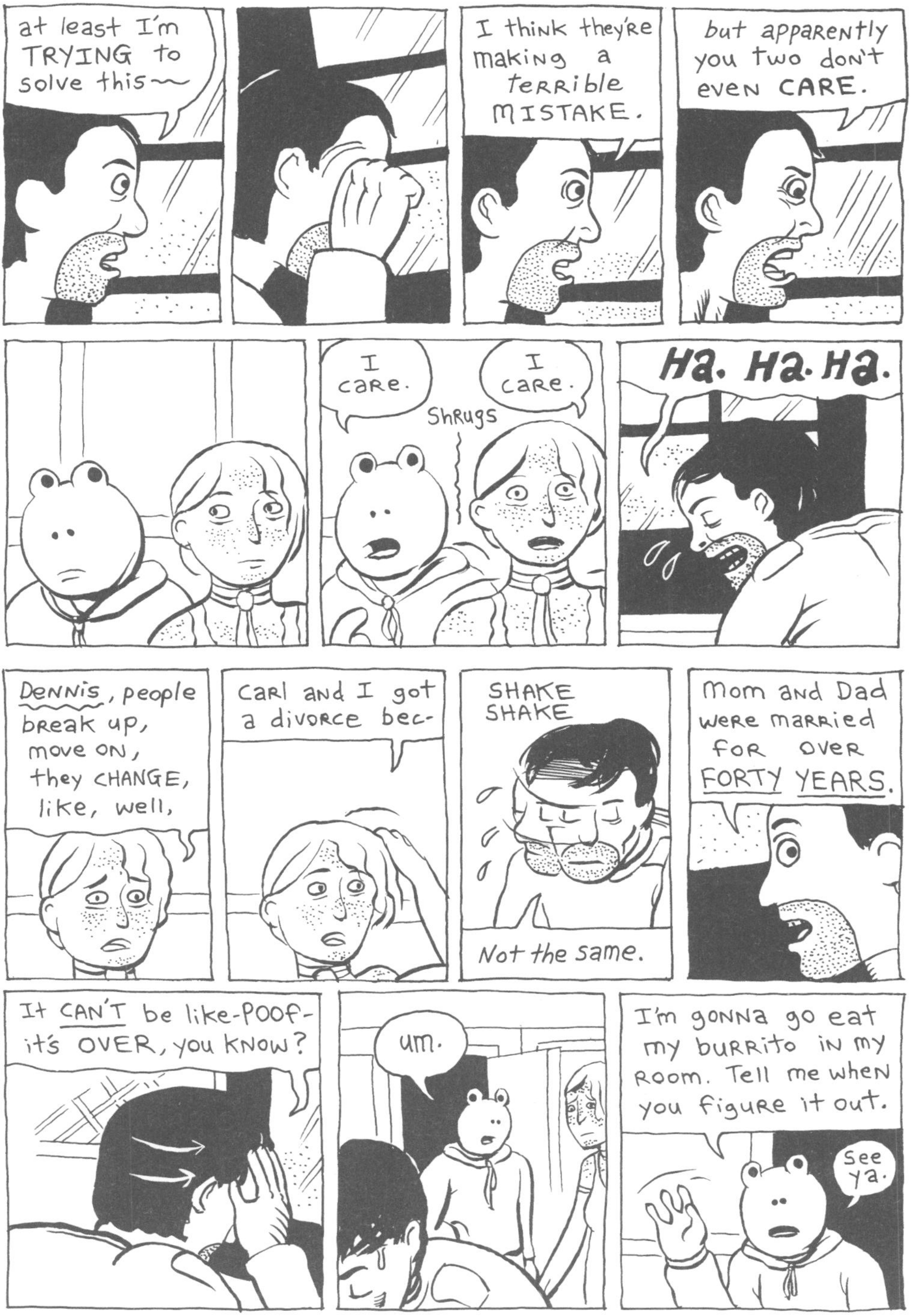
at least I'm TRYING to solve this~~
I think they're making a terrible MISTAKE.
but apparently you two don't even CARE.
I care.
I care.
Shrugs
HA. HA. HA.
DENNIS, people break up, move ON, they CHANGE, like, well,
Carl and I got a divorce bec-
SHAKE SHAKE
Not the same.
Mom and Dad were married for over FORTY YEARS.
It CAN'T be like-POOF- it's OVER, you know?
um.
I'm gonna go eat my burrito in my room. Tell me when you figure it out.
See ya.

DENNIS
DON'T CRY.
I'M TRYING NOT TO.

You make this mess, sweetie pie?
FOLD
"Terrible Twos," huh?
You'll be out of that crib soon.
FOLD

PEEKABOO!
Ha Ha
Ha Ha
hee
You're the best thing in my life.
You're so full of hope.

Smelly shirt with no cum stain.
Small cum stain, but does not stink.
Smells bad.
Holes in knees, smells so-so.

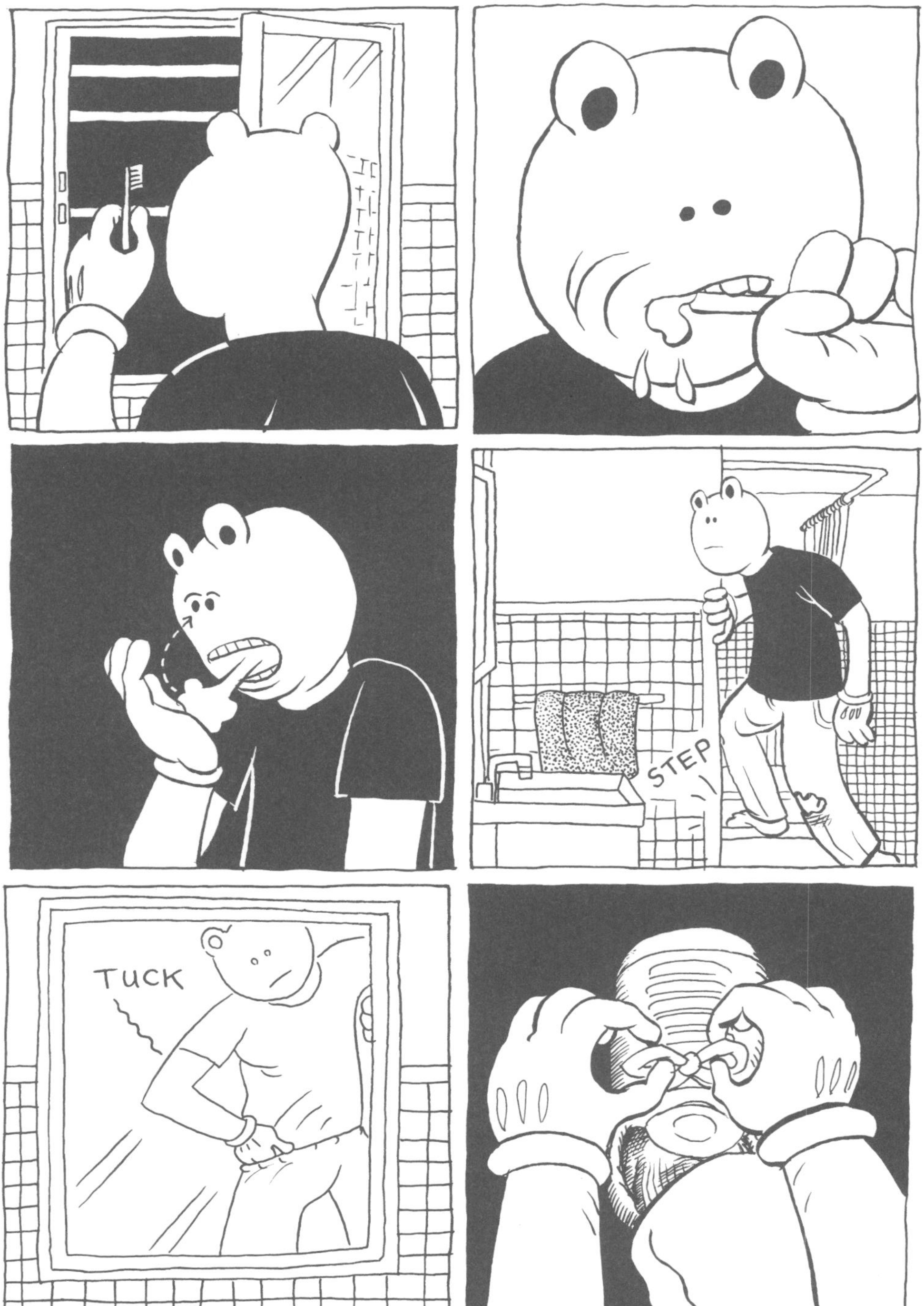
STEP
TUCK

STEP
STEP
STEP
Ha Ha Ha! So now that you got a girl you're tucking in your shirt?! Ha Ha...
No, No, I was just-
Ha Ha Ha Ha!
STEP
UNTUCK

wind
wind

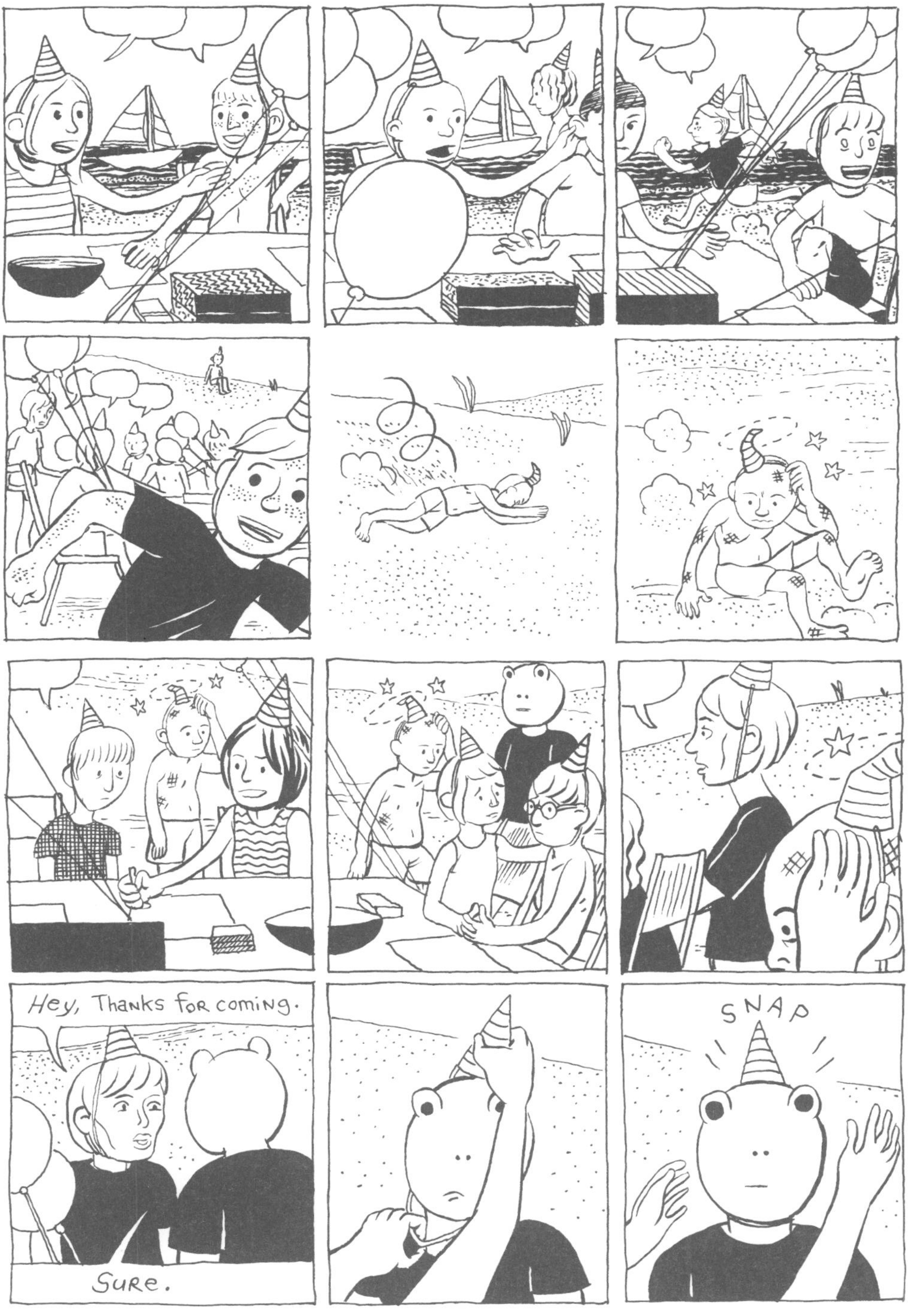
Hey, Thanks for coming.
Sure.
SNAP

TODAY'S MY BIRTHDAY!
I see that, Paul.
How old are you, if you don't mind me asking?
WOW. are you sure?
UH-HUH!
You're not just kidding me? You don't look a day over five.
You're weird.
POKE POKE
POKE
KAT KAT KAT KAT!
CAN I OPEN MY PRESENTS?!
Sure, Paul.
EVERYBODY! BRING MY PRESENTS NOW!
SIT DOWN! SIT DOWN!

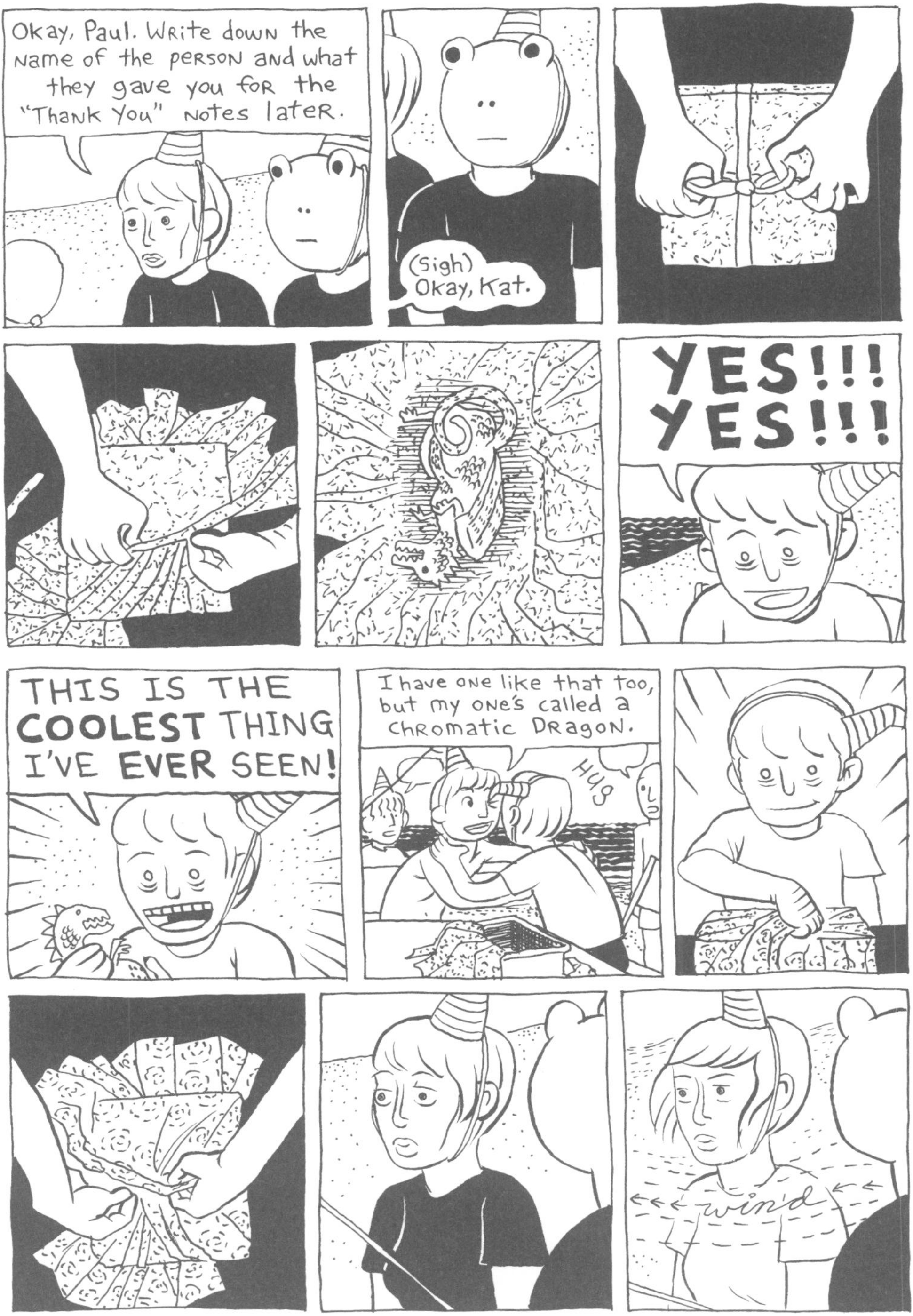
Okay, Paul. Write down the name of the person and what they gave you for the "Thank You" notes later.
(Sigh) Okay, Kat.
YES!!! YES!!!
THIS IS THE COOLEST THING I'VE EVER SEEN!
I have one like that too, but my one's called a chromatic Dragon.
HUG
wind

What?
A WRINKLE IN TIME
a book?!
NEXT!
Woah!
See? It punches and also kicks if you press-
WOW.
I have that
Peter, could you sit with the girls? They're not too interested in the boys' toys.
I'm on the job, sarge.
Not too excited 'bout the birthday party?
'sokay.
When's your birthday?
April sixth.
That's a good day.

There's gonna be cake and ice cream later.
I'm lactose intolerant.
oh.
Sorry, dude.
'sokay.
SIT
windy, huh?
Are you Kat's boyfriend?
Ha Ha.
No.
Yeah. I thought not.
What's THAT supposed to mean?
What?
So... have you met her boyfriend?

No.
Do you know if she has a boyfriend?
Why you whisperin'?
No reason.
I know she has boyfriends.
Like... multiple boyfriends at the same time? What're we talkin' 'bout here?
Do you know how to make a sandcastle?
Dude - Just be upfront with me. Answer my question.
Ha Ha
You're funny.
ha. ha. You're like a funny clown.
Oh-kay.
Can you make me a sandcastle, please?!
I'll make you an awesome sandcastle if you tell me every-thing you know about Kat.

um.
I have ta meet her first.
WHAT?! — Kat, your counselor. You know: Kat.
Can you make the castle have a tower for a princess?
No. No deal. I revoke my offer.
What's DAT mean?
No princess castle.
No.

Okay, Okay- Listen: I'll make you a sandcastle.
alright? alright?
SNIF
Look:
Princess tower.
She needs a pony.
Oh-kay.
Pony.
That's a pretty pony.
and here's a wall for the castle.
awww...

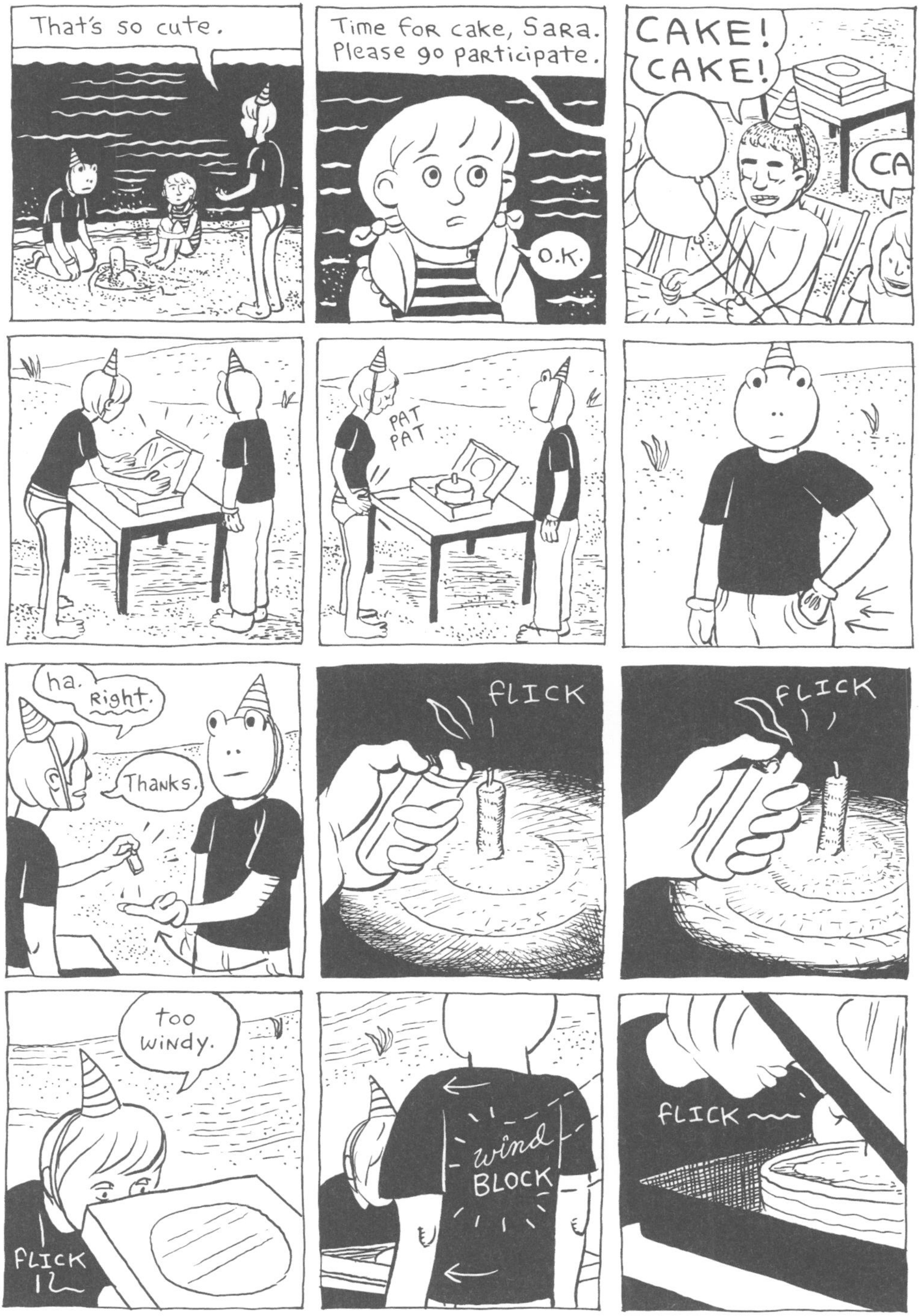

That's so cute.
Time for cake, Sara. Please go participate.
O.K.
CAKE! CAKE!
CA
PAT PAT
ha. Right.
Thanks.
FLICK
FLICK
too windy.
FLICK
wind BLOCK
FLICK

FLICK
FLICK!
YAY! YAY!
YAY!
Make a wish and blow out the candles.
Wish FOR
FOR
Wish FOR
FOR
FOR
You can't make anyone die or force someone to fall in love with you. Those are the rules.
Wish FOR
FOR
FOR
FOR
FOR
FOR
FOR
FOR
FOR
FOR
FOR
FOR
FOR
FOR
FOR
FOR
FOR
FOR

SUCK
BLOW
CLAP
CLAP
CLAP

wind
Hey, Aki.
How's the leg?
It's weird. It's all better.
No bruise at all.
DON'T TELL DENNIS.
I found my glove.

Listen. Claire, I-
Hey- You don't have to say anything.
I'm a person too, ya'know?
There's been times when I thought being content and happy was, like, BORING.

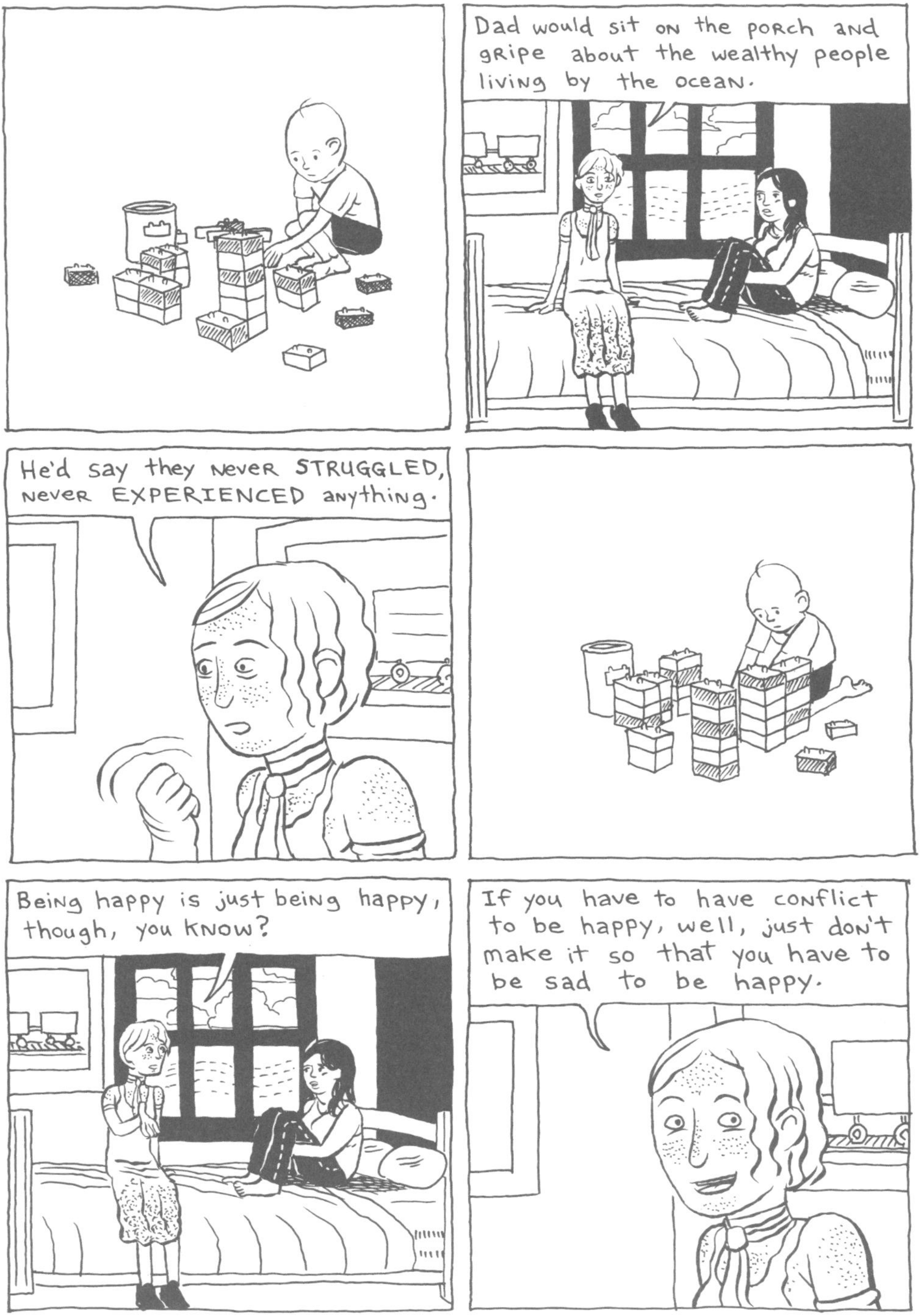
Dad would sit on the porch and gripe about the wealthy people living by the ocean.
He'd say they never STRUGGLED, never EXPERIENCED anything.
Being happy is just being happy, though, you know?
If you have to have conflict to be happy, well, just don't make it so that you have to be sad to be happy.

Because you're not happy when you're sad. You're sad.
Does that make any sense?
Ha. Ha.
It DOES, I just don't know what it has to do with ME.
huh?

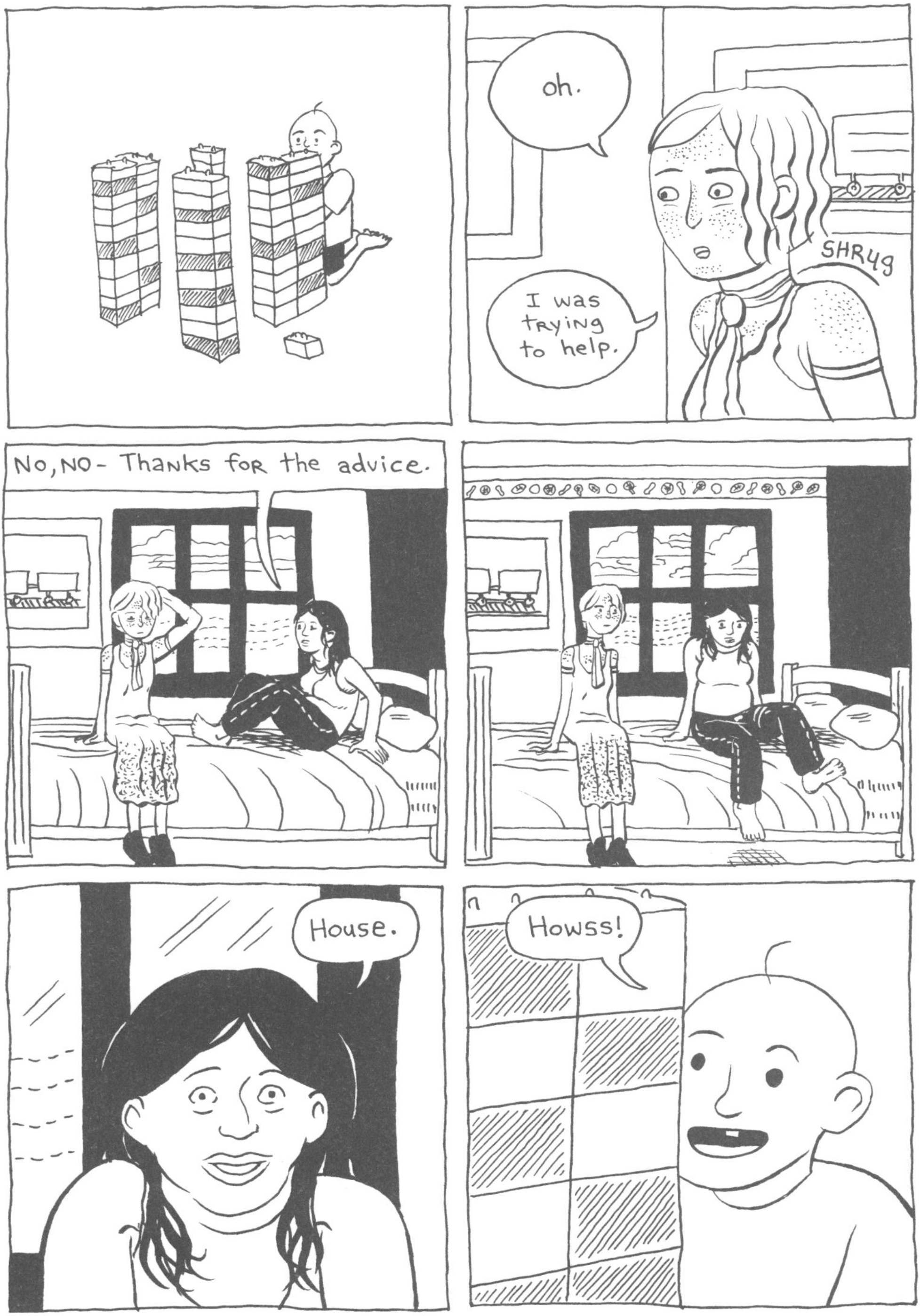
oh.
I was trying to help.
SHRUG
No, NO- Thanks for the advice.
House.
Howss!

Washer and
Dryer located
on lowest floor.
DING

SHUT
DINK
DINK

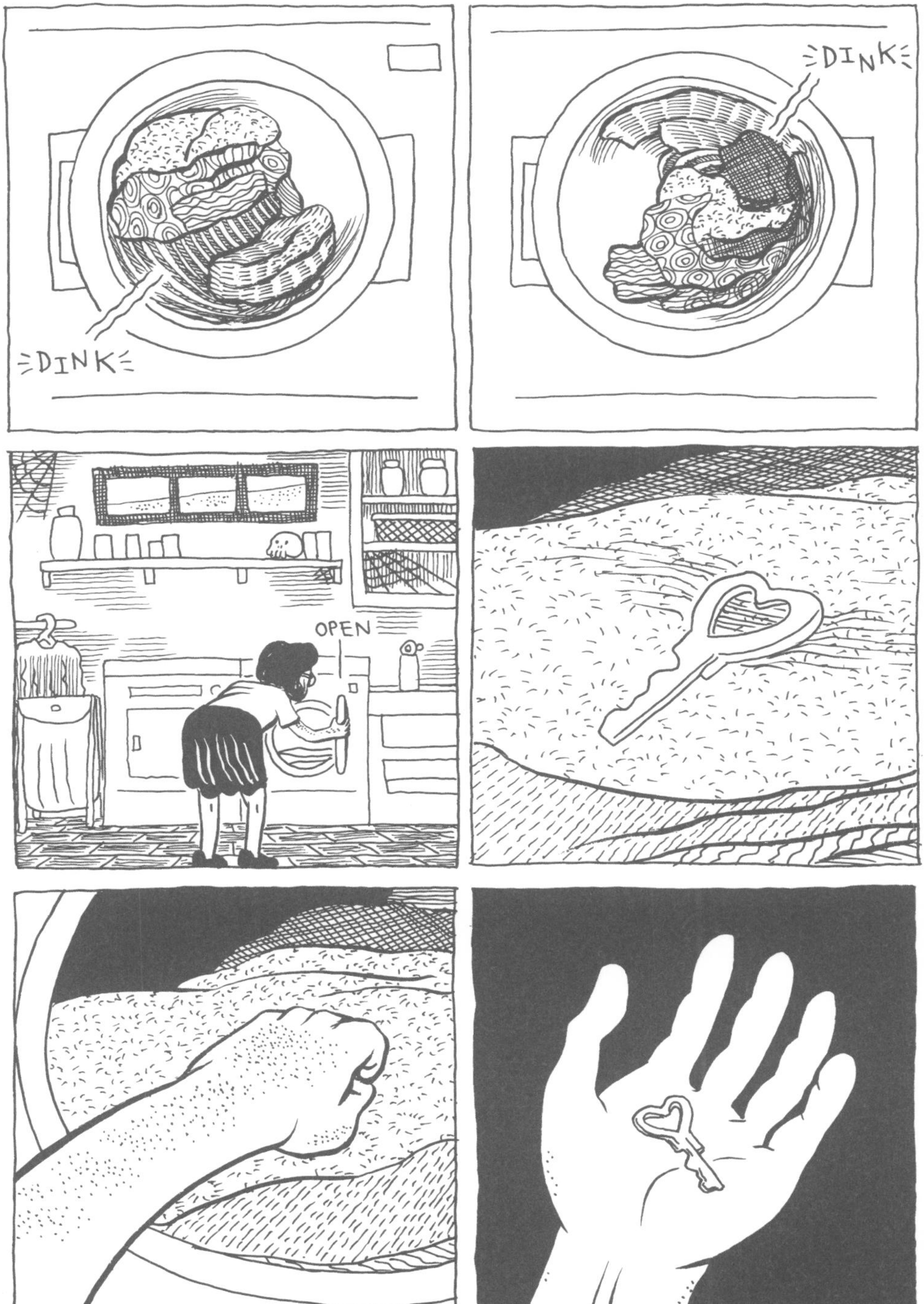
DINK
DINK
OPEN

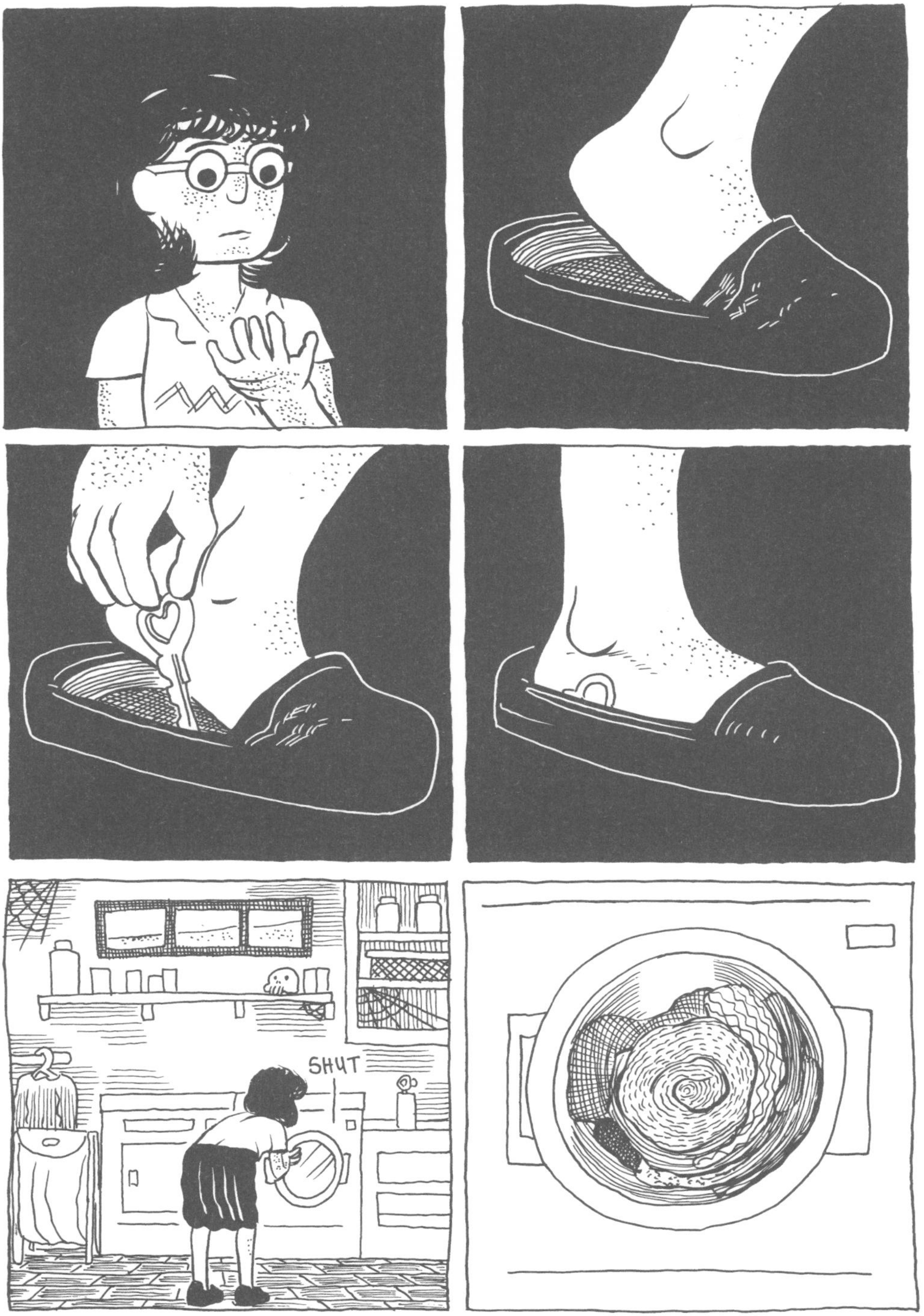
SHUT

RING! RING!
ah!
Loony Residence. Jill speaking.

ANDREW TOLD ME WHAT YOU DID AND THAT'S FUCKED-UP, JILL.
what?
I TOLD YOU THINGS, JILL, AND YOU ABUSED MY TRUST.
wait,
Let me explain.
YOU'RE A BITCH.
Listen- Andrew isn't telling you the truth about what happened. He-
AND YOU STOLE MY CIGARETTES.

That part's true, but-
YOU'RE A CUNT.
You're a cunt.
NO, YOU ARE. CLICK
CLICK
SHAKEY
BUZZ

OPEN
SHUT
PSSHT
SlidE
wind
wind
FLICK
FLICK

puff
~sip
puff
-sip
stupid cunt.

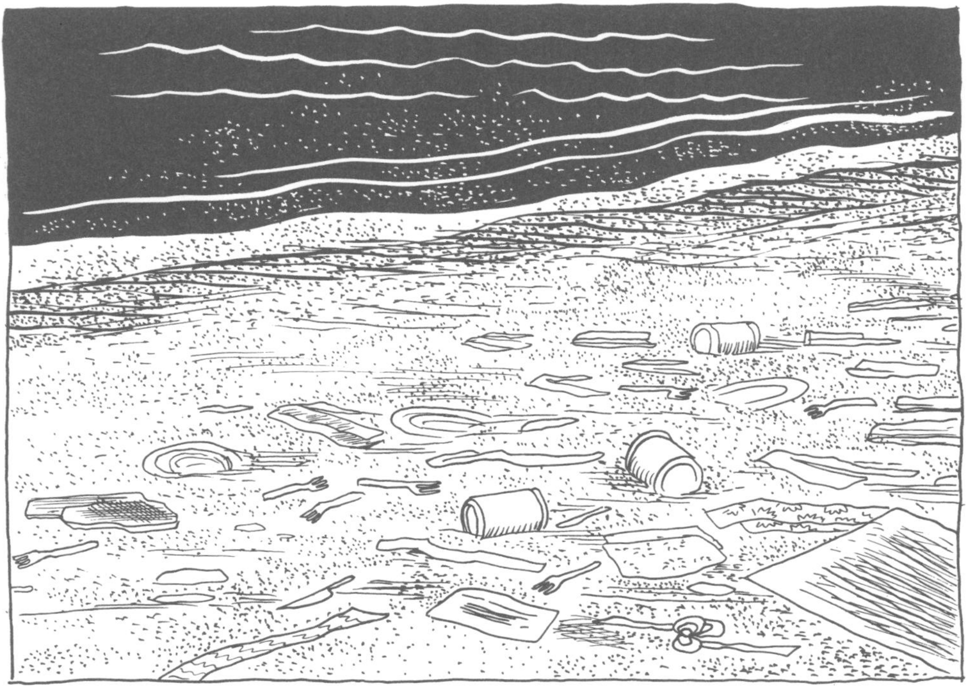
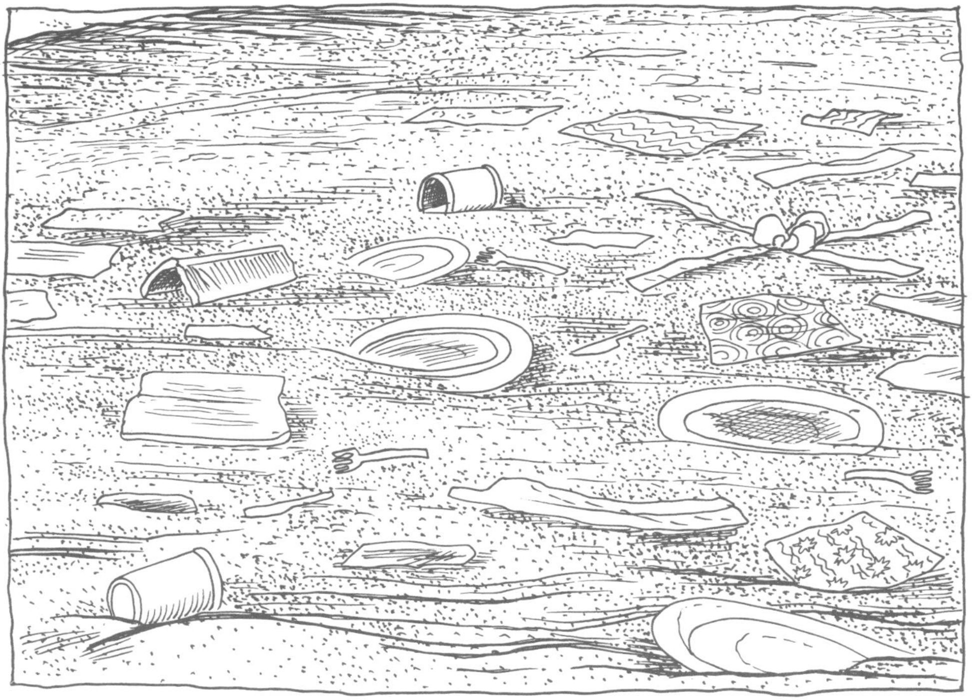

Thanks for sticking around to help clean up.
wind
wind
No problem.

Hold on to the plastic cups. We can wash them out.
wind

wind

Tie all of the balloons to that chair.
STACK
STACK
Fucking wrapping paper.

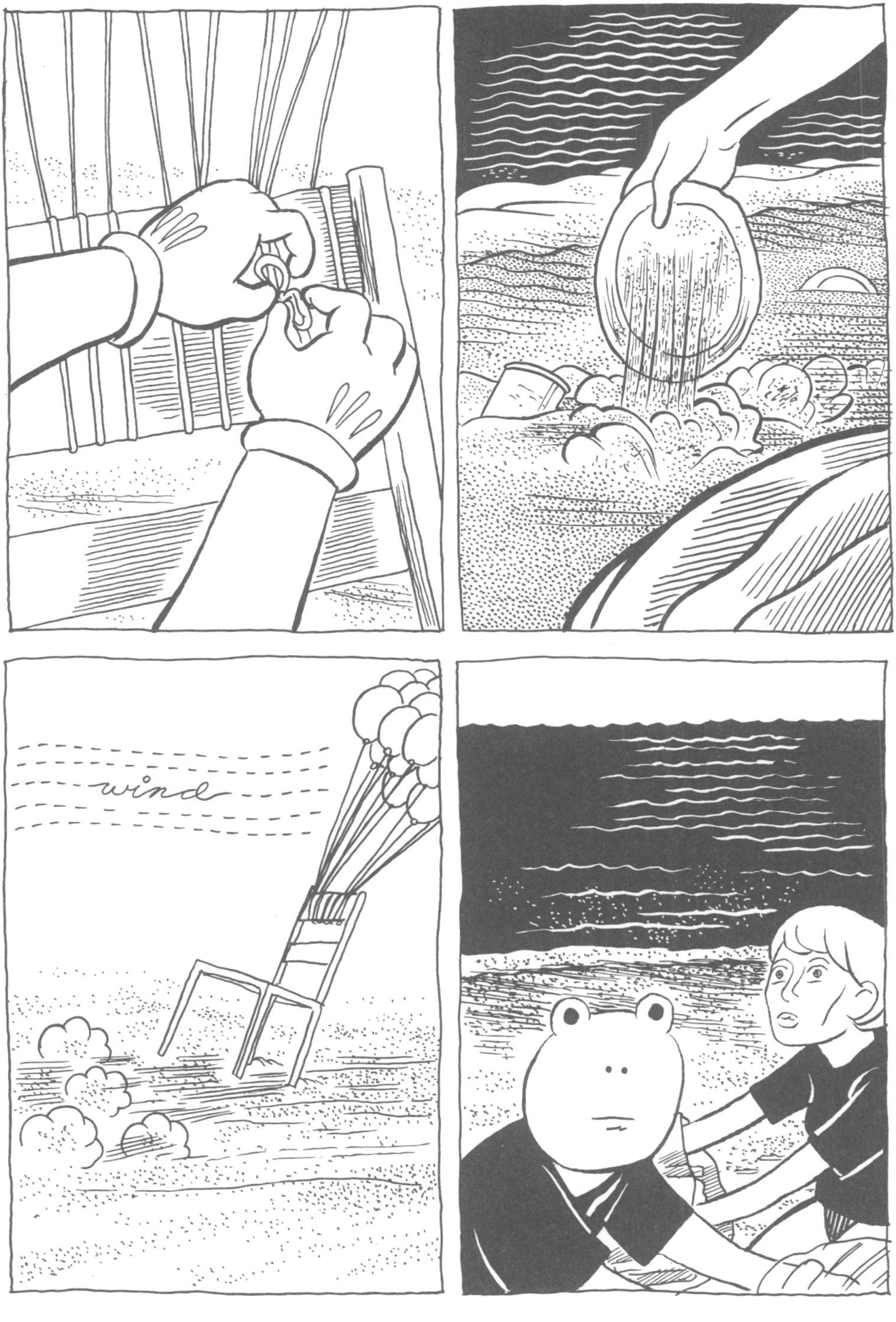
wind

wind

You look tired, sweetie. What's up?
Nothing.
Have you seen Jill?
No. Why?

Claire's freaking-out looking for her.
Why? Where is she?
Um. We don't know. Claire's looking.
RUB
RUB
How was the movie?

What movie?
Ha. That bad, huh? The movie last night. "Grey Moon."
Oh, yeah. What did Claire say? about the movie?
I didn't ask Claire.
Well, the movie was okay.
Nothing unusual.

Hey. It's clean in here.
Yeah. I picked up the mess Alex made.
Oh. Ha.
That was me, actually.
What?
What?

You threw all those things around?
Yeah.
Well,
Nevermind, Aki -
Why?! It was a pigsty in here!
I was upset.
It was-
DENNIS! YOU'RE A GROWN-UP! YOU'RE A GROWN MAN!
I'm only thirty-four.

Do you see this look I'm giving you now?
I gotta go. I'm helping Claire find Jill.
We'll talk about this more later.
KNOCK KNOCK
ma?
ma?
have you seen-
OPEN
ma?

SHUT
RIP
SMOOTHS-OUT
mom?

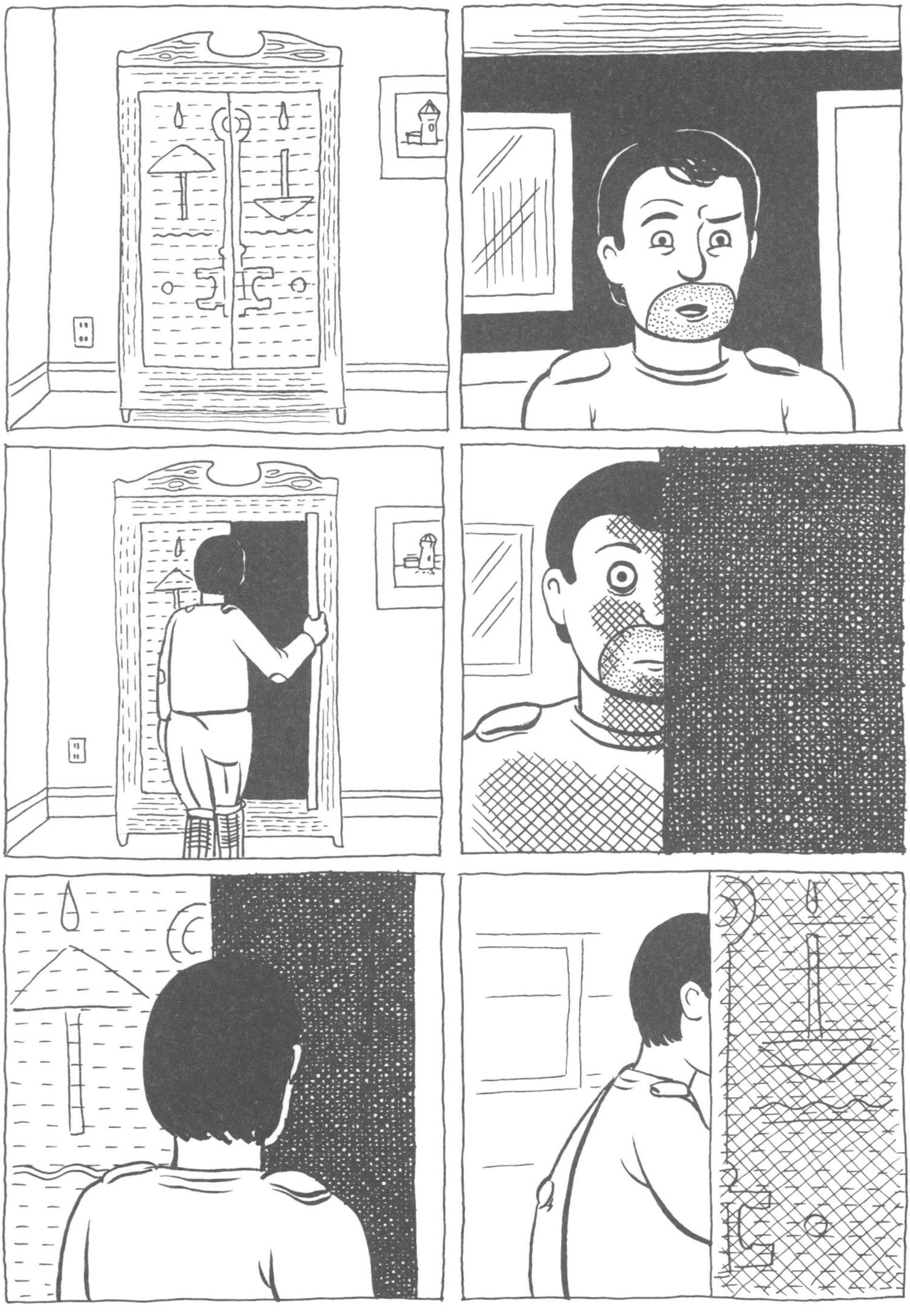

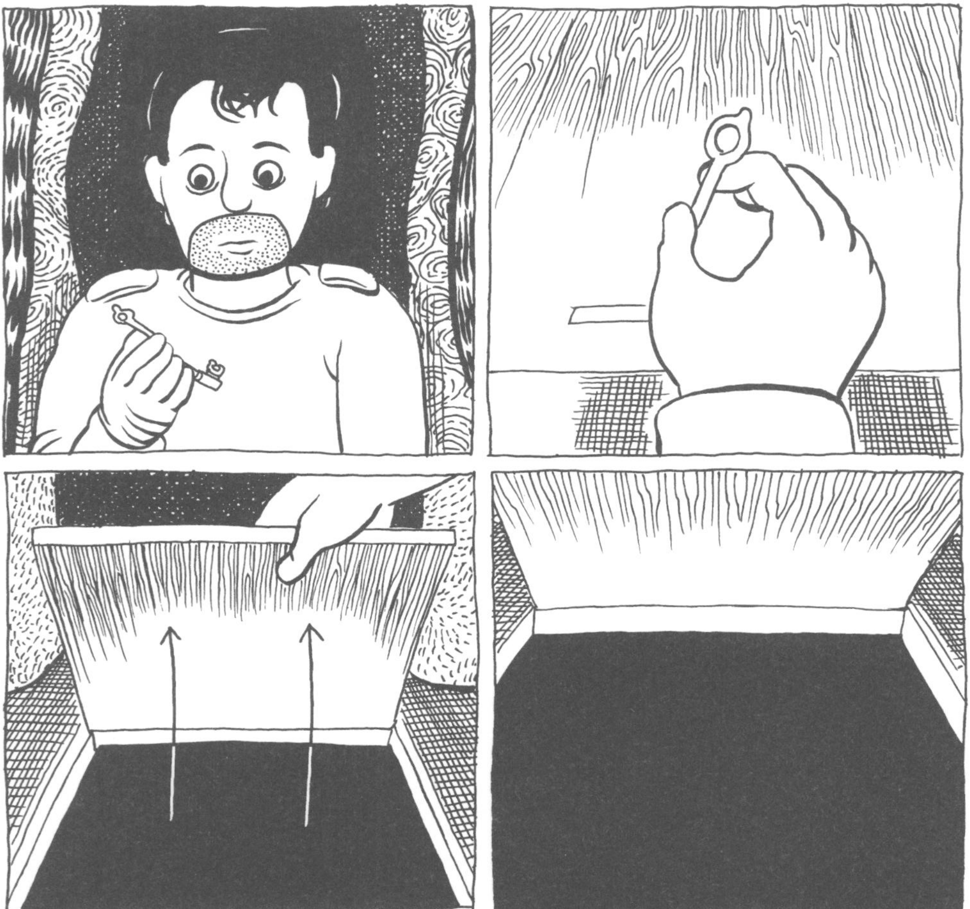

Come inside.
SHUT

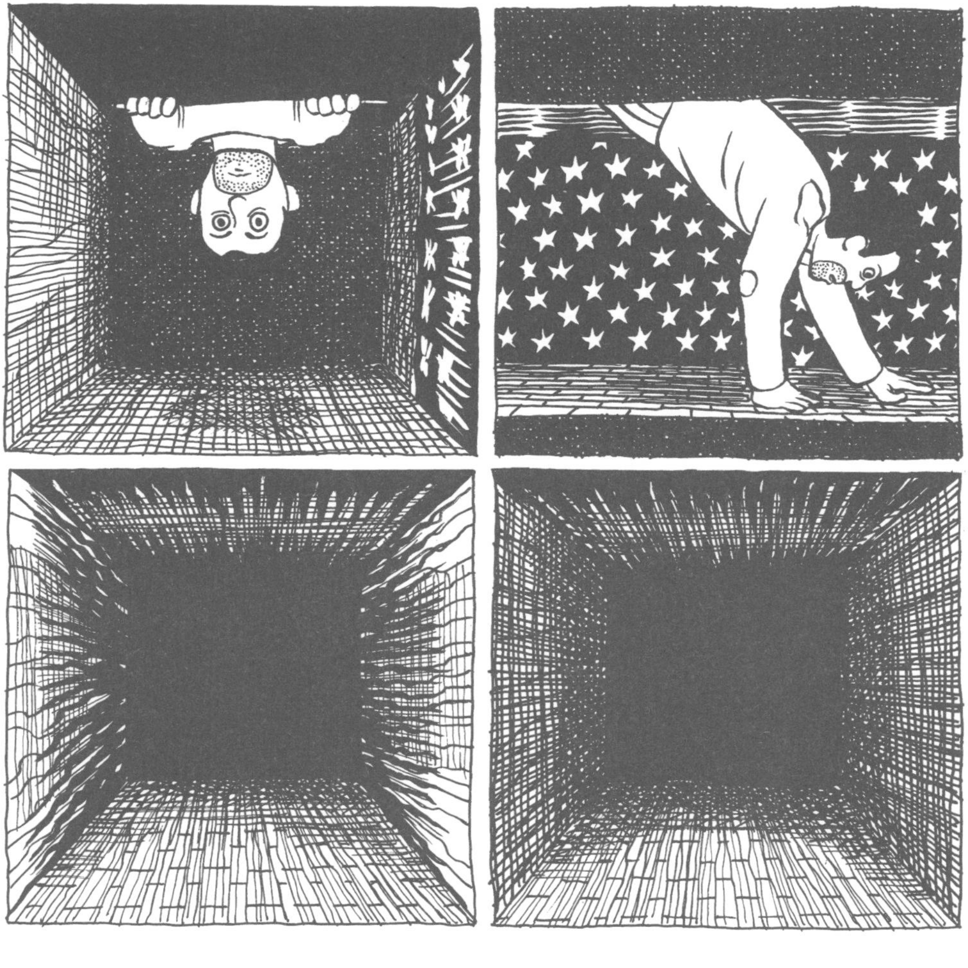

Do you know anyone in this town?
MEOW
um.
Not Really.
No-one's said anything about me, to you?
PET
um... No.
What's up?
Nothing.
PET
PET
PURRRR

PET
PET
So you just randomly walked up to me at night?
Well, I saw you the day before.
You did?
PET
Yeah.
We talked.
I don't remember that.
PET

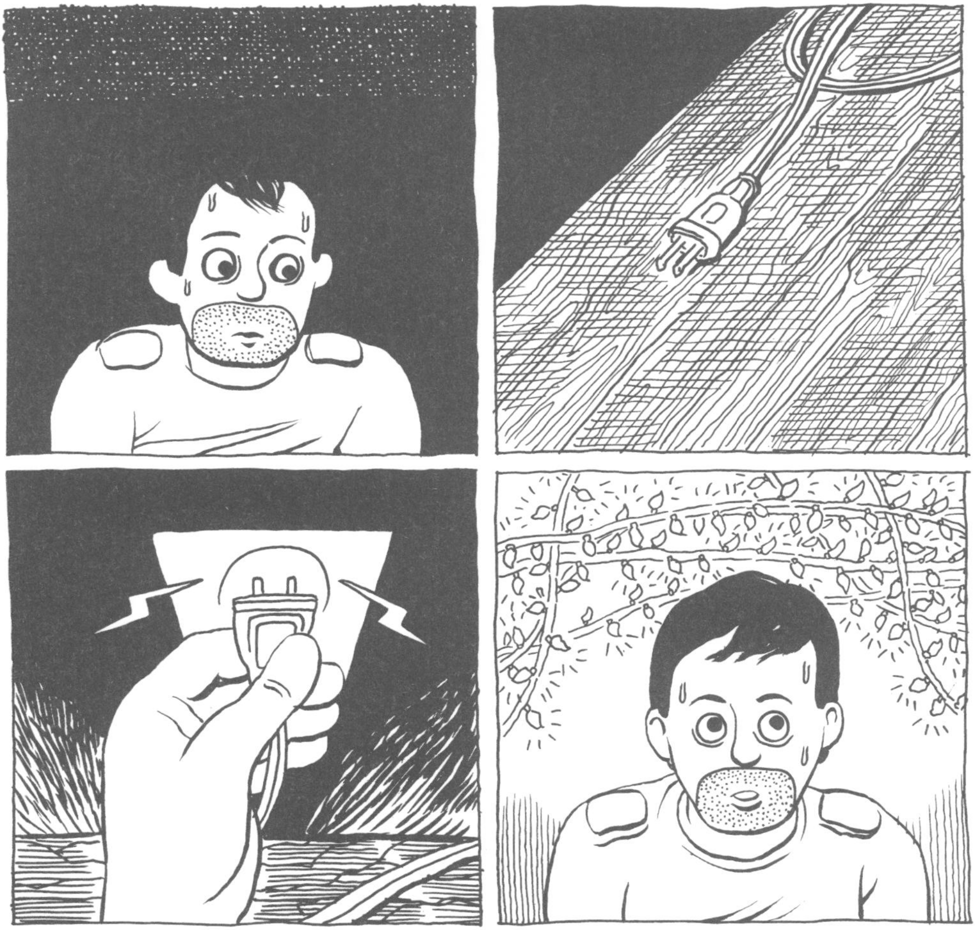

Where did you see me?
um. At the daycare.
I met Paul.
That's weird I don't remember.
Jeez.
It doesn't matter.
PURR
um.
Can I use your bathroom?
Yeah. Second door down the hall.

JILL?!
JILL?! WHERE ARE YOU?!
SHAKEY

JILL?!
Pant
GRUMBLE
SHAKEY
Jill?!
Pant
pant
pant
Pant
Pant
Pant

OW FUCK!

NOT THAT ONE!
Oh. Right.
Don't ever go in there.

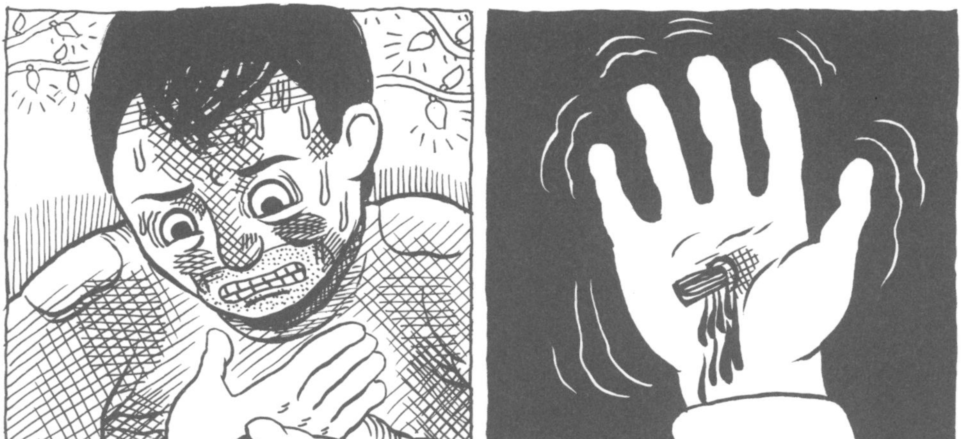
Fuck.
Fuck
Fuck
BLOW

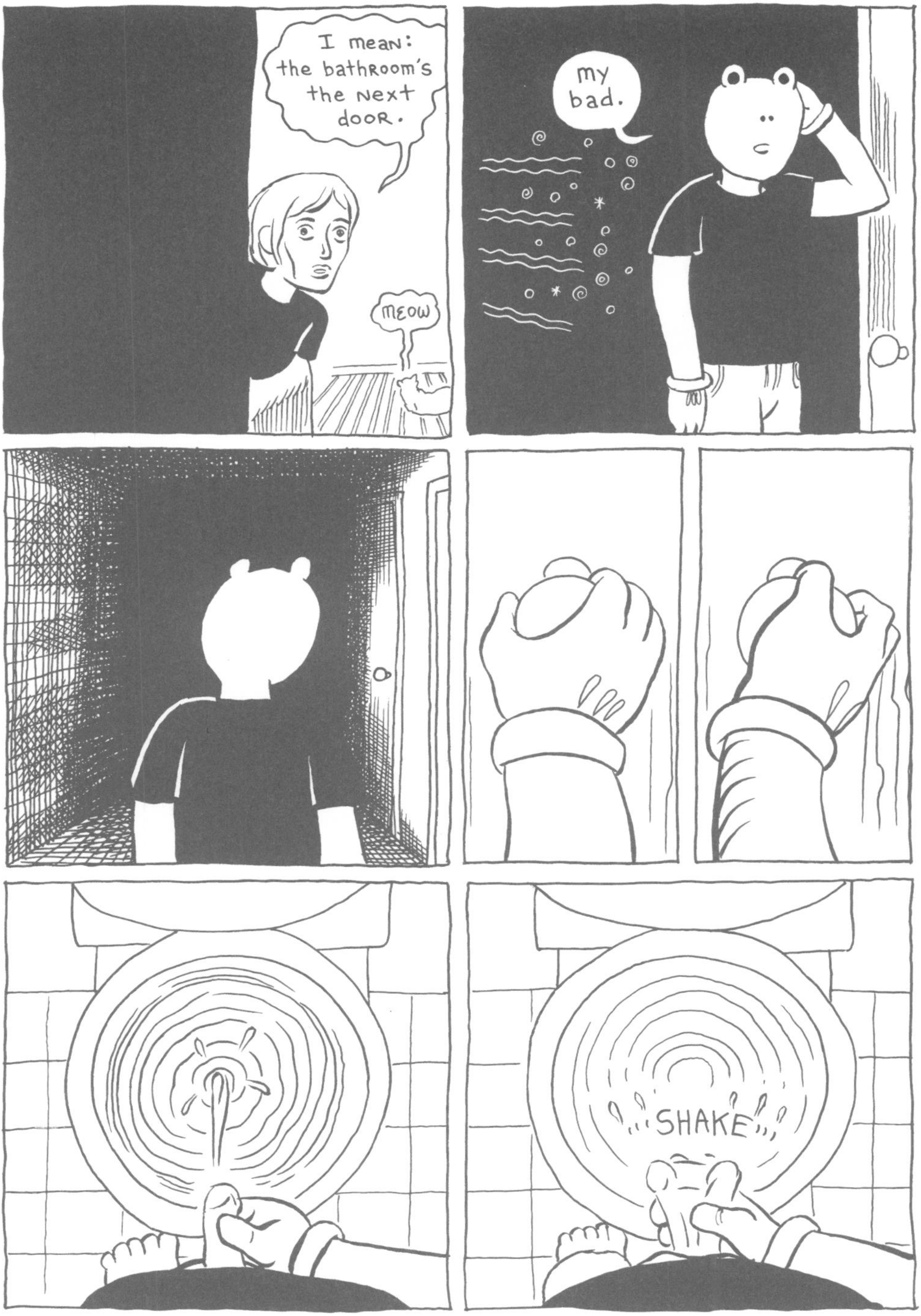
I mean: the bathroom's the next door.
MEOW
my bad.
SHAKE

SHAKE
Damn it.

WIPE
WIPE

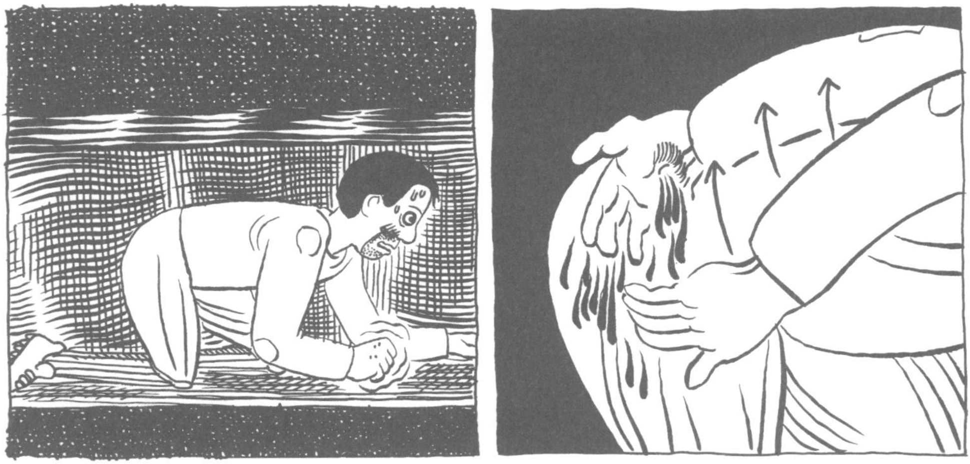
SHAKEY

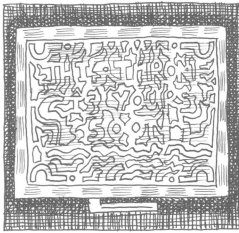

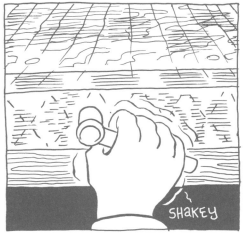

AAAAAA
FUCK!
AAAAAAA
PANT
PANT
AAAAAAA
Who's there?!
A-
PANT
AAAAAAA
PANT
Who's that?!
PANT

BURST

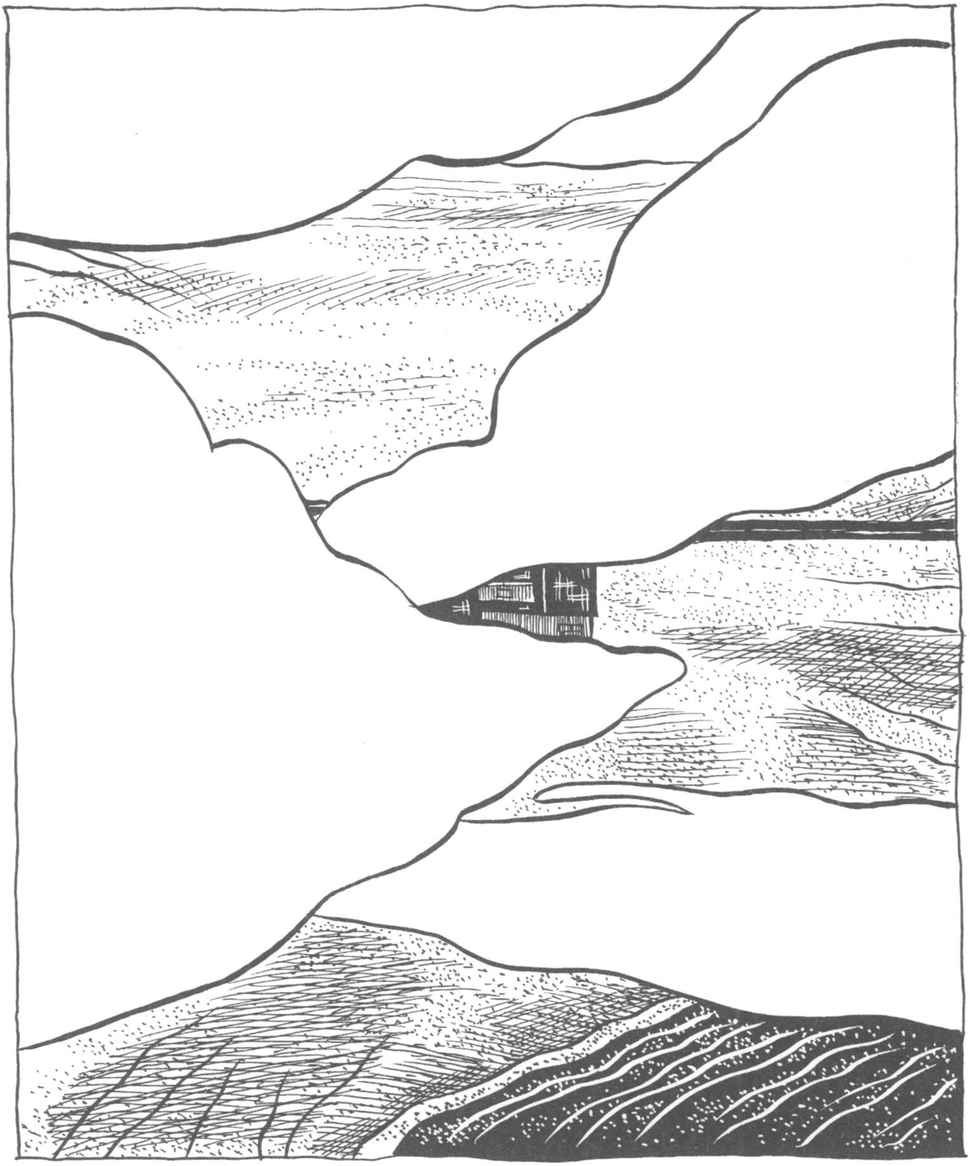

AAAAAA

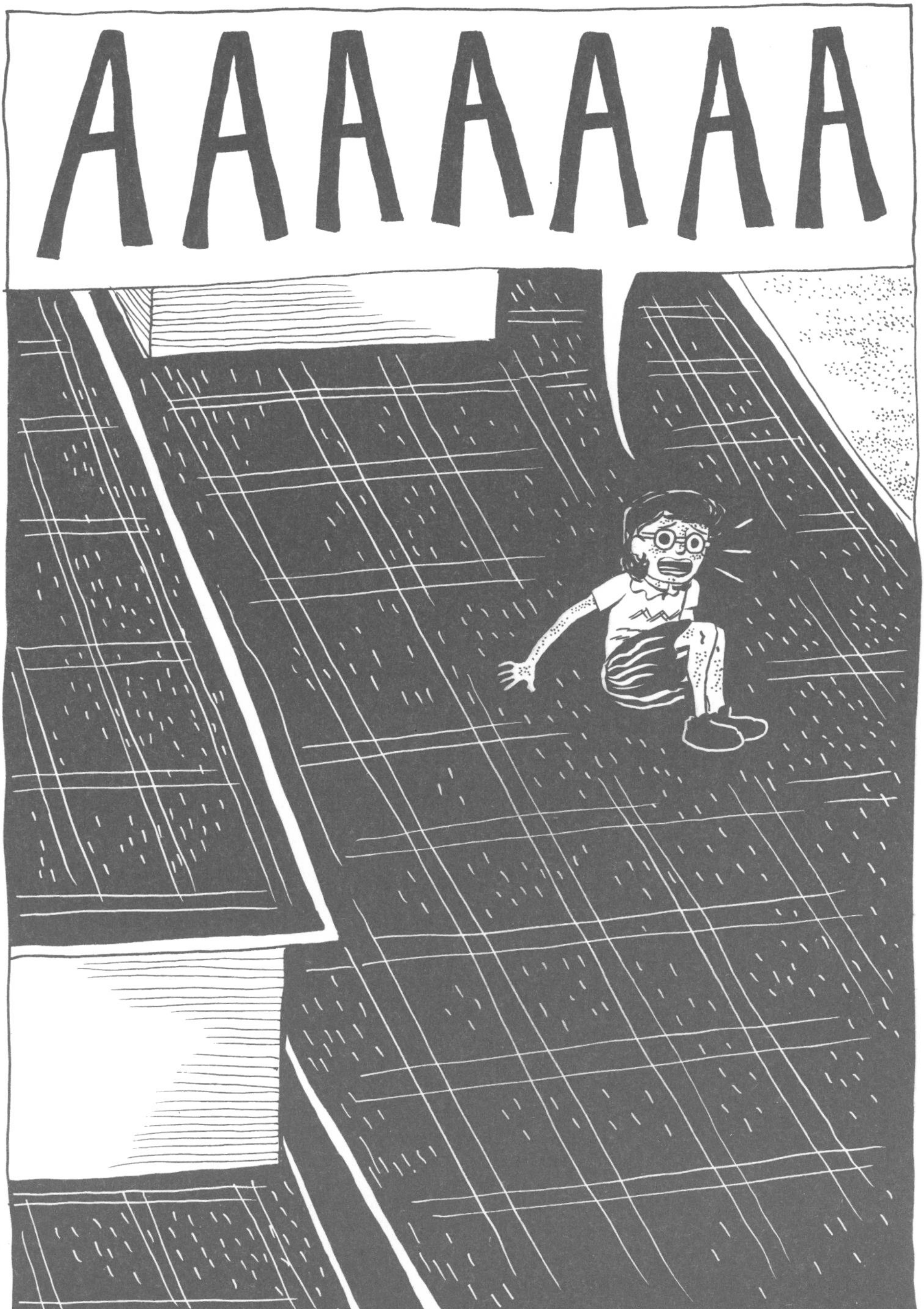
AAAAAAA

AAAAAAA

CRASH
AAAAGHH
A-
pant
pant
A

STOP
Shakey
Shakey
Pant
Pant
SHAKEY
SHAKEY
SHAKEY
PAIN
CLIMB
ROLL

SHUT
SOUND of RUNNING WATER
shhhh

Shhhhhh
Shhh
Shhh
Shhh
Shhhhhh
SIT.

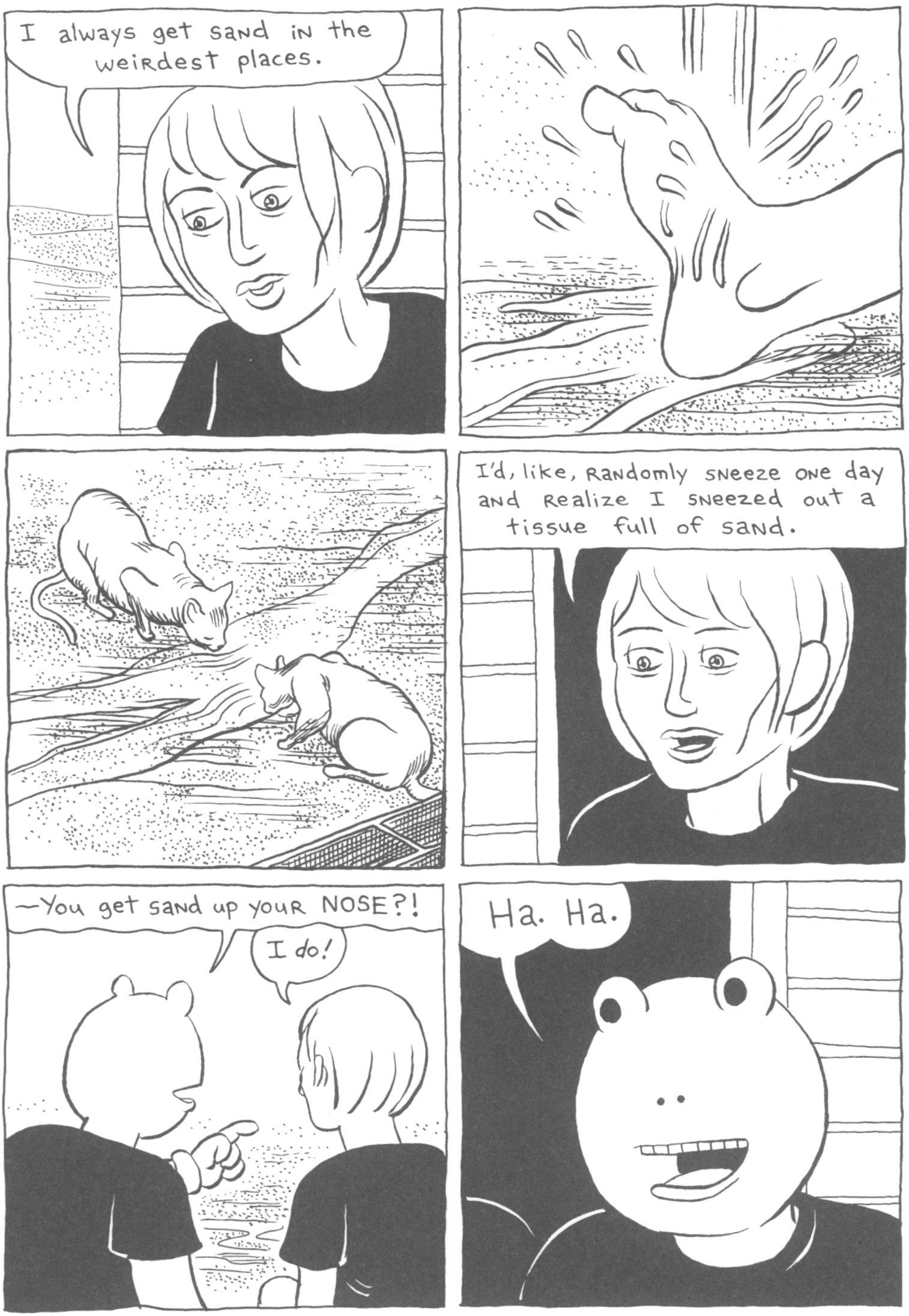
I always get sand in the weirdest places.
I'd, like, randomly sneeze one day and realize I sneezed out a tissue full of sand.
~You get sand up your NOSE?!
I do!
Ha. Ha.

RUB
PURR
I SWEAR! I'd be trying to get it out all day-
This way.
That way.
Ha.
It's hard to do in public. I mean: there's a fine line between rubbing your nose and picking your nose.

Ha. I admit I've picked my nose before and-
WOAH! WOAH!
Anyone who's said they've never picked their nose before is a god-damn liar.
I know someone who said that.
WHat? When?
In elementary school, I think.
Ha! yeah, well-
ROLL ROLL

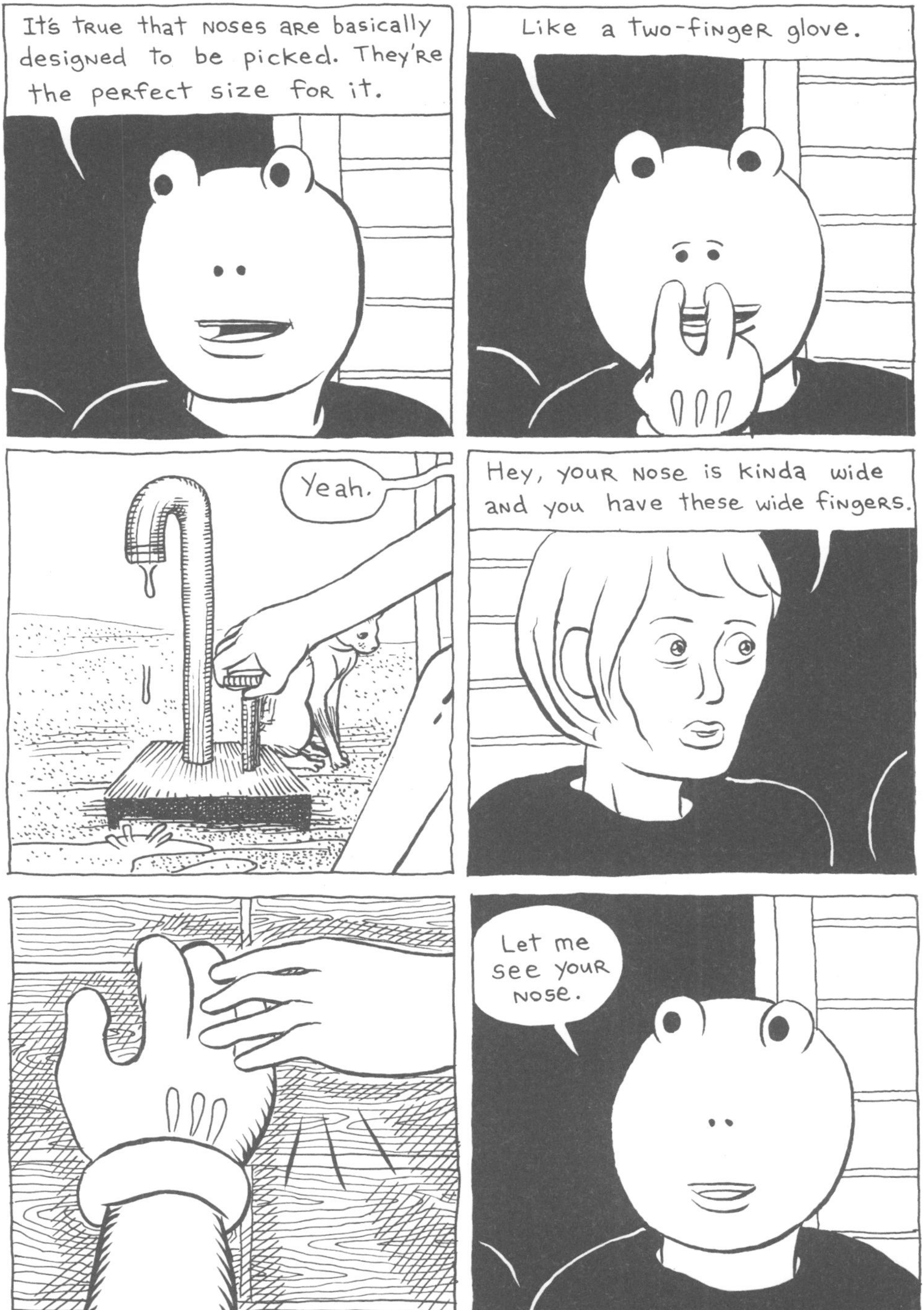
It's true that noses are basically designed to be picked. They're the perfect size for it.
Like a two-finger glove.
Yeah.
Hey, your nose is kinda wide and you have these wide fingers.
Let me see your nose.

Very curvy inside.
Like looking into a vase.
Now let me see your fingers.

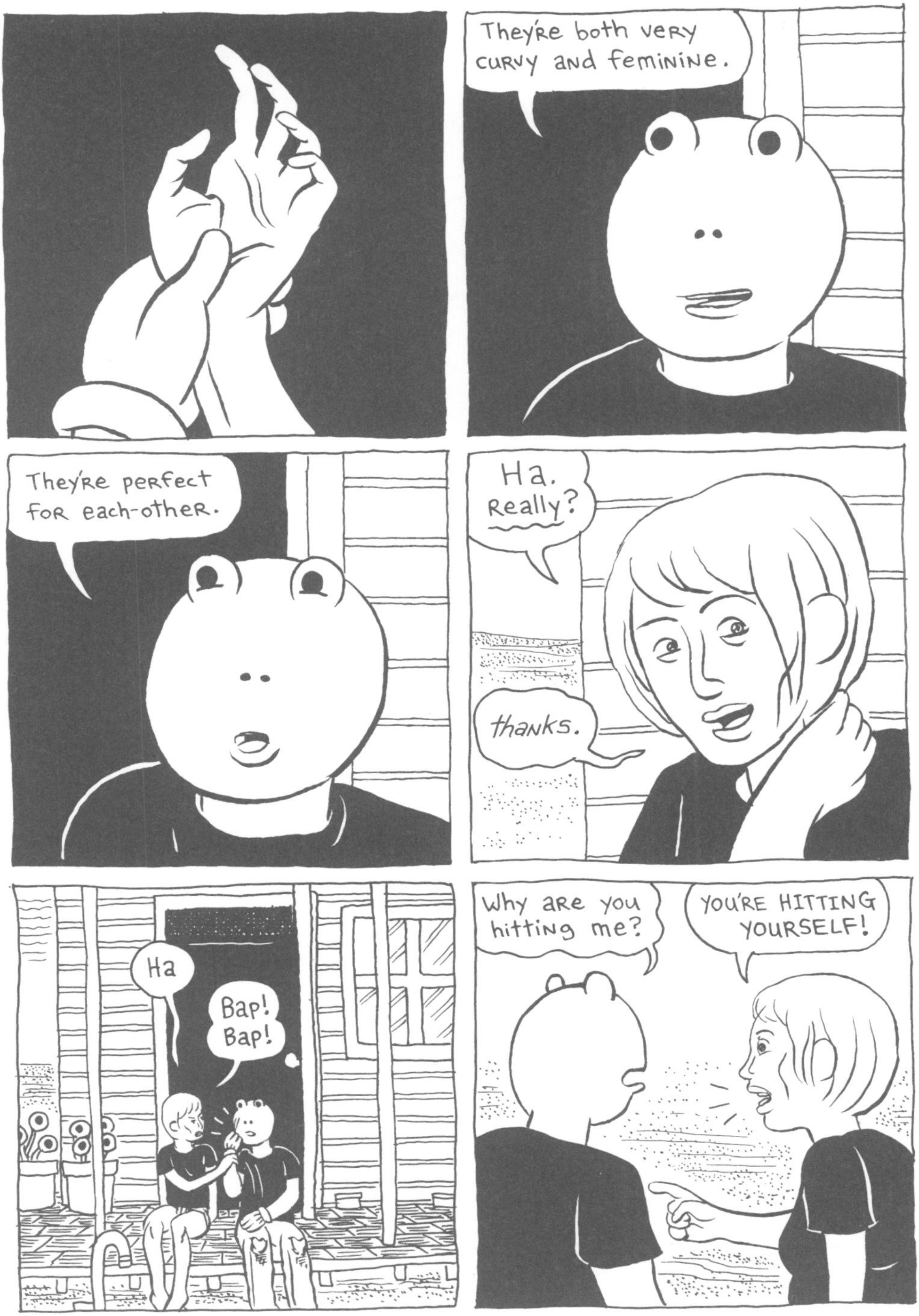
They're both very curvy and feminine.
They're perfect for each-other.
Ha. Really?
thanks.
Ha
Bap! Bap!
Why are you hitting me?
YOU'RE HITTING YOURSELF!

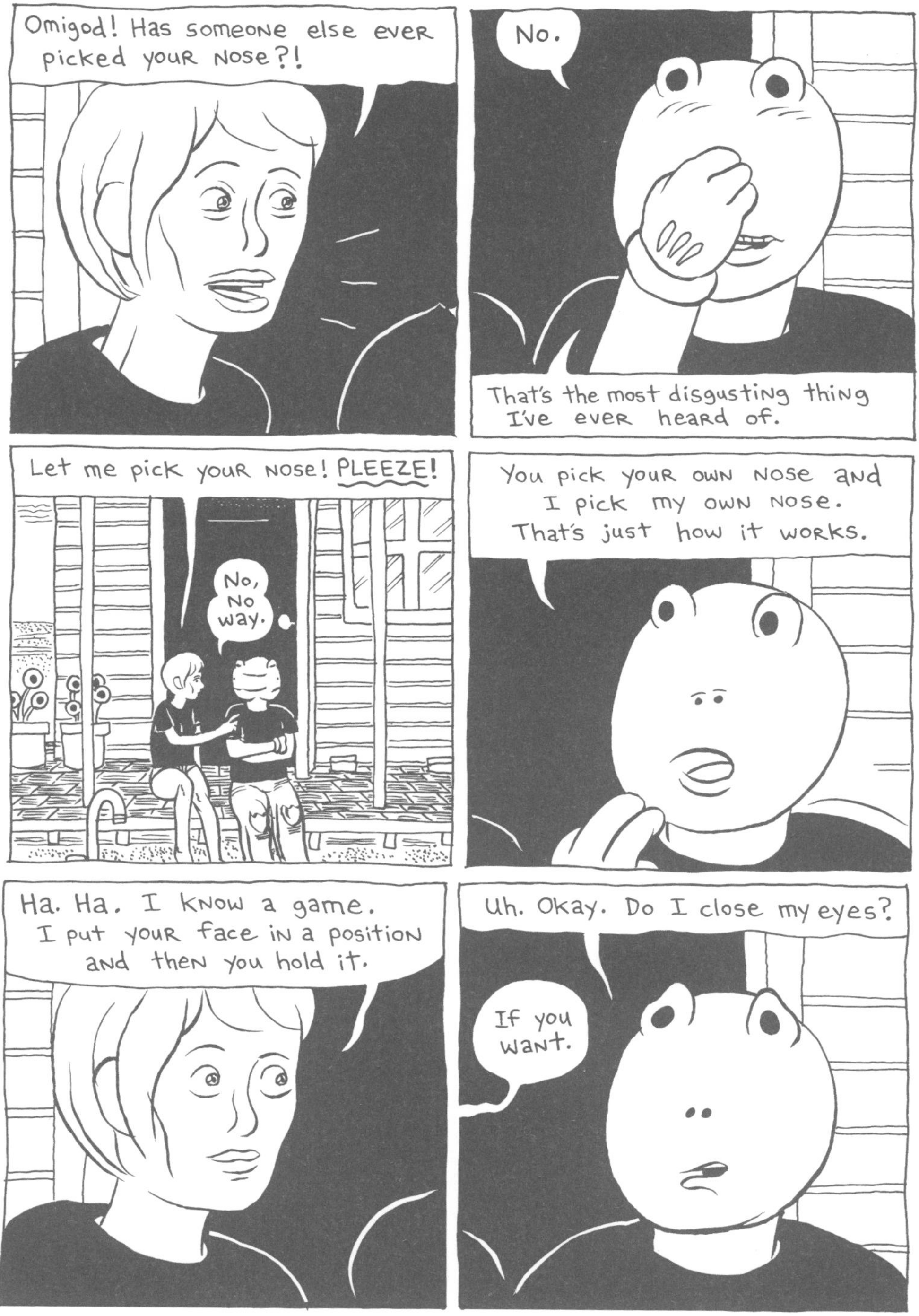
Omigod! Has someone else ever picked your nose?!
No.
That's the most disgusting thing I've ever heard of.
Let me pick your nose! PLEEZE!
No, No way.
You pick your own nose and I pick my own nose. That's just how it works.
Ha. Ha. I know a game. I put your face in a position and then you hold it.
Uh. Okay. Do I close my eyes?
If you want.

Ha.
Ha,
Ha.
Can I stop holding it now?
Ha,
Ha.
Yeah. Now do me.

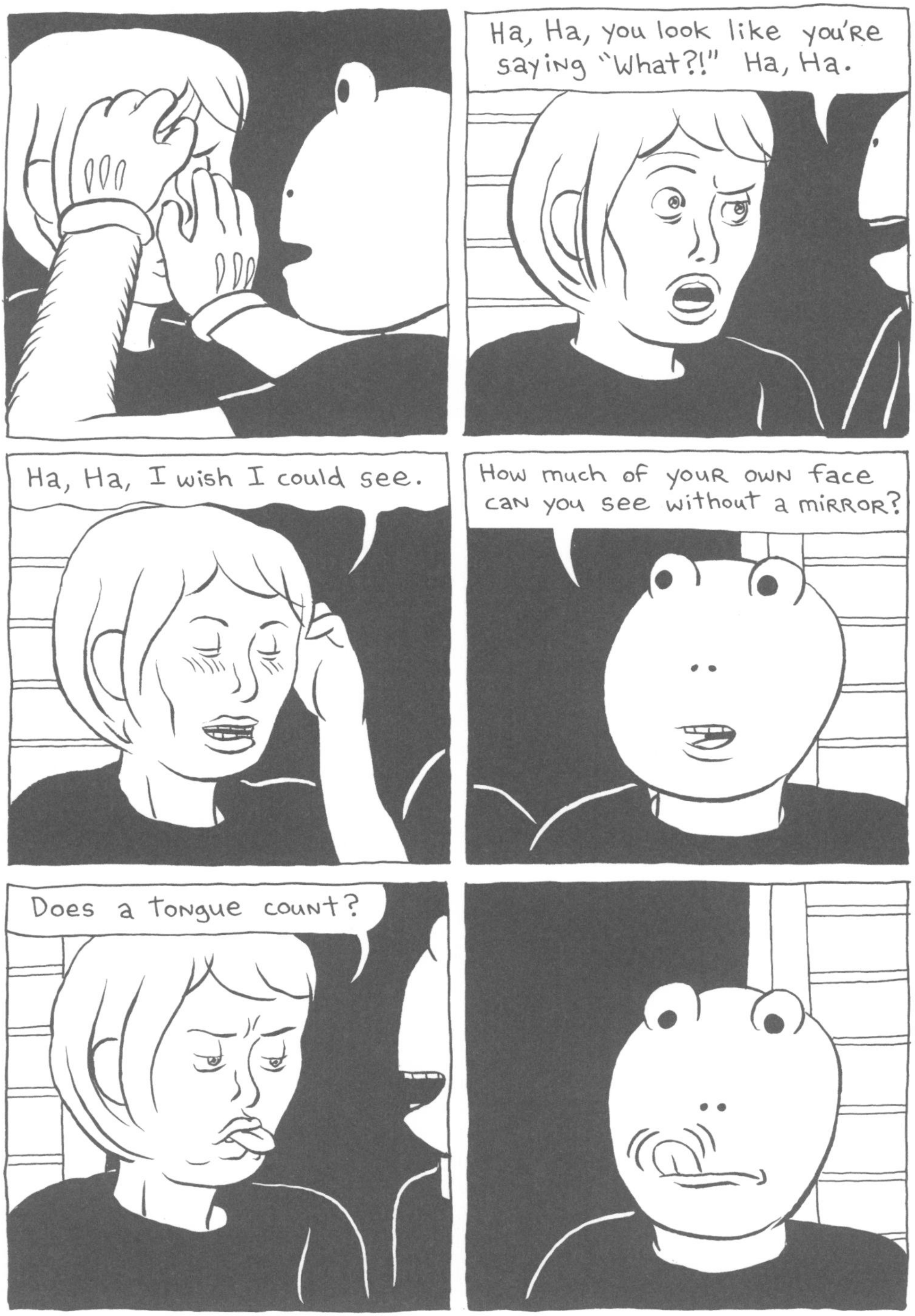
Ha, Ha, you look like you're saying "What?!" Ha, Ha.
Ha, Ha, I wish I could see.
How much of your own face can you see without a mirror?
Does a tongue count?

I can see my nose.
I can see my cheeks.

pant
pant
ENGH.
SHAKEY
JILL?!
pant

What're you doing up here?
Why were you screaming?
What was the crash?
YOU'RE BLEEDING!
What happened?
Stretch
That chair fell from the sky.

What?
It probably fell off of an airplane or maybe a hot-air balloon.
I just hope someone wasn't sitting on it.
wind
ha, ha.
wait
are you serious?
I was just having a smoke and-
YOU WERE SMOKING?!

SNIFF
SNIFF SNIFF
YOU STINK OF CIGARETTES AND YOUR LEG IS DRIPPING WITH BEER!
ARE YOU SUICIDAL? ARE YOU A SUICIDAL TEEN?
mom!
Mom, don't worry about it!

What's going on, Jill? What's up? Come inside and we'll wash you off.
No. I hate this place. It's creepy.
I totally think that house is, like, HAUNTED or something.
Don't be silly. It's not old enough to be haunted.
whatev.

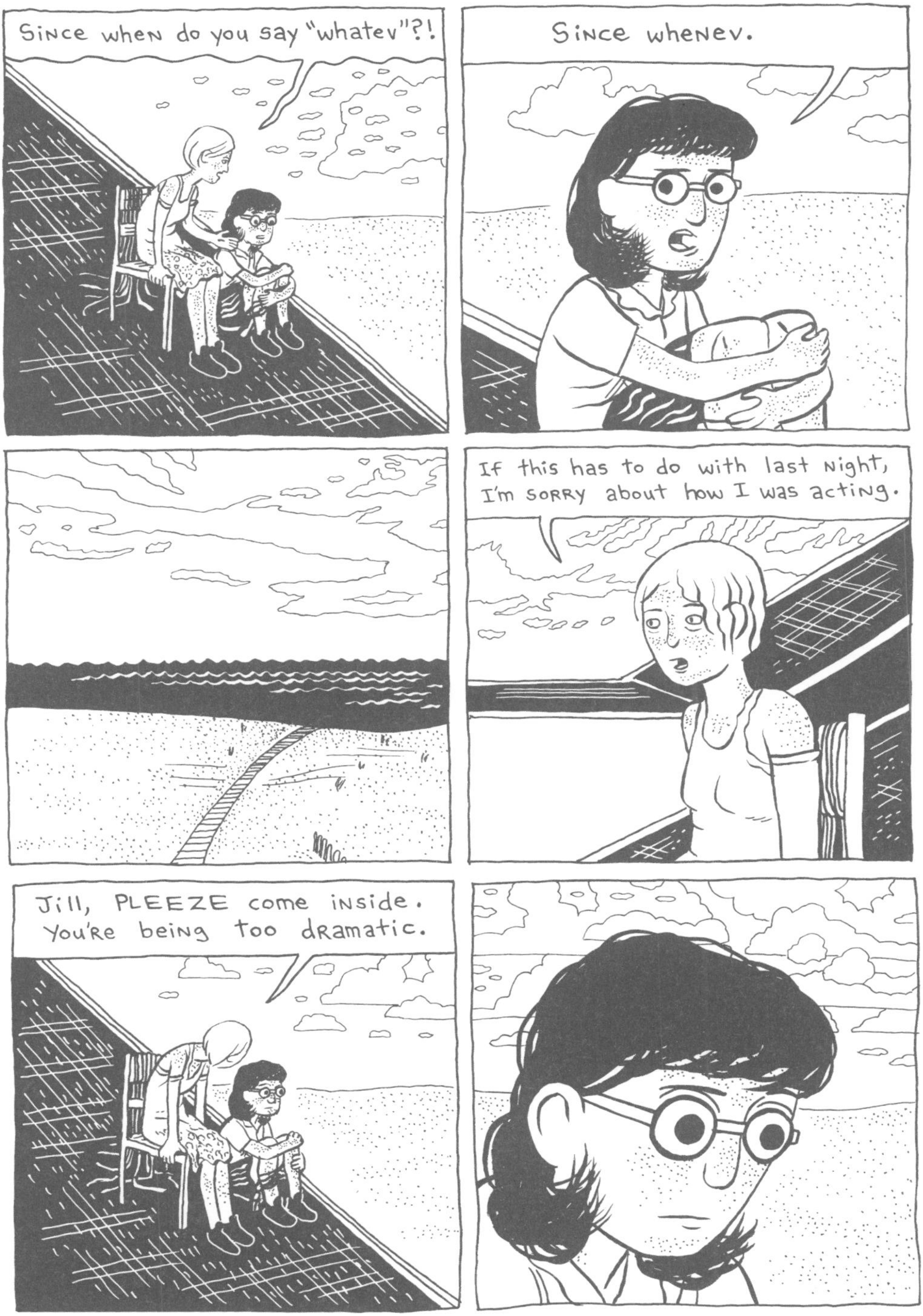
Since when do you say "whatev"?!
Since whenev.
If this has to do with last night, I'm sorry about how I was acting.
Jill, PLEEZE come inside. You're being too dramatic.

Shhhhhhhhhh
OPEN
SHUT

DAB
DAB
Do I look like a man to you?
Someone I know? Your dad?
No, No. Um. Like: mannish.
Well, I told you to change your hair. It's really goofy-looking.
DAB

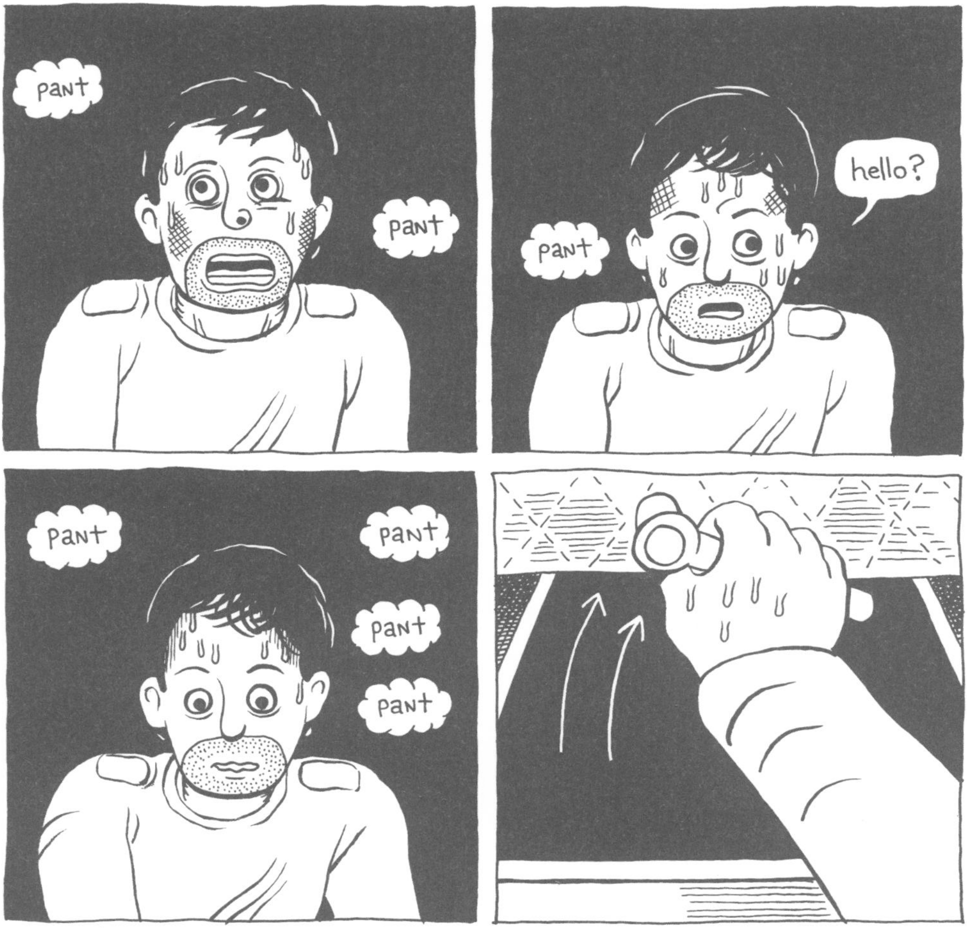
pant
pant
pant
hello?
pant
pant
pant
pant

PURR
PET
What's her name?
PURR
Jacques.
That's Farel,
Tom,
Jordan,
Jane and Mary.
Oh? I knew someone named Mary.

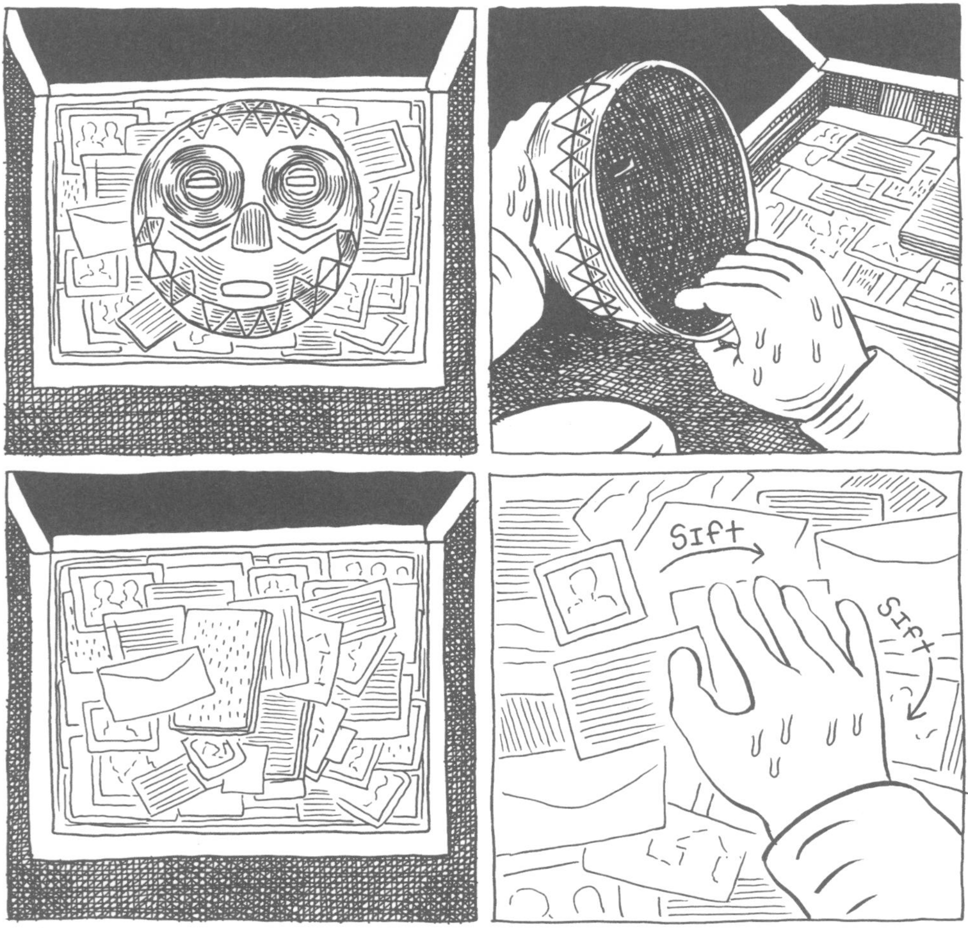
SIFT
SIFT

Mary's my mom's name.
Huh. What's your dad's name?
James... Why?
See: My mom's name is Maggie and my dad's name is David.
So: "M" for Maggie and Mom. "D" for David and Dad.
Weird, huh?
Ha. YOU'RE weird.
PET

flip
flip
flip
flip
flip
ha.
All out of order.

But NO, you don't look like a man! Where'd you get that idea?
You're very cute, Jill.
DAB DAB
ROLL
ROLL
Thanks, Mom.

Hey, Jill- This idea just popped into my head: Since you're in the tub and everything, and neither of us have any plans...
Why don't I just cut your hair now?
Huh? Neat idea, Right?
(Sigh) Okay, Mom. I don't care.

How long have you lived here? I haven't seen you around...
SHUT
Well, I was raised here.
And then went to film school and moved away, you know?
I'm just here for a week to visit my family.
wind
ROCK
ROCK
You close?
Your family?
Not really. We haven't spoken to each other in a long time.

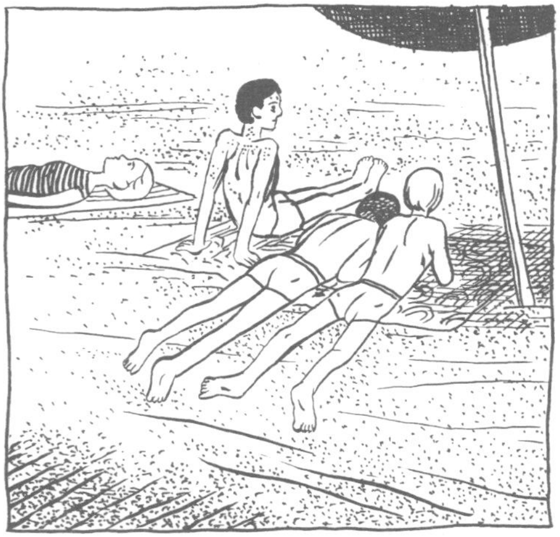

SHUT

OUIJ
Are you Religious or something? It looks like a creepy church here.
Well, I WORSHIP the DEVIL.
I'm Just KIDDING!
Oh.
ha.

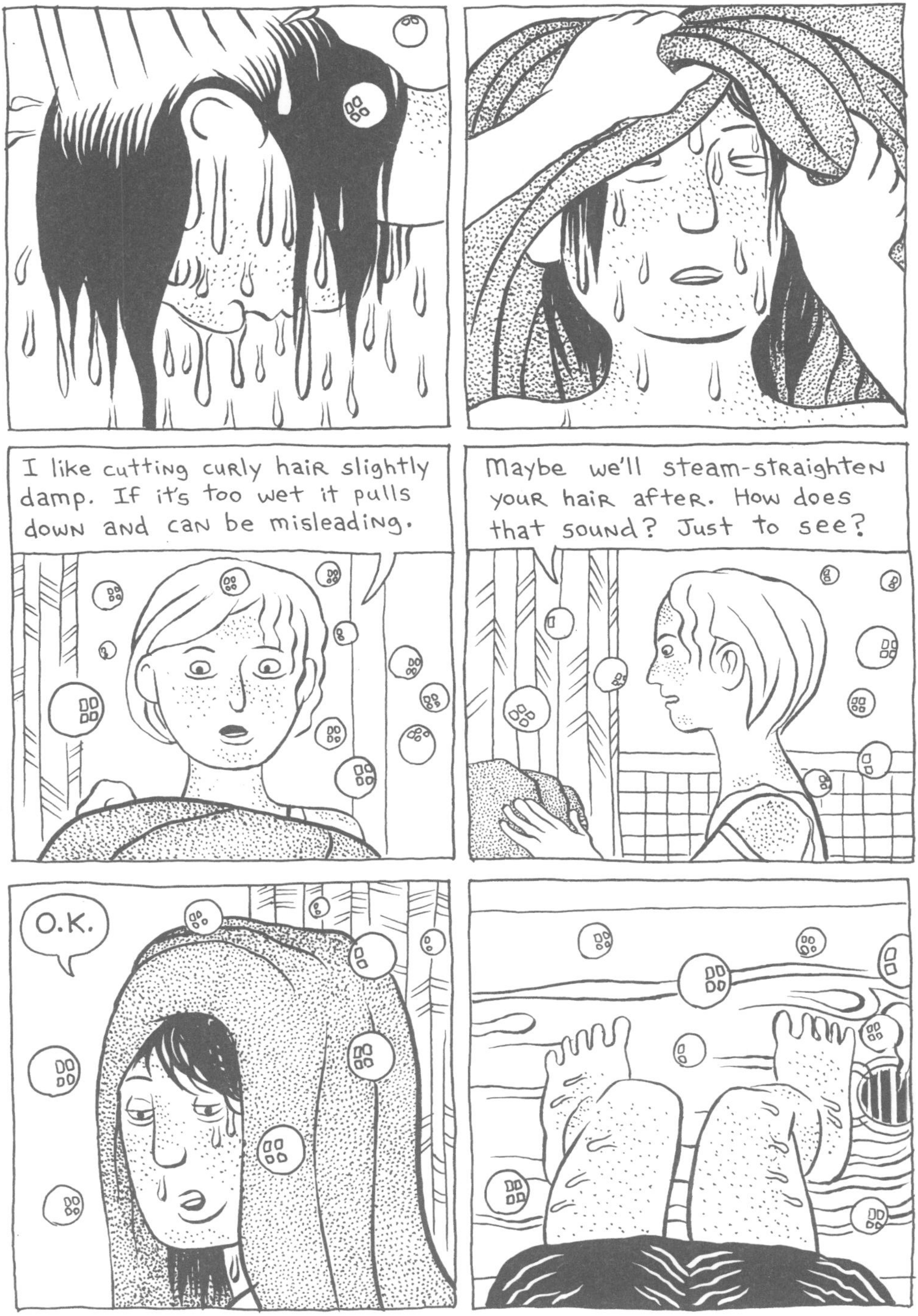

I like cutting curly hair slightly damp. If it's too wet it pulls down and can be misleading.
Maybe we'll steam-straighten your hair after. How does that sound? Just to see?
O.K.

I was Raised Catholic but I'm not anymore. I just like the way icon paintings look.
My dad's an atheist and my mom's Christian or something. I don't know what kind.
Glow-In-The-Dark Star Stickers all over ceiling
What about you?
I don't think about stuff like that.
Shrug

drape
Don't worry. I know what's "hip."

DRIP
R CONSTRUCTION
TRUCT
DRIP

Sweaty Palms
letters

DUSK LIGHT
MAROON GLOW ON WALLS
DUSK LIGHT
SUN'S down.

SNIP
Keep your chin up, Jill.
SNIP
SNIP
Chin up.

WIPE
coff
ahem.

David,

Please get me the following after class:

Ice

Cucumbers

Kelp (seaweed)

Milk

Eggs

Unsalted butter or margarine

Peaches

Asparagus

Tuna

8 cookies

<u>Search</u> for them.

it's easy.

-Maggie

wind
It's getting late. I guess I should probably start walking home. It's not too far.
SCRATCH
No.
Why don't you stay longer?
wind
Sit down?
PAT PAT
Really?
I mean,
okay.
um.
sure.

M-

I want to apologize for my behavior Sunday. In answer to your question: "No. Of course not." If I seem insensitive it's only because it's hard for me to see you so infrequantly - whenever we do meet I put so much pressure on myself to say the right thing. The time is so precious I don't want to mess things up. Anyway, I've made a new friend here - his name's Tony and I can talk to him about you. He has a girlfriend off base too.

Everyone reads science-fiction books here. We give each-other names based on the caracters and name our baseball teams on the armies in the books. You'll probobly think their stupid but I attached one so you can read it and find out, at least read page 100.

♡ - D

David,

Christmas was terrible.
I could recount the day's events:
3pm: a relative knew my name and I
couldn't remember theirs, 4pm: this,
5pm: that, but it would be
innacurate to my overwhelming reality:
I miss you terribly.
I was annoyed that we wouldn't
receive any mail on the holiday, since
that would mean maybe your letter
is sitting in the post office
undelivered, lonely. On non-holidays
I fear that some appointment would
prevent me from being home at
noon when the mail arrives. I fear
that somehow my previous letter was
lost or, somehow, misinterpreted and
you hate me.
I read the book you sent (including
page 200-but I was working then).
Sorry. I will respond as soon
as possible. I'm glad to read
anything you send me, even
outer-space stories. I want to know
you better than anyone.

with love,
truly,
-Maggie

P.S. you are an
adorable grizzly bear.

freckles →

← I can't draw.

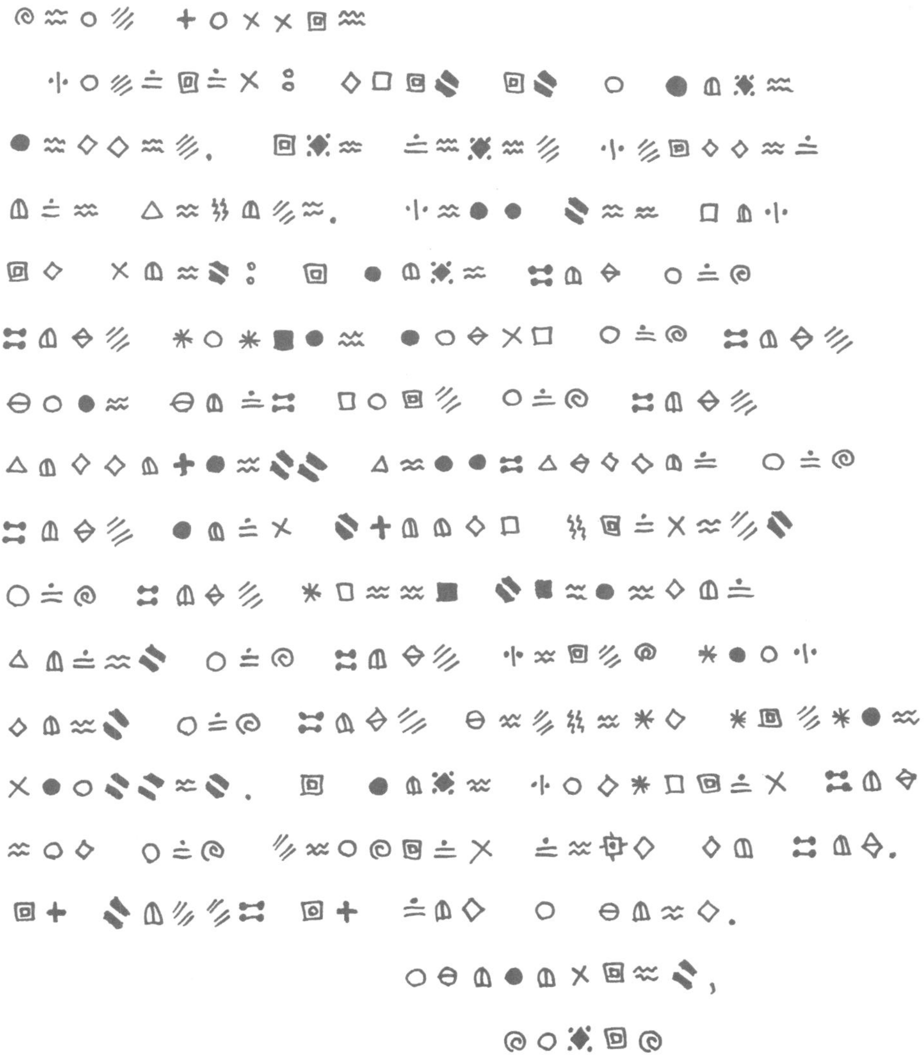

It's dangerous to have so many candles in your room.
I like candle light.
But,
Your bed could catch on fire.

wind
Ha Ha Ha
Ha, ha,
ha.
Is this your leg I'm touching?
Nevermind.
GROOVES IN WOOD

M—

Did you get
my last letter?
Hello?

—D

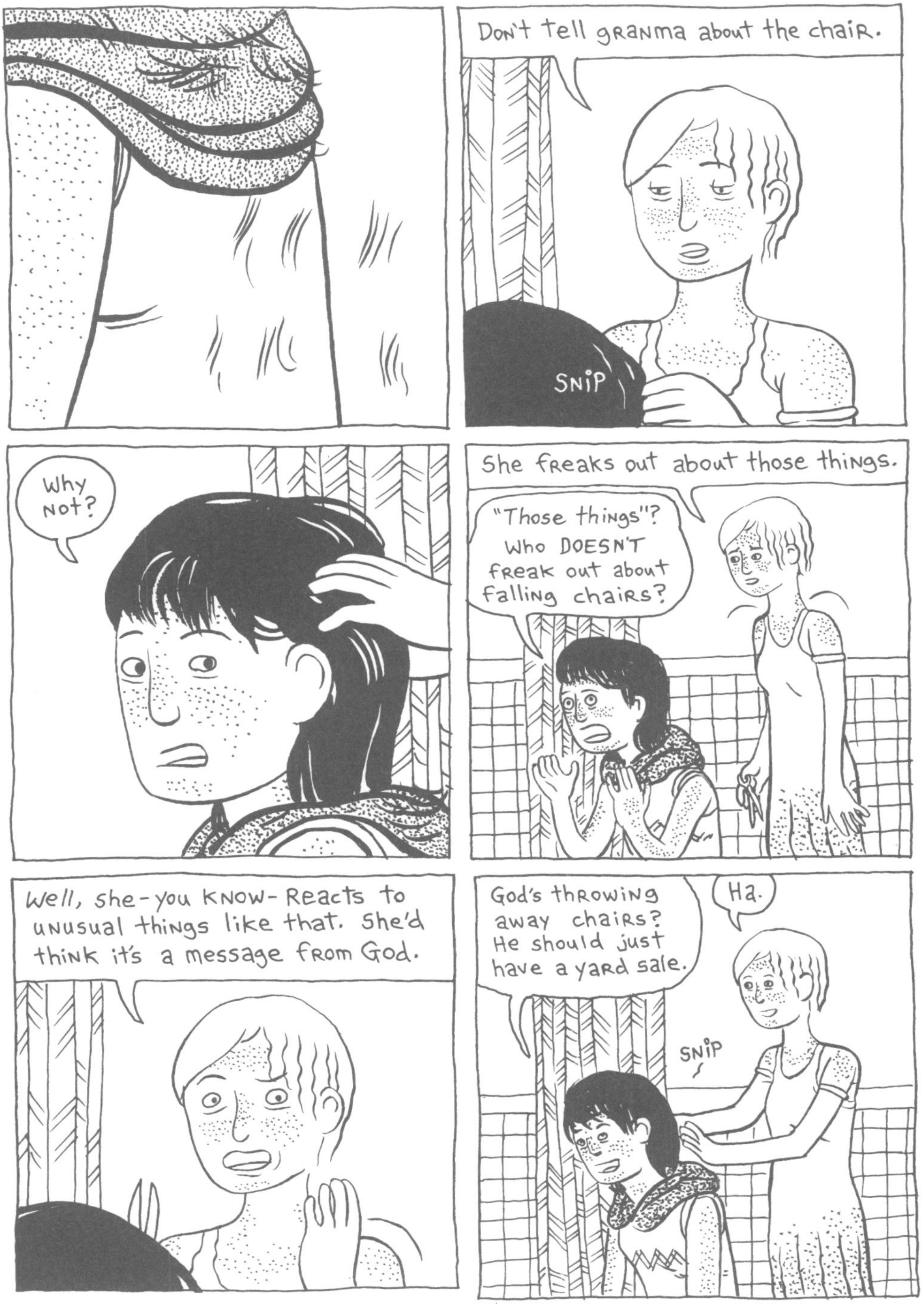

Don't tell granma about the chair.
SNIP
Why not?
She freaks out about those things.
"Those things"? Who DOESN'T freak out about falling chairs?
Well, she- you know- Reacts to unusual things like that. She'd think it's a message from God.
God's throwing away chairs? He should just have a yard sale.
Ha.
SNIP

Here's my impression of Mom: Don't you SEE, Claire? Don't you SEE what this MEANS? It means you should SIT DOWN, Relax.
Ha, Ha,
Ha.
Do Grampa!
Dad's the silent, stoic type.
Chair, Huh?
Long pause.
Stroke and scratch beard.
Ha.
Claire! You did WHAT? god DAMN it!
Ha Ha Ha
Do you know how to change a tire? Do you EVEN know HOW?!

Ha.
Ha.
Now do Peter!
SIGH
SLOUCH
Hands in pockets.
Dude, I just got an idea for a movie. It's about a depressed, lonely guy. It ends with him finally meeting a girl. Dude.
Shrug
ouch.
Ha.
That's pretty good.
Now do Uncle Dennis!
No, this is mean. Turn around. Besides: Dennis is already a parody of himself.

M -
Did you recieve
the letter? I
haven't heard from
you. please write
back.

-D

P.S. A=Z
rh sv hglkkrmt
blf ?

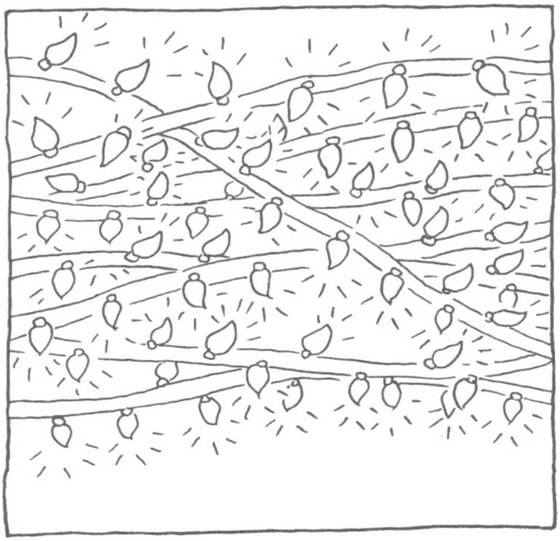

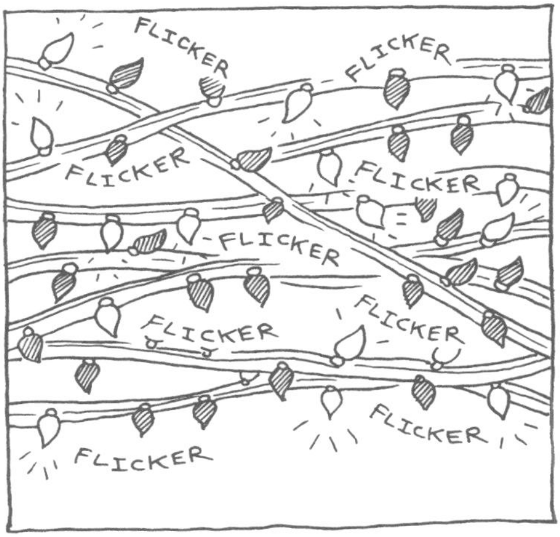
FLICKER
FLICKER
FLICKER
FLICKER
FLICKER
FLICKER
FLICKER
FLICKER
FLICKER

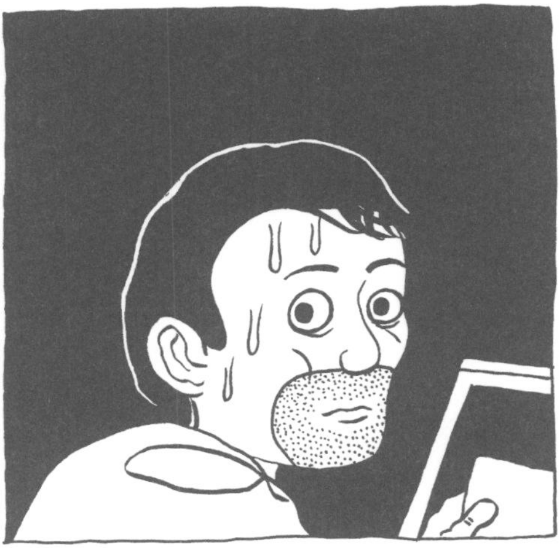

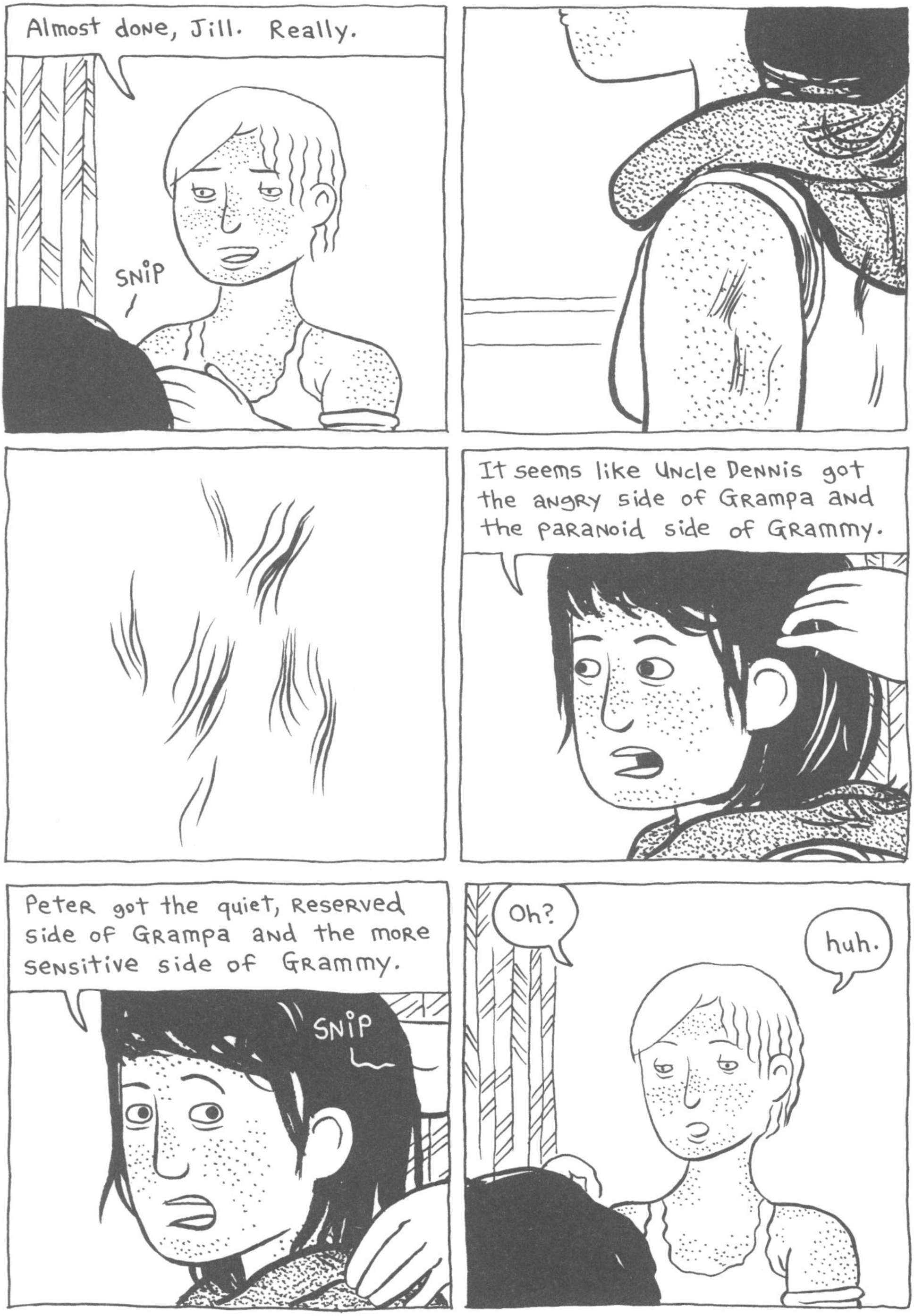
Almost done, Jill. Really.
SNIP
It seems like Uncle Dennis got the angry side of Grampa and the paranoid side of Grammy.
Peter got the quiet, reserved side of Grampa and the more sensitive side of Grammy.
SNIP
Oh?
huh.

What about me, DR. Jill? Huh?
SNIP
I dunno. You seem more like Grammy I guess. I don't know.
ROLL
ROLL
Shrug
ha.
warm.
STEAM

Sand in sheets.
ha.
ha.
Gross, heavy curtains my mom gave me.
um.
Some kind of vase?
CERAMIC
Cold window.
Something angora.
your shoulder blade.
ha.

David,

Dad's out of town so we don't have to write in code any more— although your spelling makes ~~everthing~~ everything a code! I think he knew what was going on (I told him you were an artist and he said "maybe a con artist!") I can't believe he would open our letters! It seems like he automatically hates anyone I meet outside church. You're lucky your parents are never around.

I'm sorry I didn't write sooner. I *did* write, I'd just throw it away. I'm no poet either - but I am a former spelling bee winner! I can spell "asphyxiate" (I don't know what it means, though). Finally, I decided that whatever I write, I'd immediately send off. No looking bach.

I decoded your letter — it took me forever. I like what you said about my belly-button. I'm an inny and you're an outie — we fit together.

Love, Maggie

P.S. what does "P.S." stand for?
peace soon?
please speak?
pretty swans?

Ha
Ha
um.
Where'd you go?

M-

I guess I wanted to write it and send it and (sort of) wanted you to read it but also (sort of) didn't want you to. It's pretty embarassing.

Your dad's very intimidating. His height and all-black attire doesn't help. Your dad will like me eventually. It's hard for two quiet people to talk to each-other. That's why we work well like a team (I love the sound of your voice). I want to depend on you and I want you to depend on me. Do you want to know how I wrote the long code so neatly? Tony showed me how. Tape a sheet of graph paper on a window. Then write on a sheet of paper over the graph paper when light is shining through the window. You can see through both pages. The graph is the guide.

I asked Tony to help me on the spelling of this letter. I told him you deserve the best spelling.

♡ always -D

It's "Lily of the Valley" scented.
BLOW
Can you smell it?
uh-huh.
I like saying "lily". lily lily lily.
Lilly Billy Silly Willy.
Willy-Nilly Frilly Pilly
Pickadilly Boofapilly.

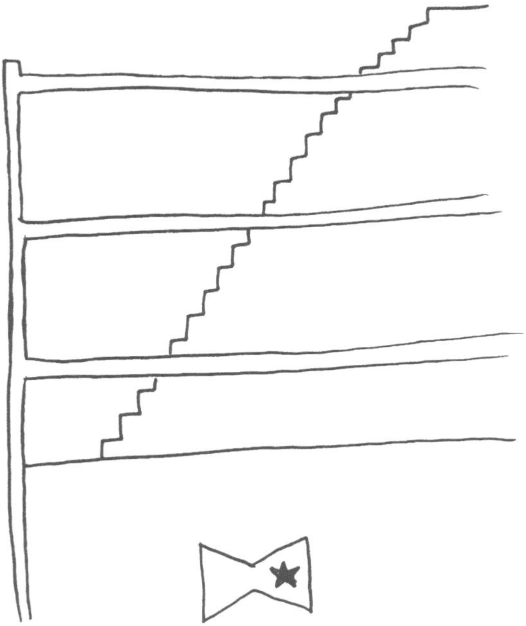

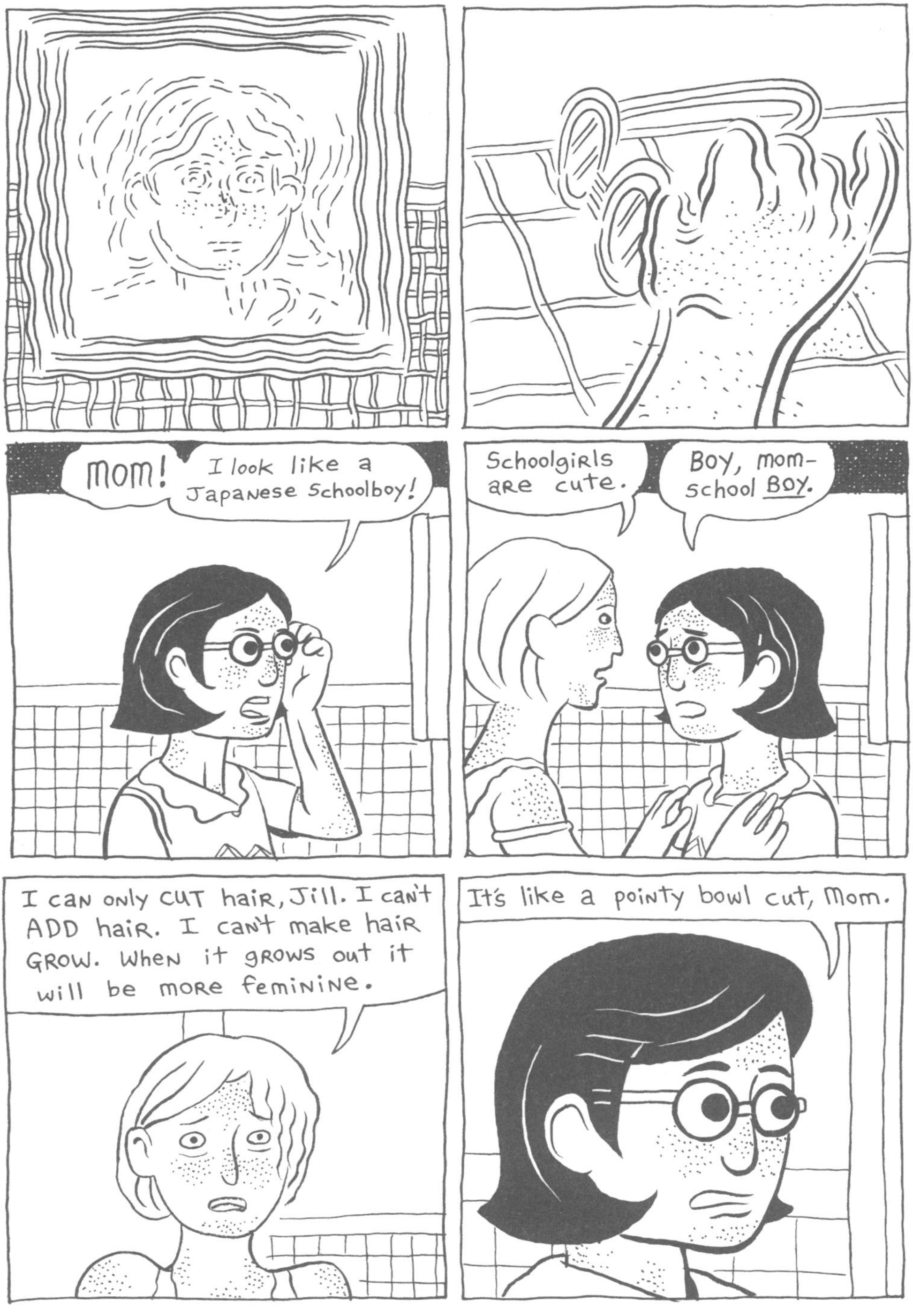
mom!
I look like a Japanese Schoolboy!
Schoolgirls are cute.
Boy, mom- school BOY.
I can only CUT hair, Jill. I can't ADD hair. I can't make hair GROW. When it grows out it will be more feminine.
It's like a pointy bowl cut, Mom.

Cof
Red-colored paper
SHAKEY
stuff
Cof
Hard to breathe.
SHUT

Jill?
I'm tired, Mom. It's been a long day, you know?
Jill?
GASP
GASP
GASP
...fuckin...
...haunted...

coff
Gasp
Pant
GASP
GASP
GASP

shhhhhhhhhh
shhhhhhhhhh

8
GASP!
GASP!
Gasp
Gasp
Gasp

um.
Can I kiss you? I can't tell.
Ha Ha Ha
Ha,
You're cute.
oh-kay.

Should I close my eyes?
Ha If you want, Peter.

I'm getting to the bottom of this.
There is no bottom, Dennis.
God, listen to yourself.
You've been on the same level ever since we arrived here.
When you get stuck on something it just gets worse and worse. You're like a little kid.
BRUSH
Aki, I-
Hey,
If you want some mystery to solve, I have a few for you.

How about this: When are we going to pull together a down- -payment? Mystery.
SHAKE
SHAKE
Alex CAN'T grow up in our neighborhood and it seems like I'm-
AKI. I KNOW.
I don't want Alex to be there any more than you do. Really.
SIT.
Listen: The newspaper thing is over, but the sports column is happening. It's all set with the editor.
I CAN do this, Aki. The father is the glue of the family.

Ha. yeah, yeah.
Smoothing-out wrinkle in table cloth
It just feels like one problem after another lately. Problem. Problem. Problem.
That's why we're a family, Aki, Right?
When everything's going wrong it's time to be a family. We all get through it.
I love you, Dennis. I, you know, you have these ideas about how families - and-
and- I LIKE your ideas, where every--one fits together,
and.
uh.
I forgot what I was saying—what I was going to say.
BRUSH
I'm so tired. I don't like it here. I want to go home.

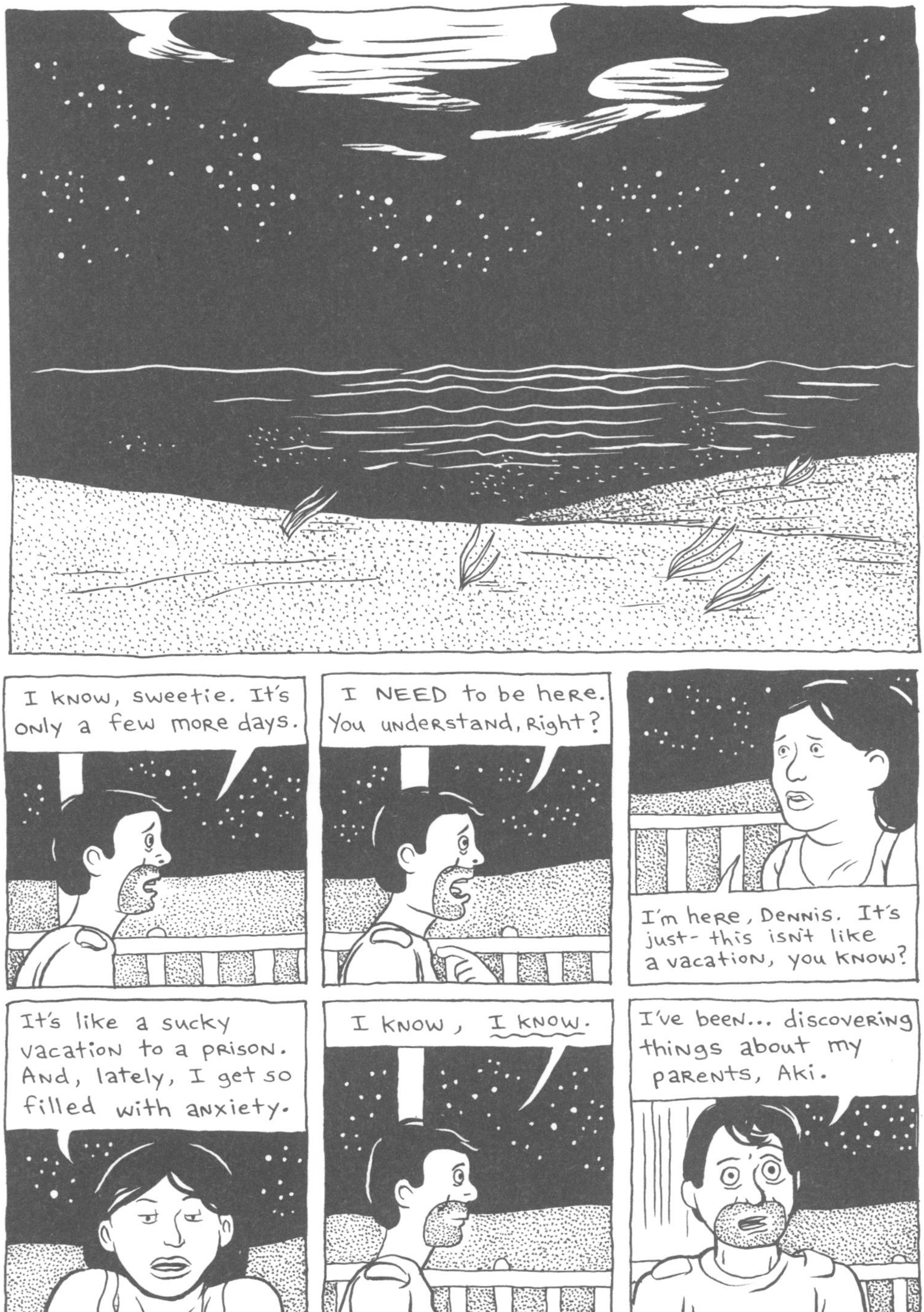
I KNOW, SWEETIE. IT'S ONLY A FEW MORE DAYS.
I NEED TO BE HERE. YOU UNDERSTAND, RIGHT?
I'M HERE, DENNIS. IT'S JUST- THIS ISN'T LIKE A VACATION, YOU KNOW?
IT'S LIKE A SUCKY VACATION TO A PRISON. AND, LATELY, I GET SO FILLED WITH ANXIETY.
I KNOW, I KNOW.
I'VE BEEN... DISCOVERING THINGS ABOUT MY PARENTS, AKI.

There's a whole history I never knew.
Secrets.
Things my parents never told me. I know you think it's crazy, but-
there is a reason for why this is all happening now.
And I'm getting deeper and deeper into it, Aki.
Sigh.
Believe what you want to believe, Dennis.
What's THAT supposed to mean, Aki? Ha.
Honey?
I'm tired.
SLIDE

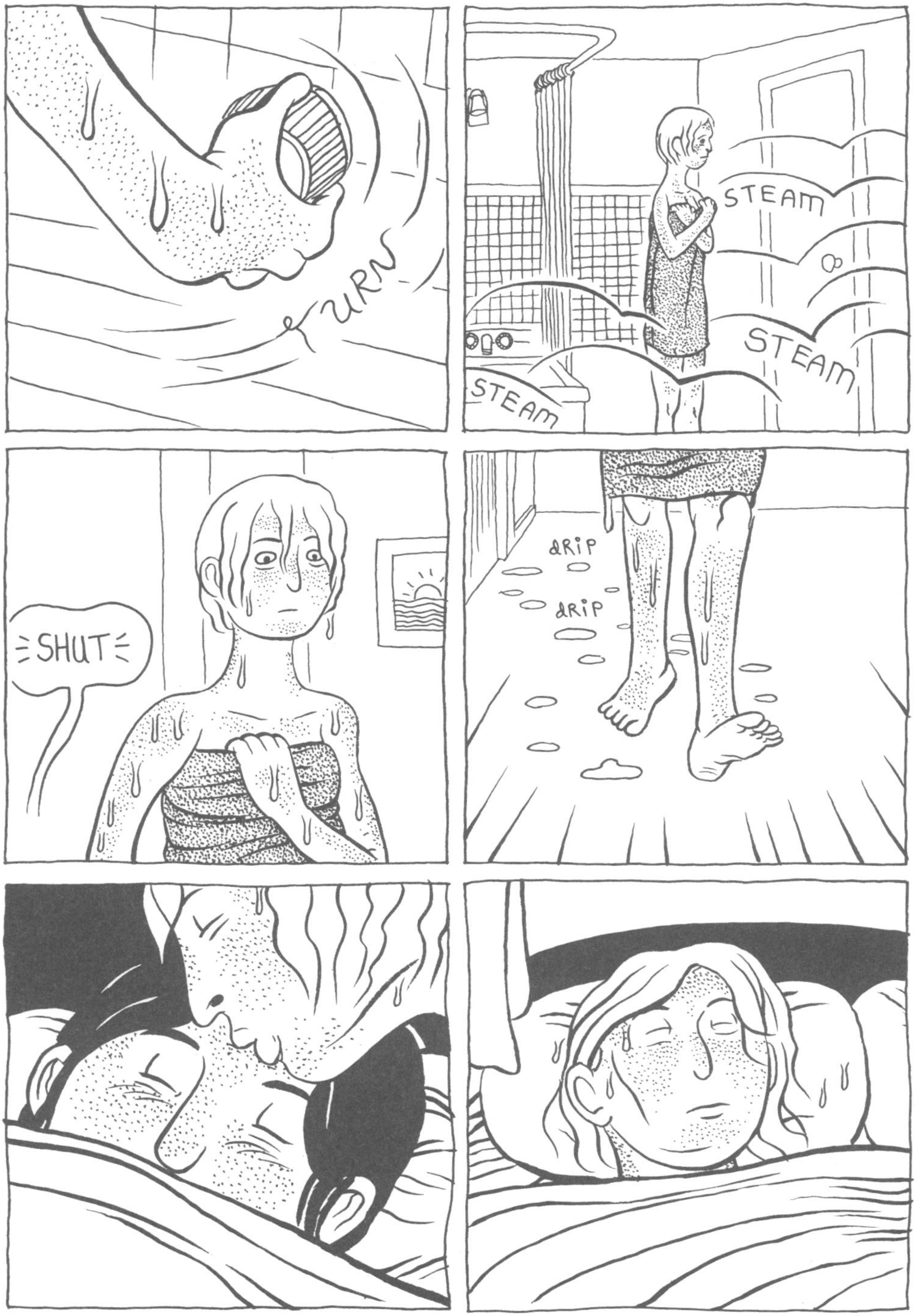
TURN
STEAM
STEAM
STEAM
SHUT
drip
drip

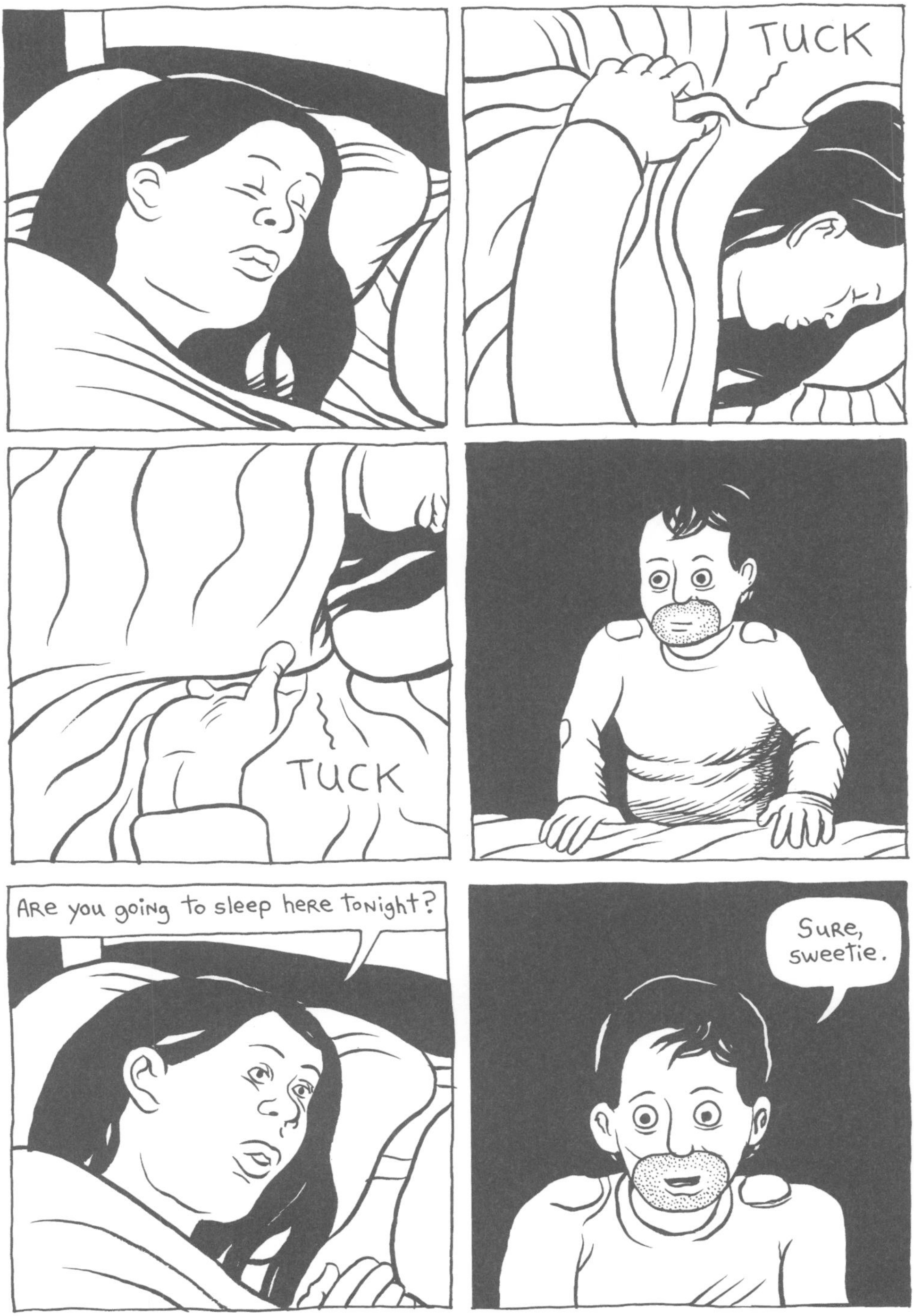
TUCK
TUCK
Are you going to sleep here tonight?
Sure, sweetie.

hot newz !
OUIJ
TWO SHOCKING STORIES IN TODAY'S HEADLINES, BOTH INVOLVING SUPER-STAR HUNK CHAD BONES.
OUIJ
BONES' LATEST FILM, "GREY MOON" SUNK AT THE BOX OFFICE.
AUDIENCES, EXPECTING TO SEE A ROMANTIC DATE MOVIE, WERE HORRIFIED BY THE FILM'S UNLIKABLE CHARACTERS AND MISOGYNISTIC UNDERTONES.

THE DIRECTOR, ANDREW LUCIDO, DEFENDS HIS FILM: "IT WAS A CASE OF MISLEADING MARKETING. THIS IS AN ART FILM THAT SPEAKS, ON A SOCIAL AND POLITICAL LEVEL, TO THE COUNTRY."
THE NEXT BIG NEWS: MODEL-TURNED-ACTRESS BRYCE GIVENS CALLED OFF HER ENGAGEMENT TO CHAD BONES EARLIER THIS MORNING. HER PRESS AGENT-
CITED "IRRECONCILA
YES, IT'S BEEN A R
FEW DAYS FOR MR.
CELEBRITY CORRE
RELATIONSHIP
DON"S FAILURE
E AND THE
ENGAGEMENT?
BU
WE
A
OU
NT
ICK

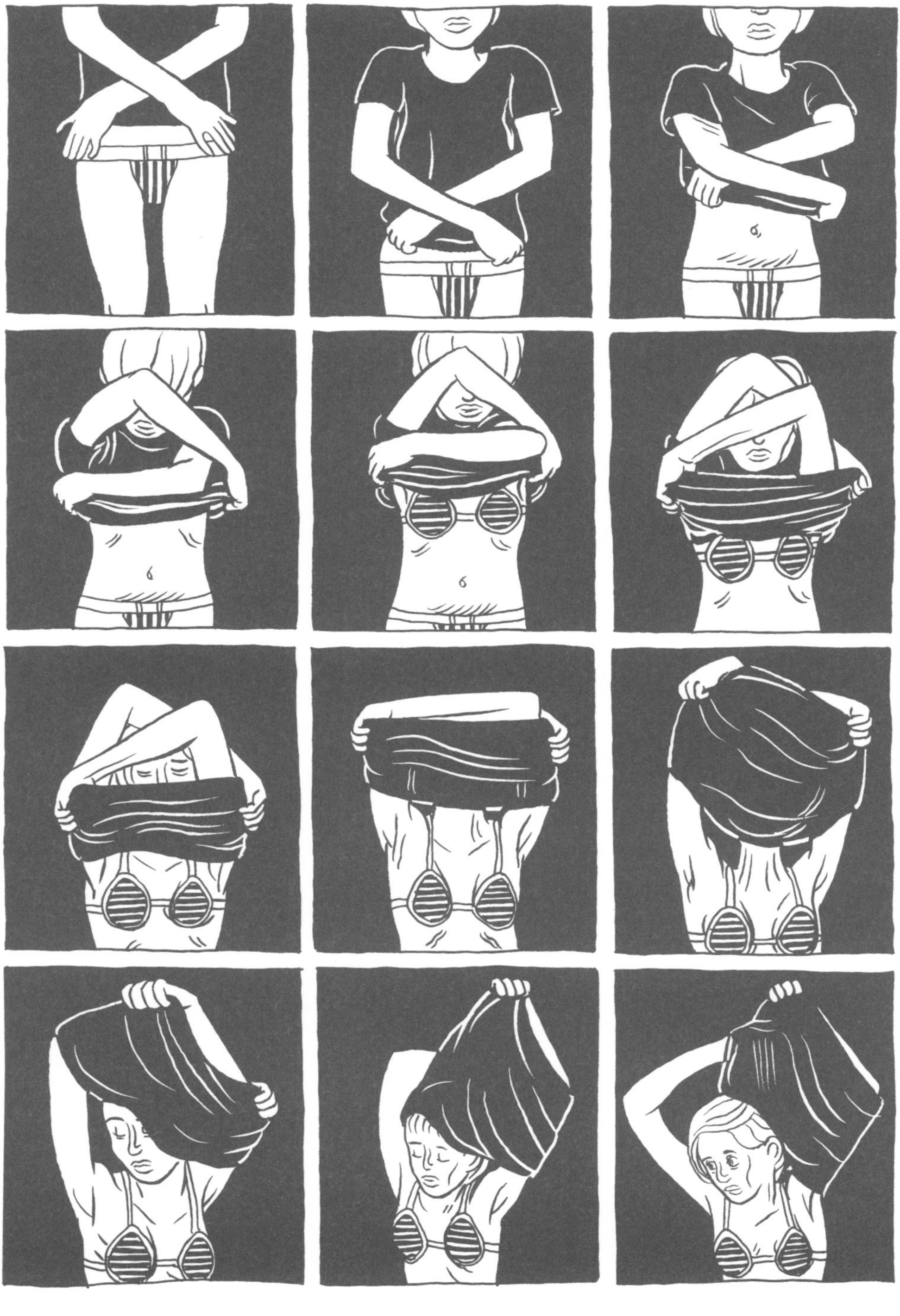

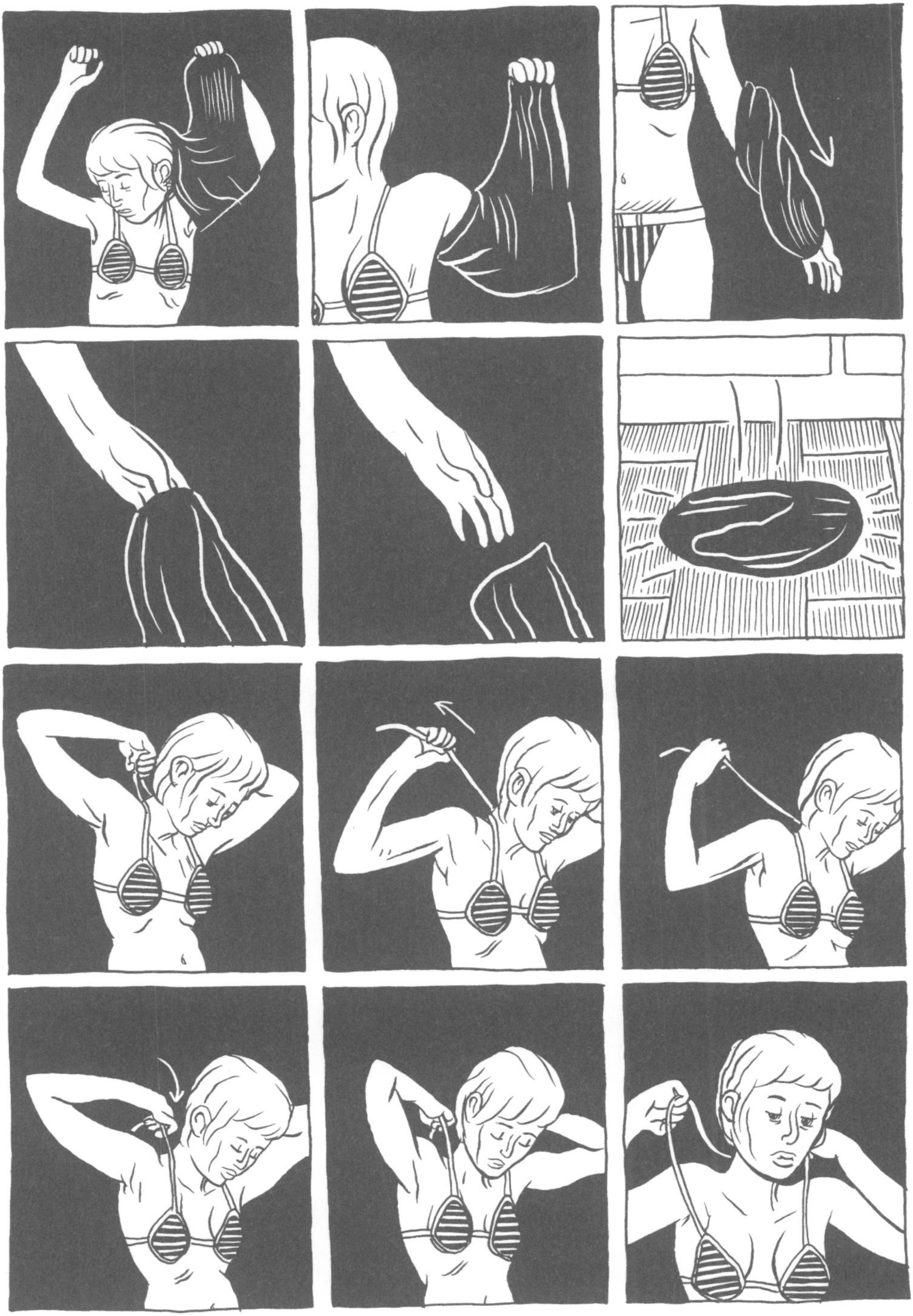

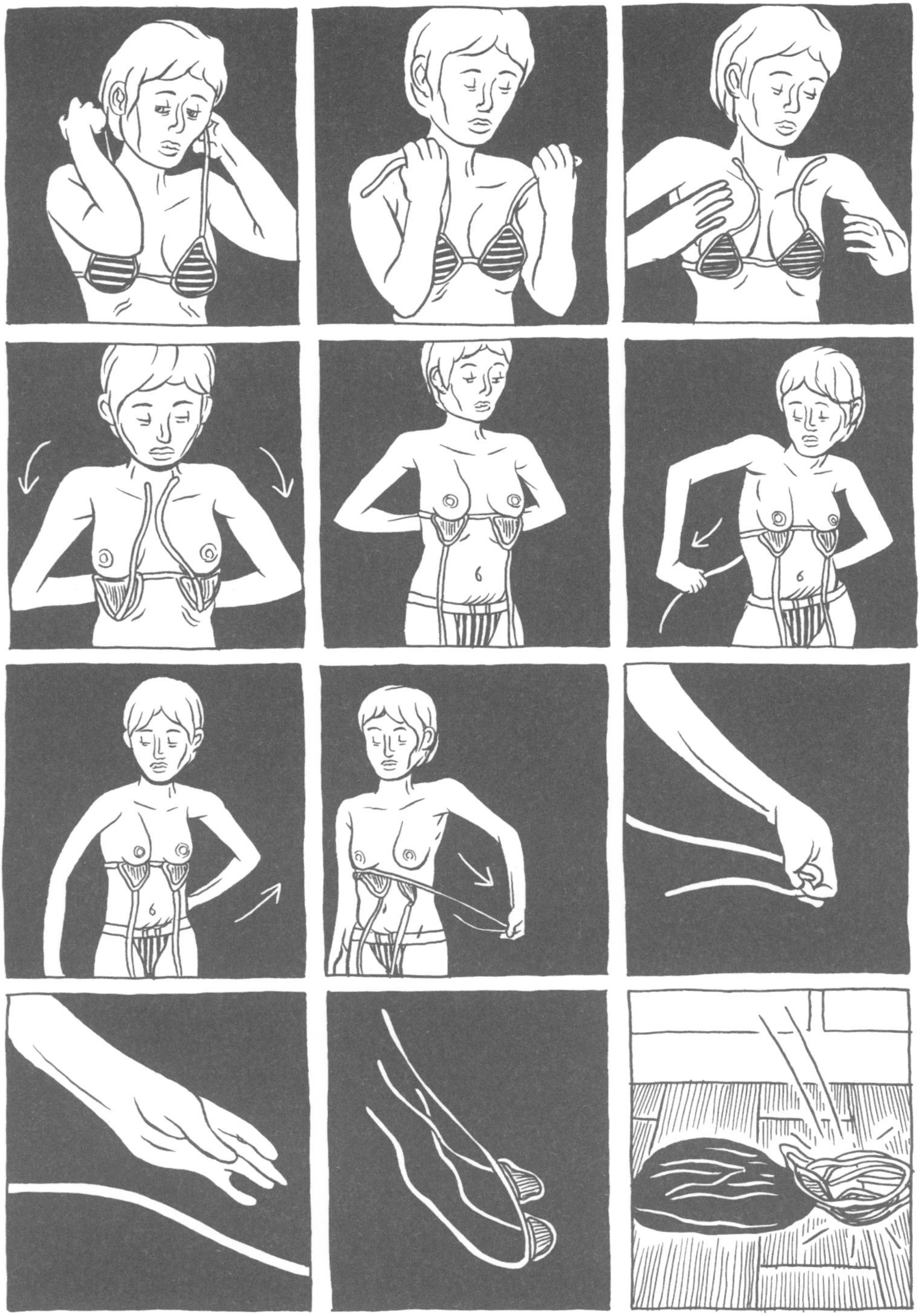

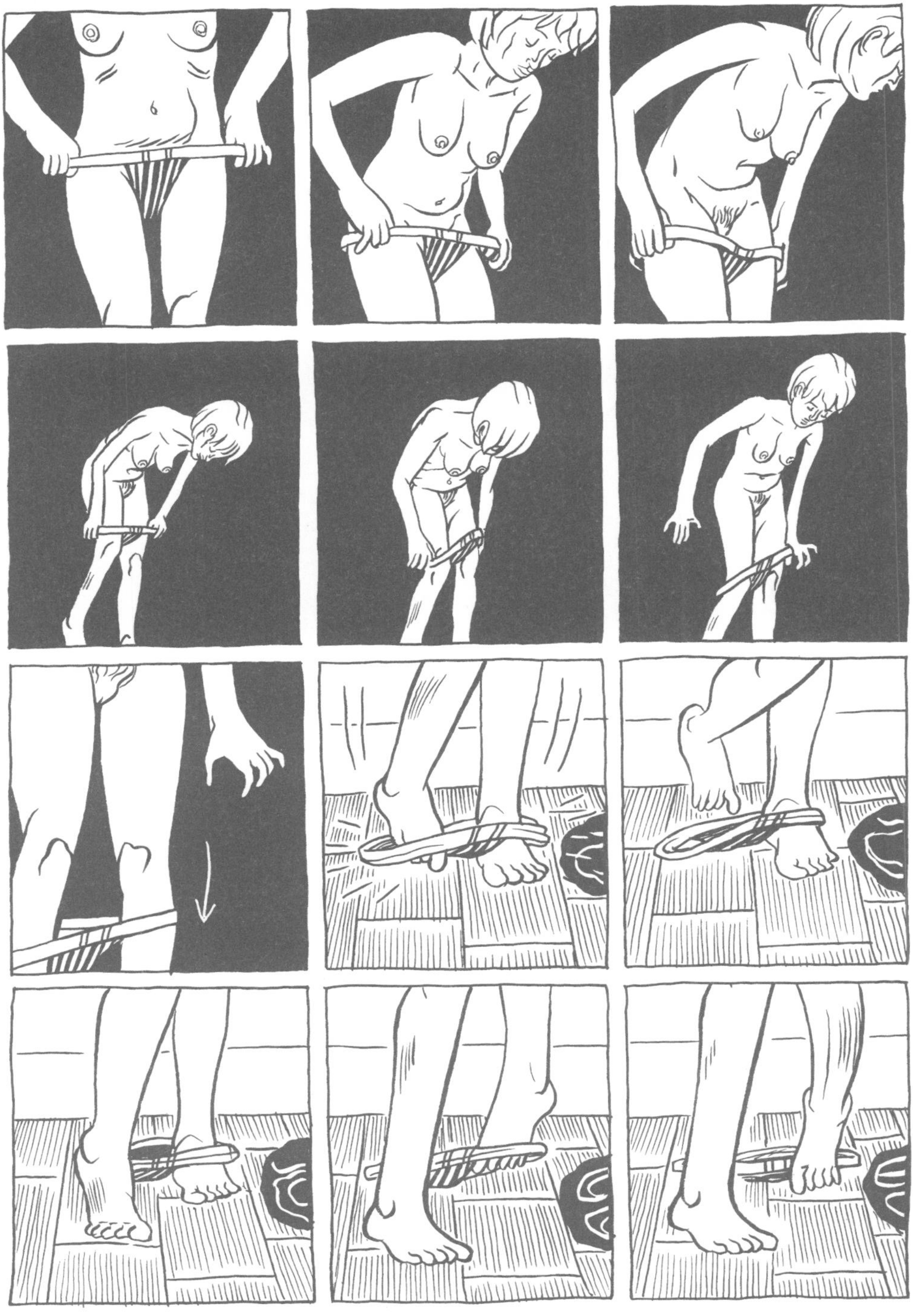

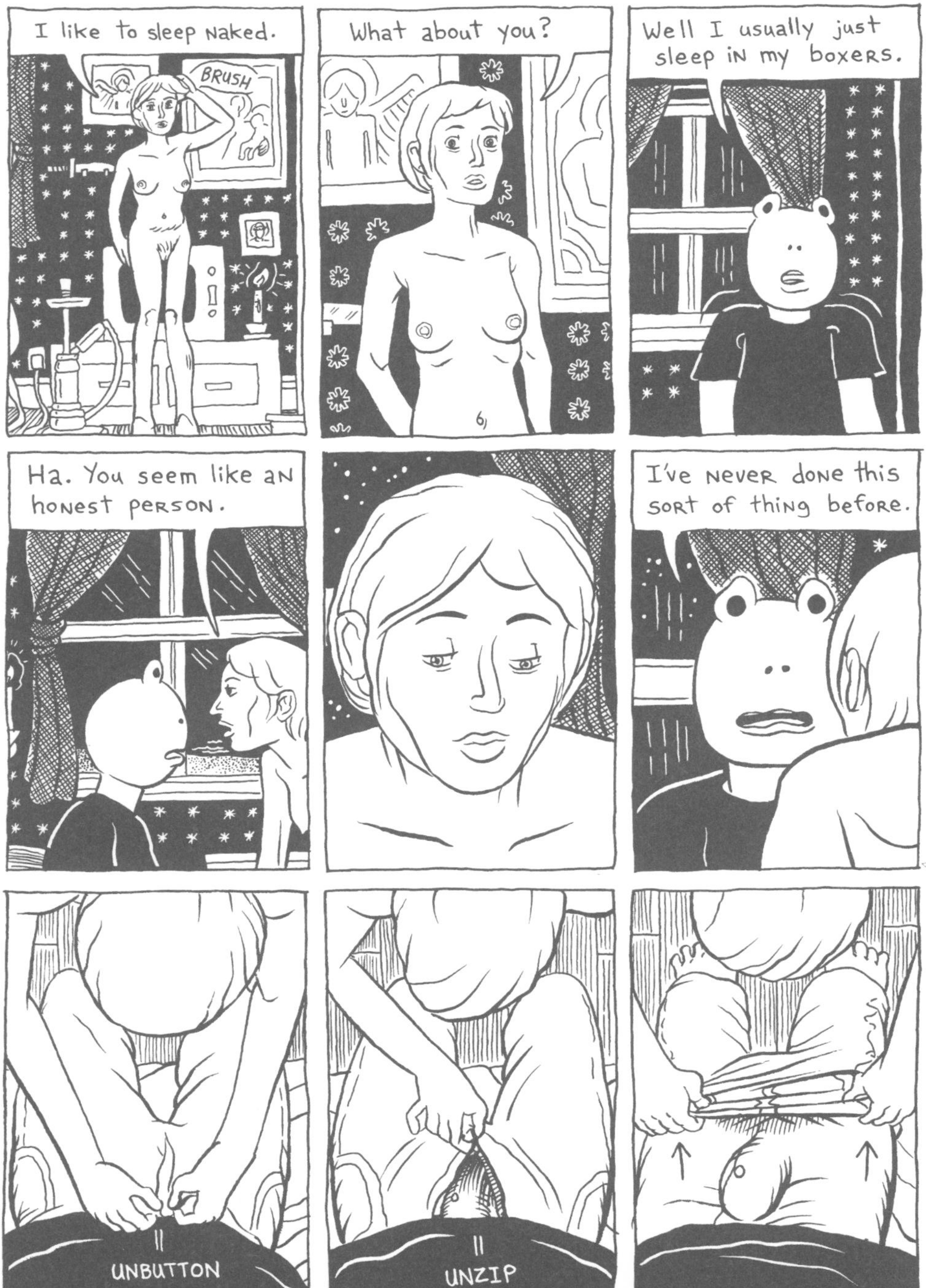
I like to sleep naked.
BRUSH
What about you?
Well I usually just sleep in my boxers.
Ha. You seem like an honest person.
I've never done this sort of thing before.
UNBUTTON
UNZIP

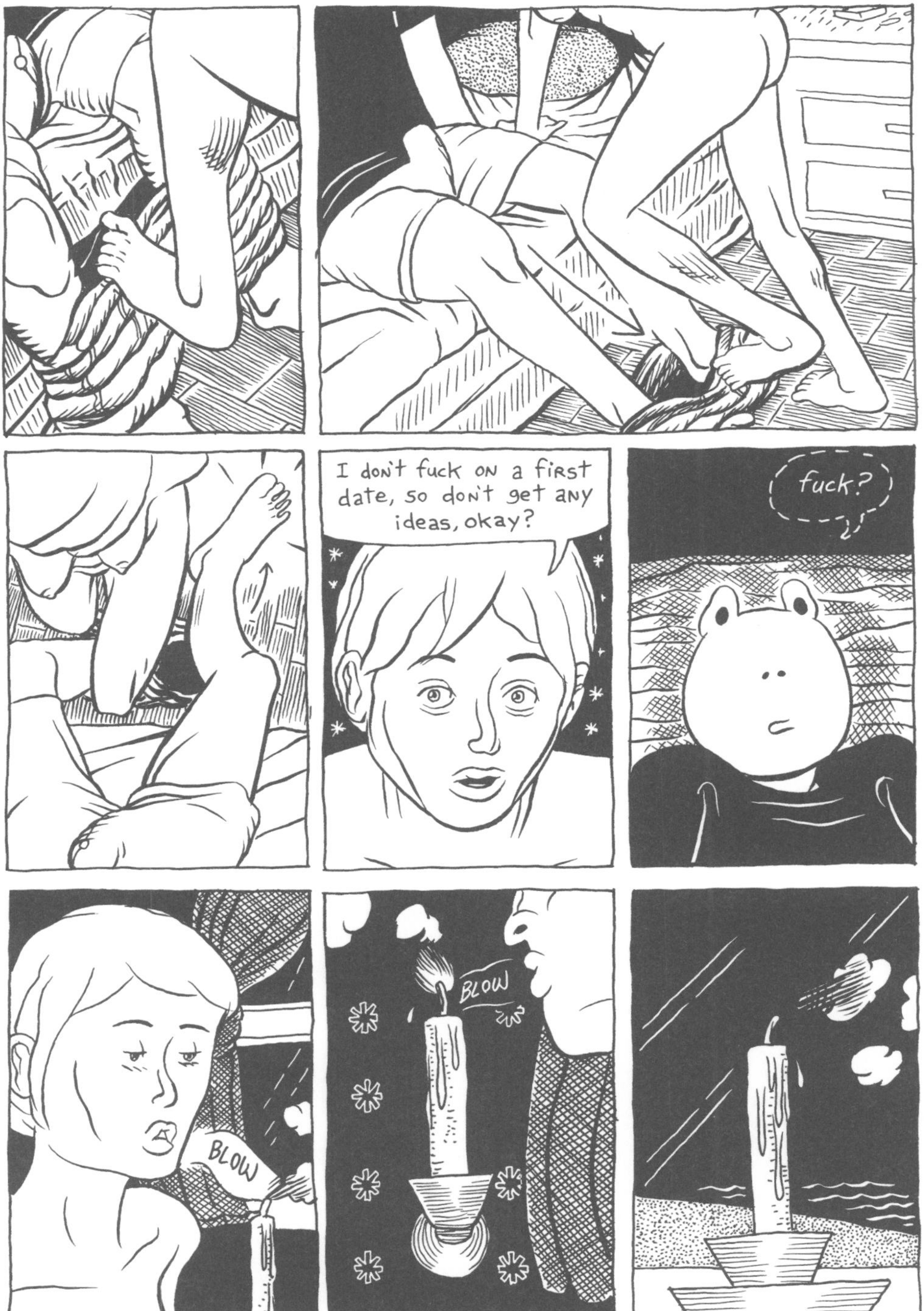

I don't fuck on a first date, so don't get any ideas, okay?
fuck?
BLOW
BLOW

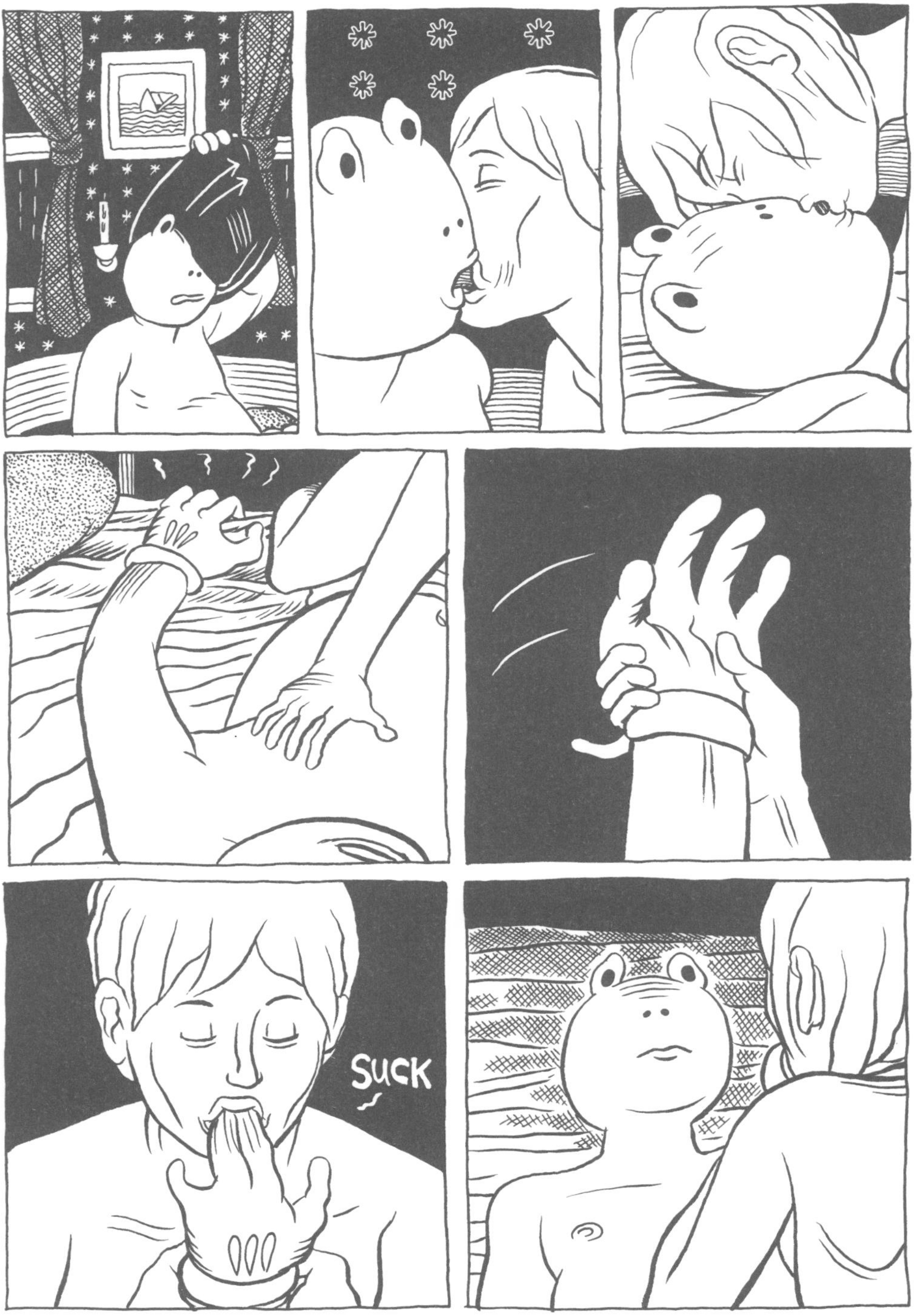
SUCK

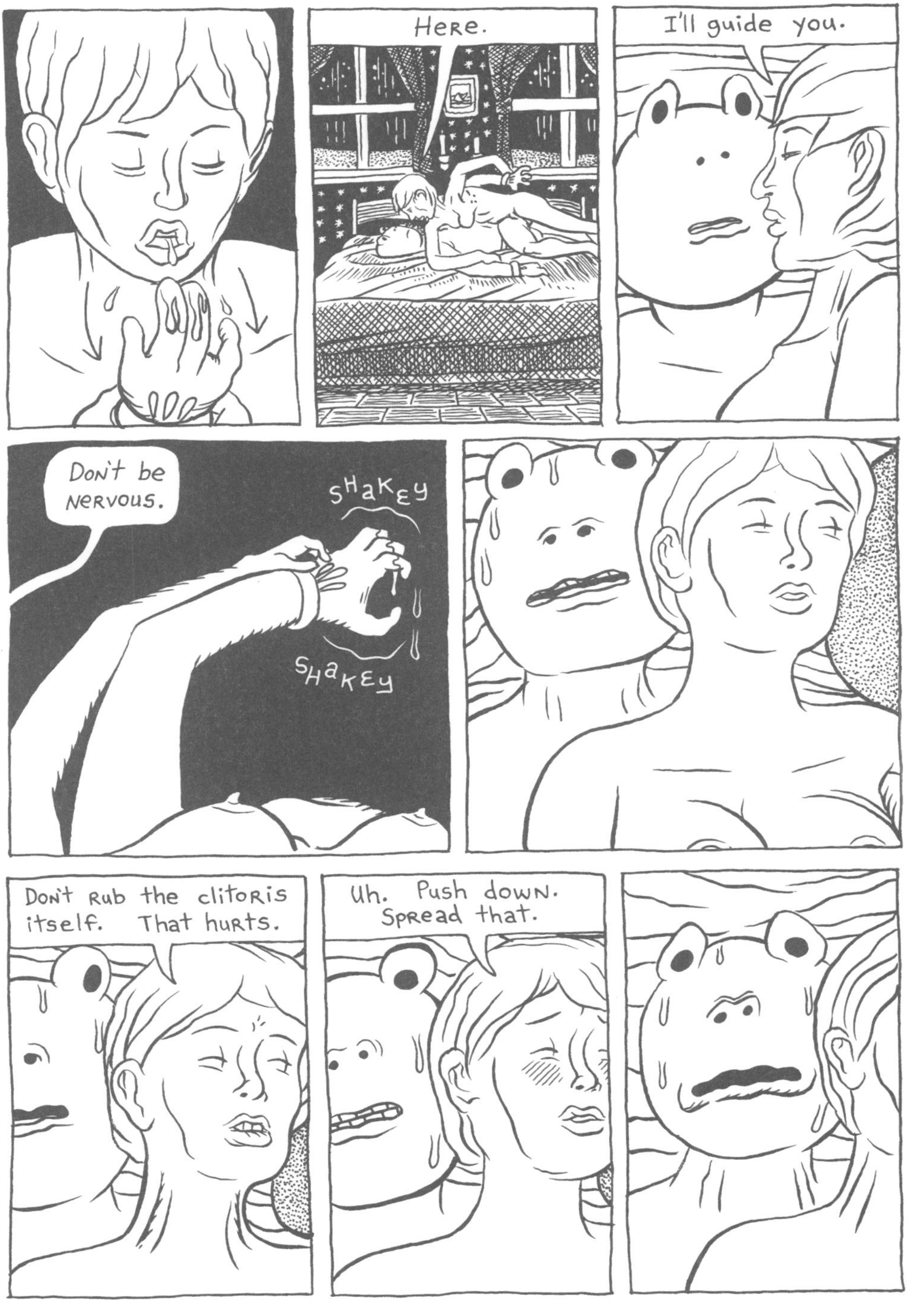
Here.
I'll guide you.
Don't be nervous.
SHAKEY
SHAKEY
Don't rub the clitoris itself. That hurts.
Uh. Push down. Spread that.

Pinch it and stretch skin over it. Like this:
PINCH
Am I doing it right? I- I don't-
Yeah, Peter.
I can feel your hard dick against my back.

SHAKEY
SHAKEY
SPIT.
BREATHES OUT.
UNBUTTON
SPURT

Oh God. Oh God.
That's probably just pre cum.
I'm SORRY,
I'll clean it up, I-
It's OKAY, Really. It means you like me, Peter. I'll clean it.
Kat- I-
I understand, Peter.
We'll stop, okay. Too much too fast. I'm not a slut you know.

DAB
DAB
I wonder what burning cum smells like.
OUIJ
What?
FWOOSH
You're Right. Bad idea.
STAMP
STAMP
OUIJ

Where are you going?
Just to the bathroom.
O.K.

TURN
WIPE
SNIF.
WIPE
STEPS BACK
AIM

AIM
AIM
AIM
FLUSH
BUTTON
WIPE
WIPE
WIPE
WIPE

Sigh.

BREATHES OUT.
Having trouble sleeping?
I - I guess so.
Take one of these.

W-What is it?
Just take one.
SHRUG
It will help you sleep.
Well, I want to know what it is.
It doesn't matter.
It'll let you sleep easy.

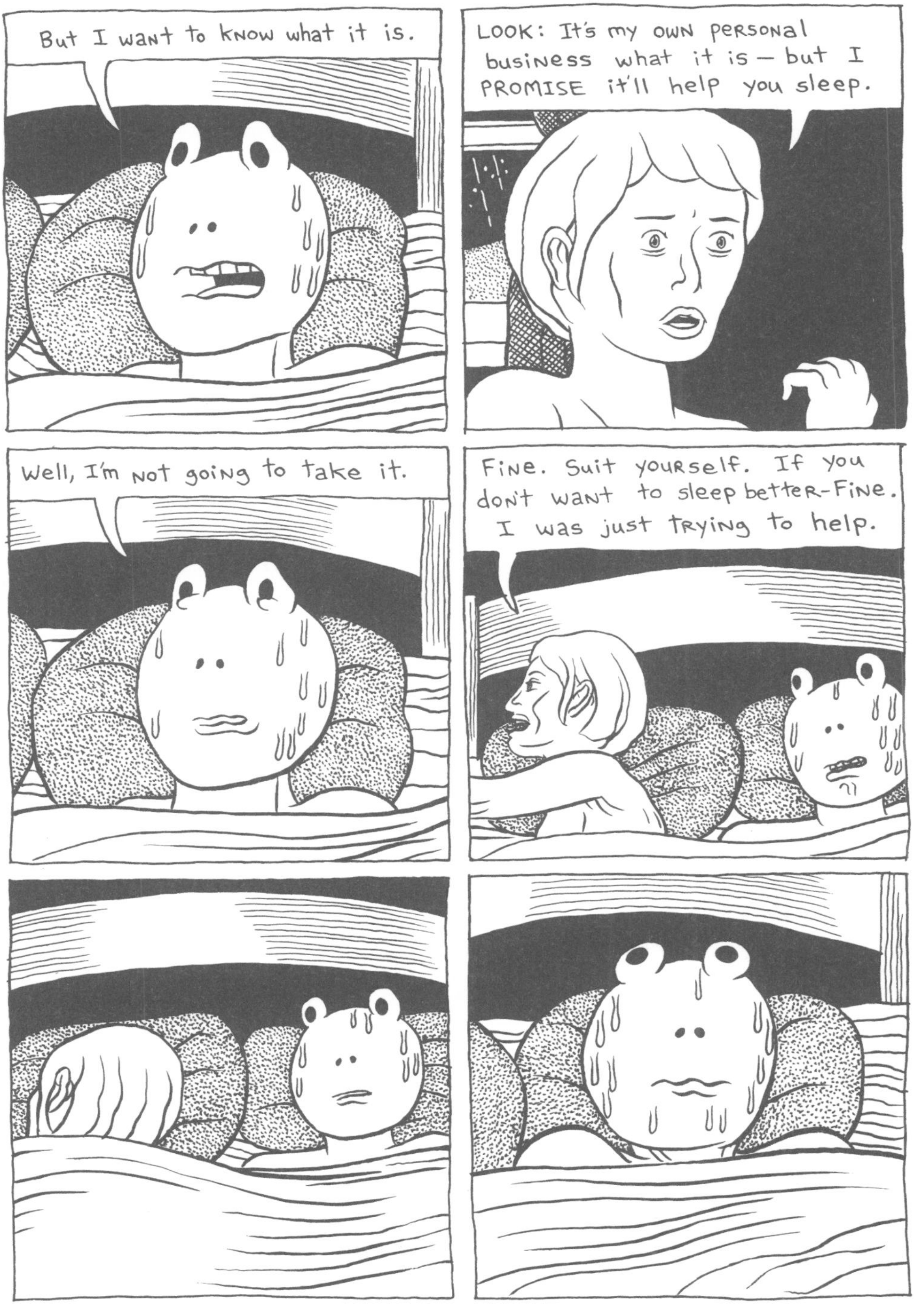
But I want to know what it is.
LOOK: It's my own personal business what it is — but I PROMISE it'll help you sleep.
Well, I'm not going to take it.
Fine. Suit yourself. If you don't want to sleep better-Fine. I was just trying to help.

Sigh.

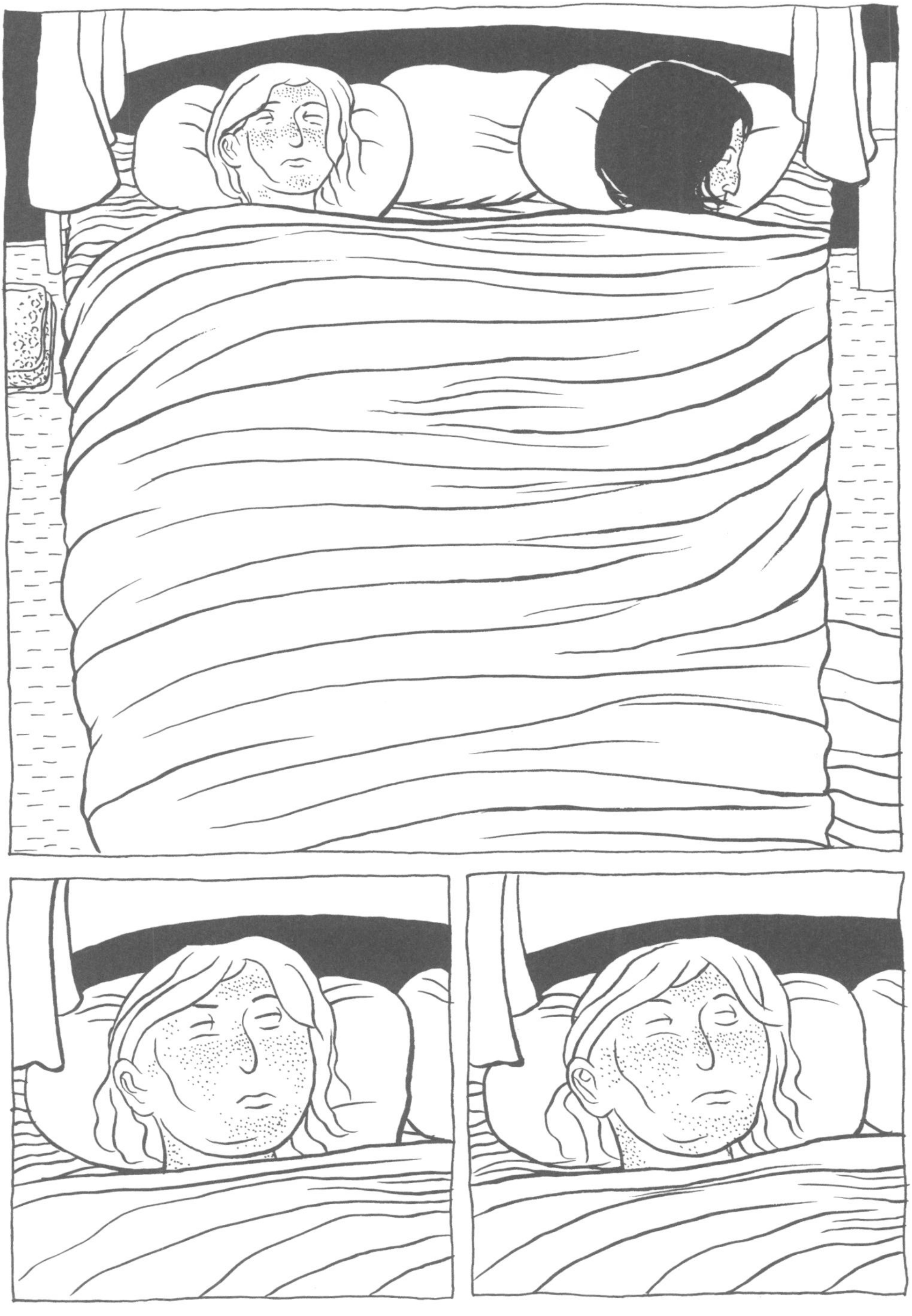

KNOCK
KNOCK
KNOCK
KNOCK
← OPEN —
Hello?

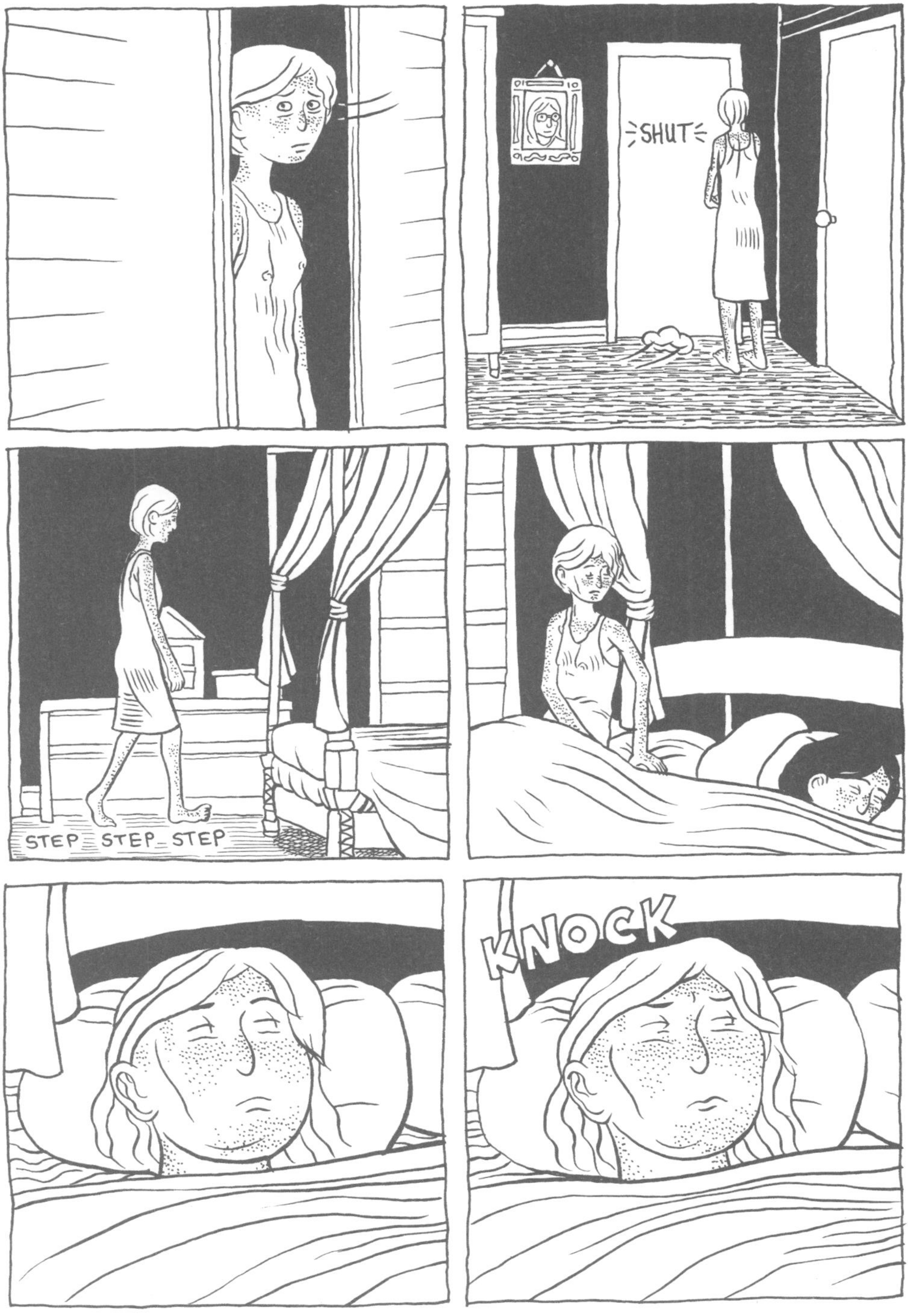
SHUT
STEP STEP STEP
KNOCK

KNOCK
KNOCK
KNOCK
C-Carl?
DRIP
DRIP
IT'S SNOWING OUTSIDE.
-DRIP
BRUSH
BRUSH

SHAKE
DRIP
DRIP
HANG
DRIP
DRIP
DRIP
DRIP
I CAN'T DO THIS. I CAN'T DO THIS.
HAVING A BABY, BEING MARRIED... IT REQUIRES A STABILITY, A FINANCIAL SECURITY I'M NEVER GOING TO HAVE, CLAIRE.

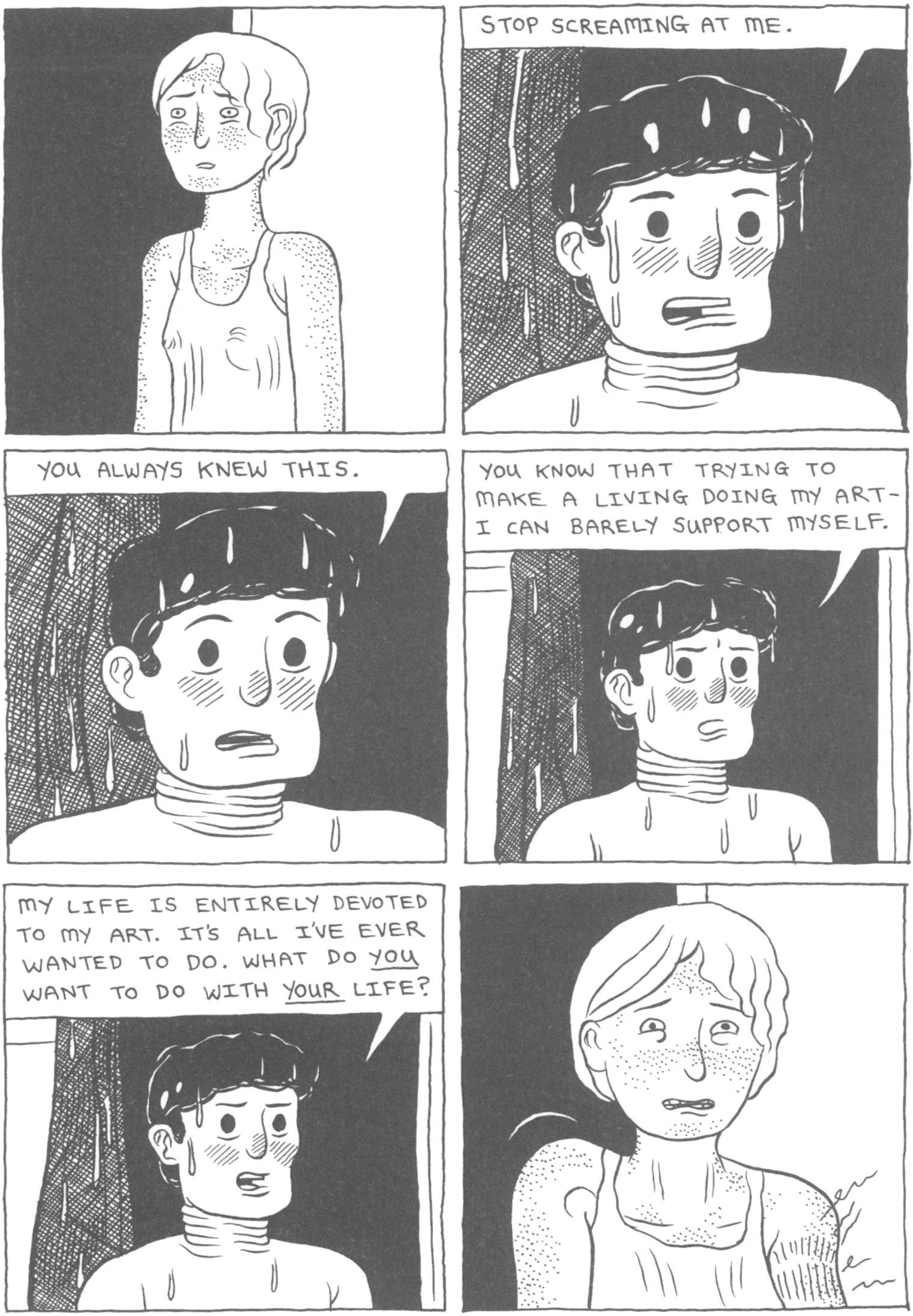
STOP SCREAMING AT ME.
YOU ALWAYS KNEW THIS.
YOU KNOW THAT TRYING TO MAKE A LIVING DOING MY ART- I CAN BARELY SUPPORT MYSELF.
MY LIFE IS ENTIRELY DEVOTED TO MY ART. IT'S ALL I'VE EVER WANTED TO DO. WHAT DO YOU WANT TO DO WITH YOUR LIFE?

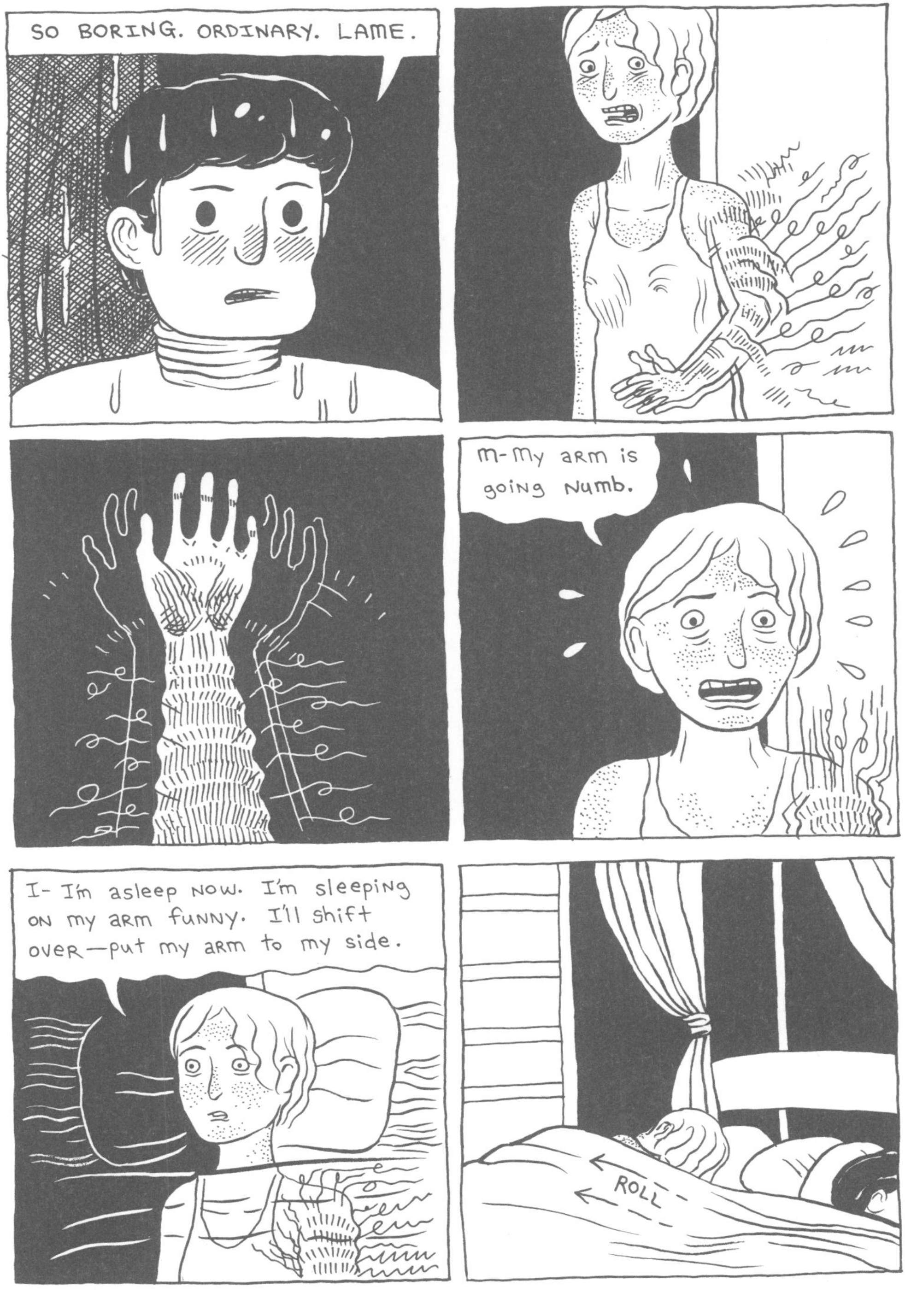
SO BORING. ORDINARY. LAME.
M-My arm is going Numb.
I- I'm asleep Now. I'm sleeping on my arm funny. I'll shift over—put my arm to my side.
ROLL

I HAVE TO GO. LATER: I HAVE TO GET OFF THE PHONE NOW.
I HAVE A GALLERY OPENING ON AN ISLAND. THERE ARE OTHER HOT BITCHES WHO WANT TO MARRY ME.
YOU THINK MY ART IS IMPORTANT AND SUBLIME, RIGHT? RIGHT?
TELL LIL' JILL I LOVE HER. THIS MAKES YOU SO MAD THAT I WOULD SAY THAT.
AND
WHEN I LEAVE YOUR APARTMENT I FORGET TO TAKE MY COAT.

OBVIOUSLY, IT'S SNOWING AND FREEZING OUTSIDE.
BUT I DON'T GO BACK, KNOCK ON YOUR DOOR, SEE YOU, TO RETRIEVE MY DRIP DRIP COAT.
SHUT

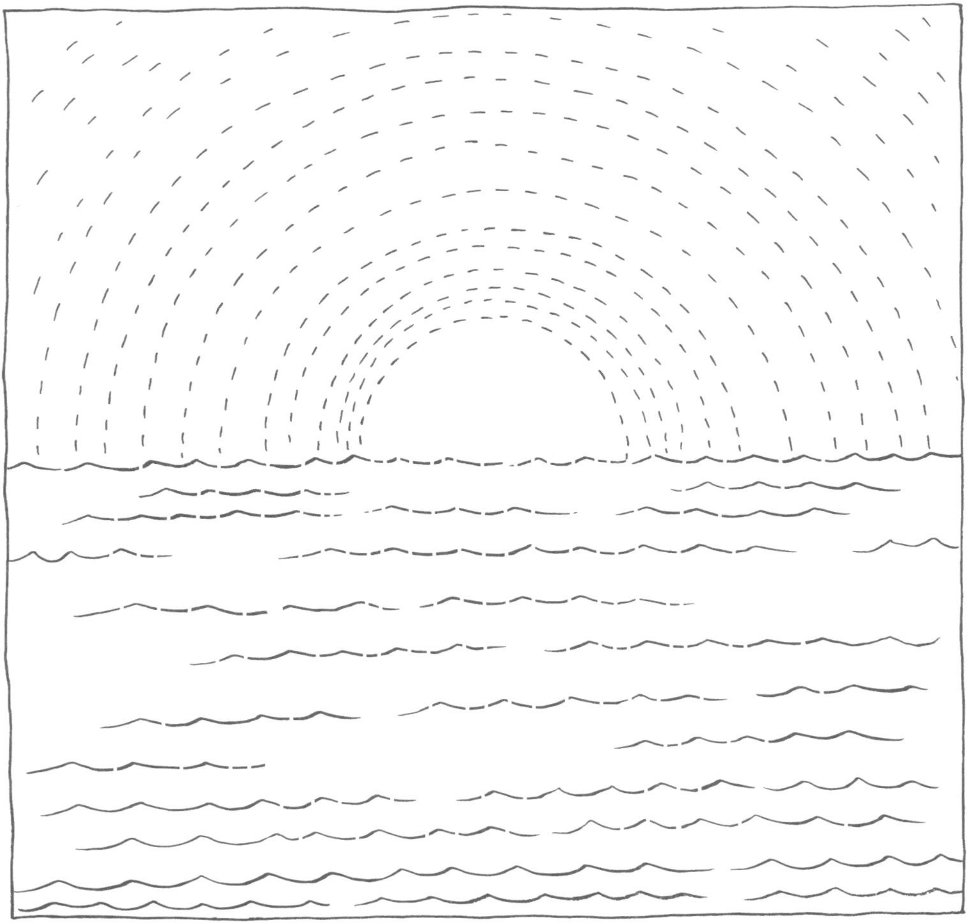

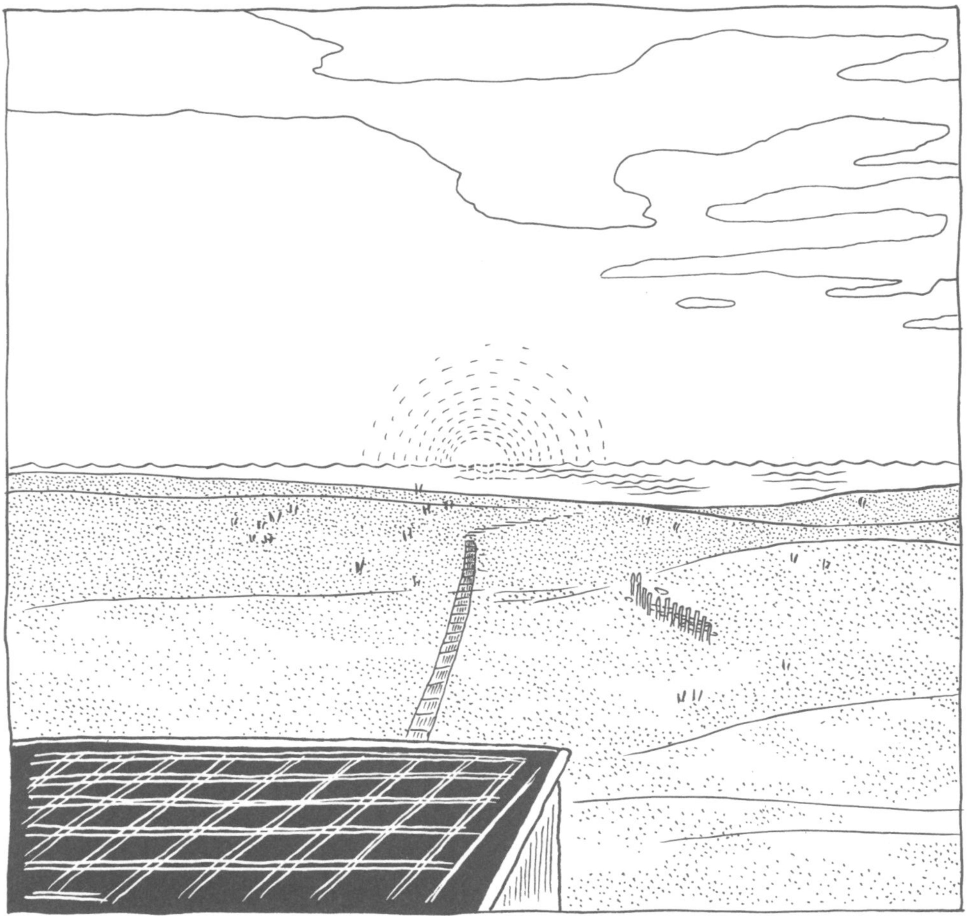

shhhhhhhhhh

shhhhhhhhhhh
ha.
SQUEEZE
FART NOISE

TURN
SQUINT
STEAM
STEAM
STEAM
STEAM
STEAM
STEAM
foggy
STEAM
STEAM
STEAM
NO TOWELS
STEAM
STEAM
STEAM
STEAM
STEAM
STEAM
STEAM
drip
drip

DRIP
DRIP
DRIP
DRIP
DRIP
Mom! Where are towels?!
DRIP
DRIP
Nn-
Hallway closet.
DRIP
DRIP

TURN

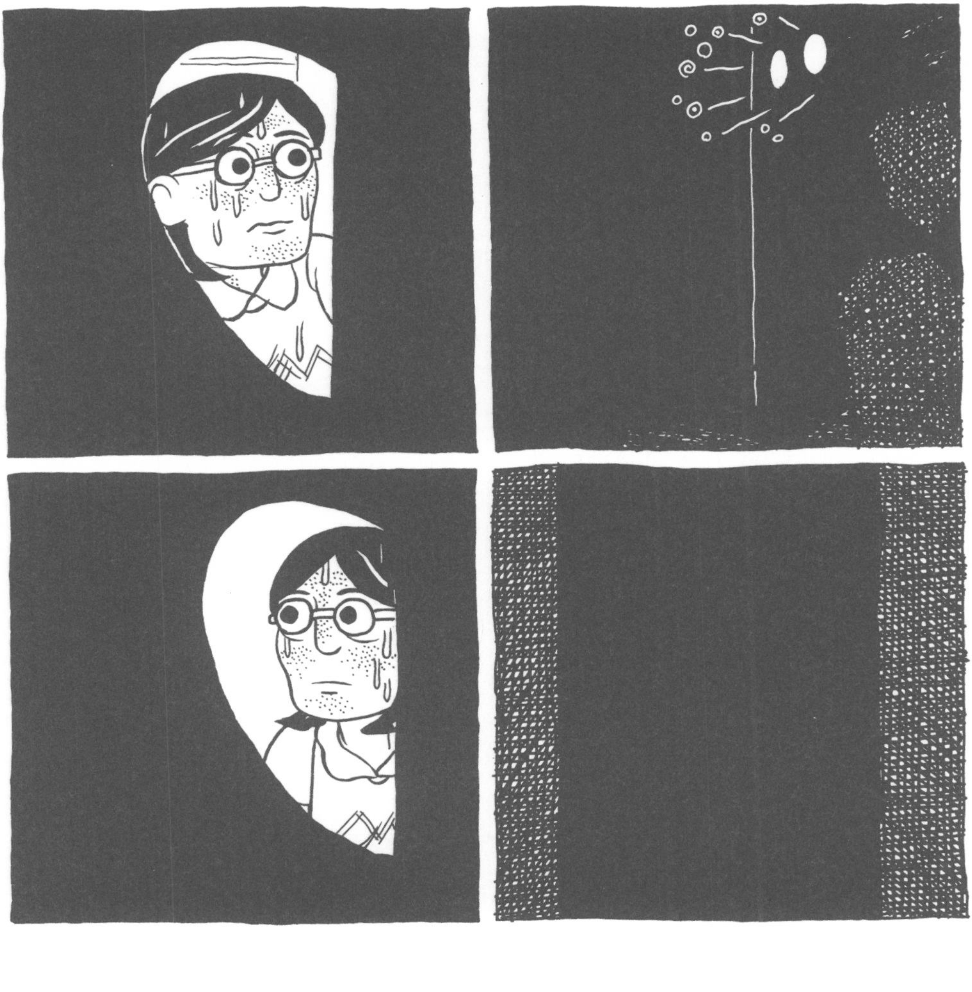

WEIRD.
SHUT
SHUT

STEP
STEP

OPEN

DATE BOOK
DUST
DUST
19
20
21
22
26
27
28
29
DUST

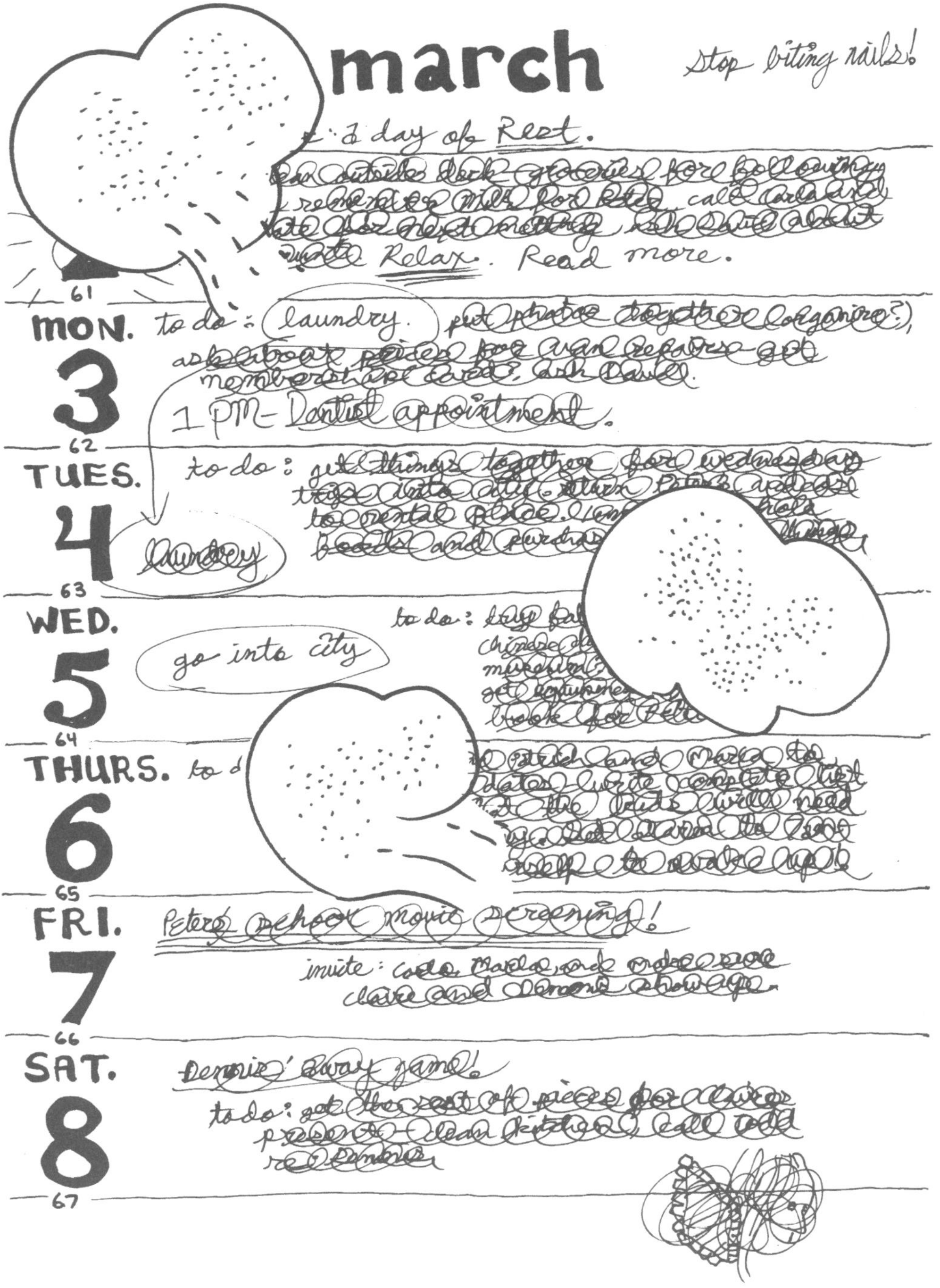
march
Stop biting nails!
A day of Rest.
Relax. Read more.
61
MON.
3
to do:
laundry.
1 PM - Dentist appointment.
62
TUES.
4
to do:
63
WED.
5
to do:
go into city
64
THURS.
6
65
FRI.
7
invite:
66
SAT.
8
todo:
67

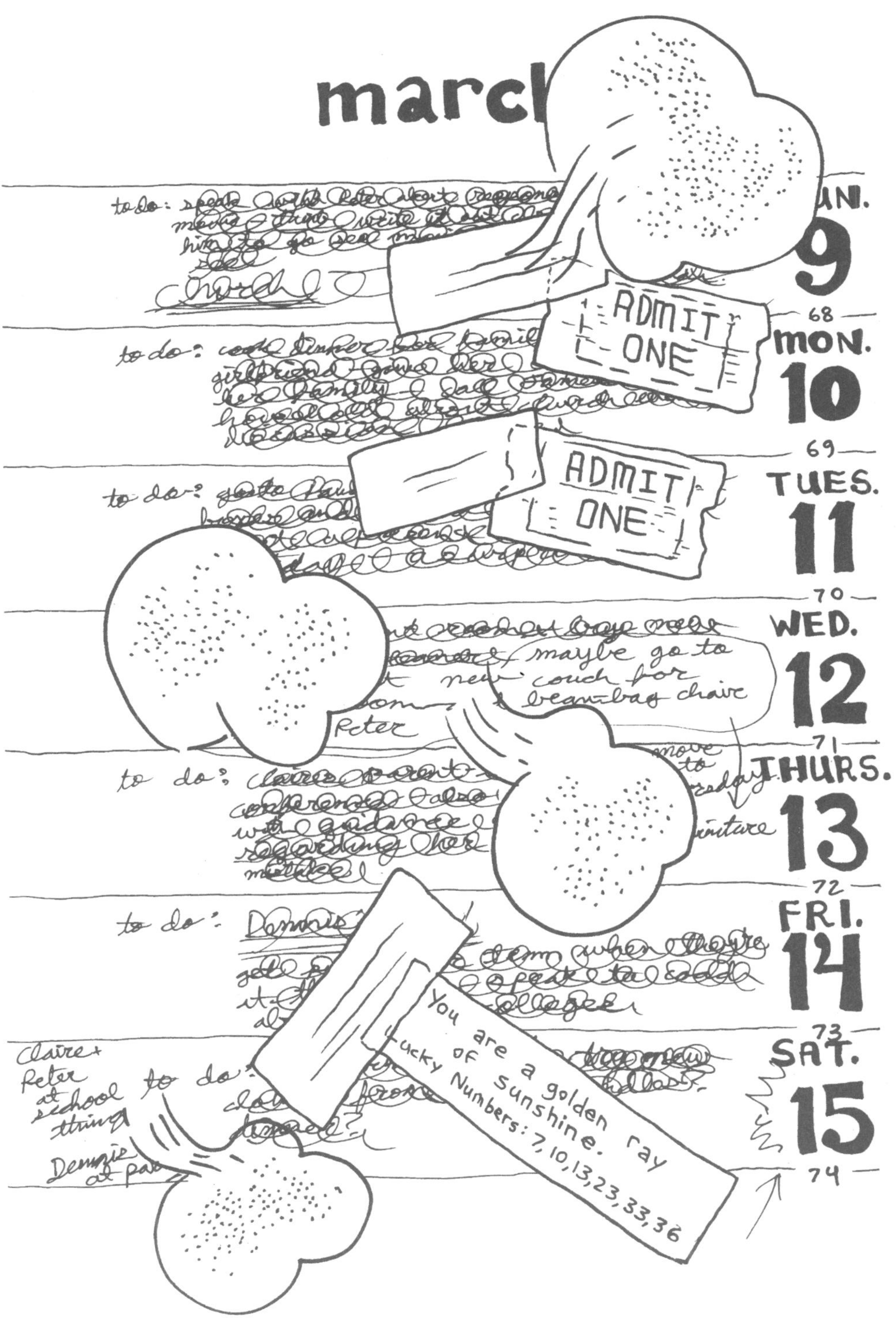
march
UN.
9
68
MON.
10
69
TUES.
11
70
WED.
12
71
THURS.
13
72
FRI.
14
73
SAT.
15
74
ADMIT ONE
ADMIT ONE
to do:
to do:
to do:
maybe go to
new couch for
bean-bag chair
Peter
to do:
to do:
Claire + Peter at school thing
to do:
Dennis at pa
You are a golden ray of sunshine.
Lucky Numbers: 7,10,13,23,33,36

march
SUN.
16
to do:
75
MON.
17
to do:
76
TUES.
18
to do:
maybe a mystery?
at library:
77
WED.
19
to do:
physical therapist for David? back? neck?
78
THURS.
20
79
FRI.
21
80
SAT.
22
81
VISIT
KNOTTING
POINT

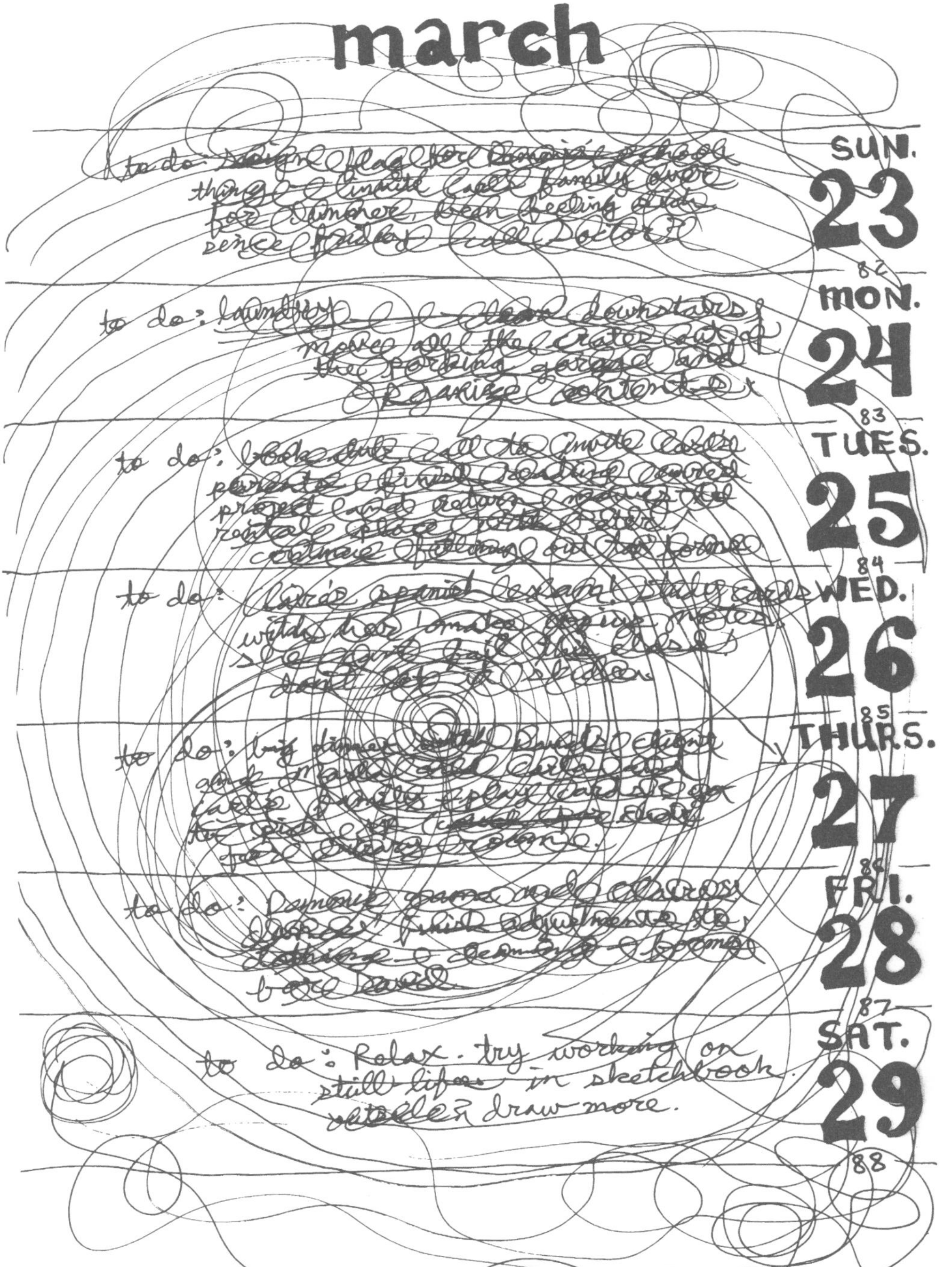
march
SUN.
23
82
to do: laundry
MON.
24
83
TUES.
25
84
WED.
26
85
THURS.
27
86
FRI.
28
87
to do: Relax. try working on still lifes in sketchbook
draw more.
SAT.
29
88

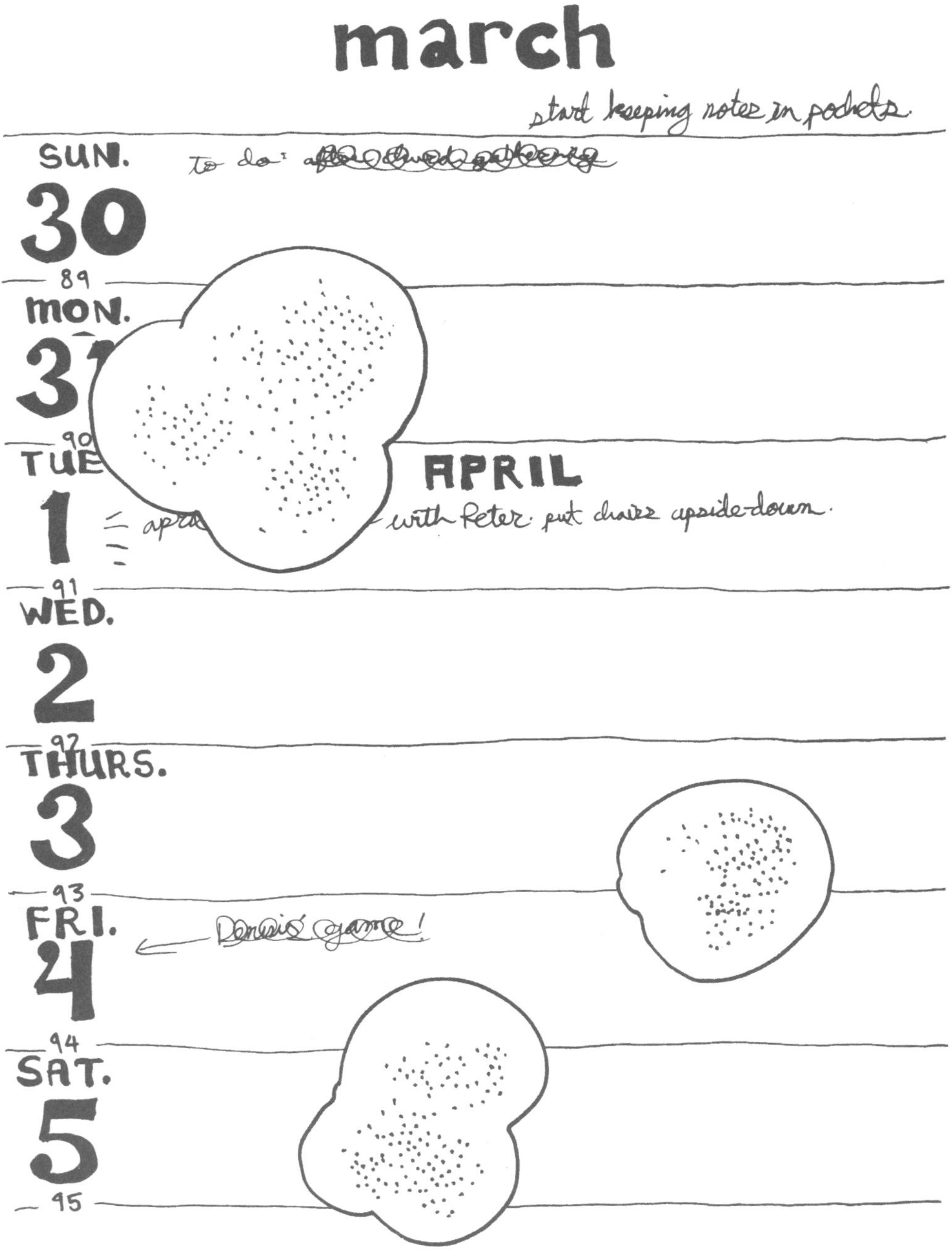
march
start keeping notes in pockets.
SUN.
to do:
30
89
MON.
31
90
TUE
APRIL
1
with Peter. put chairs upside-down.
91
WED.
2
92
THURS.
3
93
FRI.
Dennis' game!
4
94
SAT.
5
95

SHUT
DUST
DUST
DUST
cof
cof

cof
cof
cof
LIFT
LIFT

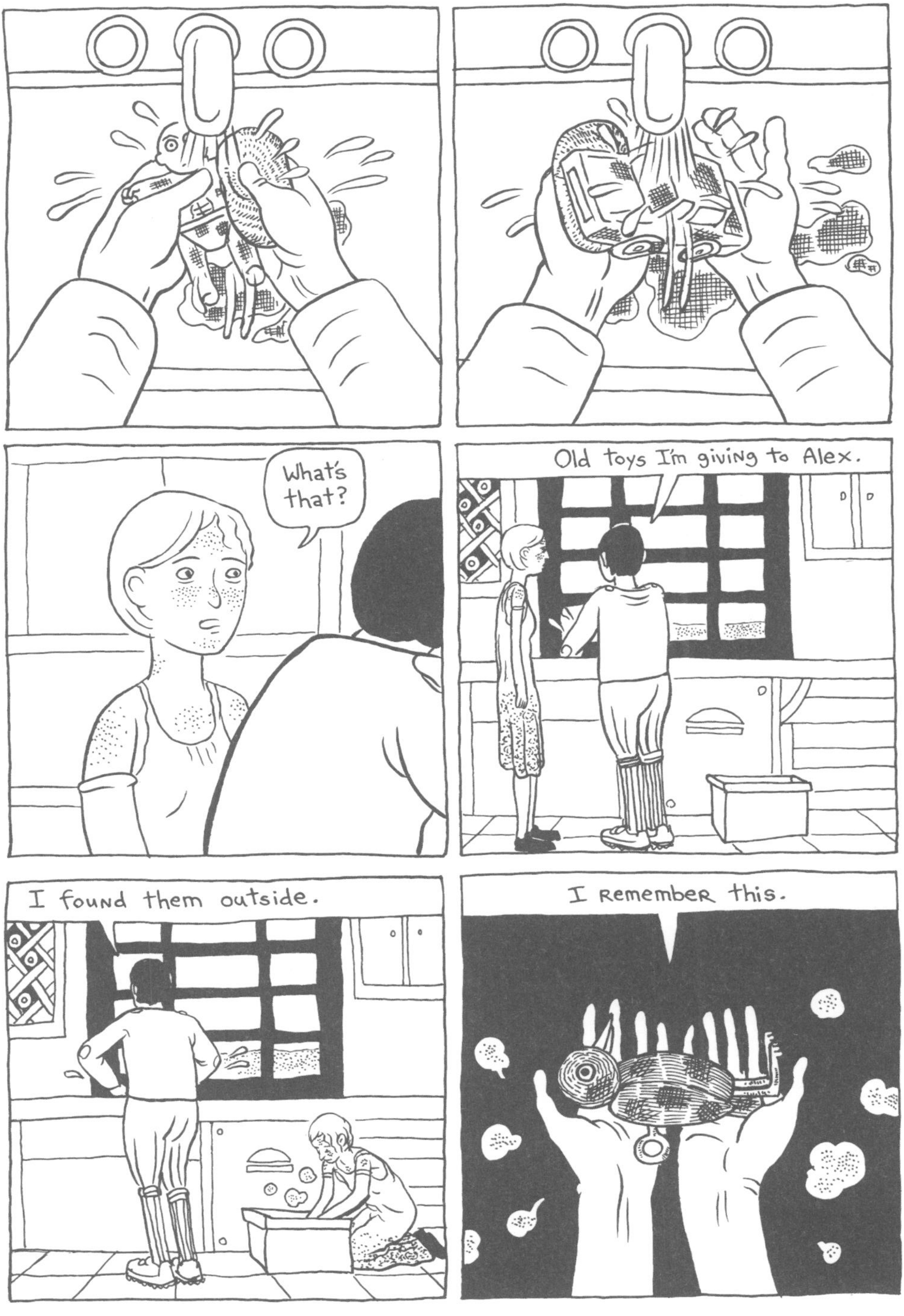

What's that?
Old toys I'm giving to Alex.
I found them outside.
I remember this.

BLINK
BLINK
YAWN
gasp
gasp
gasp
BARF

BLINK

Good Morning! 3p.m. breakfast food is on it's way. Eggs.
Three P.M.? Really? SORRY.
No. Ha. I just didn't know if I should have woken you up. If you had any appointments.
Nope. Just chillin' NON-stop.
Ha.

Family Parade
Fa
"Can I invite the delivery man to the pizza party?"
Ha
How long are you staying at your parent's place?
A few more days.
My parents are getting divorced. That's why I'm here.
Huh. How old are they?
Like seventy or something. They've been married over forty years and now they're splitting.
That's hard core.
yeah.

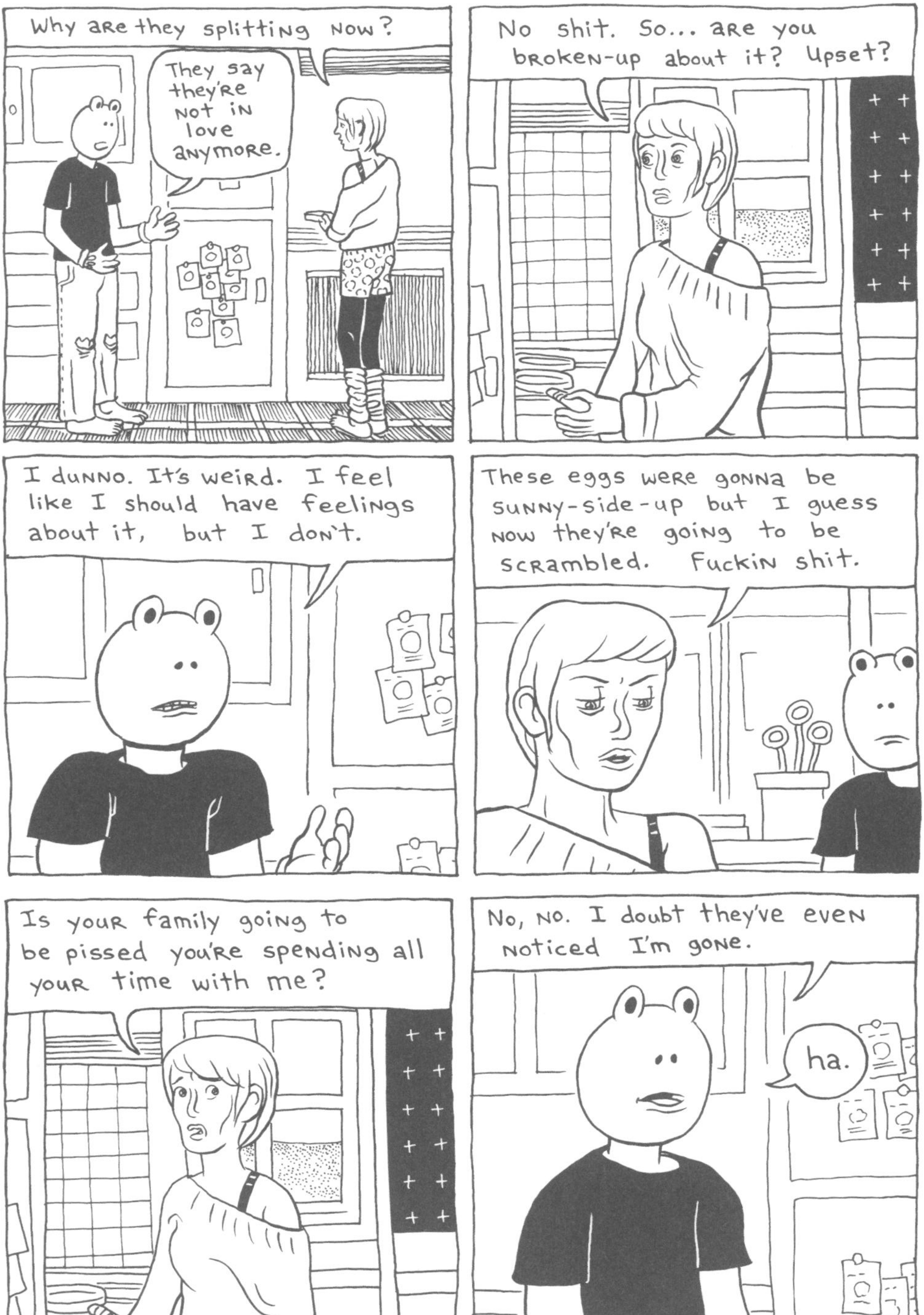
Why are they splitting now?
They say they're not in love anymore.
No shit. So... are you broken-up about it? Upset?
I dunno. It's weird. I feel like I should have feelings about it, but I don't.
These eggs were gonna be sunny-side-up but I guess now they're going to be scrambled. Fuckin shit.
Is your family going to be pissed you're spending all your time with me?
No, no. I doubt they've even noticed I'm gone.
ha.

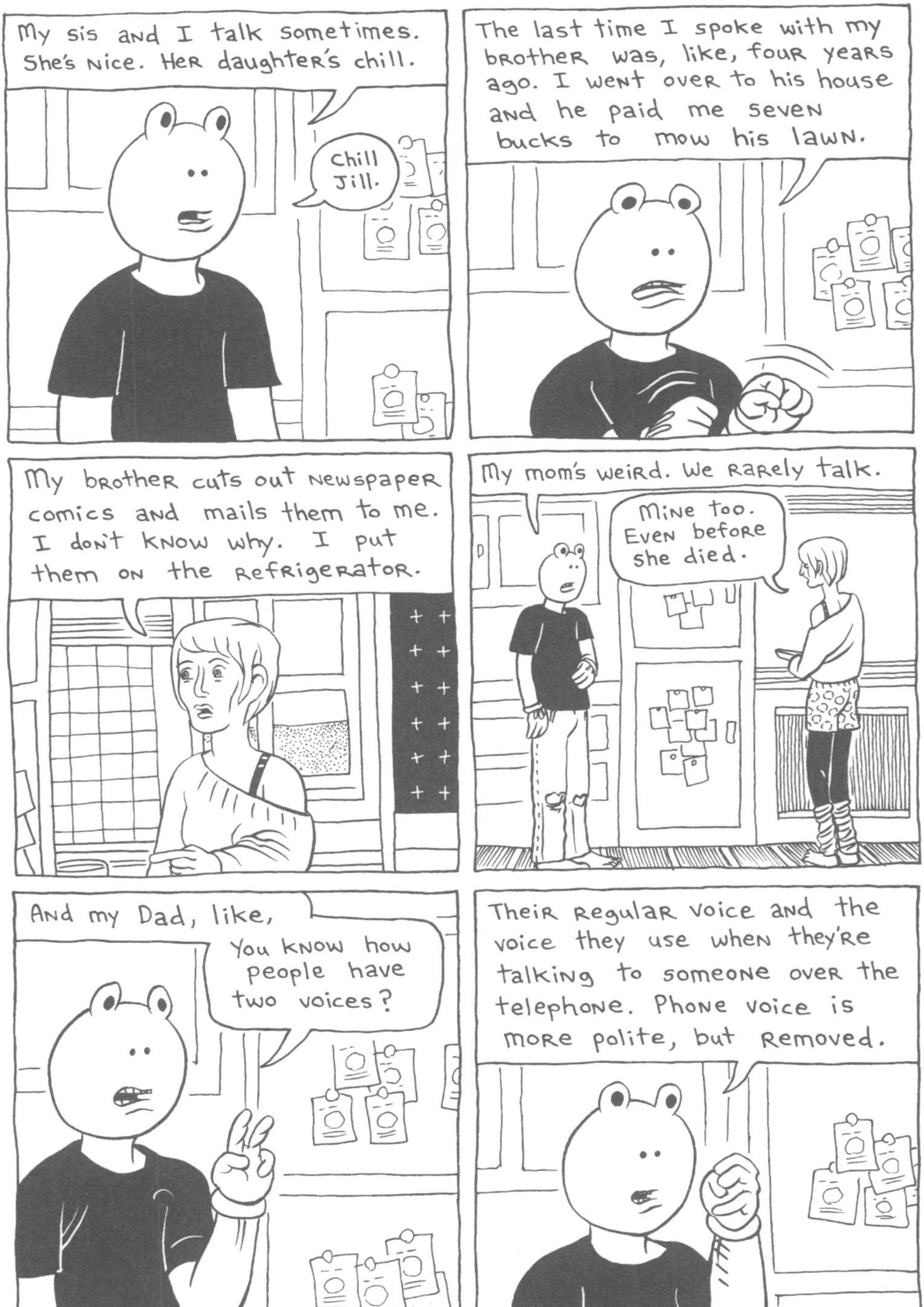
My sis and I talk sometimes. She's nice. Her daughter's chill.
Chill Jill.
The last time I spoke with my brother was, like, four years ago. I went over to his house and he paid me seven bucks to mow his lawn.
My brother cuts out newspaper comics and mails them to me. I don't know why. I put them on the refrigerator.
My mom's weird. We rarely talk.
Mine too. Even before she died.
And my Dad, like,
You know how people have two voices?
Their regular voice and the voice they use when they're talking to someone over the telephone. Phone voice is more polite, but removed.

Whenever my dad talks to me, it's like I'm a telemarketer. Only me. I noticed this when I was in middle school.
I'm the youngest child cliché. I don't belong. My whole family looks at me like I'm a dumb, weird frog.
Do I look like a frog to you? Sometimes I think I look like a frog.
I don't think so.
These eggs aren't scrambled. I don't know what's going on with these eggs, to be honest.

God, these eggs are terrible. I can't cook for shit. I'm sorry.
I like the orange juice.
Good juice.
Ha. You're funny.
I'm glad I met you, Peter. I'm so sorry about last night, I was–
Don't be sorry. It's my fault.
I'm glad I met you too.

PANT
PANT
PANT
PANT
PANT
PANT
PANT
PANT

CUT-AWAY VIEW:

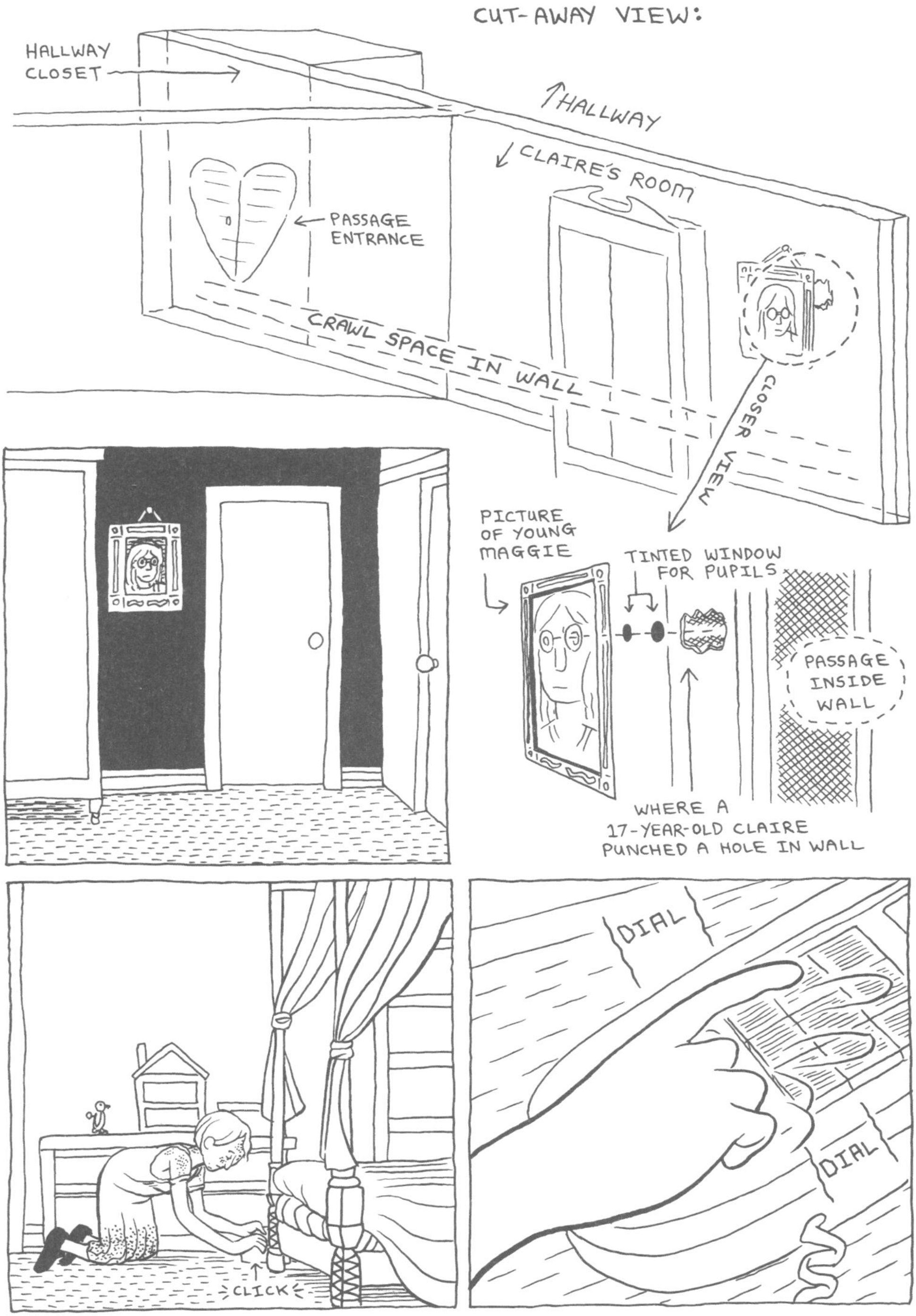
CUT-AWAY VIEW:
HALLWAY CLOSET
HALLWAY
CLAIRE'S ROOM
PASSAGE ENTRANCE
CRAWL SPACE IN WALL
CLOSER VIEW
PICTURE OF YOUNG MAGGIE
TINTED WINDOW FOR PUPILS
PASSAGE INSIDE WALL
WHERE A 17-YEAR-OLD CLAIRE PUNCHED A HOLE IN WALL
CLICK
DIAL
DIAL

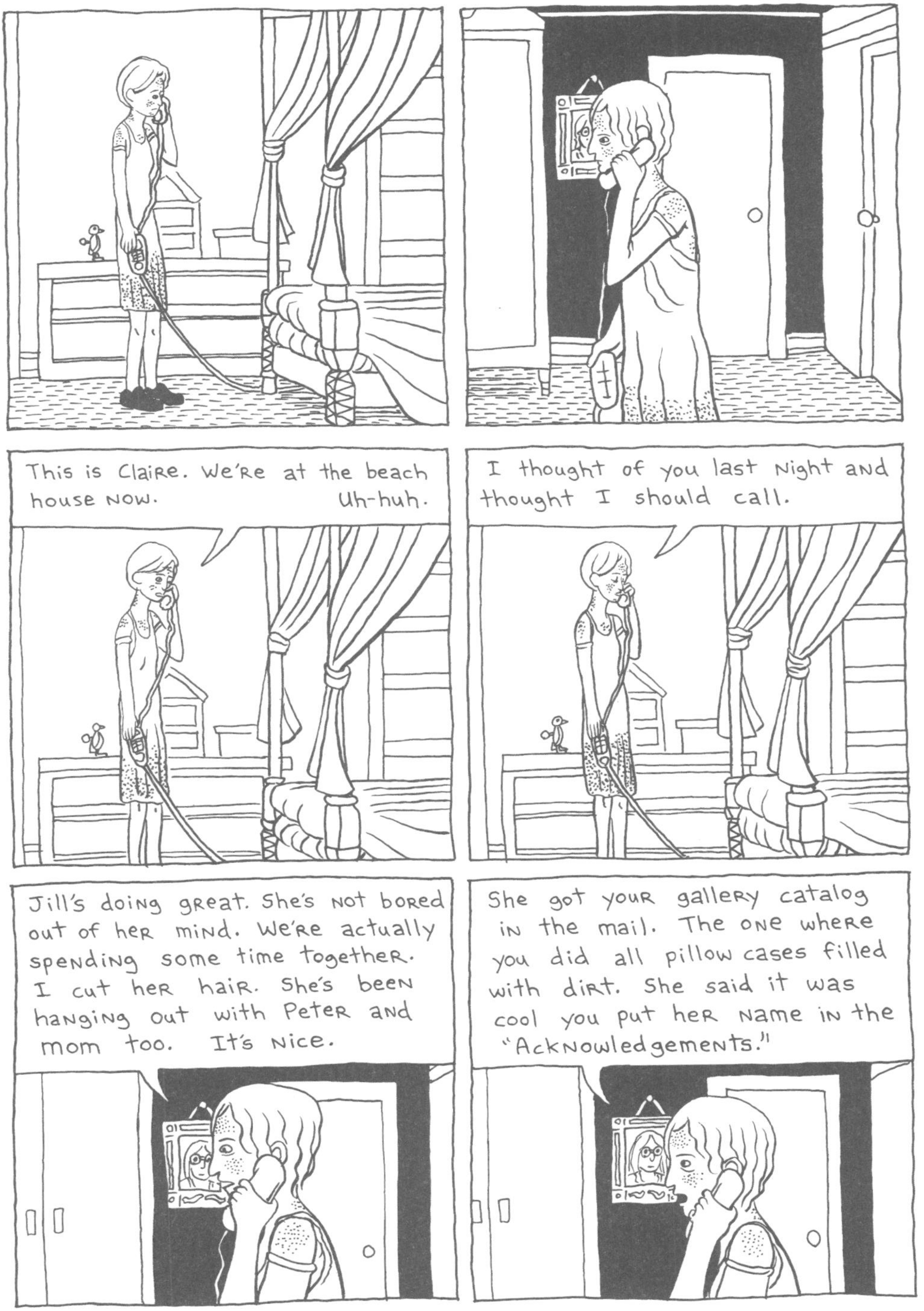

This is Claire. We're at the beach house now. Uh-huh.
I thought of you last night and thought I should call.
Jill's doing great. She's not bored out of her mind. We're actually spending some time together. I cut her hair. She's been hanging out with Peter and mom too. It's nice.
She got your gallery catalog in the mail. The one where you did all pillow cases filled with dirt. She said it was cool you put her name in the "Acknowledgements."

I'll tell her you said that. She's downstairs now.
How's it going with you?
Oh, that sounds great. Good for you.
Yeah, I understand. Well,

Okay. Bye.
CLICK
BREATHES OUT.

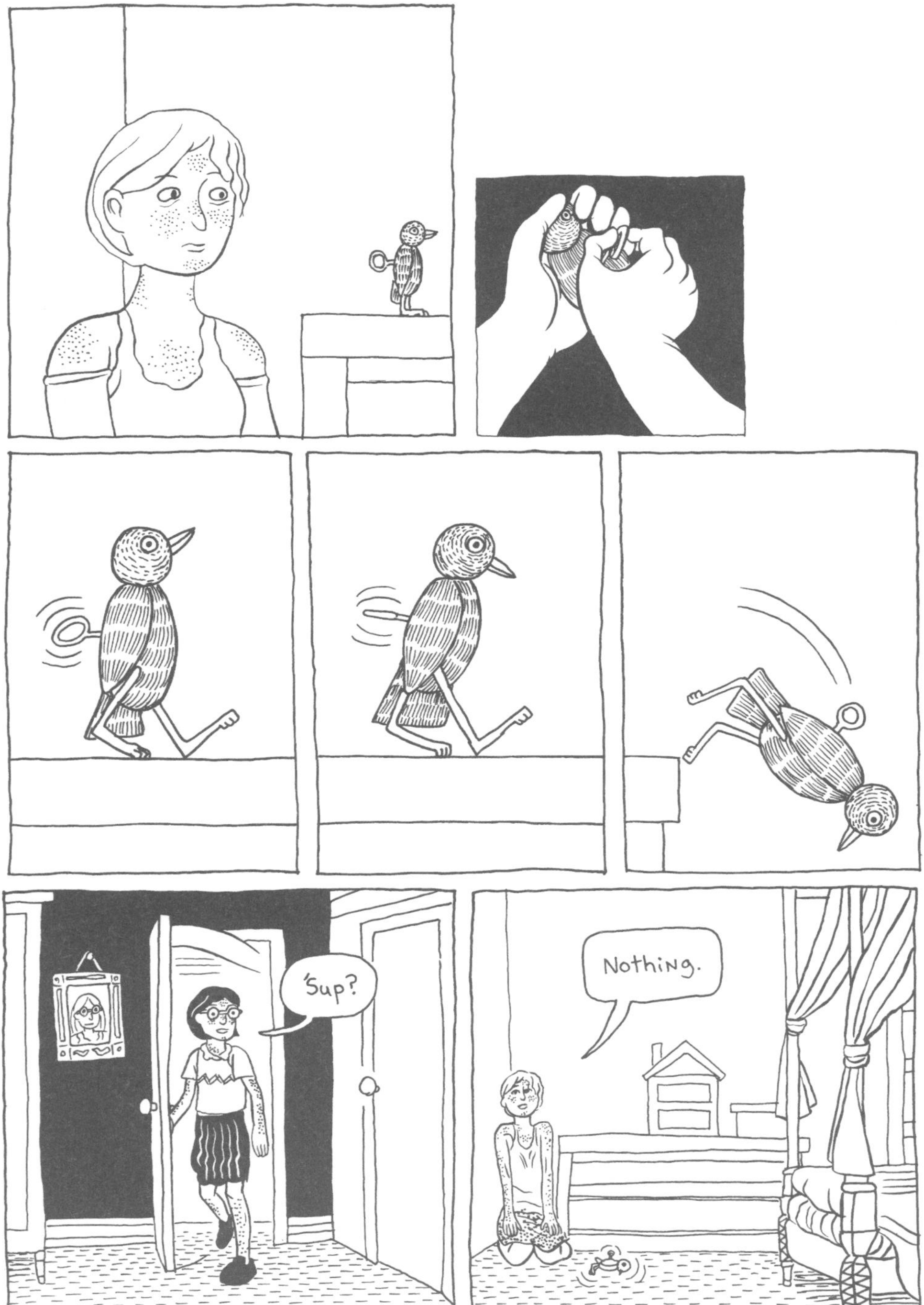
'Sup?
Nothing.

You look like you've seen a ghost. DID you see a ghost?!
Just thought I'd ask cuz this place is haunted as SHIT. I swear, if you stare at the wallpaper long enough you'll-
Where are you going?
Bathroom.
Ha.

hmm.
KNOCK
KNOCK
Someone in there?
OPEN
All yours.
SHUT

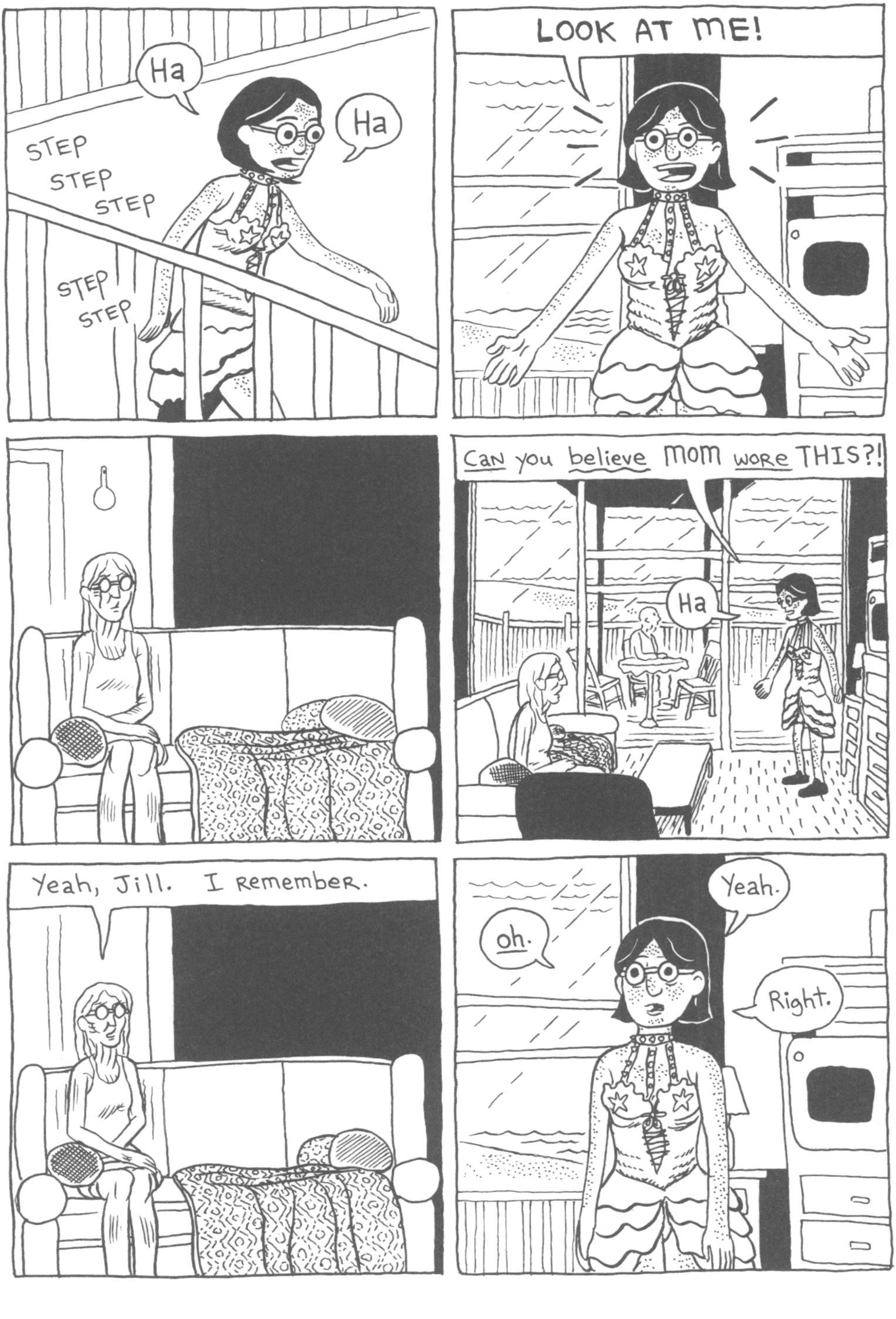
Ha
Ha
STEP
STEP
STEP
STEP
STEP
LOOK AT ME!
Can you believe mom wore THIS?!
Ha
Yeah, Jill. I remember.
oh.
Yeah.
Right.

I got some old toys for Alex.
SPORTS CARDS
CARDS
Did you know there was BLOOD on your pillow?
um.
YES
No.
I'm gonna change the sheets.
I'm sleeping down-stairs with Dad tonight, O.K.?
K.
KISS
Cold nose.

Goodnight.
Goodnight.
Hey Dad.
You, uh, have a good day? I didn't see you.
SHRUG
Yeah.
same here.
WRAP
WRAP
Goodnight.

PULL
PULL
SCOOT
PULL
SCOOT

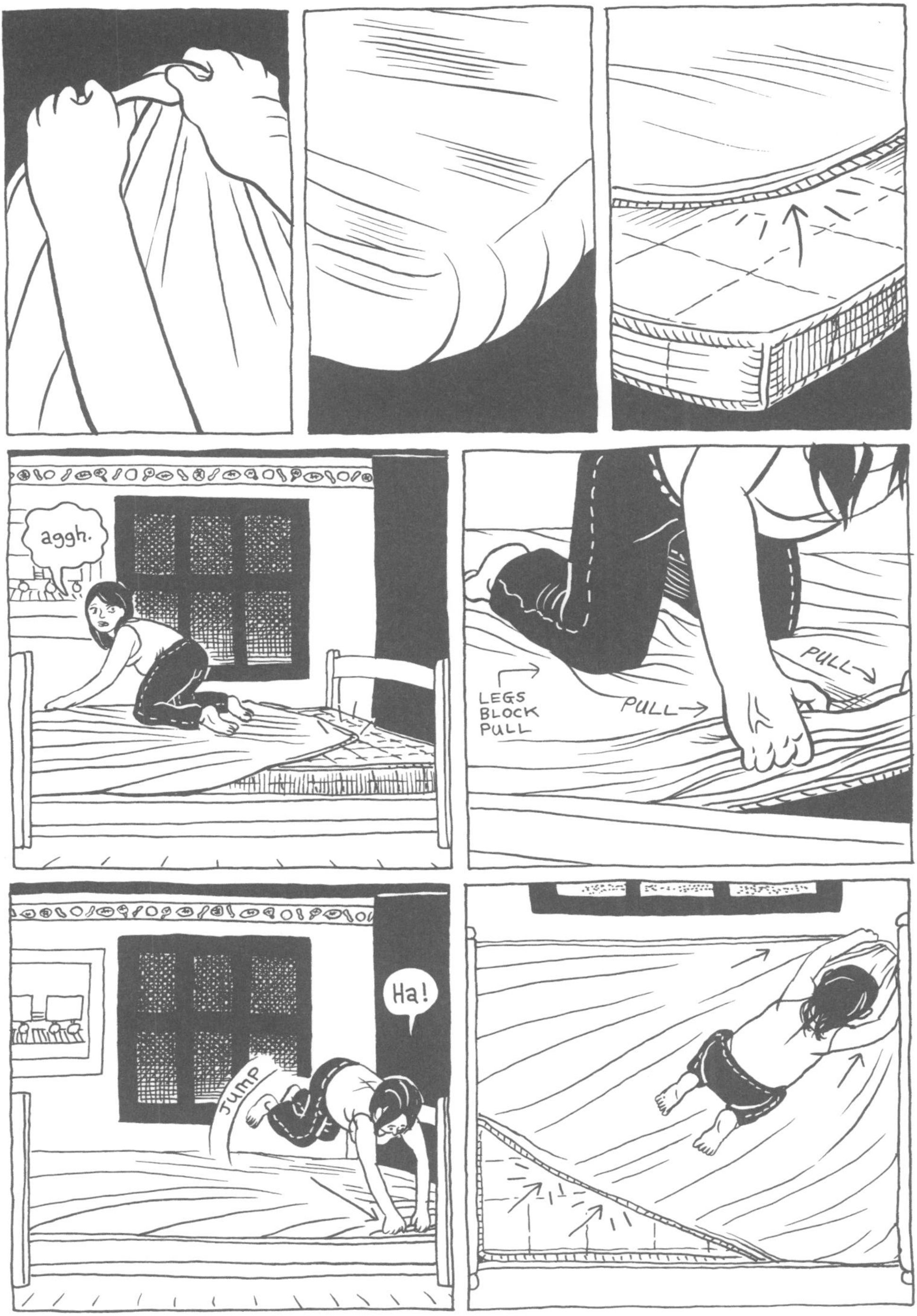
aggh.
LEGS
BLOCK
PULL
PULL
PULL
JUMP
Ha!

Fucking shit!
FUCK!
JUMP
WAAAAAAAAAAAA
AAAAAAAAAAAAAA
SHAKEY
PULL
SHAKEY
AAAAAAAAAAAAA
Aggh.
AAAAAAAAAAAAAA
Shhh!
ALEX!

AAAAAAAAAAAA
aggh...
PULL
AAAAAAAAAAAAAAA
FUCK!
THROW
AAAAAAAAAAAAAAA
ALEX!
SHUSH!
AAAAAAAAAAAAAAAAAA
ALEX!
AAAAAAAAAA
AAAAAAAAAA
AAAAAAAAAA

Ha.

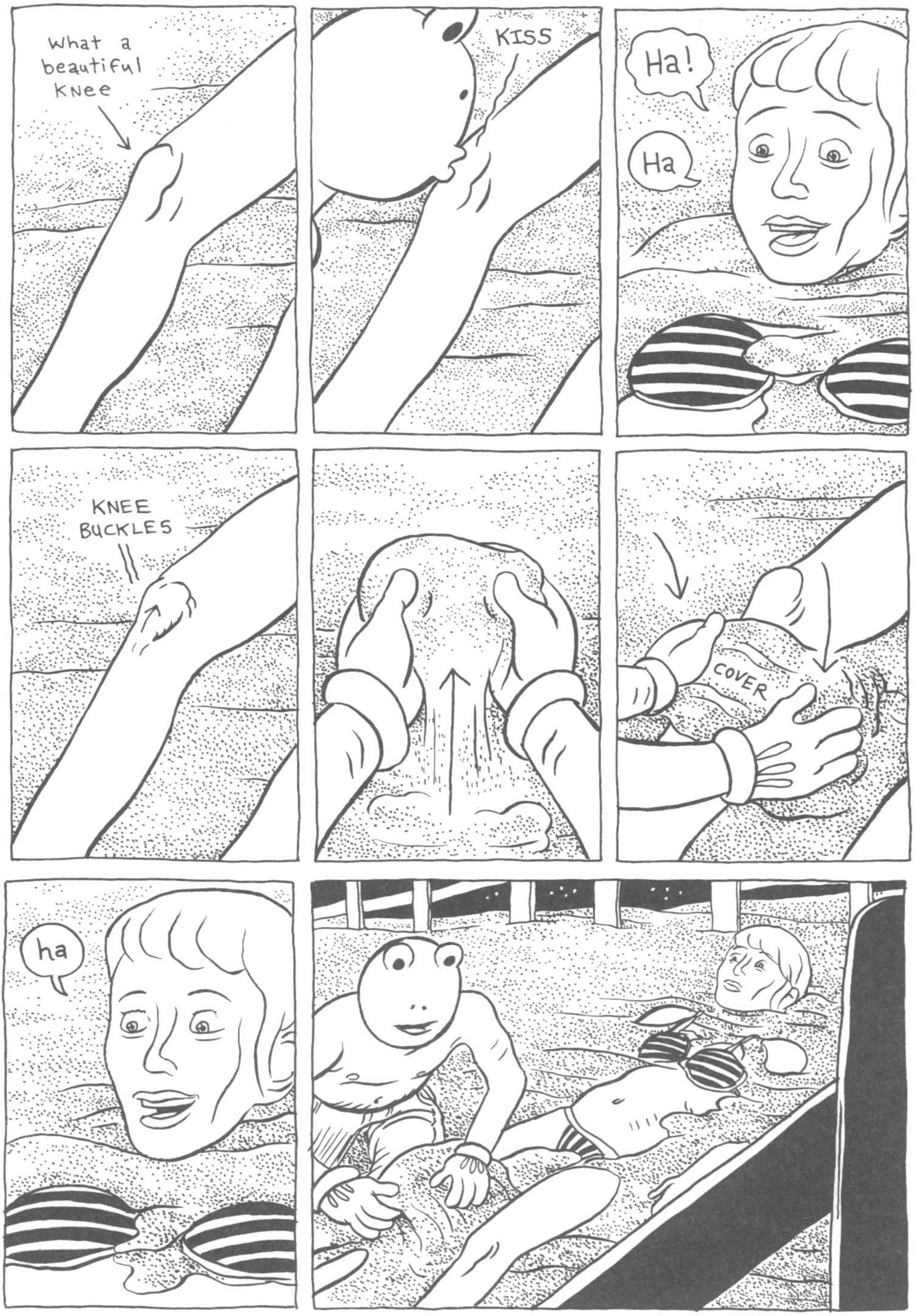
What a beautiful knee
KISS
Ha!
Ha
KNEE BUCKLES
COVER
ha

Ha!
Stomach moves up and down when she laughs
Ha
SMOOTH OVER
I think that I'm falling in love with you.
I would like it if we had both said that simultaneously.
heh.
That'd be ideal.

But I'll settle for you saying something similar in the next minute or so.
Maybe that's a lot to ask.
Ha. You're a sweetie, Peter. How could anyone NOT love you?
A storm's coming.

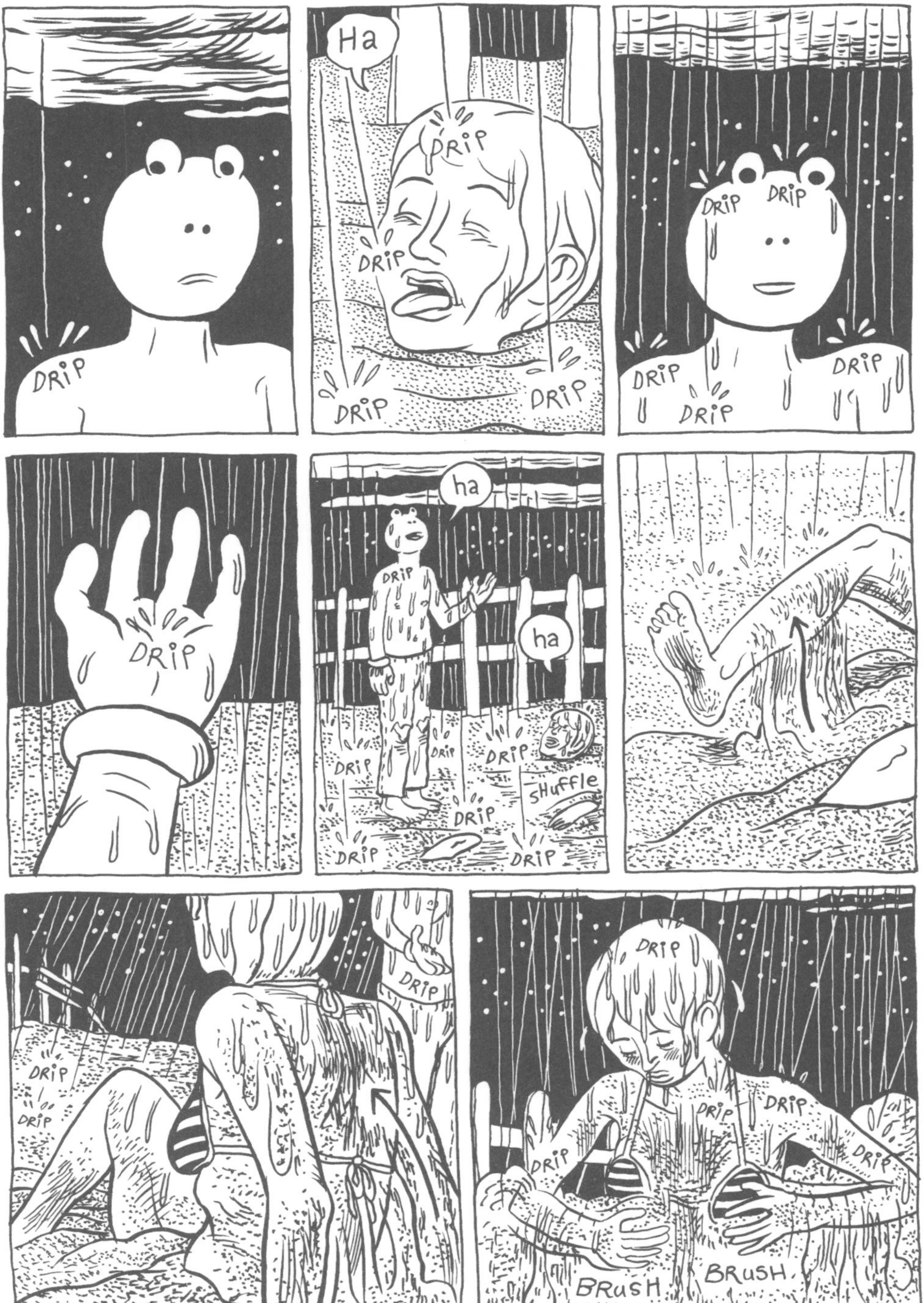
DRIP
Ha
DRIP
DRIP
DRIP
DRIP
DRIP
DRIP
DRIP
DRIP
DRIP
DRIP
DRIP
ha
DRIP
ha
DRIP
DRIP
DRIP
shuffle
DRIP
DRIP
DRIP
DRIP
DRIP
DRIP
DRIP
DRIP
DRIP
DRIP
DRIP
BRUSH
BRUSH

KRAKOW
LET'S GO SWIMMING!
KRAKOOM
WAIT! I HAVE A BETTER IDEA! LET'S GO TO MY HOUSE!
OKAY!
Ha
SLOSH
SLOSH
SLOSH

Ha
Ha
This reminds me of that scene in that movie, you know?
Did you ever see that movie?
No.
KRAKOOM
meow
DRIP
DRIP
DRIP
SHAKE
SHAKE

Sit.
KRA-KOOM
You like to sit on the floor? Ha. Sit HERE.
How'd you get holes in your knees?
I dunno. I crawl around a lot, I guess.
UNZIP
Wha- What are you doing? Kat?
KRAKOW
Ha
PULL

KRAKOW
SUCK
SUCK
SUCK SUCK
BREATHES OUT.
You don't-
GRIP
What should
I
WHAT TO DO?
KRAKOOM

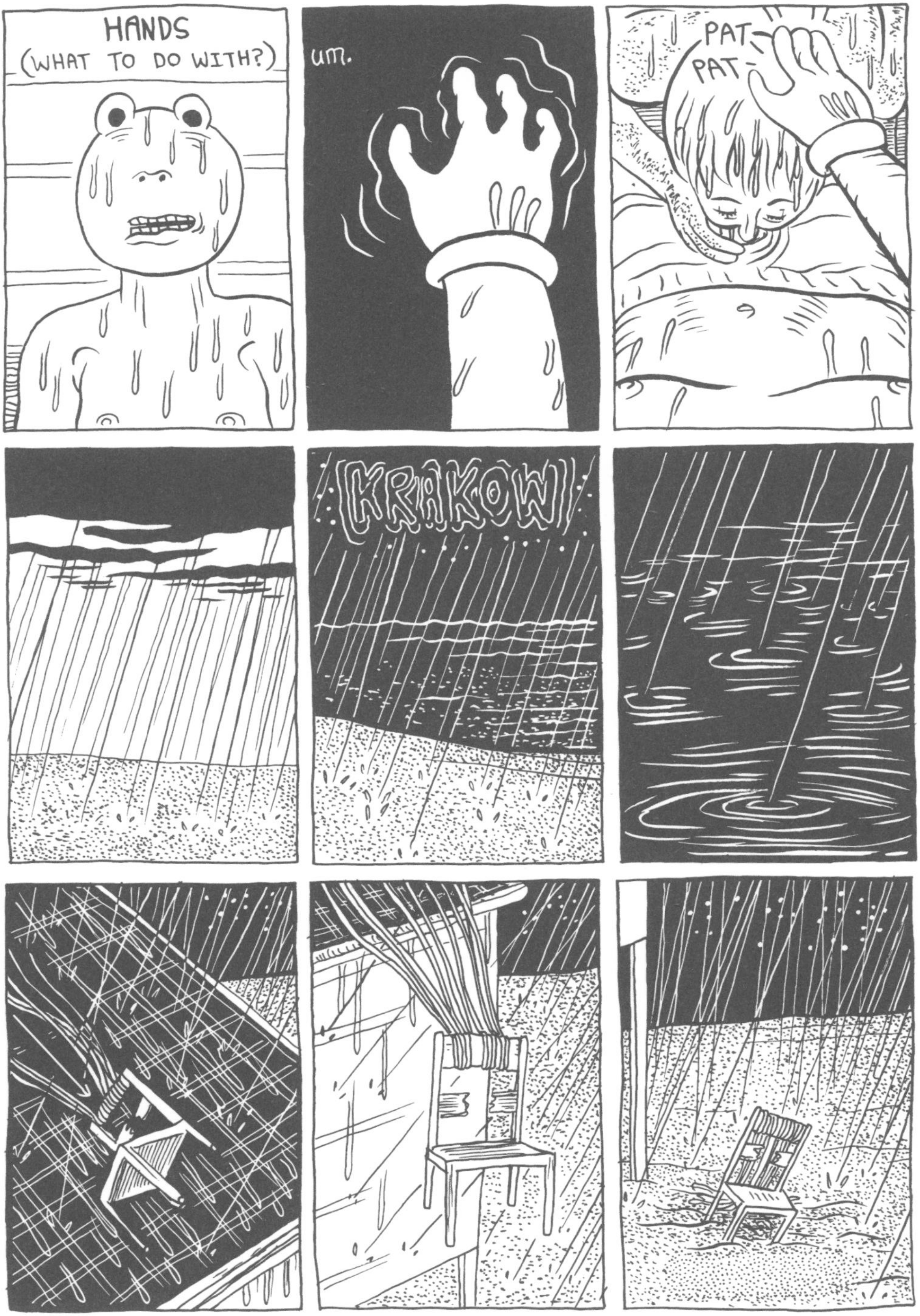
HANDS
(WHAT TO DO WITH?)
um.
PAT-
PAT-
KRAKOW

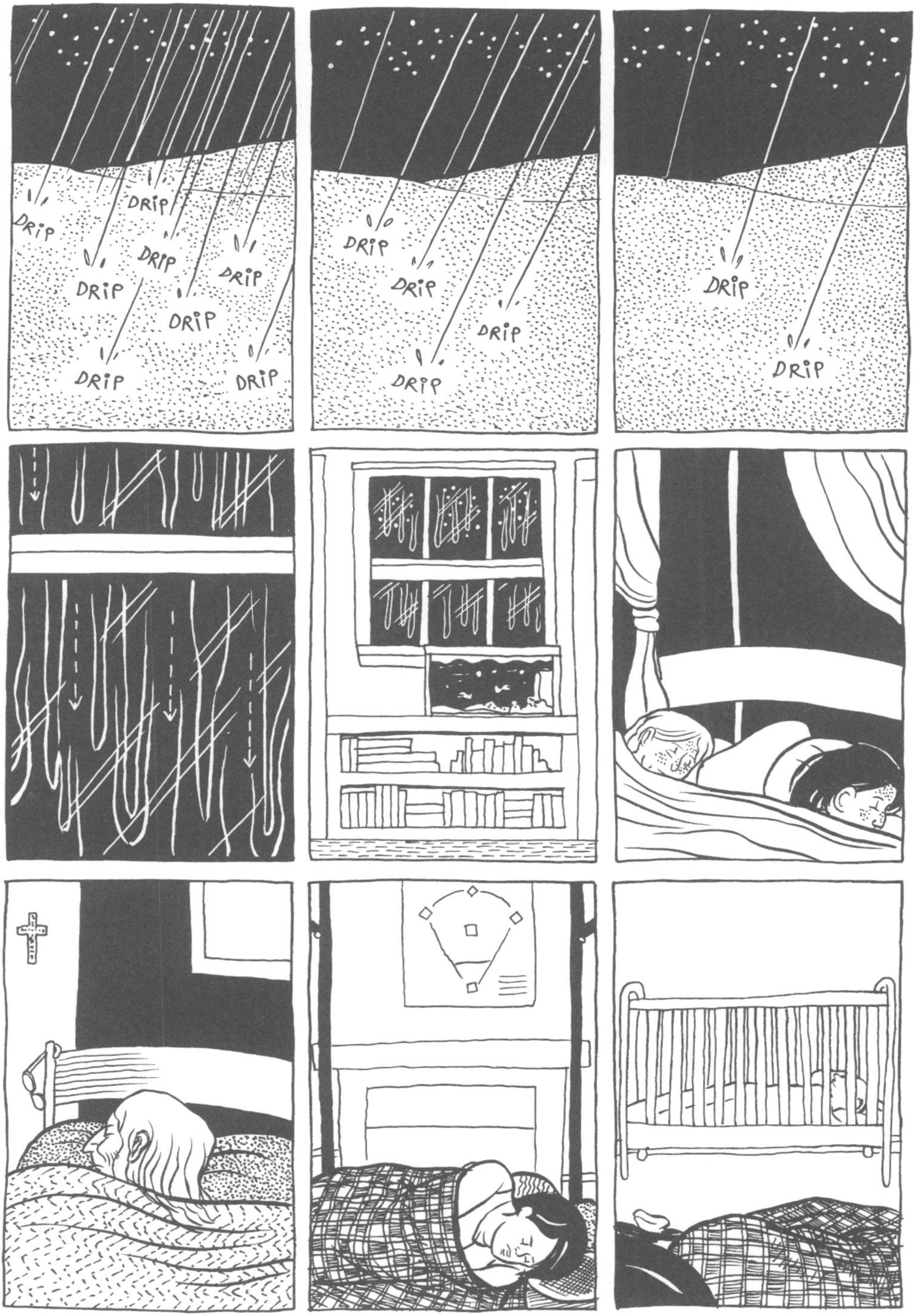
DRIP
DRIP
DRIP
DRIP
DRIP
DRIP
DRIP
DRIP
DRIP
DRIP
DRIP
DRIP
DRIP

OPEN
WIND
WIND
WIND

WIND

Dad?
SHUT
LOON

SLOSH
SLOSH

fog
fog

fog
OCEAN SOUNDS
pant
pant
fog
SLOSH
SLOSH

FOG
FOG
FOG

THUMP

DAD?!
DAD?!
fuck.
uh. I-

PANT
PANT
PANT

PANT
SLOSH
SLOSH

MOM! AKI! CLAIRE! COME DOWN!
COFF COFF

WHAT HAPPENED?
DAVID?
HE FELL.
I'M FINE.
DAD?
GET AWAY FROM ME.

Grampa fell sleepwalking. He denies it, of course.
I miss home.

End of Part Two

Part Three

There are many
types of water.

Morning dew.

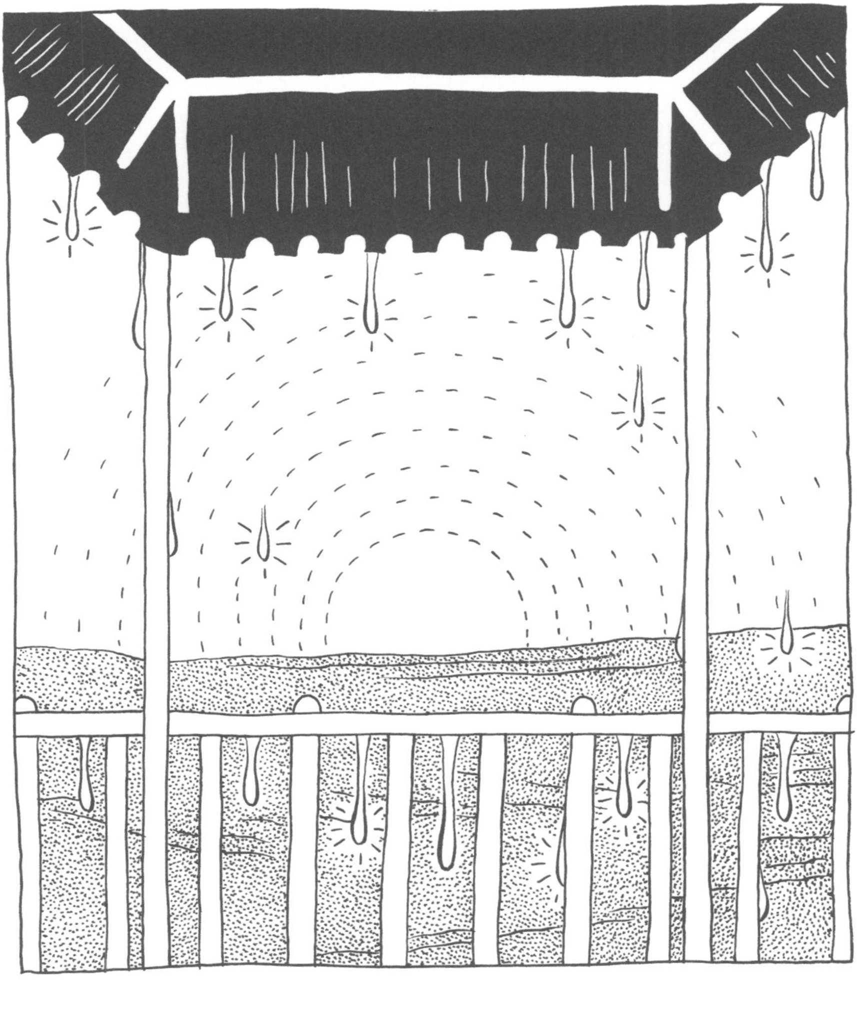

Evaporating water.

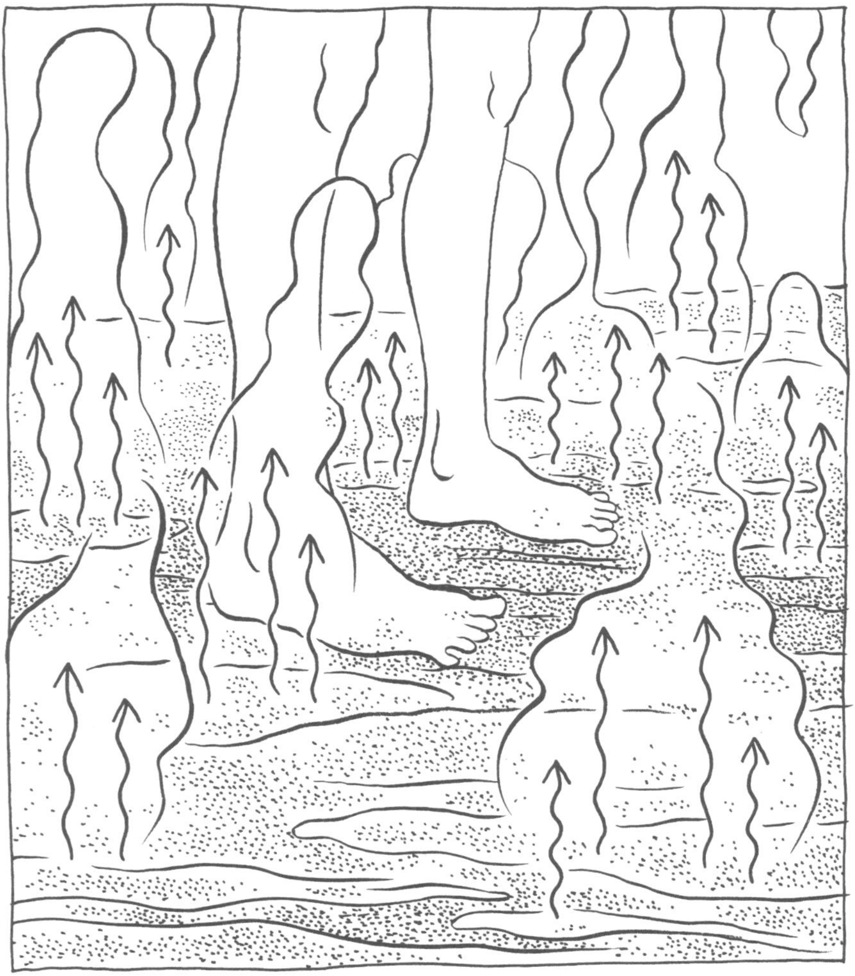

Water vapor.

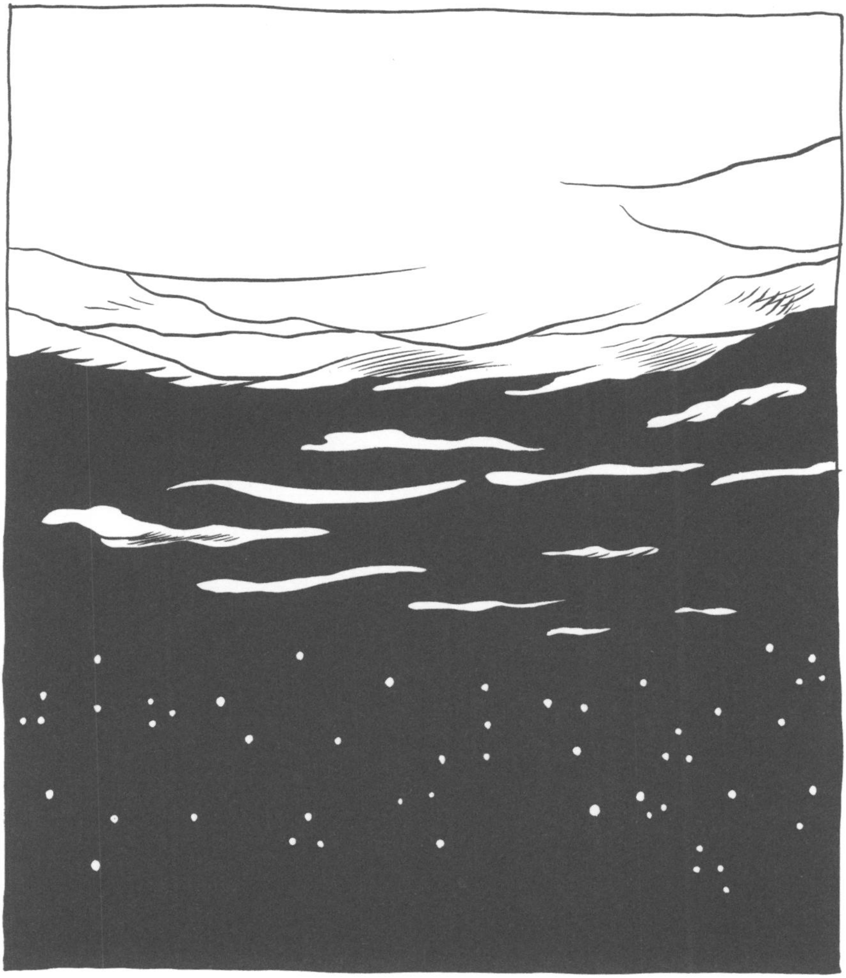

Rain.

Runoff.

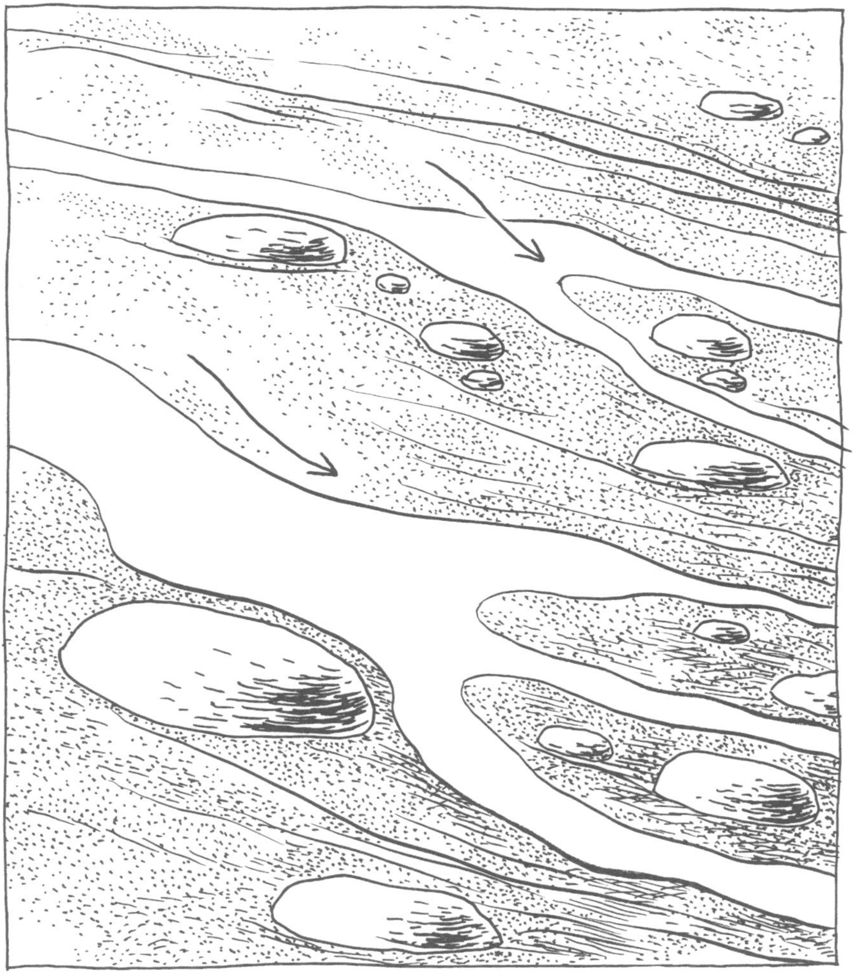

River water.

Ground water.

Saltwater (Low Tide.)

POKE
POKE POKE
GROSS.
STEP
STEP
STEP

Thanks for going on my walk with me.
I didn't have anything else to do. Ha.
Well,
me neither.
What are you going to do when you're single?
Are you gonna meet someone?
Do old people have parties?

I don't know. I never liked parties. Even when I was your age.
I feel the same way now. Exactly the same.
KICK
I just have a wrinkly body now.
This skin hanging off of my neck.
huh.
I meet people at church sometimes.

I know Claire never takes you to church. And that's okay.
uh-huh.
But think about this:
Your spirit never changes. It's the only thing that's ALWAYS with you.
You move cities, get older, lose a leg— The only thing that's YOU is your spirit.
Yeah.
That makes sense.
Someone told that to me once, and I liked it.

I didn't mean to sound preachy.
S'okay.
What about you? Do you have parties?
No.
I like one-on-one talking, you know?
Uh-huh.
HEY, I found a key in the dryer.
And some passage in the hallway closet.

oh?
YEAH. What's up with THAT?
Well, if you find a key, and then a door for the key, you should go inside.
Ha.
You're KOOKY, Grammy.
STOPS

I guess we should start walking back now.
TURN
O.K.
HEY.
my stick.
DRAG

You should get a cane and a cape.
No thanks.
DRAG
SNAP
Why's there a chair outside?
Oh.
uh...

I found it on the beach and broke its hind legs and back piece and, uh, tied strings to it.
Why?
SHAKE
JUST CUZ.
You're an artist. Like your father.

Basal tears.

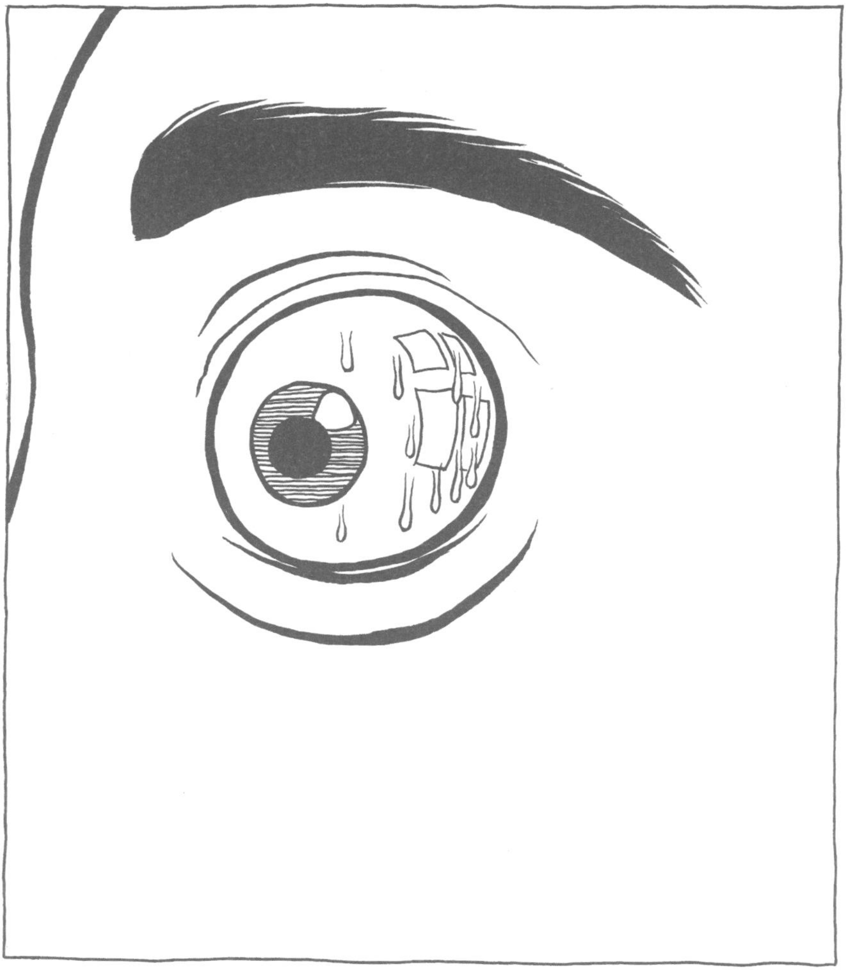

Reflex tears.

Physic tears.

PANT
PANT
PANT
SEARCH
DUST
SEARCH
SEARCH
DUST
DUST
a Rusty bicycle?
a trash bag full of empty bottles?
Hundreds of "To-Do" Lists?
A box full of "Time Management" books?
TIME IS MADE, NOT "FOUND"
GET AN EXTRA DAY EACH WEEK

SEarch
DUST
This CAN'T be ALL that's here.
CAN'T.
KICK
DUST
DUST
DUST

KICK
COUGH
COUGH
DUST
COUGH
COUGH
SIT=
KICKS
SHUT
cough
SHAKEY

CRUMPLE
CRUMPLE
CRUMPLE
TOSS
BRUSH
(RUB)
PACE

SIGH
This is so stupid.
KICK
stupid shit.
COUGH
SNif
KICK
KICK
KICK
KICK
KICK
KICK
Step up.

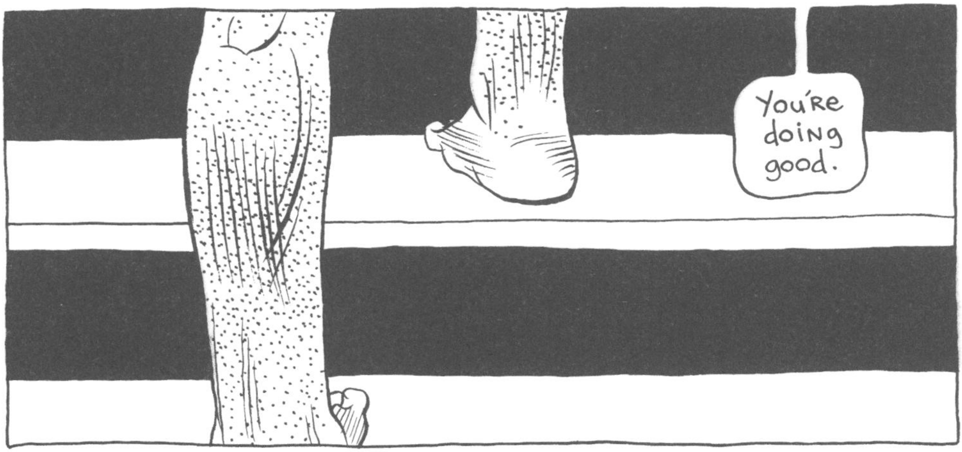
You're doing good.

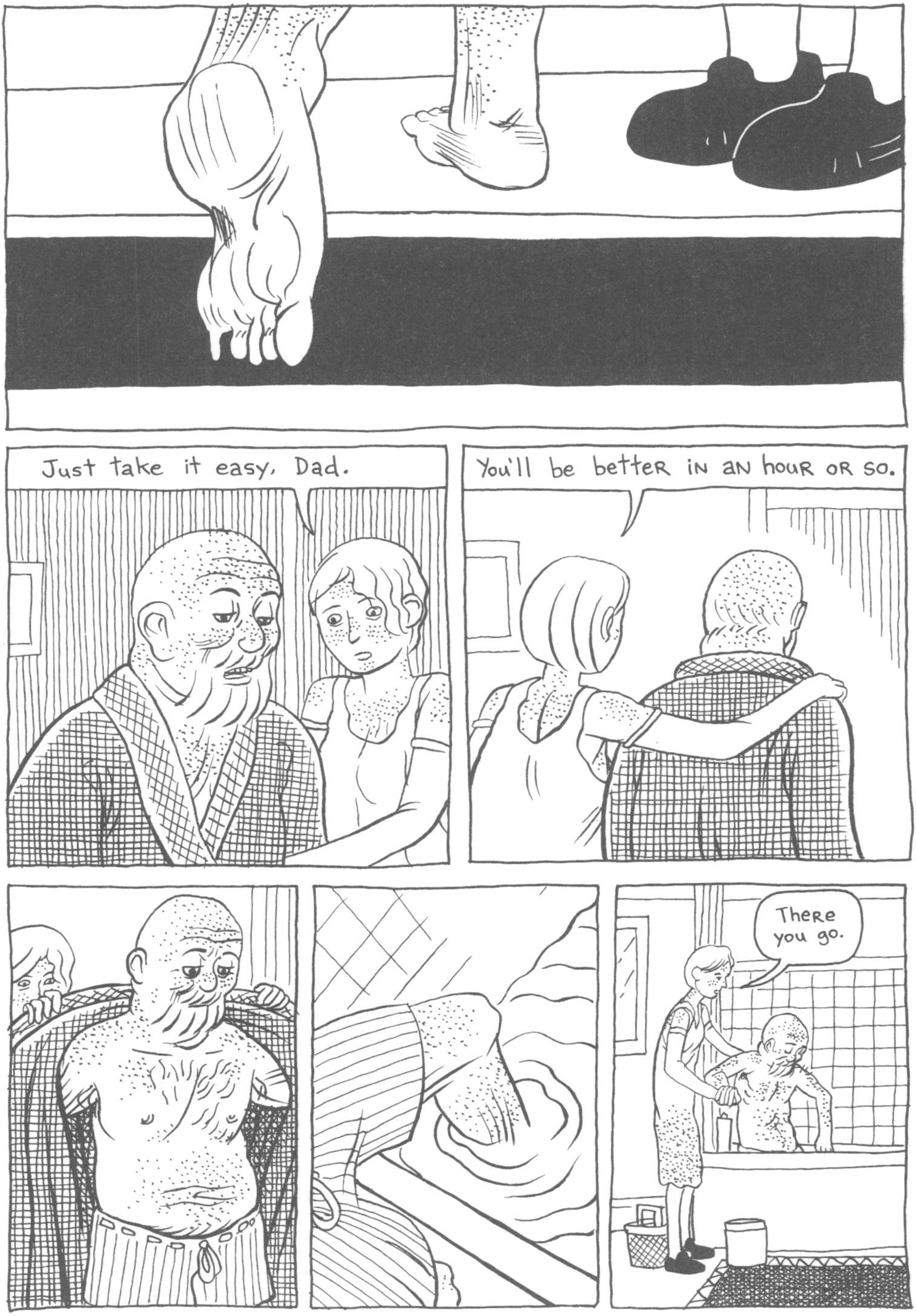
Just take it easy, Dad.
You'll be better in an hour or so.
There you go.

Bath water.

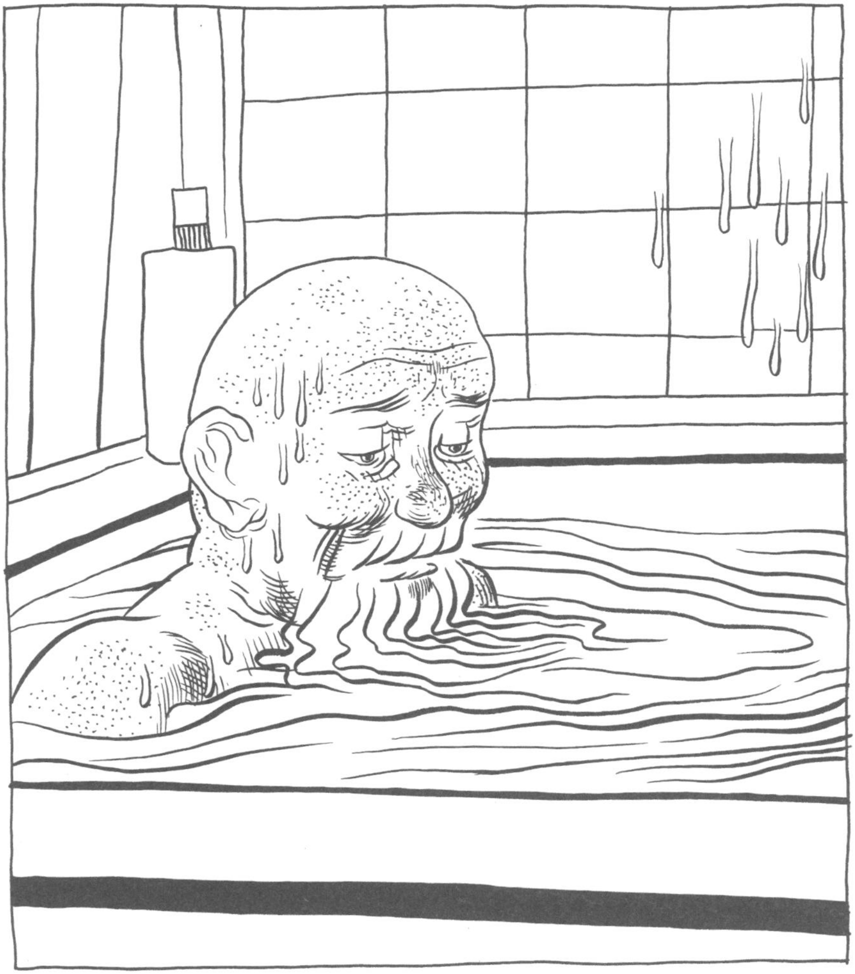

BREATHES IN.
Bubbles through beard hairs.
Sigh.
SCOOT
How's it going, Dad?

My whole body's so tired.
I'm going to die soon.
WHAT?! Did you see a doctor?
No.
I just have a feeling.
I don't think you're going to die soon! You're so healthy
I can tell.
I just know it.

Why do you want to get a divorce if you think you'll die soon?
That's a lame reason to stay together. It wouldn't be right.
hm.
Did you do marriage counselling?
No point.
Carl and I saw a therapist.
HOT WATER
We don't want to be married. Just like you and Carl.

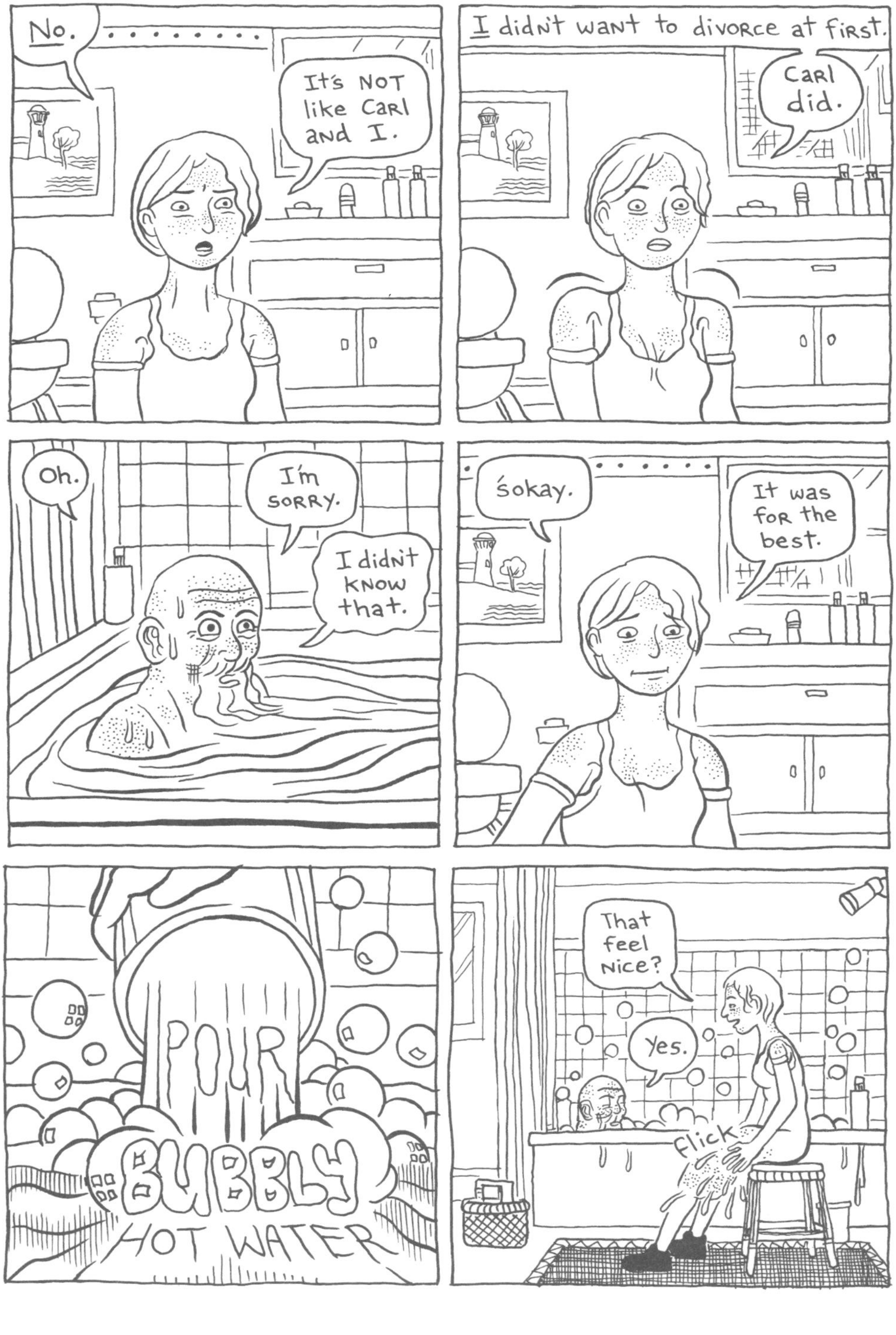
No.
It's NOT like Carl and I.
I didn't want to divorce at first.
Carl did.
Oh.
I'm SORRY.
I didn't KNOW that.
'sokay.
It was for the best.
POUR
BUBBLY
HOT WATER
That feel nice?
Yes.
flick

Remember this?
Ha.
Maggie'd do that and you kids loved it.
Ha.
COUGH
COUGH
Do you think you know what love is?

I love YOU.
I love DENNIS.
um.
I admit I don't KNOW Peter very well.
SPLISH SPLASH
I Regret that.
SPLISH
He'd always lock himself up in his Room, watching tee-vee.
Sigh.
I don't GET Peter.

If I got to know him better, I'd probably love him too.
SHRUGS

Tap water.

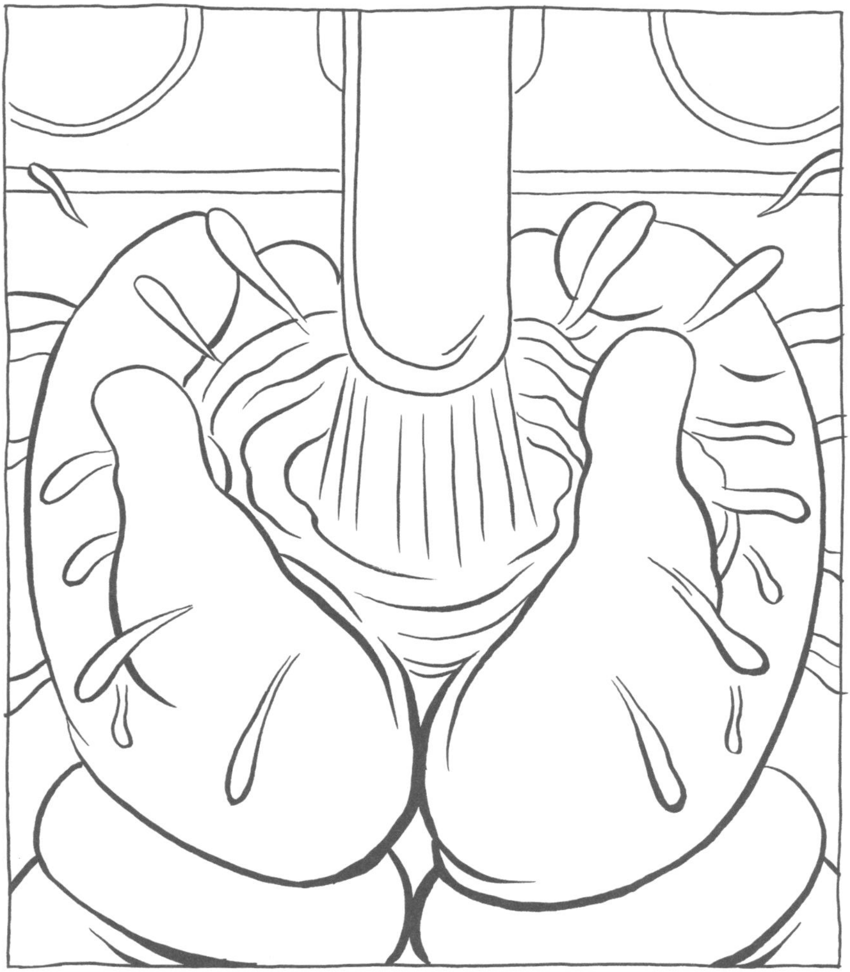

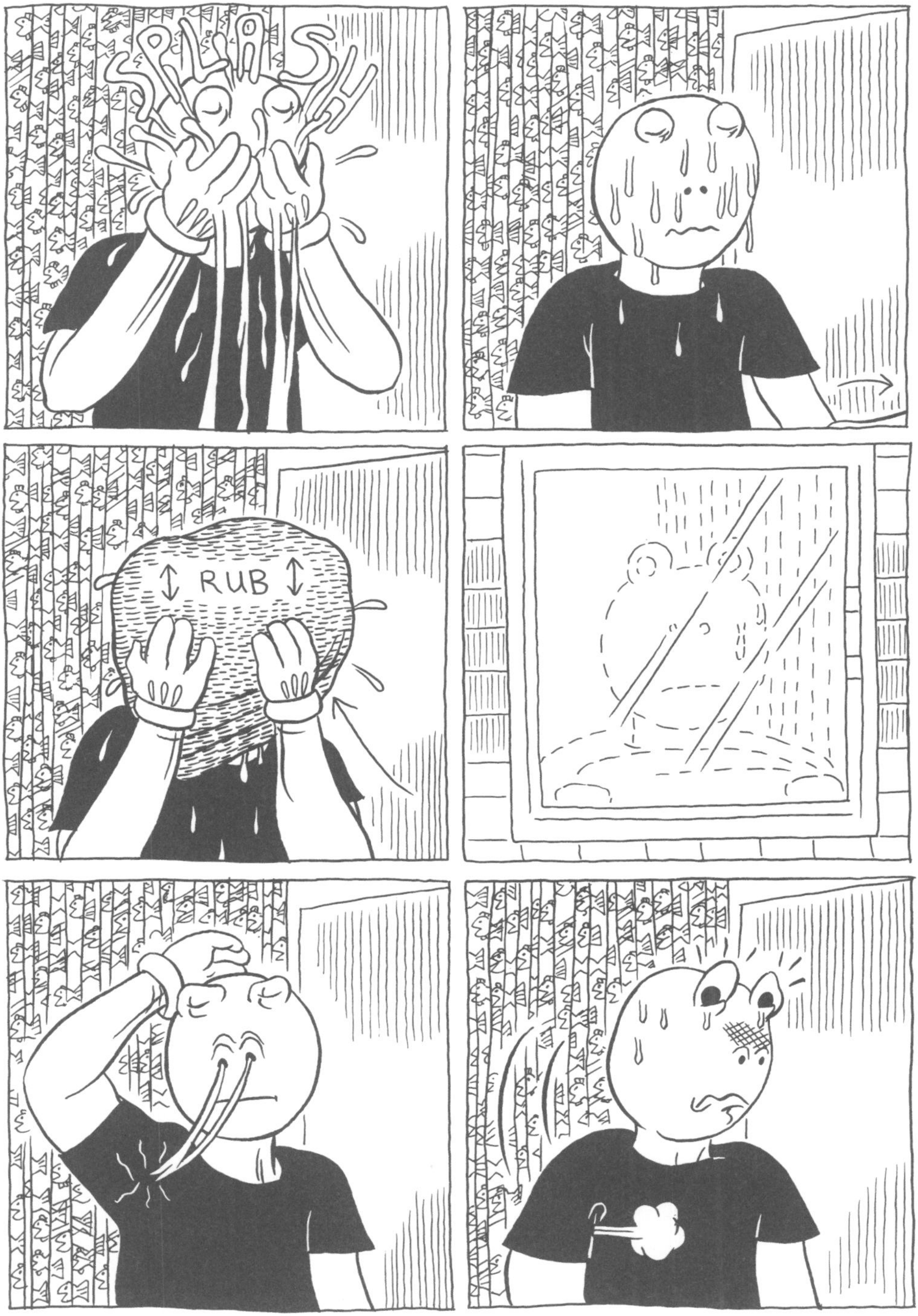
SPLASH
RUB

DEODORANT?
NO DEODORANT
hm.
TOOTHPAS

MINTY
FRESH
SMELL

You don't have to go to work with me if you don't want to.
No, No.
I want to.
KISS
Nice air.
SNIF
SNAP SNAP
PET

We're late.
We better RUN.
SNAP
BYE, FAREL!
ROLL ROLL

Near-boiling water.

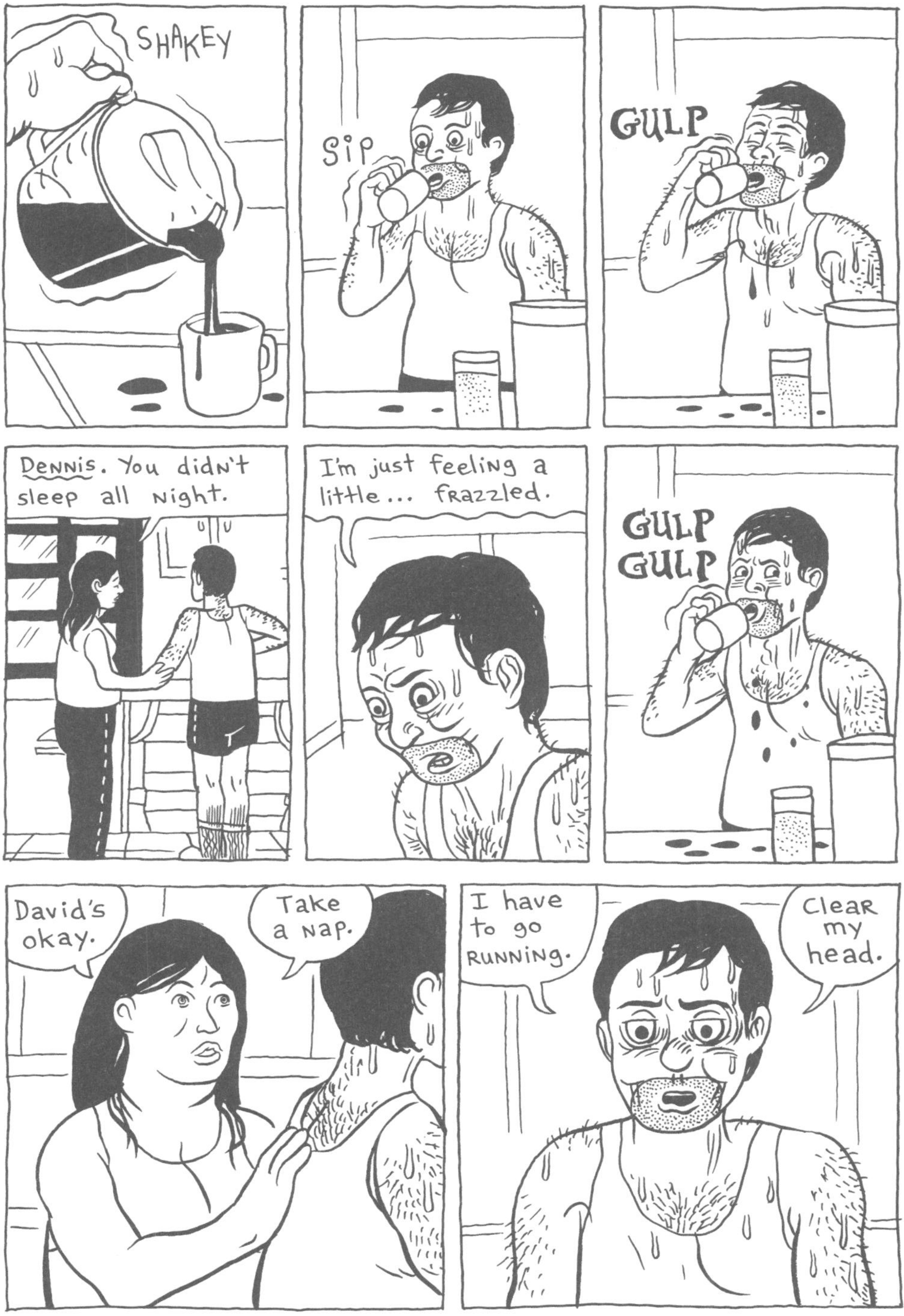
SHAKEY
SIP
GULP
DENNIS. You didn't sleep all night.
I'm just feeling a little... frazzled.
GULP GULP
David's okay.
Take a nap.
I have to go RUNNING.
Clear my head.

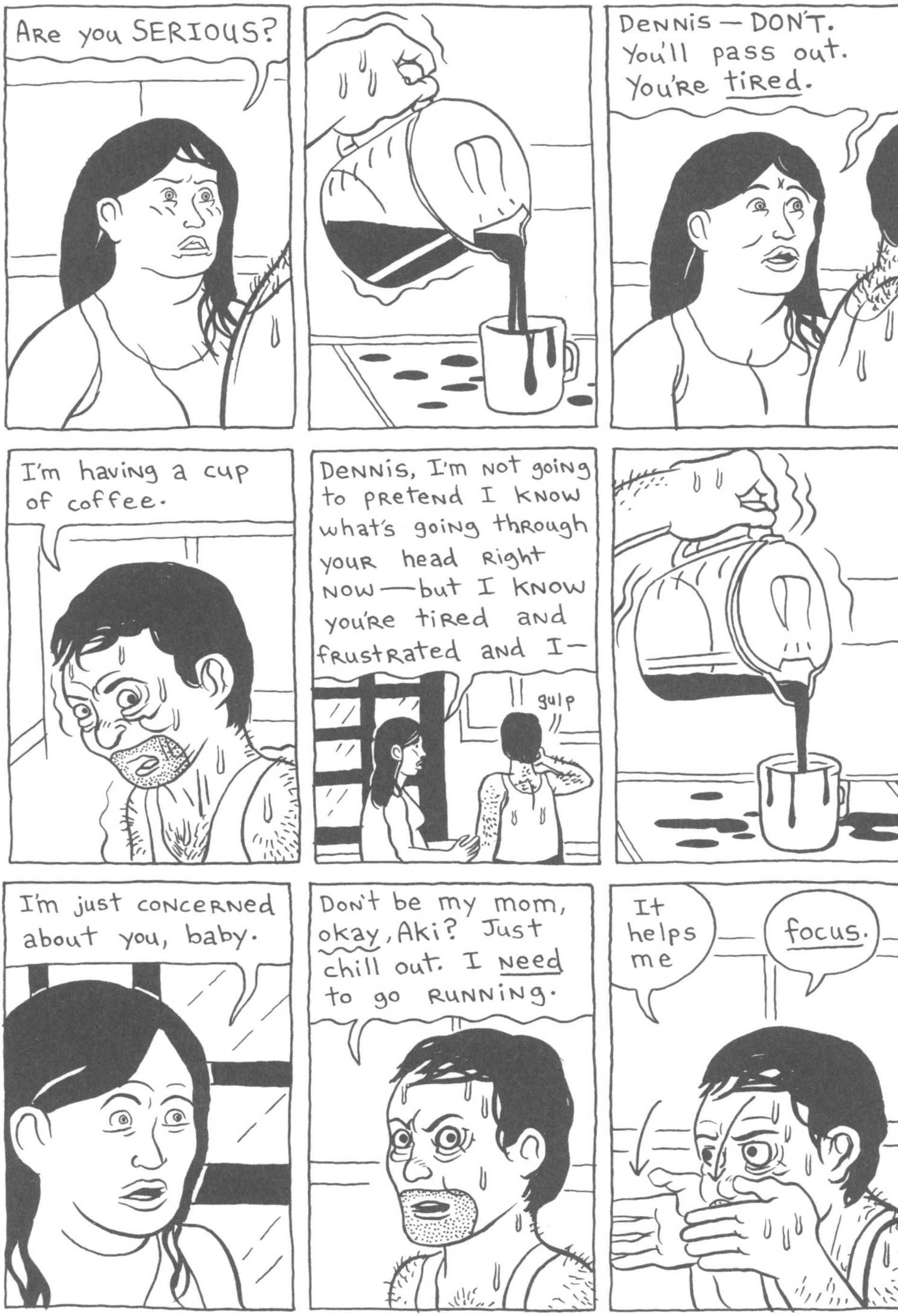
Are you SERIOUS?
DENNIS — DON'T. You'll pass out. You're tired.
I'm having a cup of coffee.
DENNIS, I'm not going to pretend I know what's going through your head right now — but I know you're tired and frustrated and I—
gulp
I'm just concerned about you, baby.
Don't be my mom, okay, Aki? Just chill out. I need to go running.
It helps me
focus.

okay, sweetie.
Just be safe.
BREATHES OUT.
cough cough

Nnh.
TRIES TO OPEN
PICK PICK

HIT
HIT
KNOCK
KNOCK
SCRATCH
SCRATCH
Shit.

NO KEY
STEP STEP
PUNCH
SIT.
BREATHES OUT.

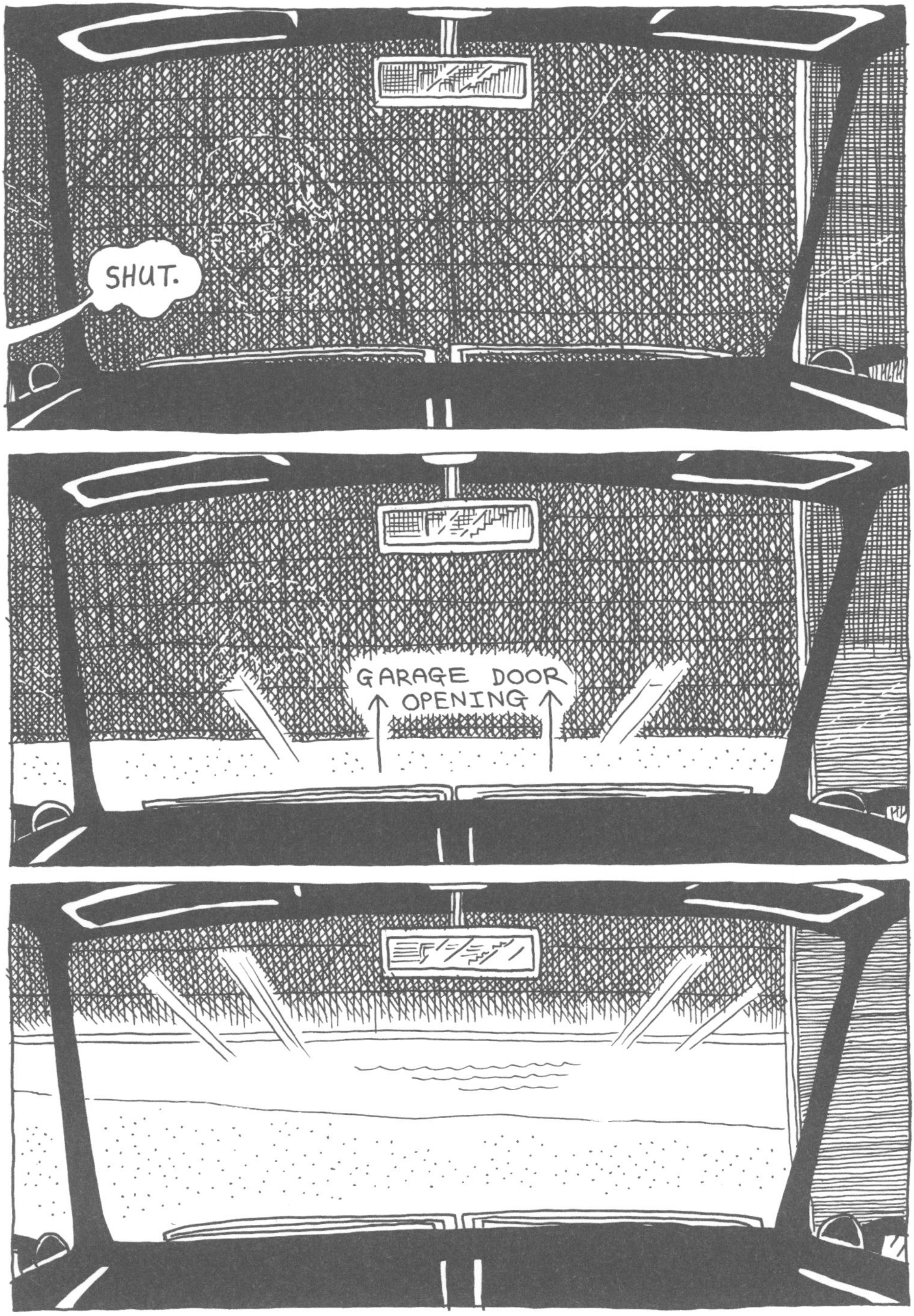
SHUT.
GARAGE DOOR OPENING

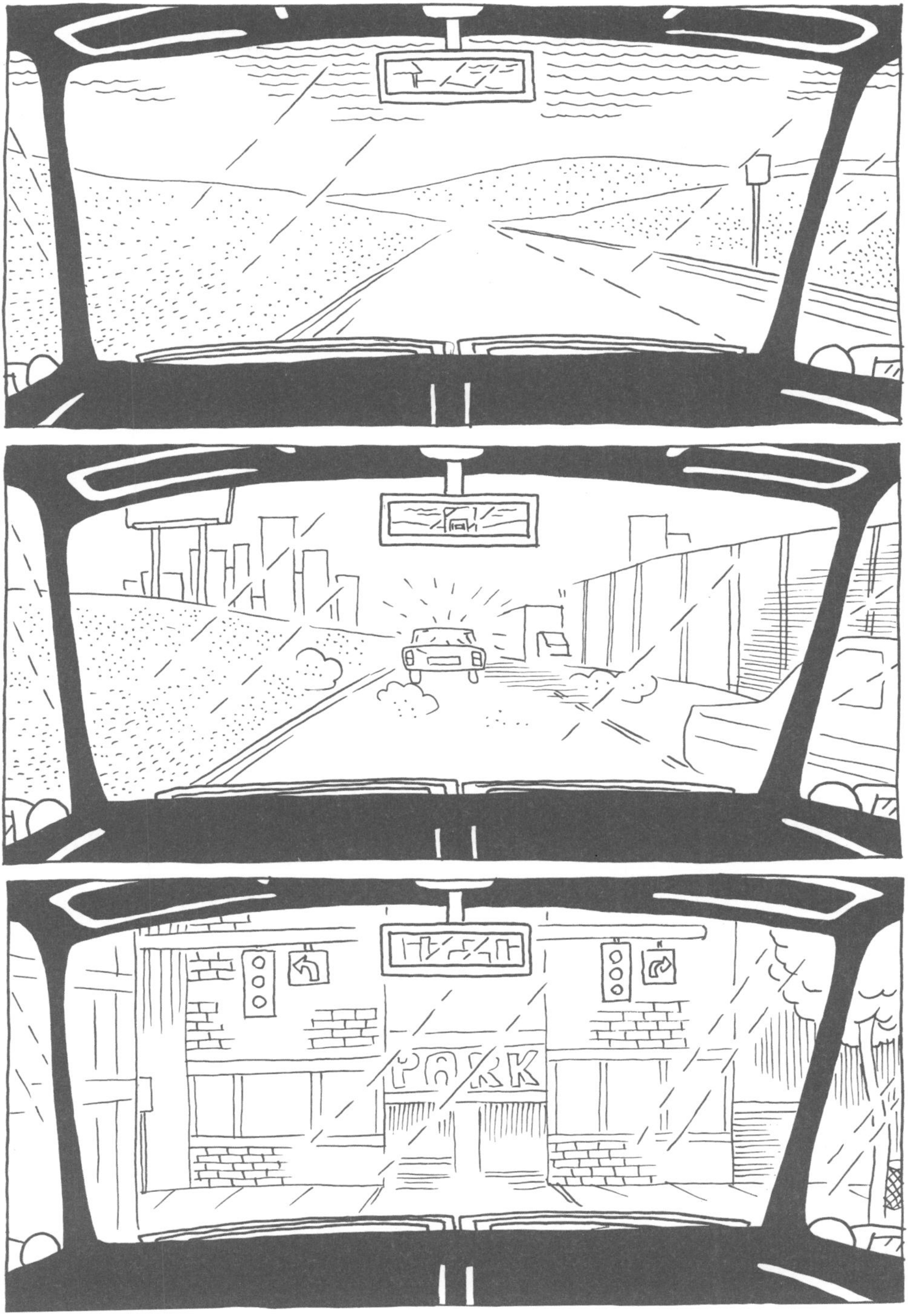
PARK

Ink.

Case Name: Loony/Farmer
Case Number: 326479
FINAL DECREE ON PETITION FOR DIVORCE OR LEGAL SEPARATION

☐ Other: ______________________________

15. Other Real Property ☒ N/A

☐ The real estate located at ______________________ is awarded to the ______________, free of any right, title or interest of the other party, but subject to any encumbrance thereon.

☐ Other: ______________________________

16. Enforceability after Death ☒ N/A

☐ The terms of this decree shall be a charge against each party's estate.

17. Signing of Documents ☐ N/A

☒ Each party shall, within thirty (30) days, sign and deliver to the other party any document or paper that is needed to fulfill or accomplish the terms of this decree.

18. Restraining Order ☒ N/A

☐ ______________ is restrained and enjoined from entering the home or the place of employment of the other party, and from harassing, intimidating or threatening the other party or his/her relatives or other household members.

☐ Other: ______________________________

19. Name Change (Divorce Only) ☐ N/A

☐ Margaret Farmer Loony may resume use of her/his former name: Margaret Addams Farmer

20. Other Requests

☐ Attorney's Fees: Any party that unreasonably fails to comply with this decree or other court orders (including "Uniform Support Order") may be responsible to reimburse the other party for whatever costs, including reasonable attorney's fees, that may be incurred in order to enforce compliance.

☐ Tax Refunds: Any tax refund due or anticipated by the parties resulting from their having filed a joint federal and/or state income tax return for this or any prior year shall, upon receipt, be endorsed by both parties and equally distributed between them.

☐ Disclosure of Assets: The parties warrant that they have fully disclosed all assets within their knowledge on their respective Financial Affidavit, specifically including any pension, profit sharing or retirement account, along with reasonable estimated values of each asset. The financial information contained on each party's Financial Affidavit has been relied upon by the other party.

FOLD
and here.
FOLD
Mag

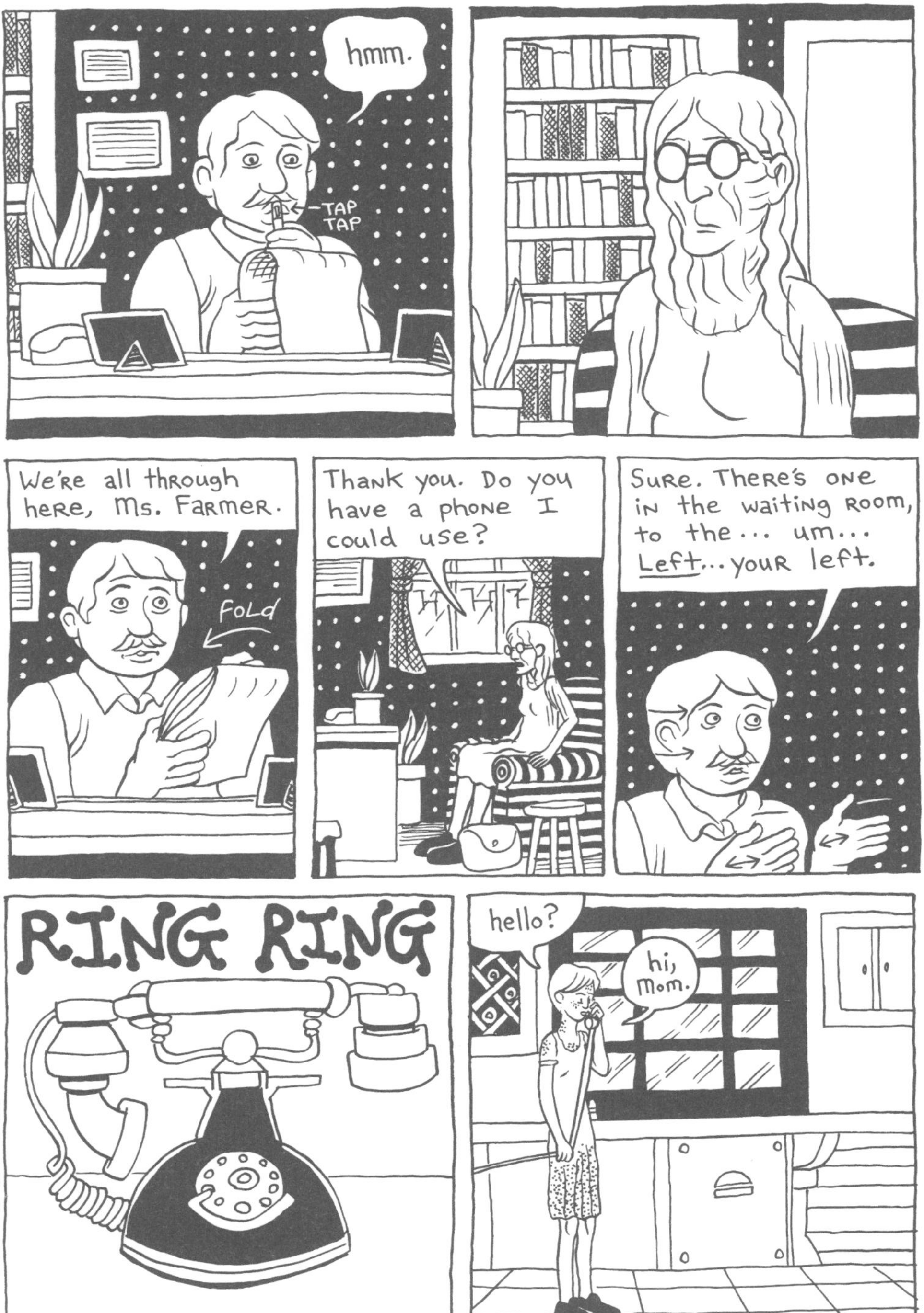
hmm.
TAP TAP
We're all through here, Ms. Farmer.
FOLD
Thank you. Do you have a phone I could use?
Sure. There's one in the waiting room, to the... um... Left... your left.
RING RING
hello?
hi, Mom.

Could you tell David the final paperwork is done?
Uh.
O.K.
-and I'm going to the grocery store to pick up some things. Is there anything you or Jill want?
um.
Jill likes bagels and cream cheese.
I'm writing it in my book so I won't forget.
bagels and cr
Red-colored paper
Thanks, Ma.
Okay.
see ya.

GROCERY STORE
FLOURESCENT LIGHTS

MILK
MILK
MARK TO AISLE 4. MARK TO AISLE 4.
MUSIC SOFTLY PLAYING IN BACKGROUND.
EGGS
EGGS
EGGS
EGGS

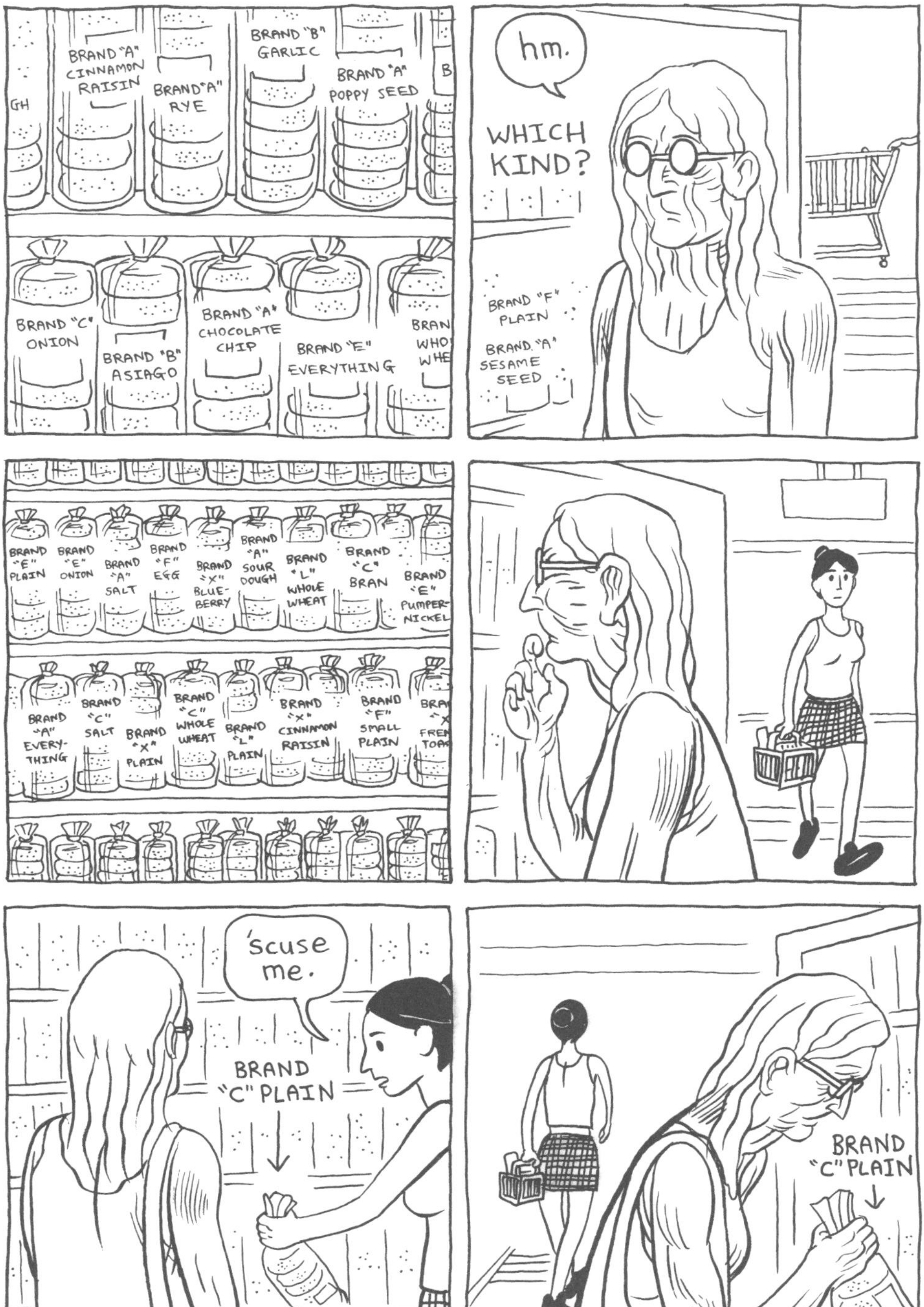
BRAND "A" CINNAMON RAISIN
BRAND "A" RYE
BRAND "B" GARLIC
BRAND "A" POPPY SEED
BRAND "C" ONION
BRAND "B" ASIAGO
BRAND "A" CHOCOLATE CHIP
BRAND "E" EVERYTHING
hm.
WHICH KIND?
BRAND "F" PLAIN
BRAND "A" SESAME SEED
BRAND "E" PLAIN
BRAND "E" ONION
BRAND "A" SALT
BRAND "F" EGG
BRAND "X" BLUE-BERRY
BRAND "A" SOUR DOUGH
BRAND "L" WHOLE WHEAT
BRAND "C" BRAN
BRAND "E" PUMPER-NICKEL
BRAND "A" EVERY-THING
BRAND "C" SALT
BRAND "X" PLAIN
BRAND "C" WHOLE WHEAT
BRAND "L" PLAIN
BRAND "X" CINNAMON RAISIN
BRAND "F" SMALL PLAIN
'scuse me.
BRAND "C" PLAIN
BRAND "C" PLAIN

CREAMCH
CHEESE
AM CHEE
REAMCH
CREC
ESE
CHECK OUT
BREATHES IN.

0 EGGS
-BEEP-
Would you like paper or plastic?
um.
plastic.
BEEP
BEEP

Do you have a preferred customer card?
Yes.
Um. Wait. I mean: No. I just have a regular credit card.
Would you like a preferred customer card?
uh.
okay.
I'll just need your phone number and-
um.
Can I get it later?
Uh, yeah.
sure.
I'm sorry.
You won't be able to save on this purchase.

I'm SORRY.
I
I'm just Not up for
that sort of thing Right now.
fine.
BREATHES OUT.
That'll be $14.86
SWIPES CARD
SIGNS
Thank you.
Bye.
Have a good day.
BEEP

SH UT
SIGH.
SUNLIGHT
OUTSIDE AIR
COUGH
COUGH
SHUT.
STORE PARKING ONLY

CAR WASH
CAR WASH
CAR WASH
THANK YOU

FLAP
FLAP
FLAP
FLAP
FLAP
FLAP
BREATHES IN.
FLAP
FLAP
FLAP
FLAP
BREATHES OUT.
WHIRR
WHIRR

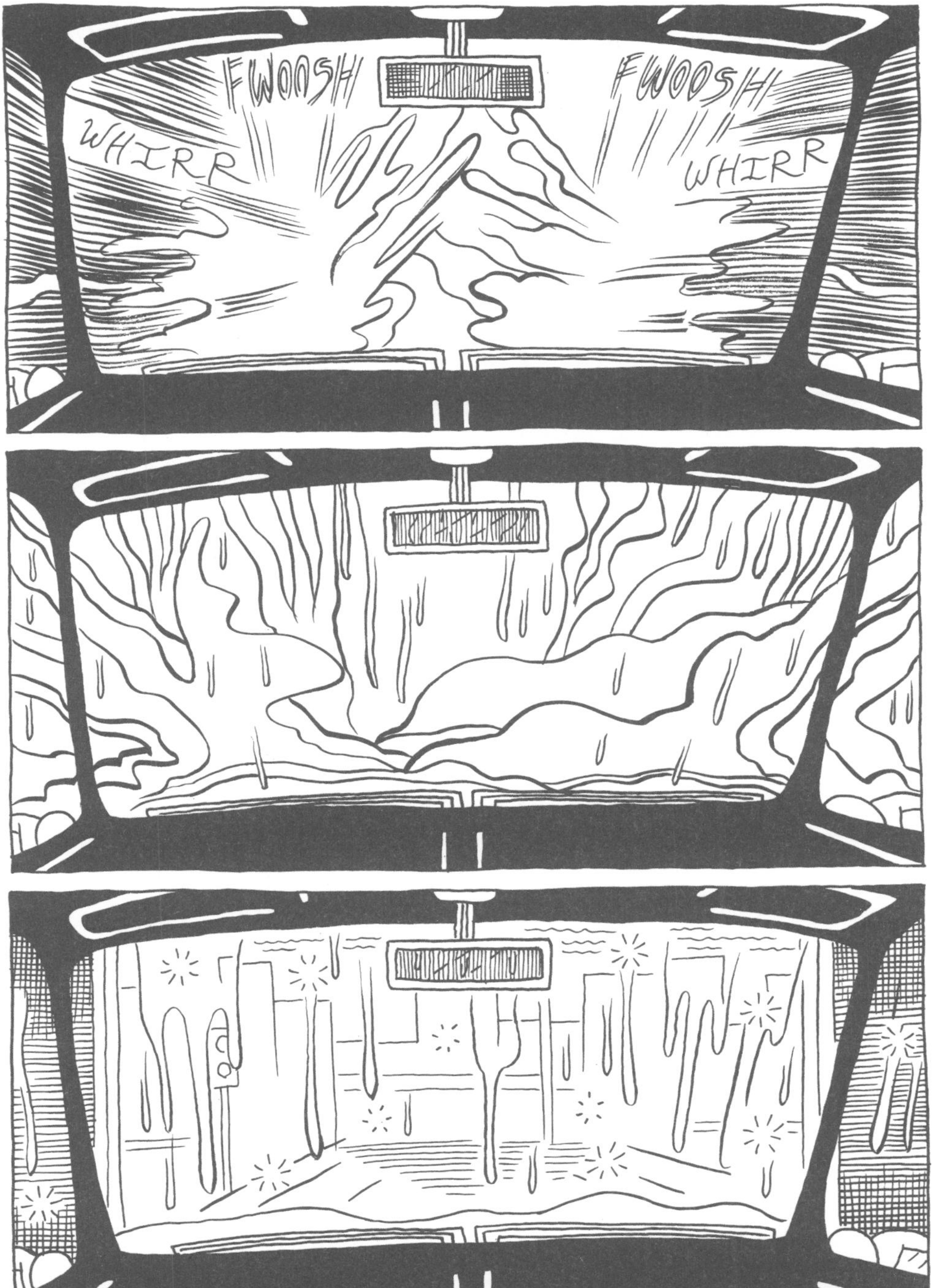
FWOOSH
FWOOSH
WHIRR
WHIRR

Saltwater (High Tide.)

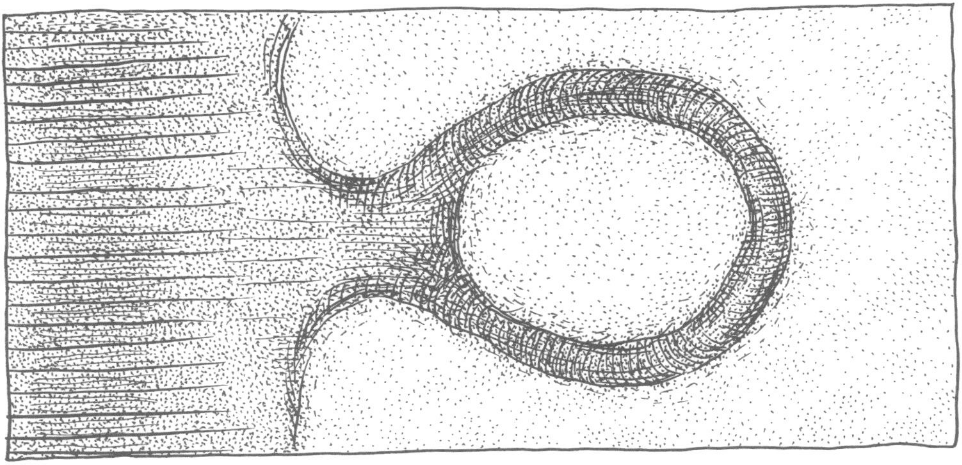

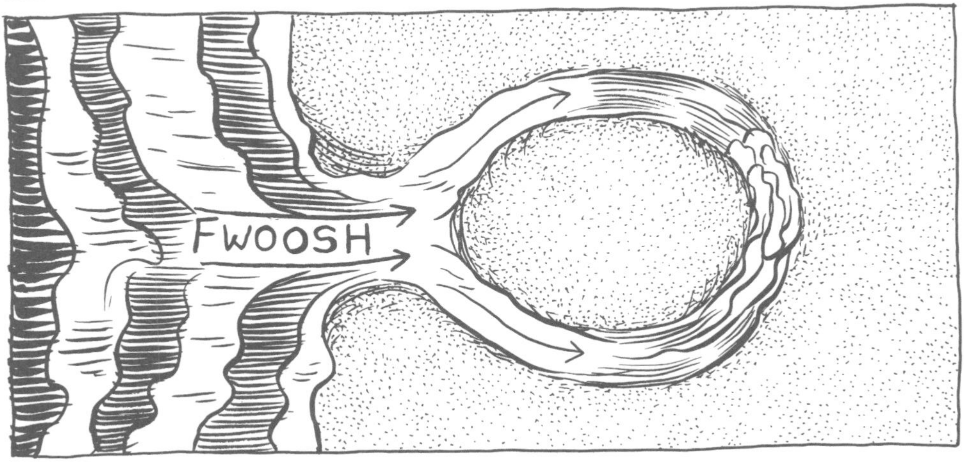
FWOOSH

WOAH!
awesome!
WOW!
COOL!
WOW!

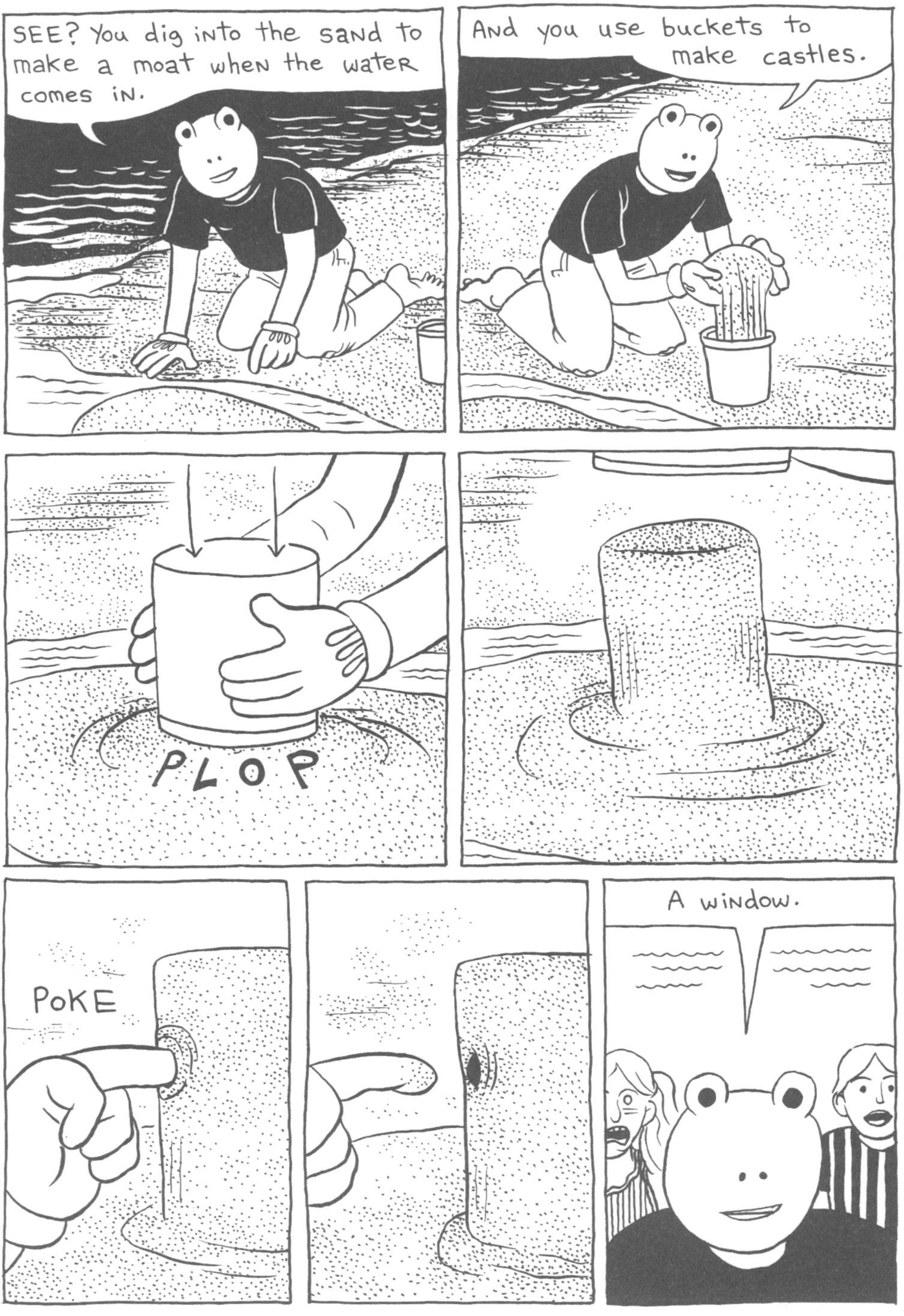
SEE? You dig into the sand to make a moat when the water comes in.
And you use buckets to make castles.
PLOP
POKE
A window.

Miss Kat, Your friend Peter's a GENIUS!
Tug
Tug
Tug
How are you feeling today, Sara?
"HIGH FIVE?"
I'm so-so.
I thought you made castles just for me.
oh.
I share. Sharing.
"HIGH FIVE?"
Don't leave me hanging, dude.
"HIGH FIVE?!"
Ha.
alright.
"FIVE."

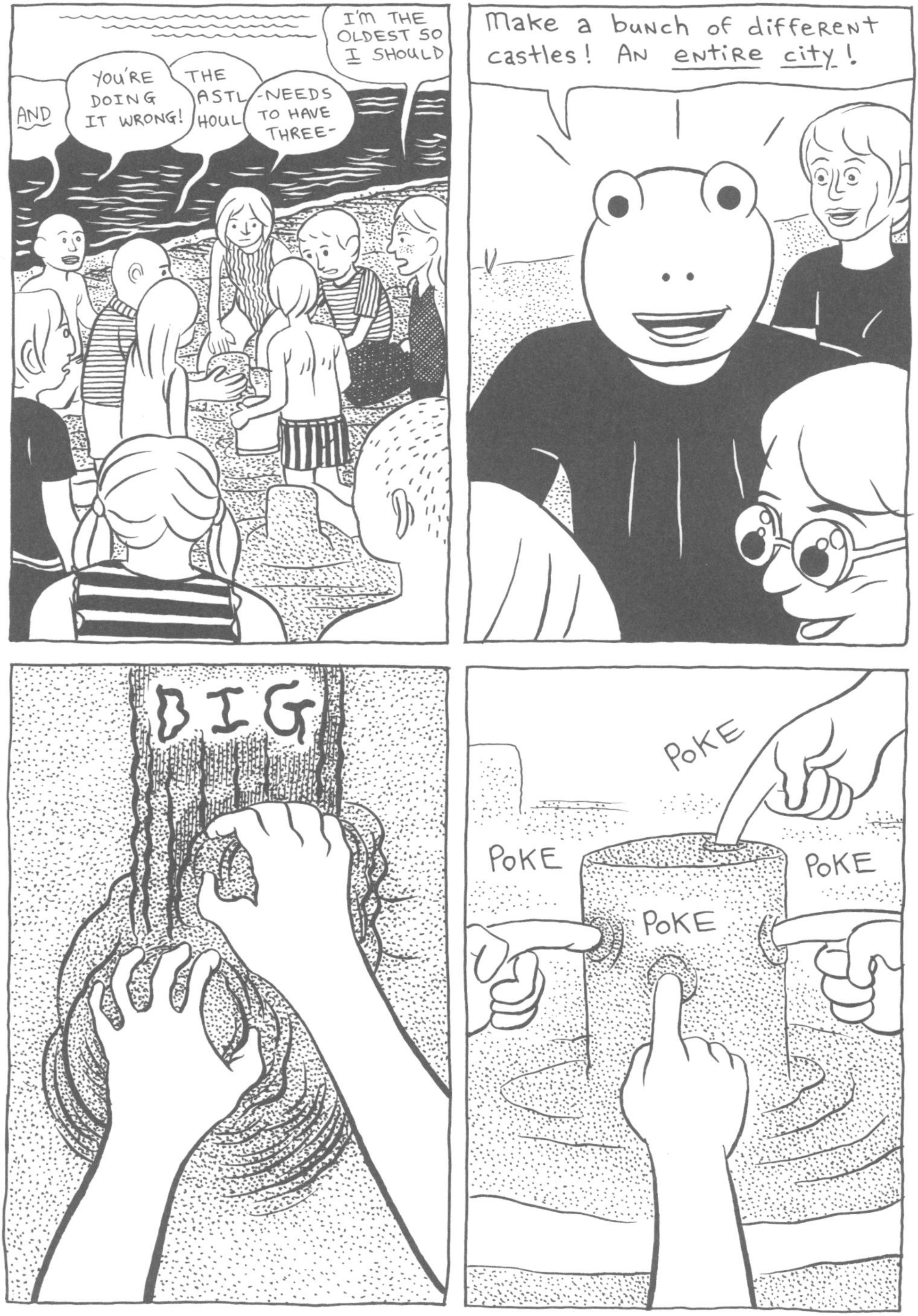
AND
YOU'RE DOING IT WRONG!
THE ASTL HOUL
-NEEDS TO HAVE THREE-
I'M THE OLDEST SO I SHOULD
Make a bunch of different castles! An entire city!
DIG
POKE
POKE
POKE
POKE

You're so good with kids.
Thanks.
I want to have, like, a kajillion million kids.
Ha.
um.
Hey, when I was in your bathroom, I-
uh.
-Noticed-
What?

YOU TOOK MY TOOTH!
NO I DIDN'T!
I KNOW YOU DID! YOU WANT THE FAIRY MONEY SO YOU STOLE IT AT MY PARTY!!
YOU'RE AN IDIOT RETARD!
I SAW YOU!
KICK

I saw a photo of you and some guy.
Yeah?
So, that's not... like... your boyfriend or anything, right?
heh.
Ha. No, No. That's my BROTHER.
oh.
Ha, ha.
Right.
I told you about him. The comic strips.
Yeah.
Right.
SORRY.

SUCK
SMACK
GIVE IT!
GRAB—
Ha Ha
GIVE IT!
Ha Ha

I just have an imagination and I worry and-
Shrug
Shrug
's cool.
Ha.
Yeah.
Sorry.
Shrug
My boyfriend's out of town.
What?
's okay. He's cool with it. He knows I like to party.

Ha Ha
YOU'RE GONNA GET IN TROUBLE!
CATCH!
SHOVE
YOU WANT IT?
GO GET IT!
I HATE YOU!
PUSH

um.
I- I don't-
He's always out of town.
What? Well, how is he your boyfriend? Do you write?
No, not really. I don't even know where he is right now.
This is confusing me.
SCRATCH
We never see each-other.
What do you mean? You NEVER see each-other?

COUGH
COUGH

pant
pant
pant

He's never in town. We never talk.
He's not even really my boyfriend.
Huh.
So you broke up with him?
I could. I could call him when I get off work.
Well,
I'd like that.
Yeah, okay. It'd be kind of weird calling him out of the blue, cuz we never talk.
HEAD ACHE

I didn't know it'd be such a huge mondo deal.
ha.
So, like, does HE have a girlfriend?
I donno.
Shrug
Well, what's he like? How'd you meet?

COUGH
WHEEZE
COUGH
COUGH
WHEEZE

Through a friend. Why?
Curious. What's his name?
Otis.
SCRATCH
What's he do? What's his job?
He's, like — a graphic designer I think... Yeah.
I hate his fucking guts.

SSSSSHH
ffff fff--
ffff-f-f-ff
F
F
F
FF
?
f
f
f
-DINK-
SLOSH
SLOSH

STILL WATER
SLIMEY
SOMETHING
ENH~
SSHLOOP
PSSSHH
SPLAT
SPLAT

CLAP
CLAP
CLAP
CLAP
ha
CLAP
ha ha ha ha ha

MISS KAT
MISS KAT
TUG
TUG
What's up, honey pie?
Tom and Jim took Paul's inhaler thingie and threw it into the water and then Paul went after it and probably drowned and died.
WHAT?!! Where is he?!
uh...
I dunno. swimming.
PAUL!
um. what should-
SHRUGS
PAUL!
Kat?
SPLOOSH

Paul?!
Paul?!
uh.
THINK.
um.
DON'T PANIC.
THINK. THINK.
Hey. Is there an office or something? You know?
uh-huh.
Run there and tell them it's an EMERGENCY. Tell them to call someone and to come here. EMERGENCY. "For real."— say that. "No joke" — don't laugh or anything. Go.
um.
Go.
Run.

pant
pant
pant
STOMACH CRAMP
hoo...
BREATHES IN.
~RUB
WHO THREW PAUL'S INHALER?! THAT WAS MEAN, DUDES.
HE SAID I STOLE HIS TOOTH WHEN I DIDN'T— AND THEN KICKED JIM AND PUSHED ME DOWN.
oh MAN.
You look SICK, Peter.

PAUL?!
~PAUL?!
PAUL?!

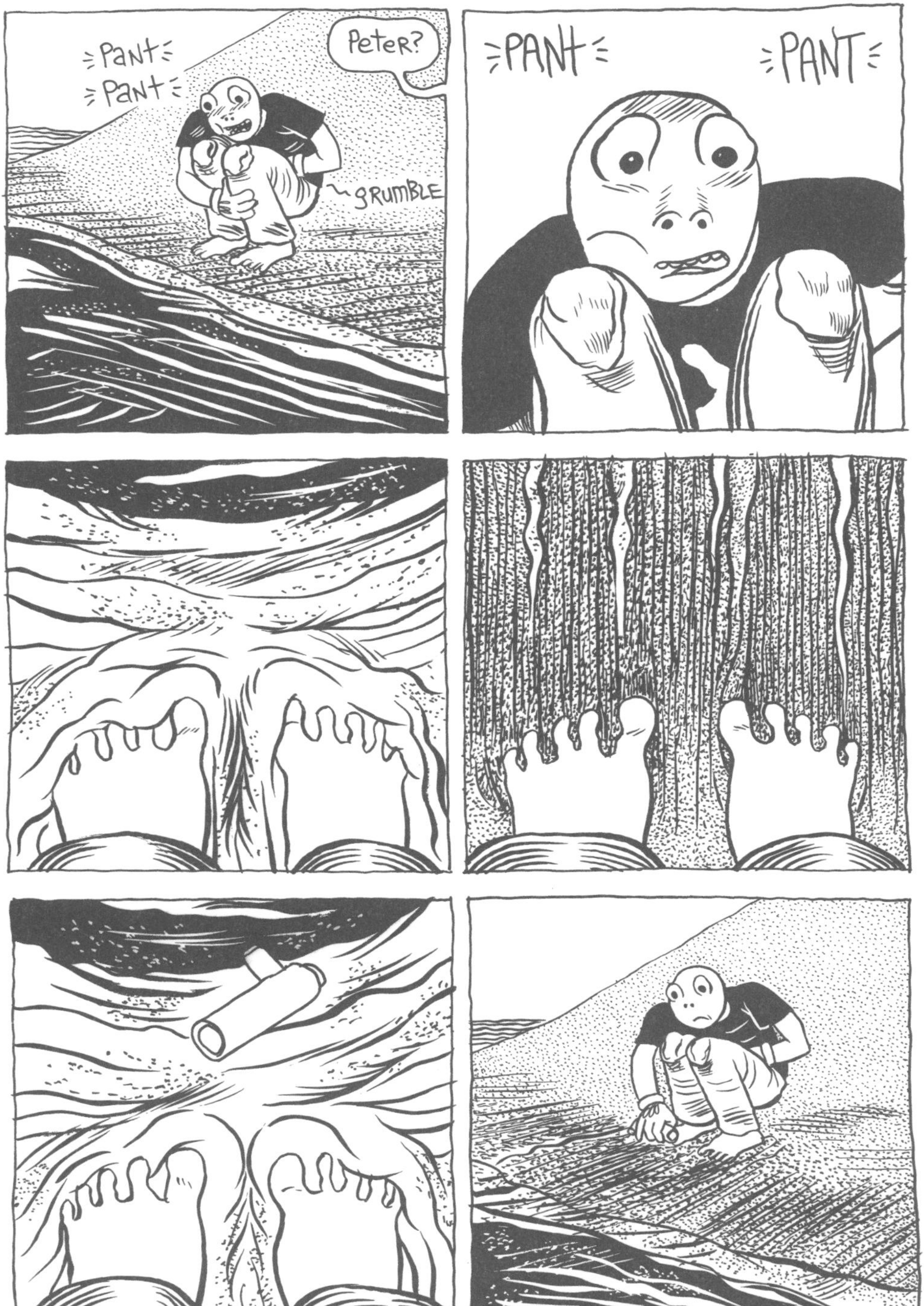
Pant
Pant
Peter?
GRUMBLE
PANT
PANT

cough
cough
cough
Hey dude.
Everyone's
looking
for you.

Shhhhhhhhhh
Shhhhhhhhhh

TURN
STEAM
STEAM
STEAM
STEAM
STEAM
STEAM
RUB
STEAM
STEAM
RUB RUB
STEAM
STEAM

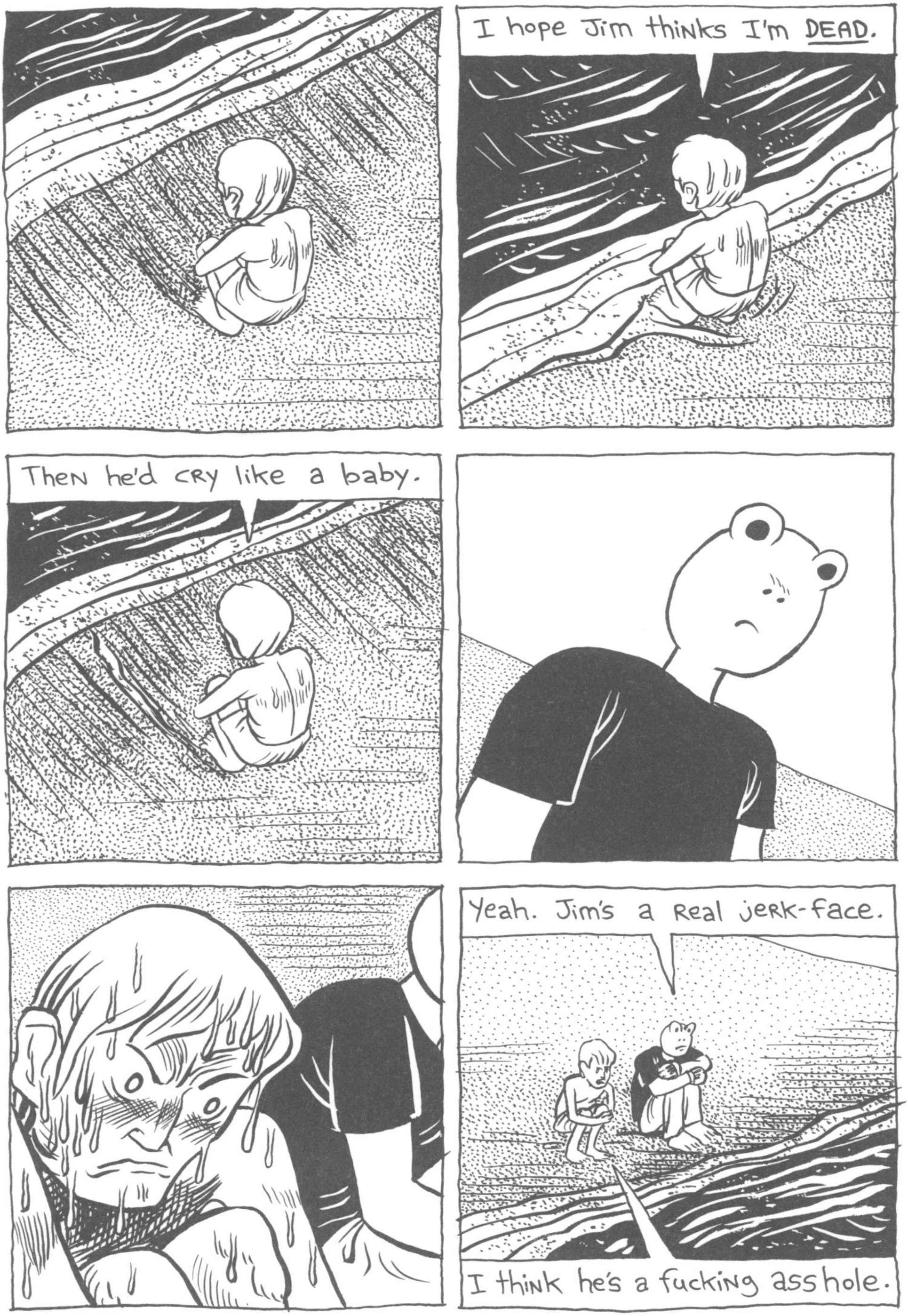
I hope Jim thinks I'm DEAD.
Then he'd cry like a baby.
Yeah. Jim's a real jerk-face.
I think he's a fucking asshole.

Well, you had ME really scared.
I was sweating.
My hands were SHAKING.
Ha Ha
My stomach was GRUMBLING.
HA HA HA
My head was THROBBING.
HA HA
Ha Ha
PLOP

I found your inhaler.
SUCK
I also have your tooth.
You can keep it.

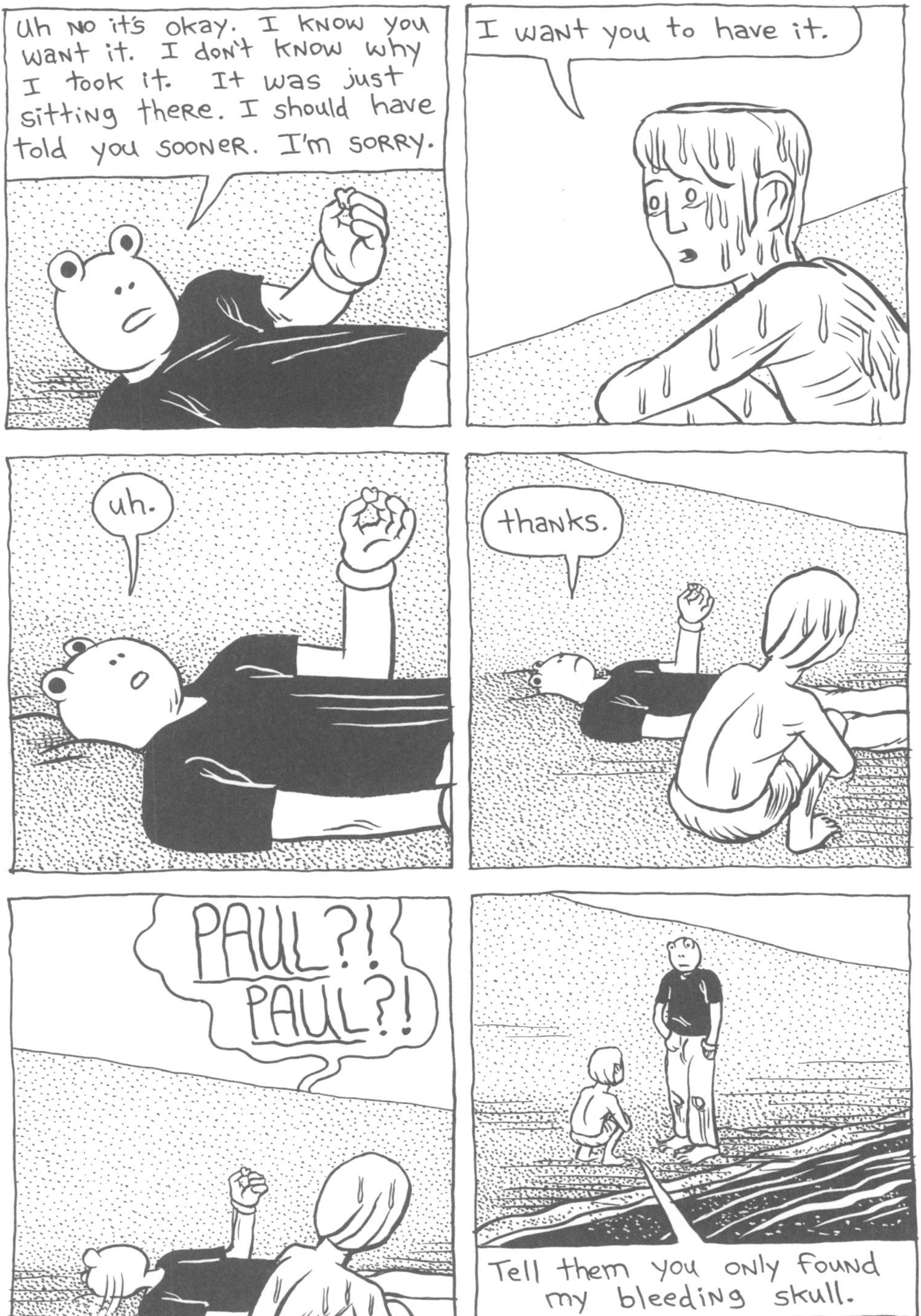
Uh no it's okay. I know you want it. I don't know why I took it. It was just sitting there. I should have told you sooner. I'm sorry.
I want you to have it.
uh.
thanks.
PAUL?! PAUL?!
Tell them you only found my bleeding skull.

Sweat.

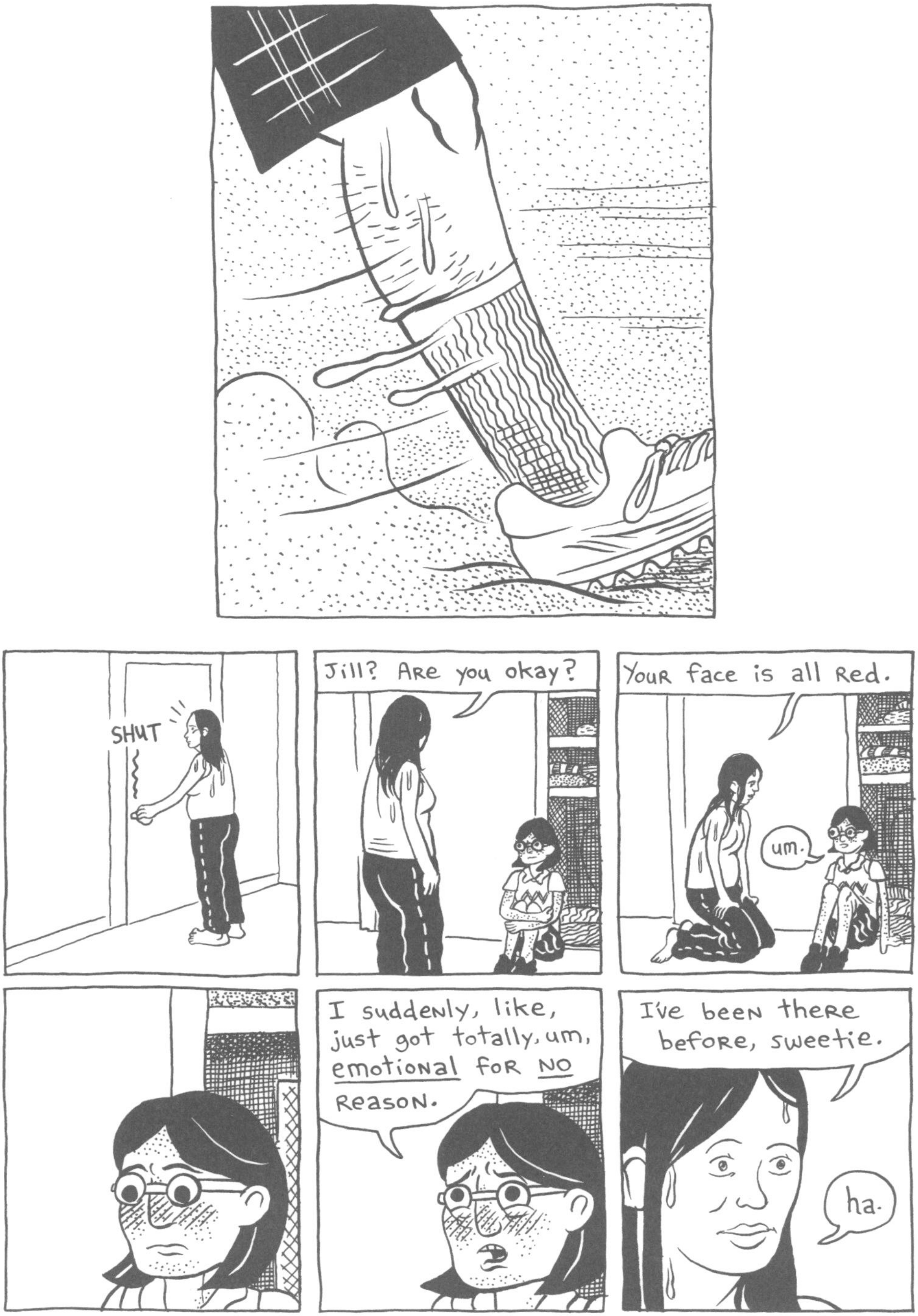
SHUT
Jill? Are you okay?
Your face is all Red.
um.
I suddenly, like, just got totally, um, emotional for NO Reason.
I've been there before, sweetie.
ha.

WIPE
I was so NERVOUS, I-
I know,
They got it. Let's go home.

Pant
I've been feeling a lot of weird anxiety here too.
I know.
You can tell?
Sort of.
I'm gonna watch T.V. —Kill time before we leave tomorrow.
ha.
Sounds like a plan.

Why did he give it to me?
He was just trying to be nice.

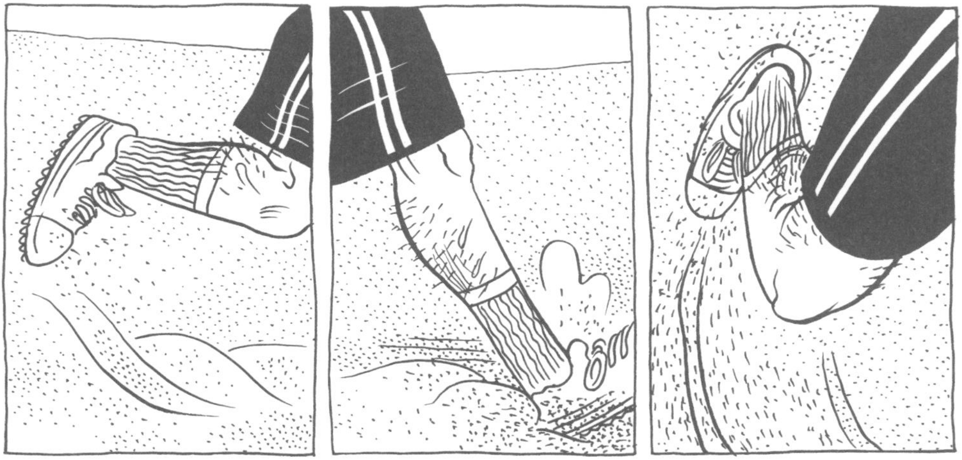

PANT
PANT

PANT
PANT
LIGHT HEADED
oh.
PANT
PANT
PANT

HOT
HOT
HOT
dry skin
CLAMMY DRY_SKIN
ah.
SIT.

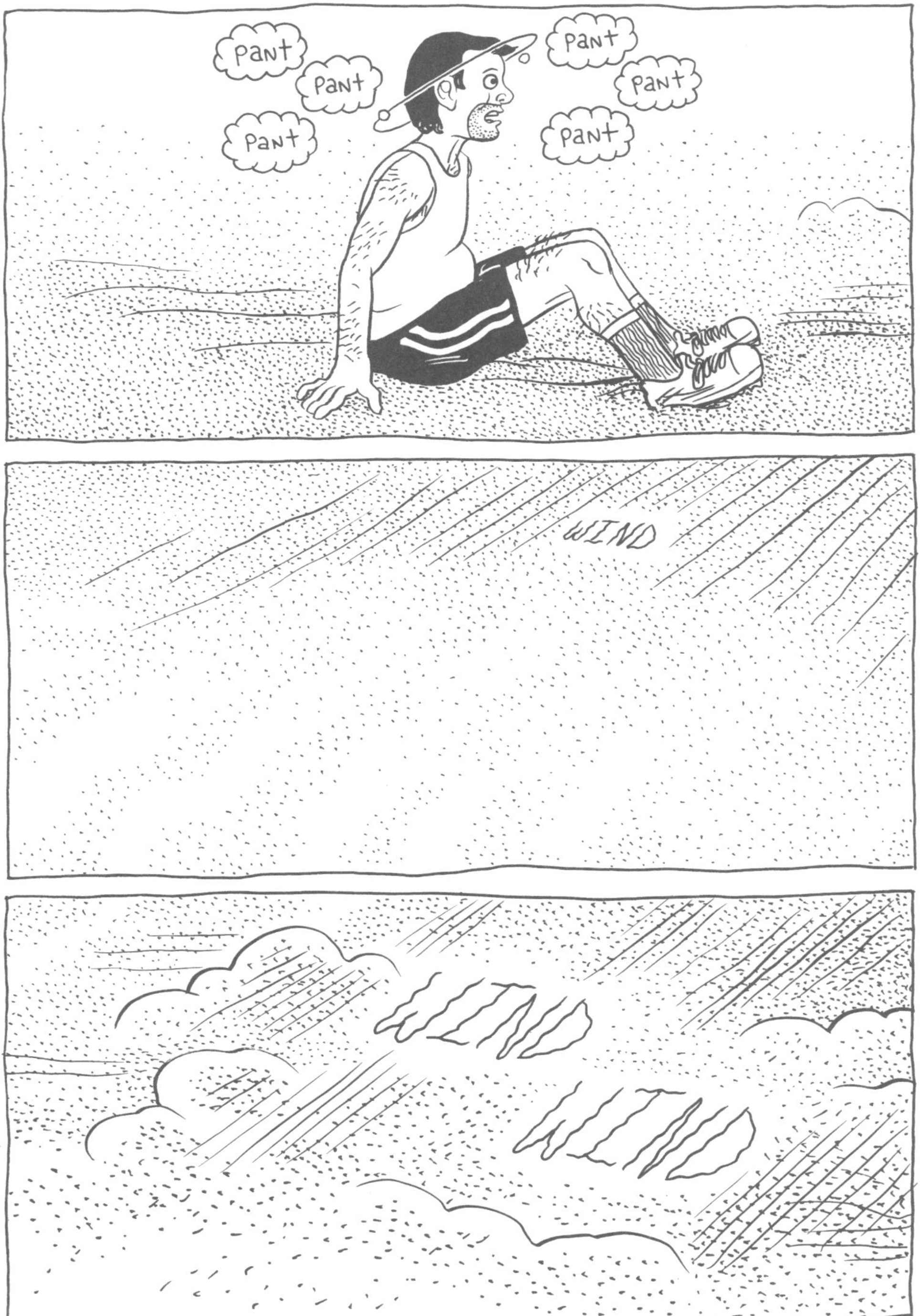
pant
pant
pant
pant
pant
pant
WIND

HEAT HEAT HEAT HEAT HEAT HEAT HEAT HEAT HEAT
=BREATHES IN.
HEAT HEAT HEAT HEAT HEAT HEAT HEAT HEAT HEAT HEAT HEAT HEAT
Enh.
STANDS
Pant
STUMBLE
Pant
pant
STUMBLE
STUMBLE

PANT
BLOWN-OUT VISION
STUMBLE
TUNNEL VISION

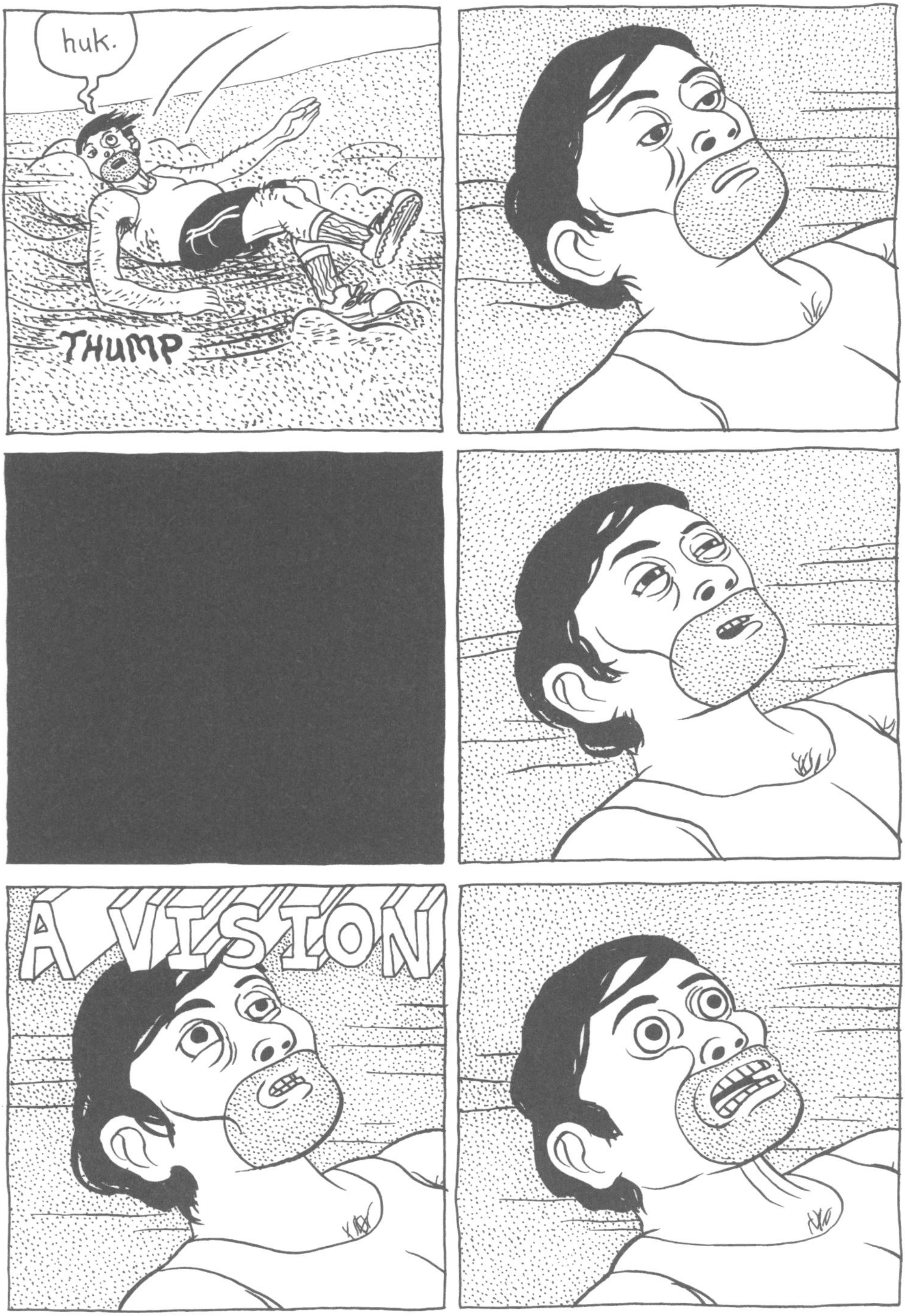
huk.
THUMP
A VISION

ha
ha
Enh.

pant.
pant.

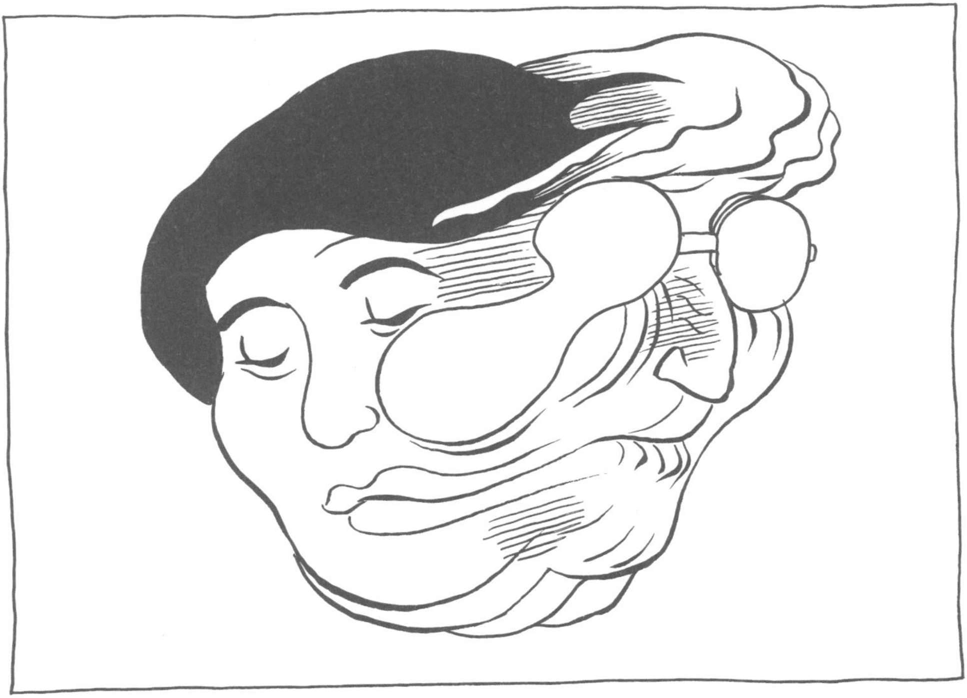

Pant.
pant.
pant.
pant.
pant.

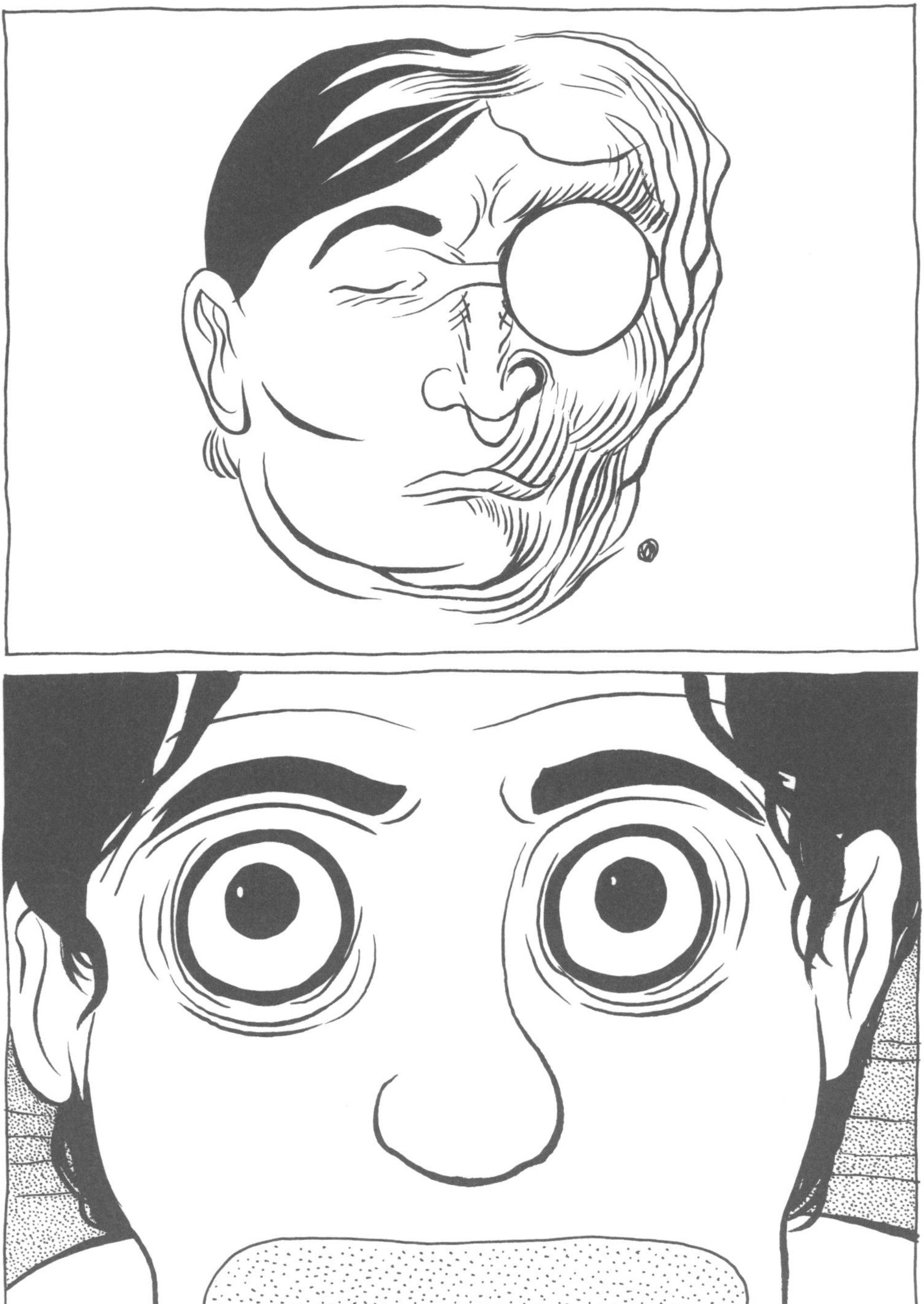

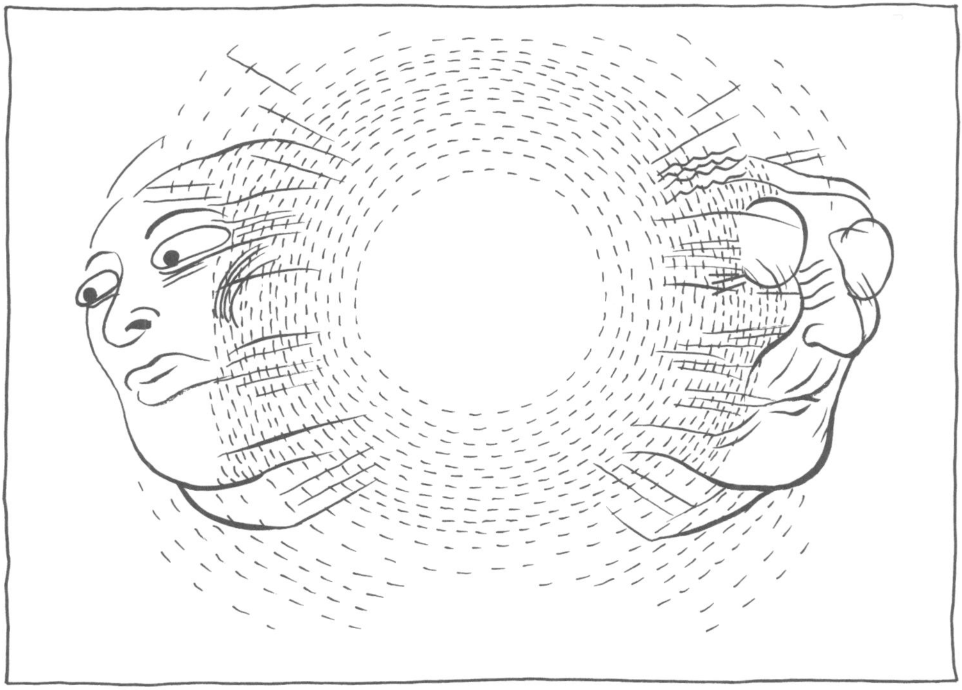

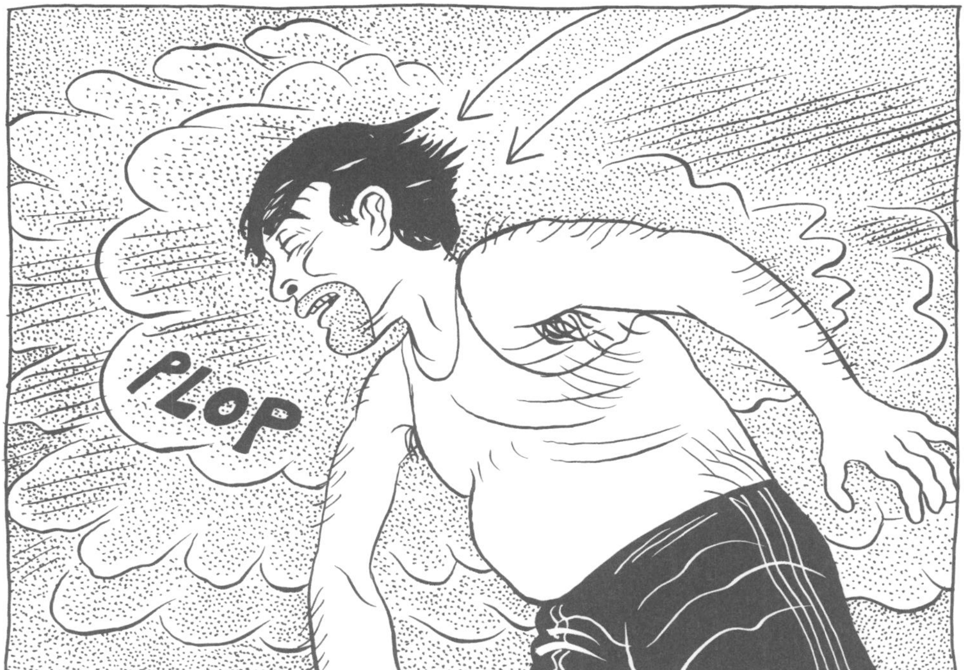
PLOP

BREATHES IN.
BREATHES OUT.
BREATHES IN.
BREATHES OUT.
SWEATING AGAIN.

Enh.
Pant
Pant
Pant
hoo.
STUMBLE
STUMBLE

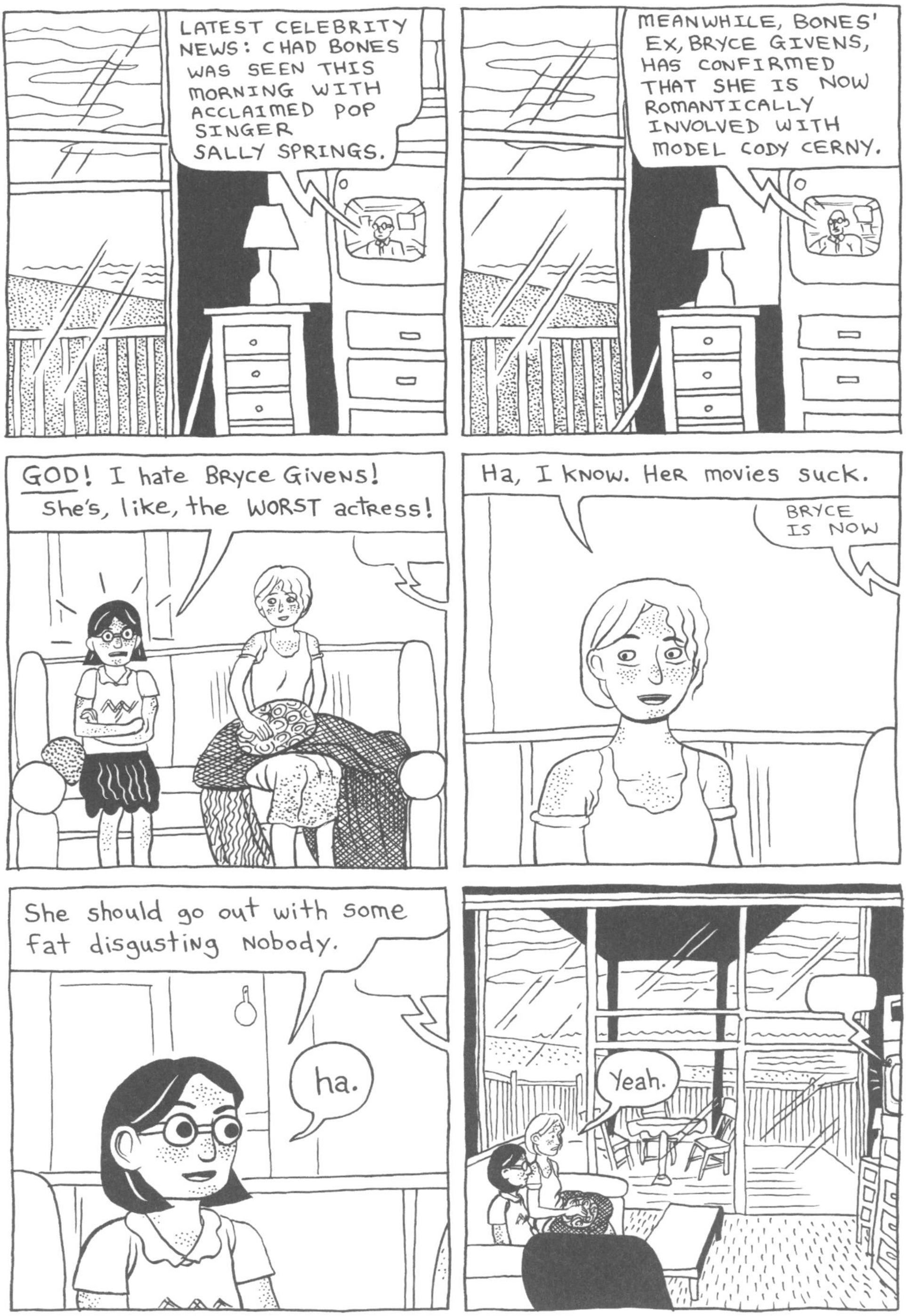
LATEST CELEBRITY NEWS: CHAD BONES WAS SEEN THIS MORNING WITH ACCLAIMED POP SINGER SALLY SPRINGS.
MEANWHILE, BONES' EX, BRYCE GIVENS, HAS CONFIRMED THAT SHE IS NOW ROMANTICALLY INVOLVED WITH MODEL CODY CERNY.
GOD! I hate Bryce Givens! She's, like, the WORST actress!
Ha, I know. Her movies suck.
BRYCE IS NOW
She should go out with some fat disgusting Nobody.
ha.
Yeah.

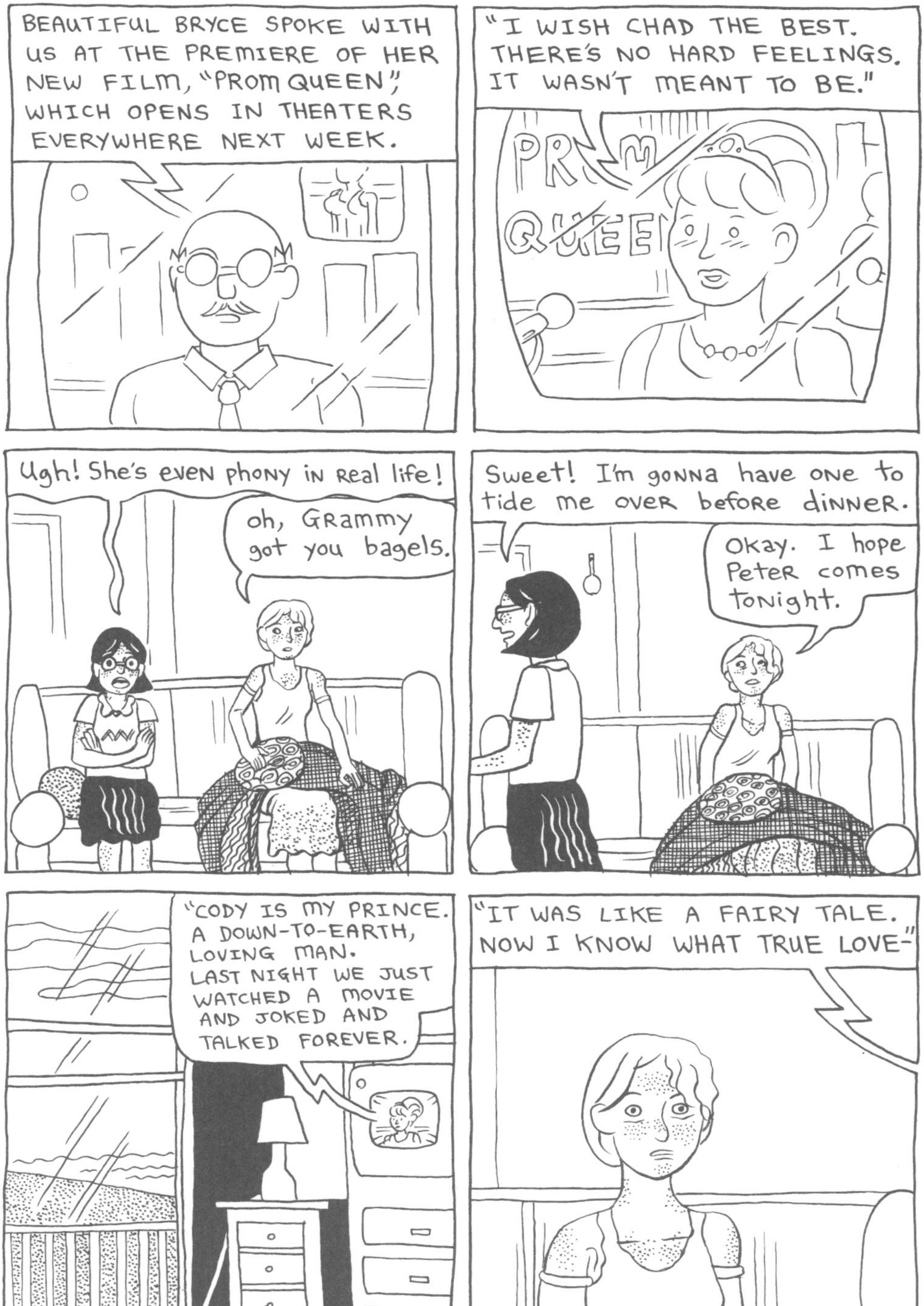
BEAUTIFUL BRYCE SPOKE WITH US AT THE PREMIERE OF HER NEW FILM, "PROM QUEEN", WHICH OPENS IN THEATERS EVERYWHERE NEXT WEEK.
"I WISH CHAD THE BEST. THERE'S NO HARD FEELINGS. IT WASN'T MEANT TO BE."
PROM QUEEN
Ugh! She's even phony in real life!
oh, Grammy got you bagels.
Sweet! I'm gonna have one to tide me over before dinner.
Okay. I hope Peter comes tonight.
"CODY IS MY PRINCE. A DOWN-TO-EARTH, LOVING MAN. LAST NIGHT WE JUST WATCHED A MOVIE AND JOKED AND TALKED FOREVER.
"IT WAS LIKE A FAIRY TALE. NOW I KNOW WHAT TRUE LOVE-"

STUMBLE
STUMBLE
DENNIS?!

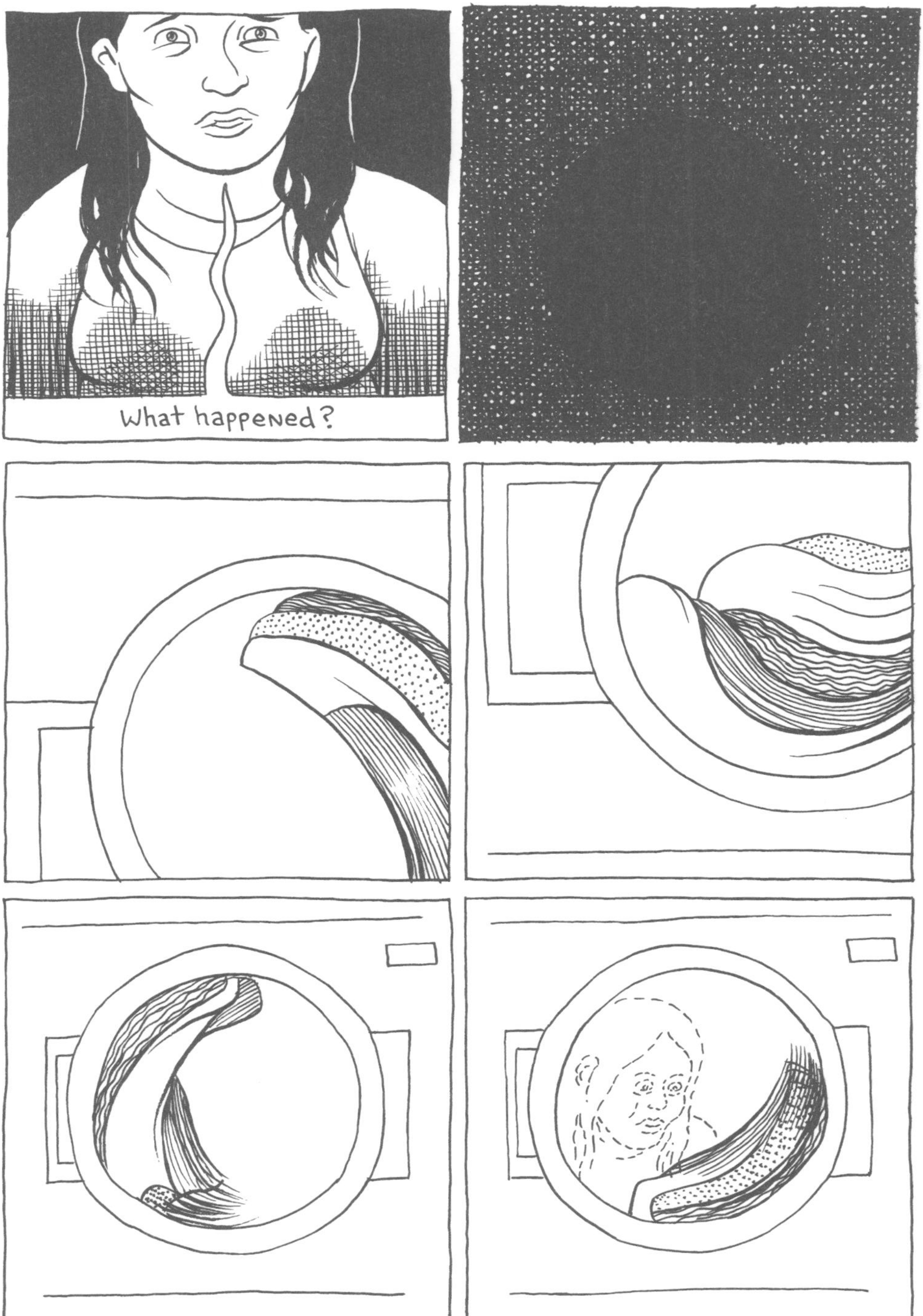
What happened?

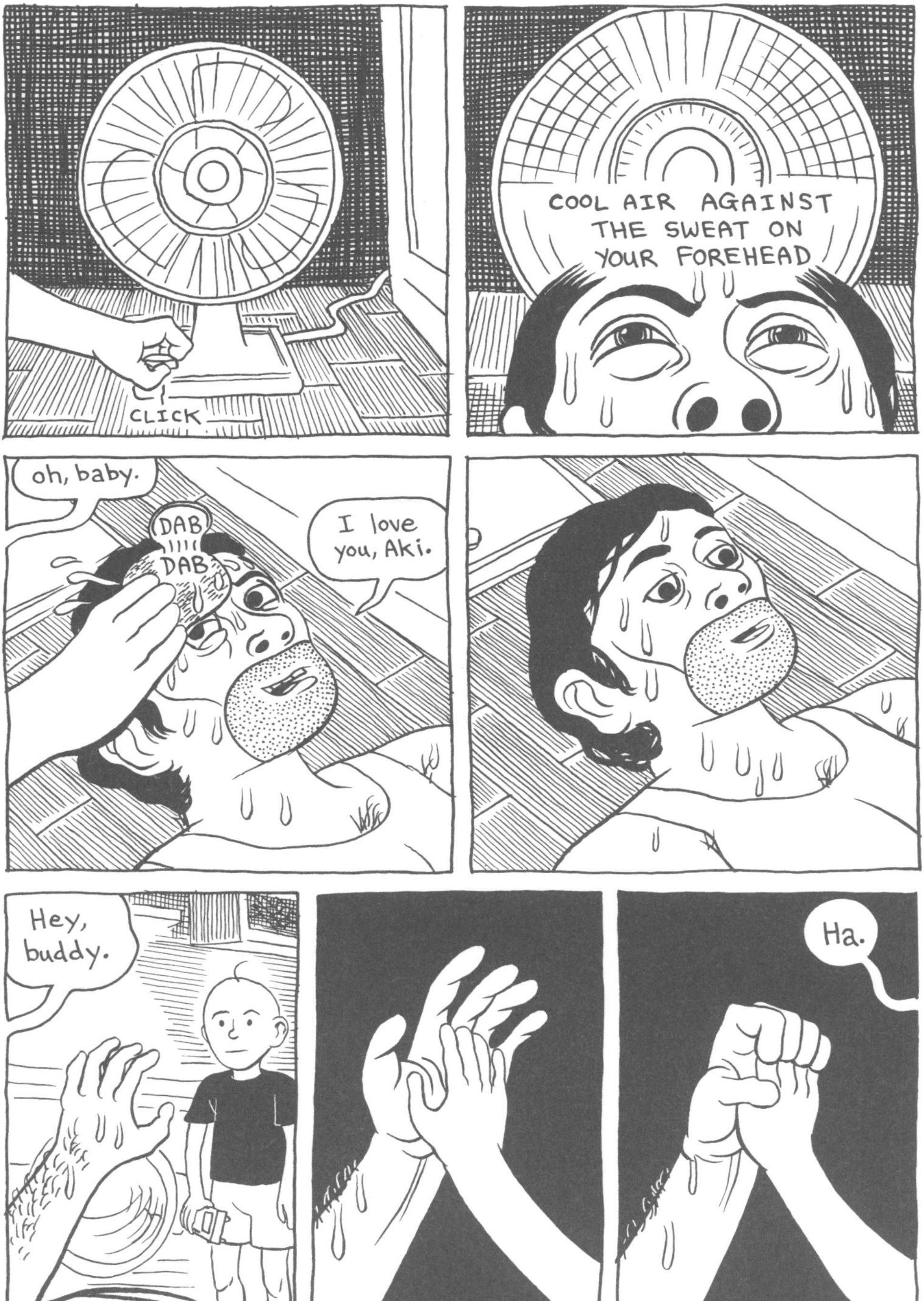
CLICK
COOL AIR AGAINST THE SWEAT ON YOUR FOREHEAD
oh, baby.
DAB DAB
I love you, Aki.
Hey, buddy.
Ha.

I was RUNNING, and, something happened.
It was like a "RUNNER'S high."
My head cleared.
I could feel my body.
Maybe it was just the heat.
I don't KNOW.
But I had a vision.
I KNOW why they're divorcing. It was like a weird puzzle and my mind filled the gaps.

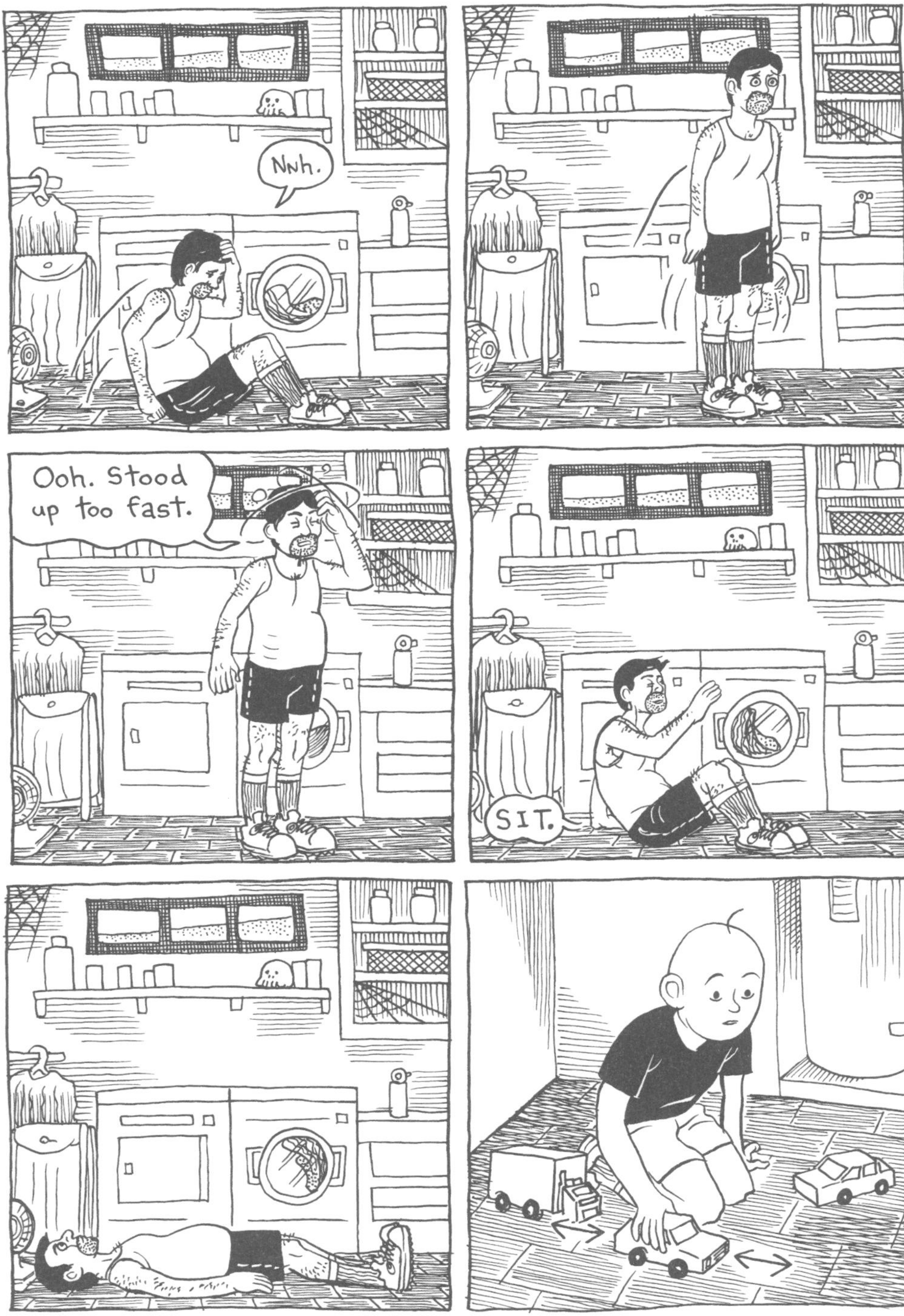
Nnh.
Ooh. Stood up too fast.
SIT.

ROLL
STOPS
Mom loves us kids. She stuck through it for us. But she, like, hates us too. Because we ruled her life for so long, you know?
She finds marriage claustrophobic. That she got into it too soon, that, somehow, she was never "free." She doesn't share the concept of a FAMILY.
She sees people as seperate beings. No glue.
And now that we're grown up, she can be "free" again.
Start her life.

D- DENNIS.
Maybe she genuinely loved Dad at first. I don't know.
Maybe she's been with other guys. Flirting around.
Probably.
I don't know who divorced who.
But it's Mom's FAULT.
um.
DENNIS.

Do you honestly think you're talking about Mom right now?
about Maggie?
Because it doesn't sound like her at all.

RING RING
RING
RING
RING

RING-
Yeah. And Kat's coming too. ...
Thanks, Claire.
BEEP

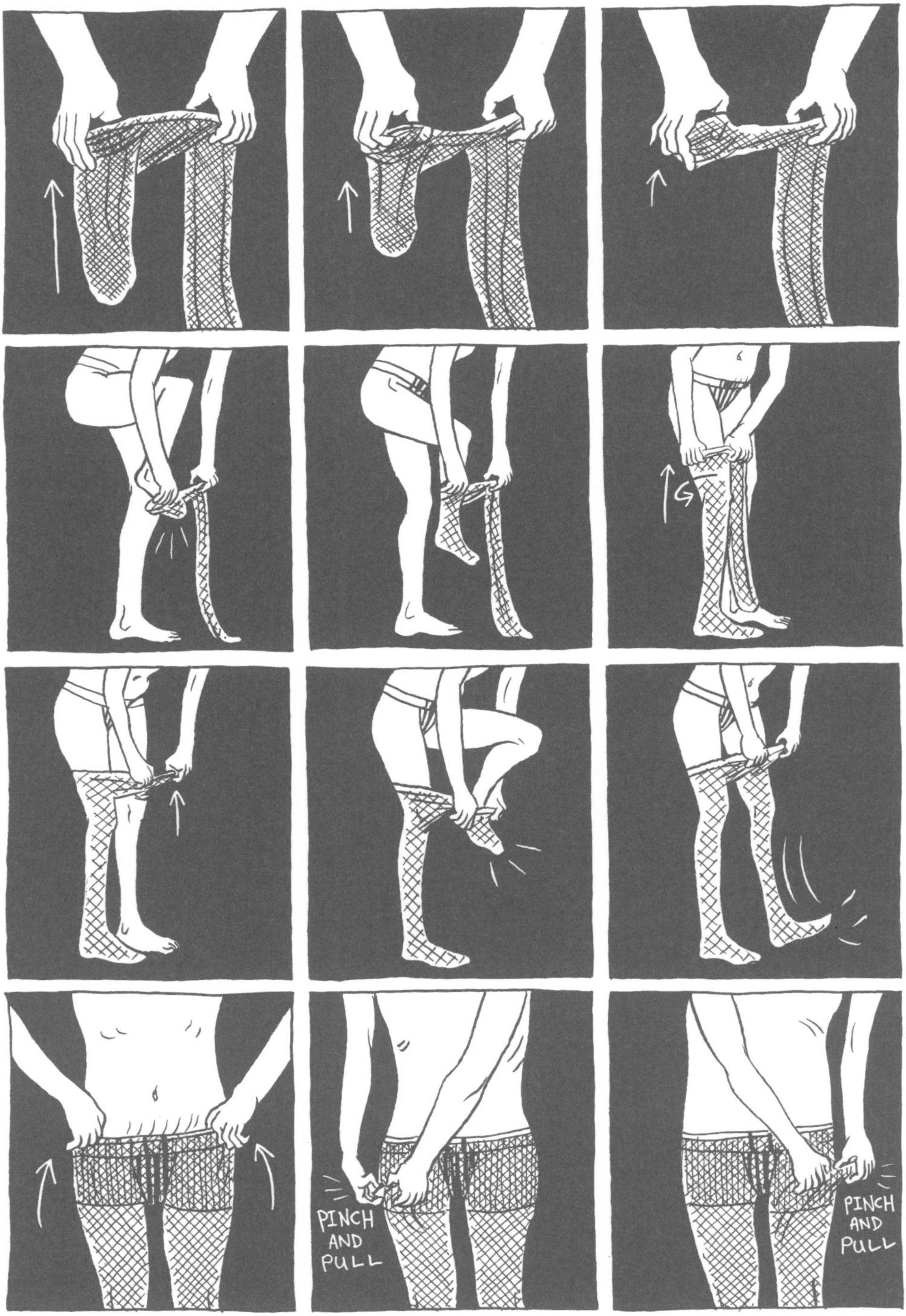
PINCH AND PULL
PINCH AND PULL

You were amazing with Paul today.
No.
You were the hero.
Will your parents like this?
Of course. It's pretty.
Nice color.
It's white.
You look good in anything.

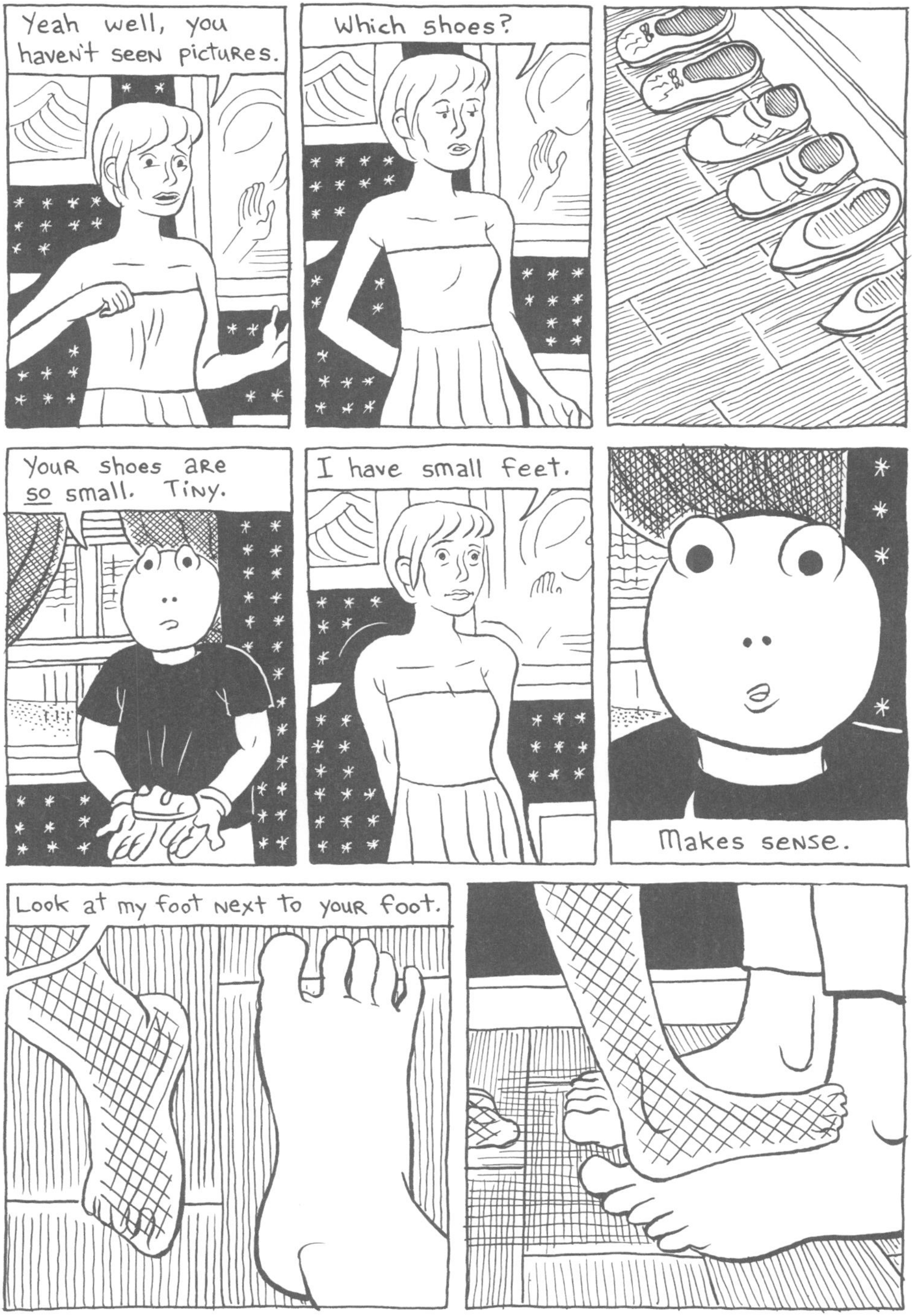

Yeah well, you haven't seen pictures.
Which shoes?
Your shoes are so small. Tiny.
I have small feet.
Makes sense.
Look at my foot next to your foot.

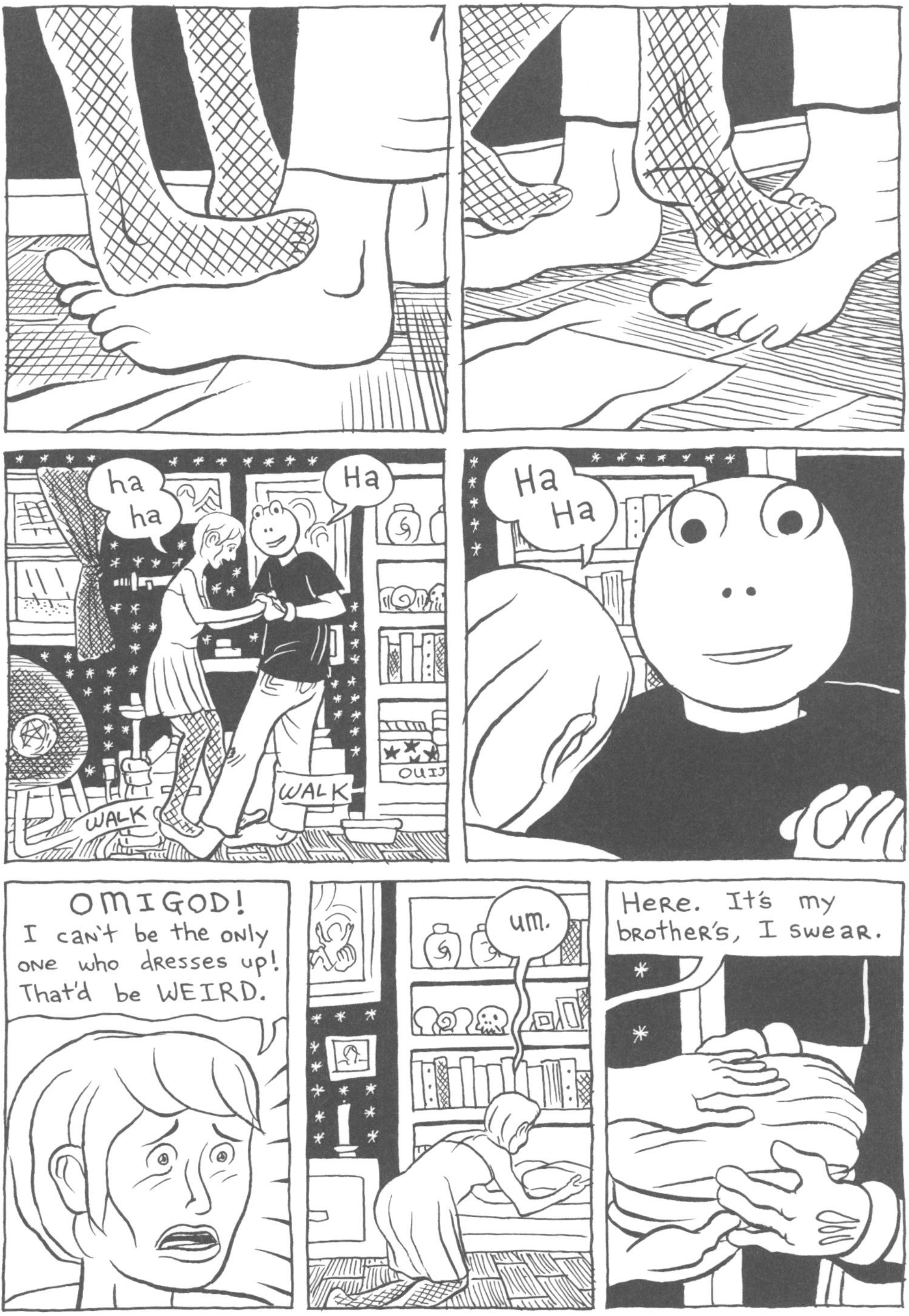

ha
ha
Ha
WALK
WALK
OUIJ
Ha
Ha
OMIGOD! I can't be the only one who dresses up! That'd be WEIRD.
um.
Here. It's my brother's, I swear.

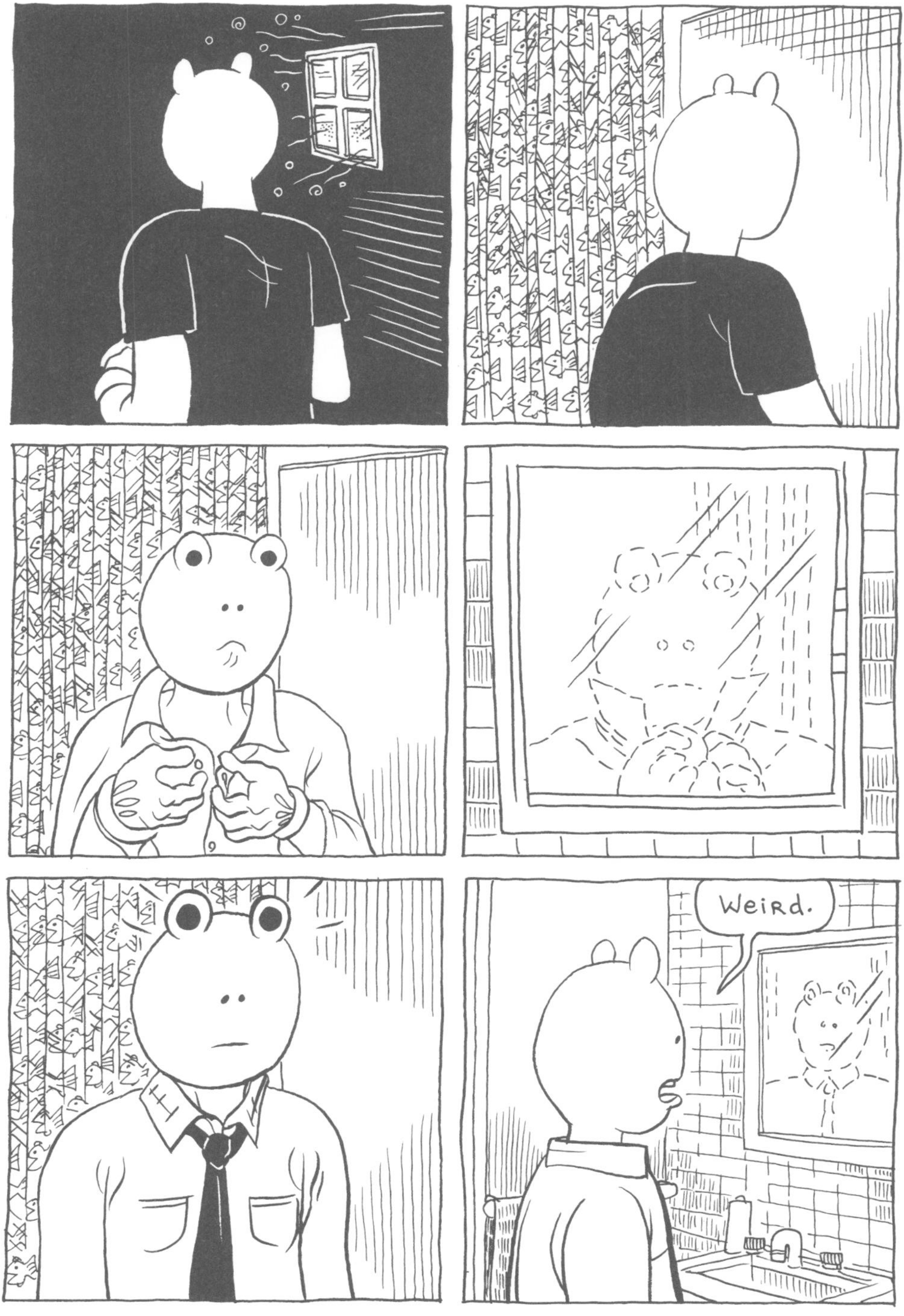
Weird.

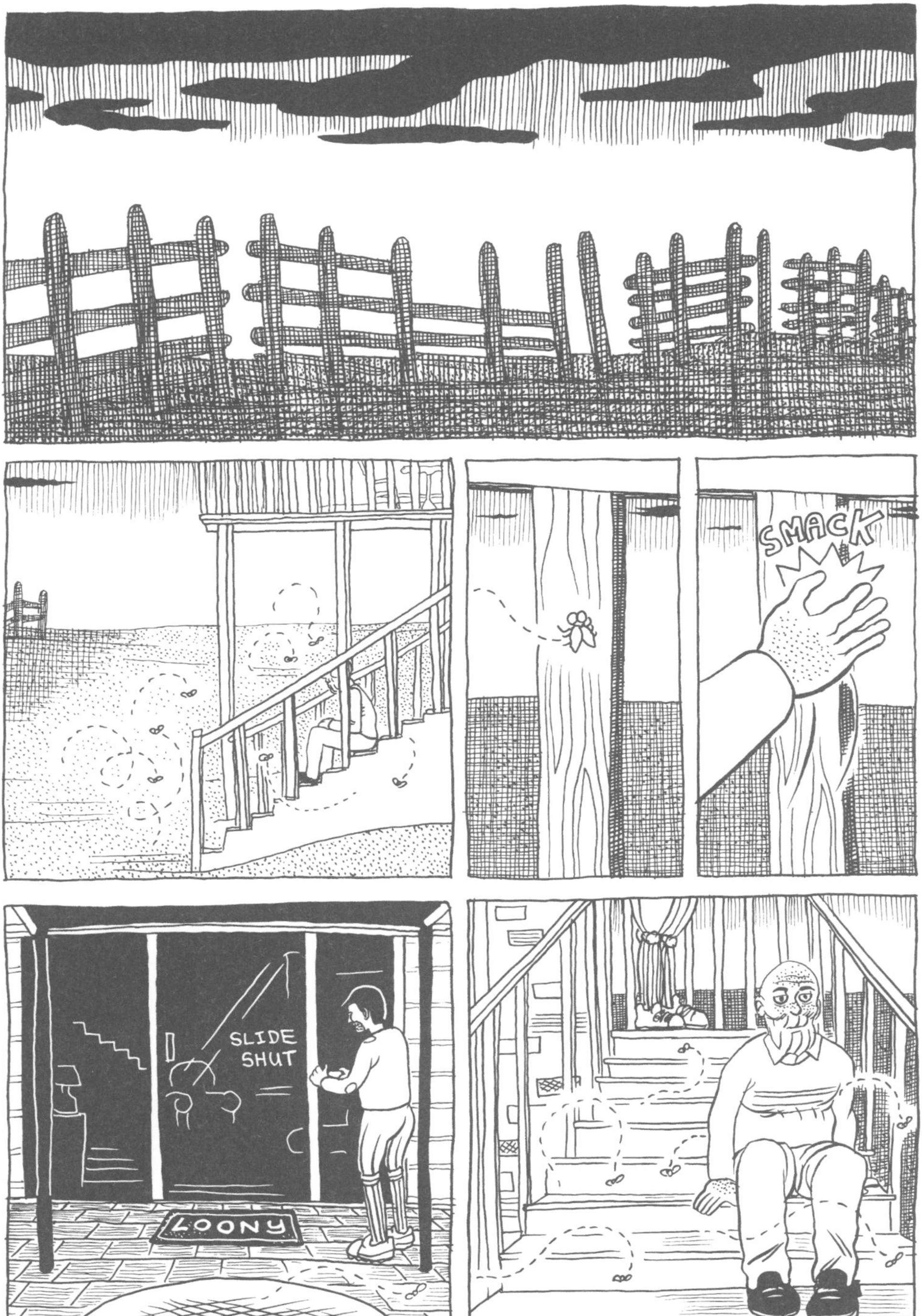
SMACK
SLIDE SHUT
LOONY

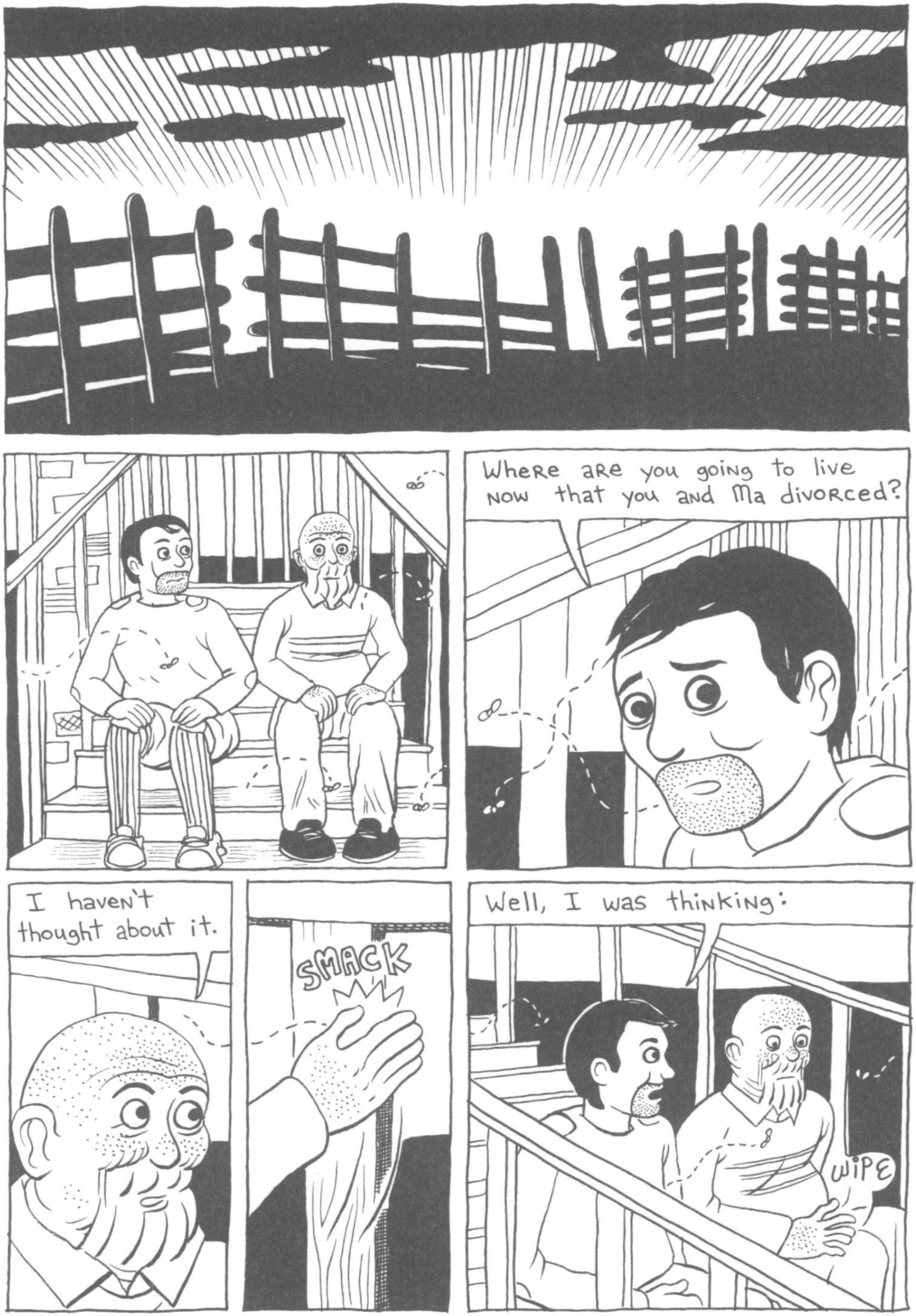
Where are you going to live now that you and Ma divorced?
I haven't thought about it.
SMACK
Well, I was thinking:
WIPE

PURPLES
PURPLES
PINKS
PINKS
PINKS
Why don't you live with Aki and I?
Until you get your feet on the ground, you know? We have a mattress—better than a couch, right?
We could take some of your things in our car on the ride back, and then Mom could mail the rest.
What do you think?
SHOO

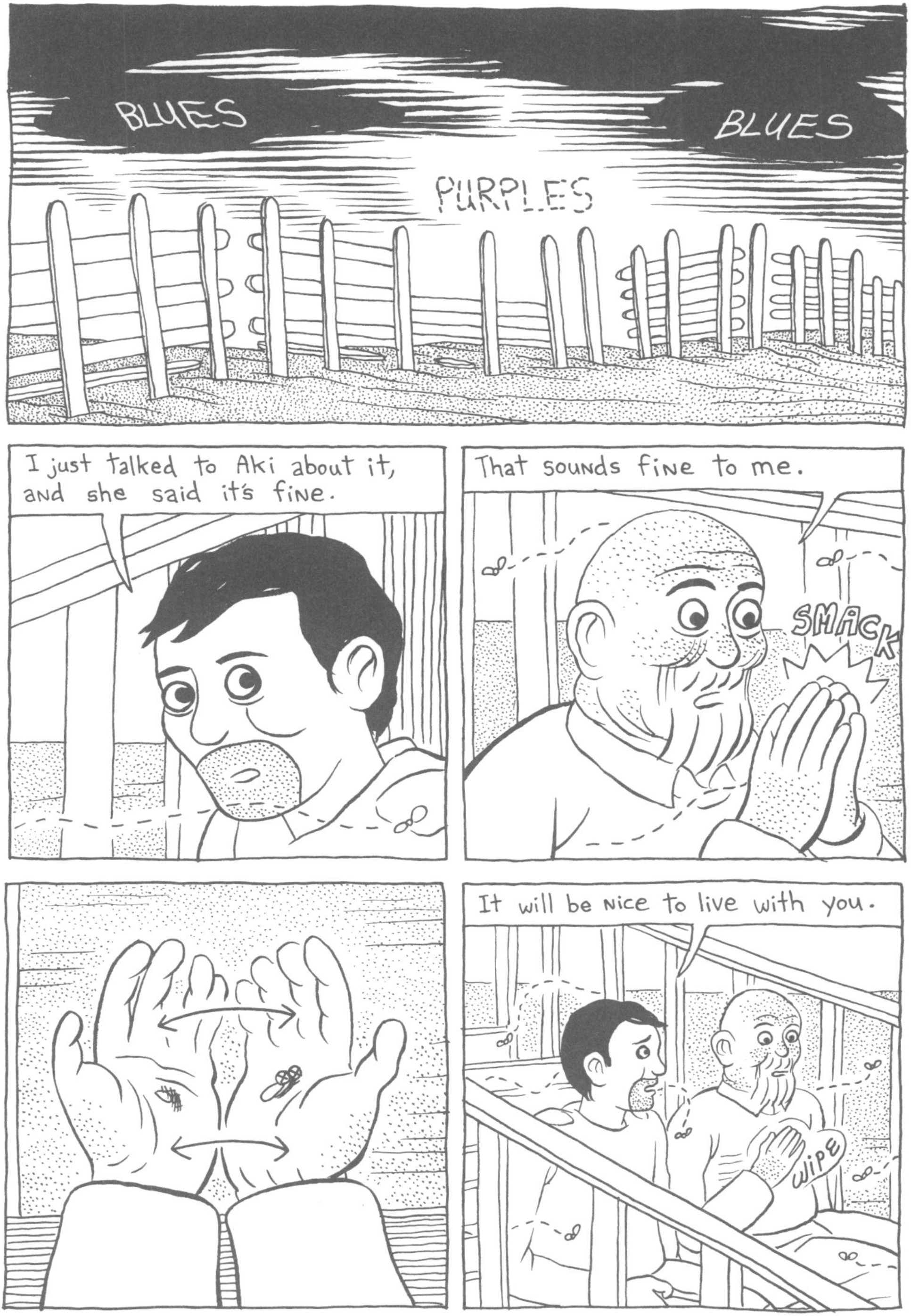

BLUES
BLUES
PURPLES
I just talked to Aki about it, and she said it's fine.
That sounds fine to me.
SMACK
It will be nice to live with you.
WIPE

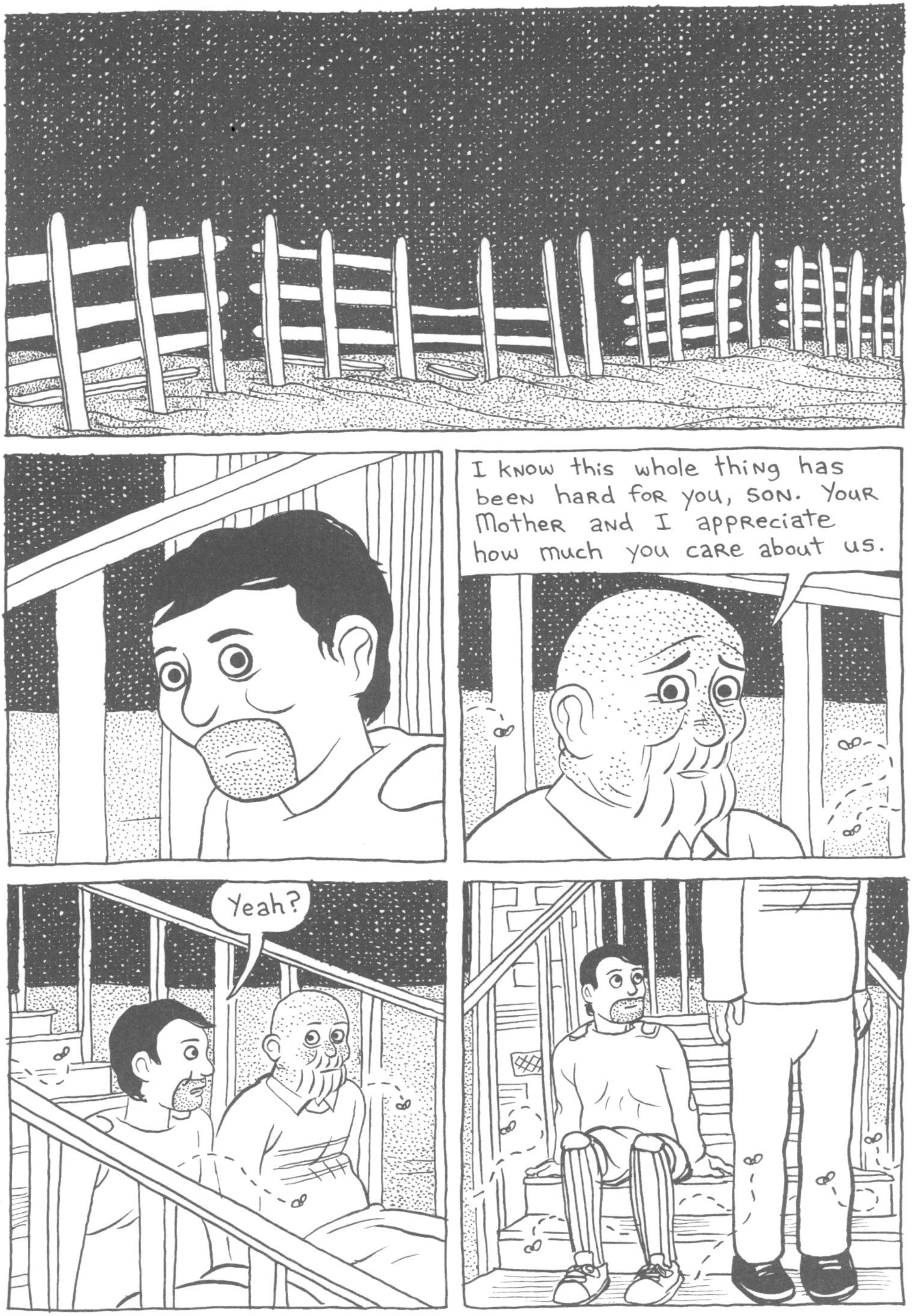
I know this whole thing has been hard for you, son. Your Mother and I appreciate how much you care about us.
Yeah?

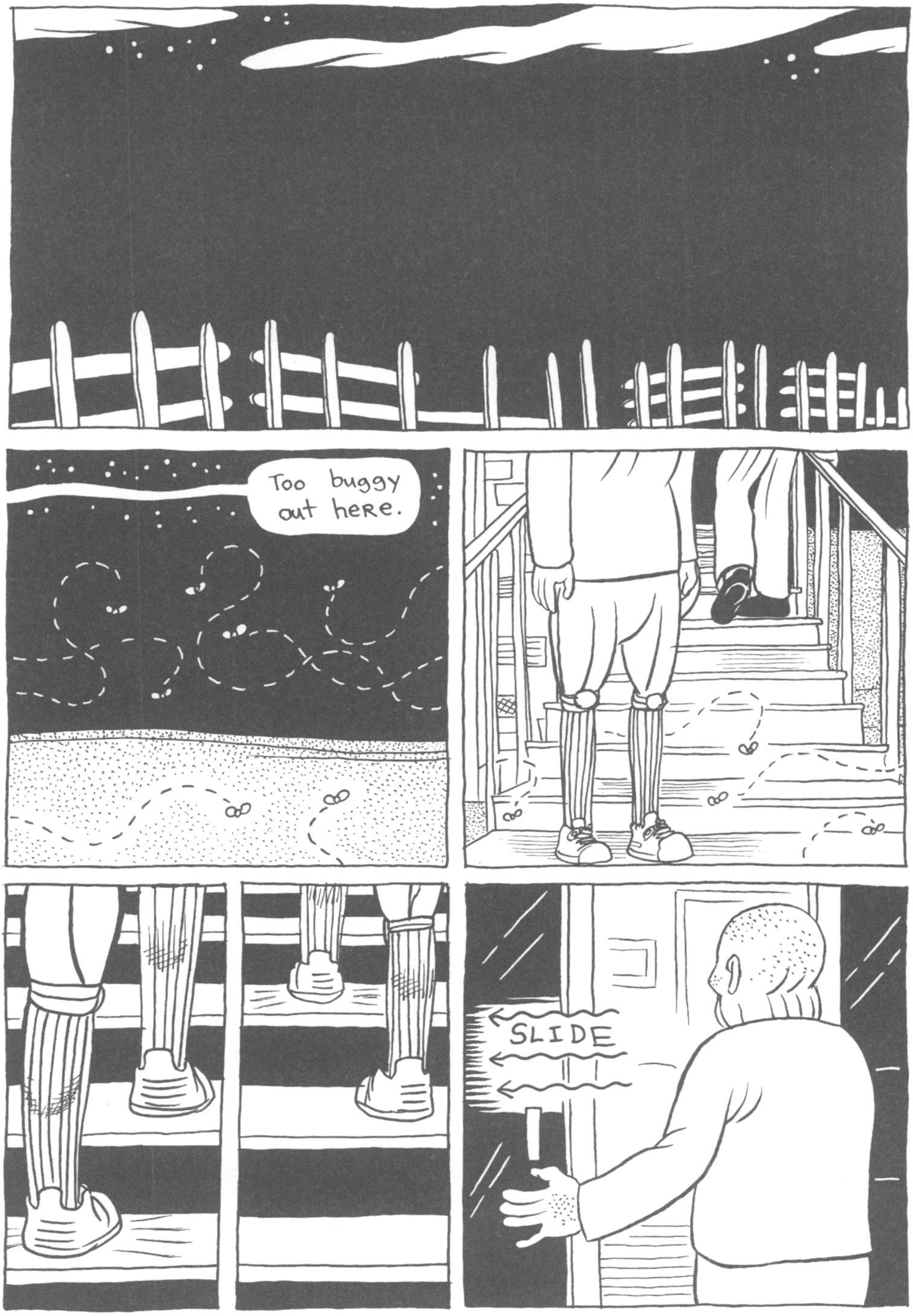
Too buggy out here.
SLIDE

Jill! Come inside to help cook.
Just a sec.

SHUT
flick
flick
creepy.

ah.
BREATHES IN.
Love is in the air.
uh-huh.

POUR
OPEN
SHUT

Kat, this is my Mom and my brother, Dennis.
Nice to meet you.
Hi.
Sister-in-law Aki.
Hi.
Hi. Kat.
My Dad and my sister, Claire.
Kat?
Hi.
And my niece, Jill.
Have we met before?
You look familiar.
Do you know Andy?
Petey?
What?
Your lady's a LOOKER, bro.
GRIP
uh... thanks.
Good work.
SQUEEZE

What would you like to drink, Peter?
Just a beer.
OPEN
SIP
And how about you, Kat? We have Merlot, Shiraz, Chardonnay, -
Ha. No- I'm nineteen.
HUK!
You're NINETEEN?
I'll be twenty in sixty-five days.
How old are you?
I'm twenty-six.
Oh, shit - that means that when I was eighteen, you were...

um
ELEVEN. Eleven years old! That's elementary school.
oh, shit.
I'm not eleven years old NOW
Ha.
I don't get it. How do you live by your-self? Have a house?
I live with my Dad. He's on a business trip right now.
So THAT's the room? Why didn't you tell me sooner?
I didn't know you were older — What's the big deal anyway? I don't care.
I'm not a creep now, am I?
I don't think that you're a creep.
SHRUG
DINNER'S READY!!!
SCOOT

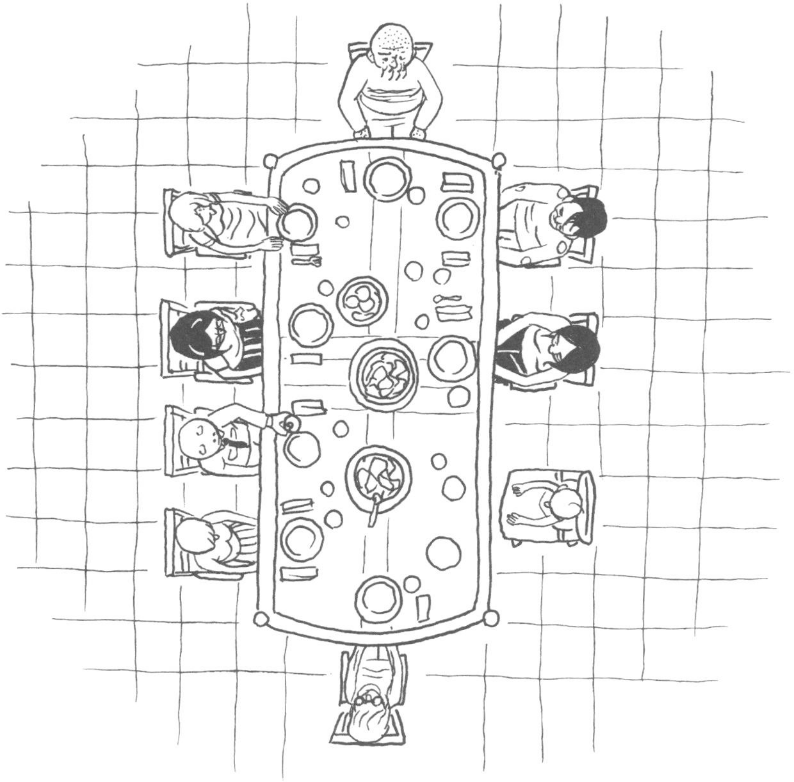

And then there was one night when Dennis came home so drunk he puked into the plant in the living room.
Ha.
Ha Ha
I don't think this is suitable dinner conversation.
Yeah. Ha ha ha.
I don't remember that at all.
Obviously.
I guess he was sober enough to decide to water the plants. Ha.
Ha.
Did the plant die?
I don't know.
Dennis was a good kid, though. Really.
In scouts once, I forgot to pack enough socks and my tent got rained in. Flooded. So I asked Dennis if he had any extra socks.
Ha, Ha. I remember this story. Jeez.
Go on.
He said he did and gave me a pair.
The next day, during a hike, I noticed he had tighty-whities wrapped around his feet.
Ha Ha.
Ha Ha Ha Ha
He'd given me his only pair.

Ha.
Ha.
Dennis got his trouble-maker spirit from his father, you know.
What do you mean?
Well, David was always doing crazy things. Ha.
'cuz my parents, well—they didn't particularly like David—
AT FIRST.
So he was always sending messages, climbing up to my window at night.
How Romantic.
Or just throwing things up to tap my window and ask me to sneak out.
-Only, once, he accidently hit my Dad's office window. Ha.
Yeah...
Ha. What'd you do?
I jumped into the bushes and hoped he didn't see me.
Ha. Ha
One time I was hiding in Maggie's closet and her Dad actually opened the door! Ha.
He didn't notice me, though. I did my best coat impression and held my breath.
Ha. Ha.

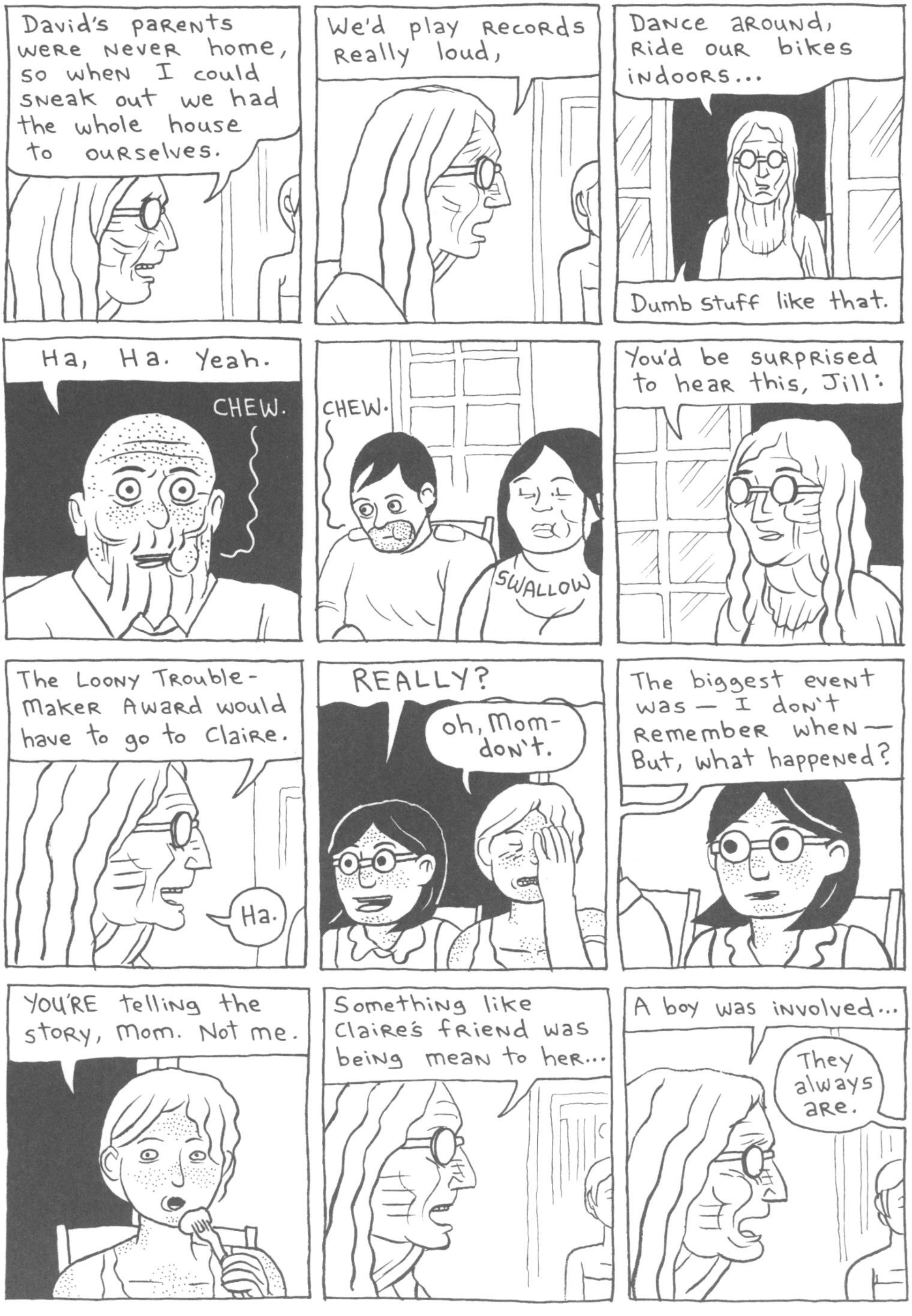
David's parents were never home, so when I could sneak out we had the whole house to ourselves.
We'd play records really loud,
Dance around, ride our bikes indoors...
Dumb stuff like that.
Ha, Ha. Yeah.
CHEW.
CHEW.
SWALLOW
You'd be surprised to hear this, Jill:
The Loony Trouble-maker Award would have to go to Claire.
Ha.
REALLY?
oh, Mom-don't.
The biggest event was — I don't remember when — But, what happened?
YOU'RE telling the story, Mom. Not me.
Something like Claire's friend was being mean to her...
A boy was involved...
They always are.

Anyway, Claire came home late at night. I could tell she was upset—
She ran up to her room and I heard a loud CRACK!
Ha. Ha.
What happened?
I run upstairs, open the door to her room—
First I see Claire sitting in the corner of the room,
Then I see blood on the carpet and on her hand.
What?
I turn around and see a pretty big hole in the wall.
She had just - POW! -
CLAP
Punched a hole right through the wall!
Ha Ha
What?
Like a super hero.
Why?!
CHEW
I was upset.
Ha
Ha Ha

That night David said we'd never have to worry about guys messing around with Claire.
She was "a fighter."
I never got into any fights.
Peter did, but I'm not sure "fight" is the right word for it.
Ha
Ha
Ha
Har-dee-har har.
HA
HA
Ha
You WERE feisty, though, Claire.
A lot of energy.
Always bouncing off the walls.
Ha.
Maybe.
CHEW
SWALLOW
Pass the dressing?
Italian or Ranch?
Ranch.
SQUEEZE
CHEW

So.
"so" what?
"So what" what?!
What?

You said "so what" – what don't you care about? ~~~ me?
No No No — I thought you were saying something.
Nevermind, I guess,
I should spend the night here. It's probably the last time I'll ever sleep in my room.
okay.
Will you come say "goodbye" to me tomorrow morning? I leave at, like, 8 A.M.
Of course. I have a shift tomorrow morning, but I should be able to come.

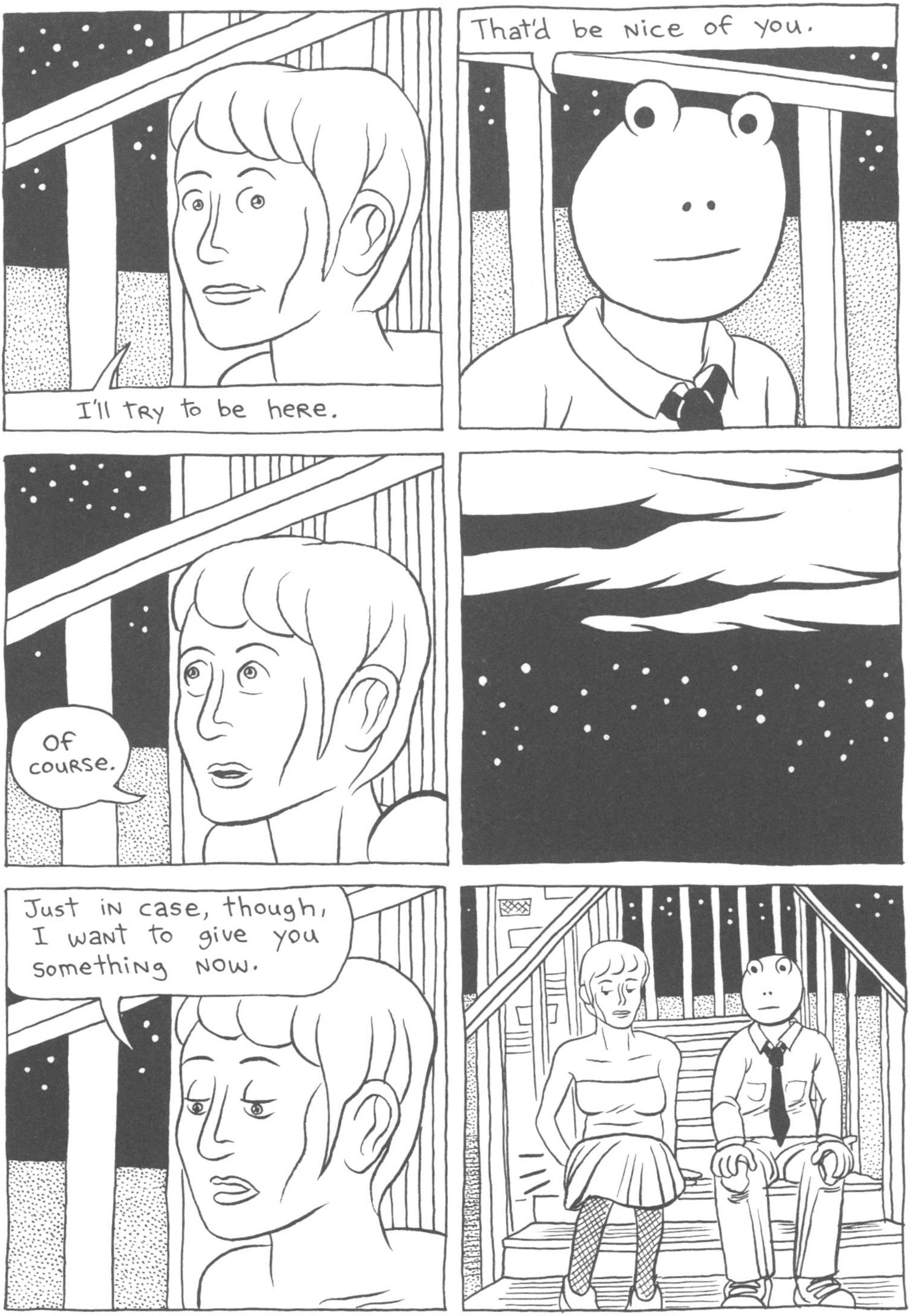
I'll try to be here.
That'd be nice of you.
Of course.
Just in case, though, I want to give you something now.

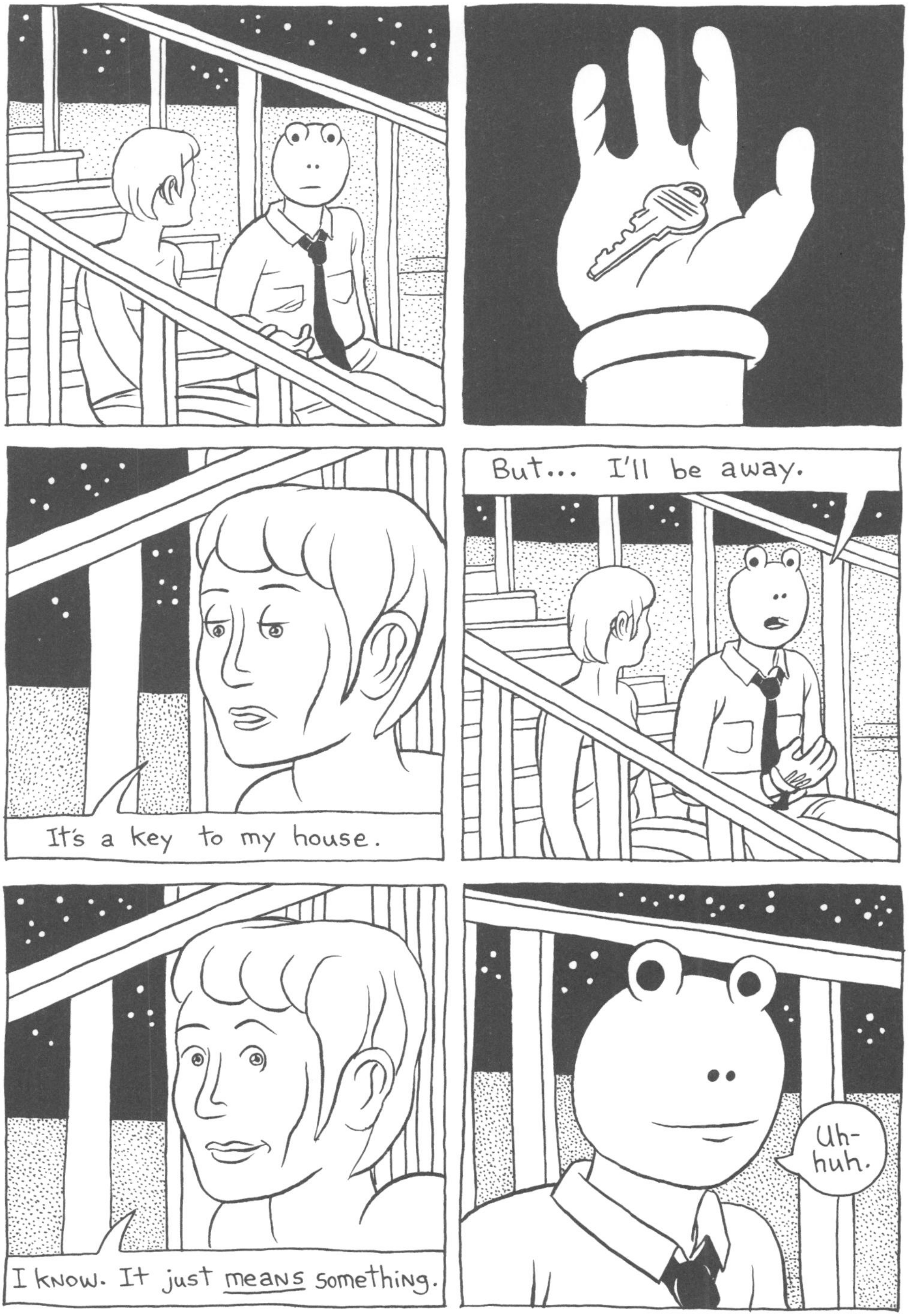
It's a key to my house.
But... I'll be away.
I know. It just means something.
Uh-huh.

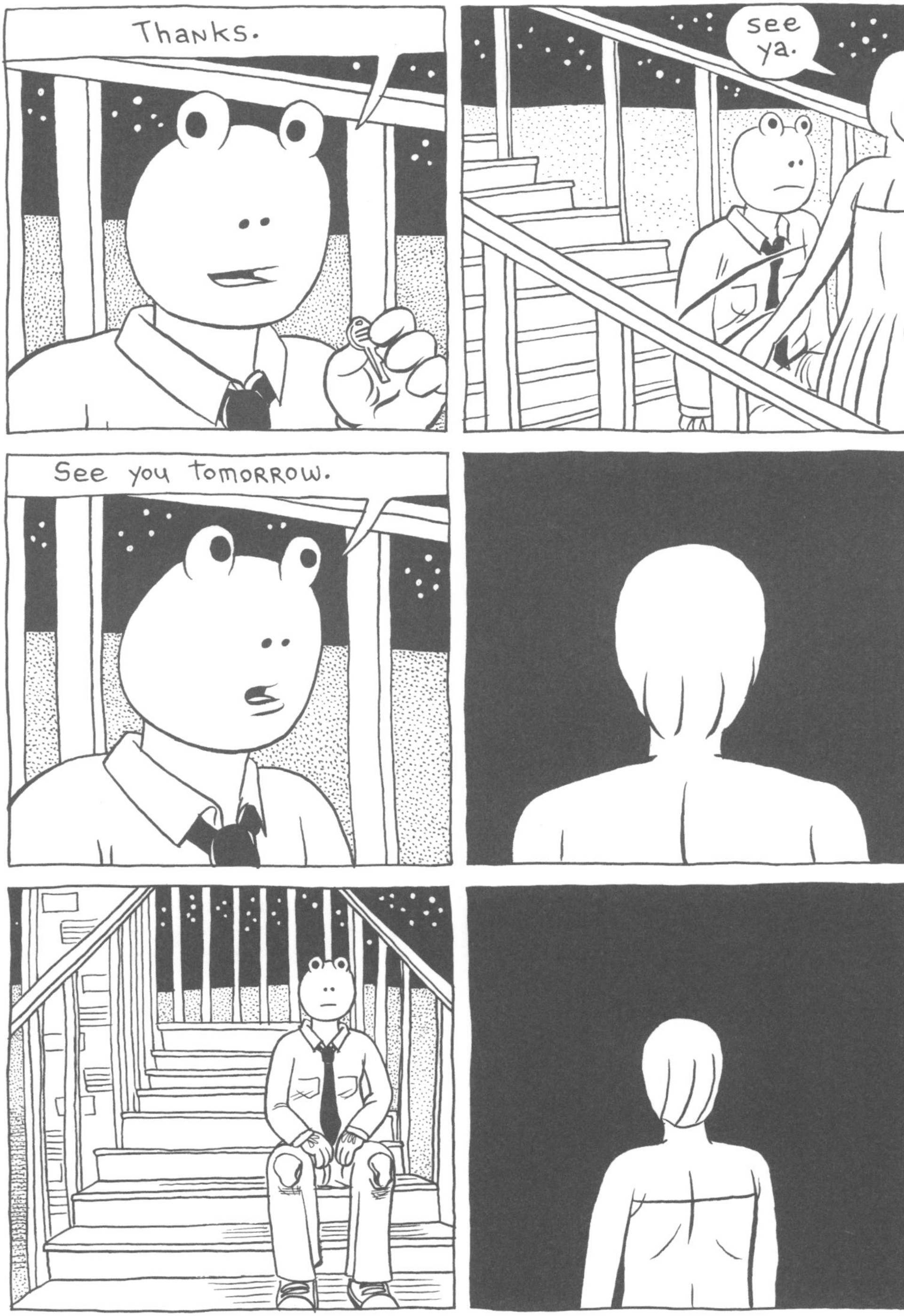
Thanks.
see ya.
See you tomorrow.

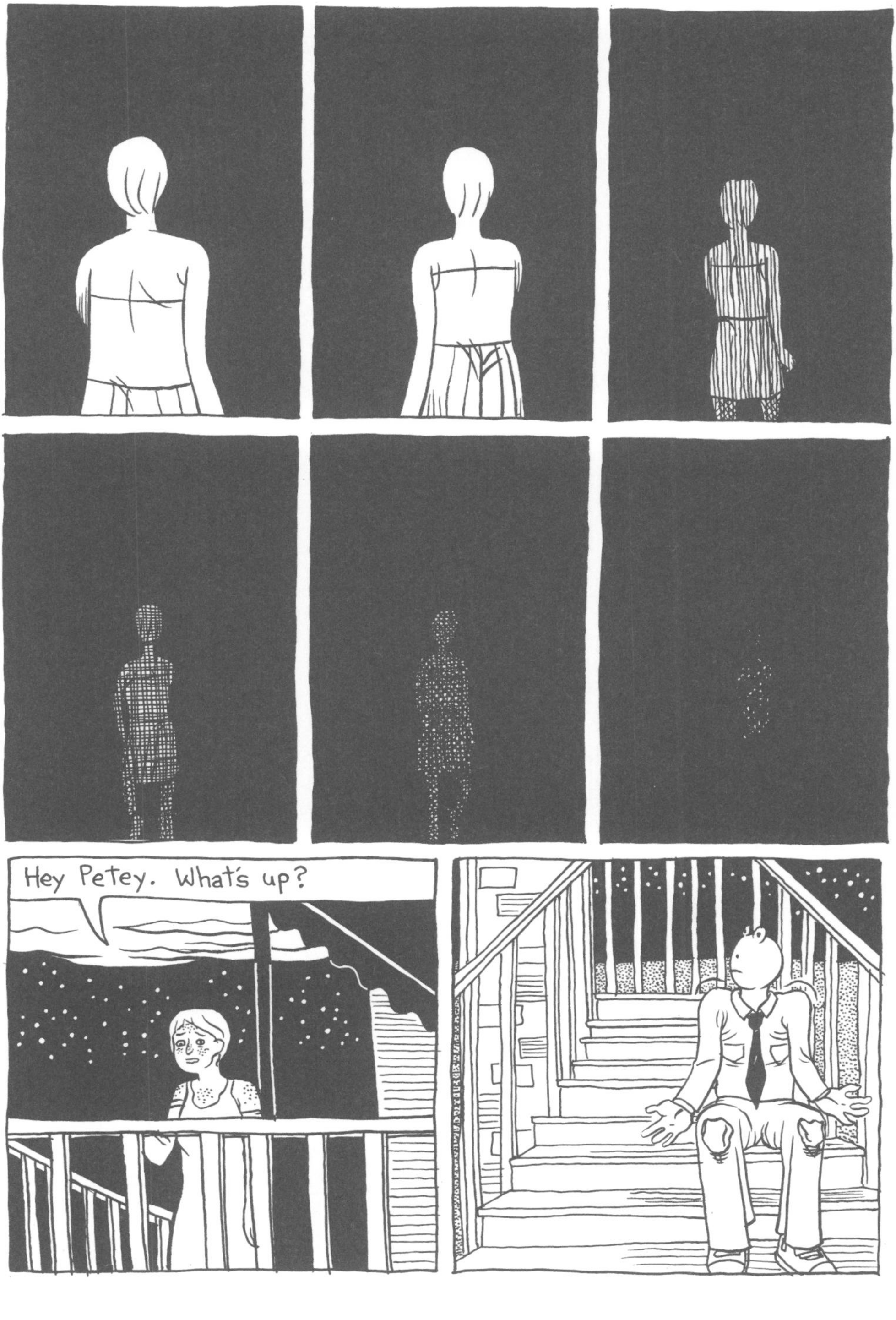
Hey Petey. What's up?

Shhhhhhhhhhhhh

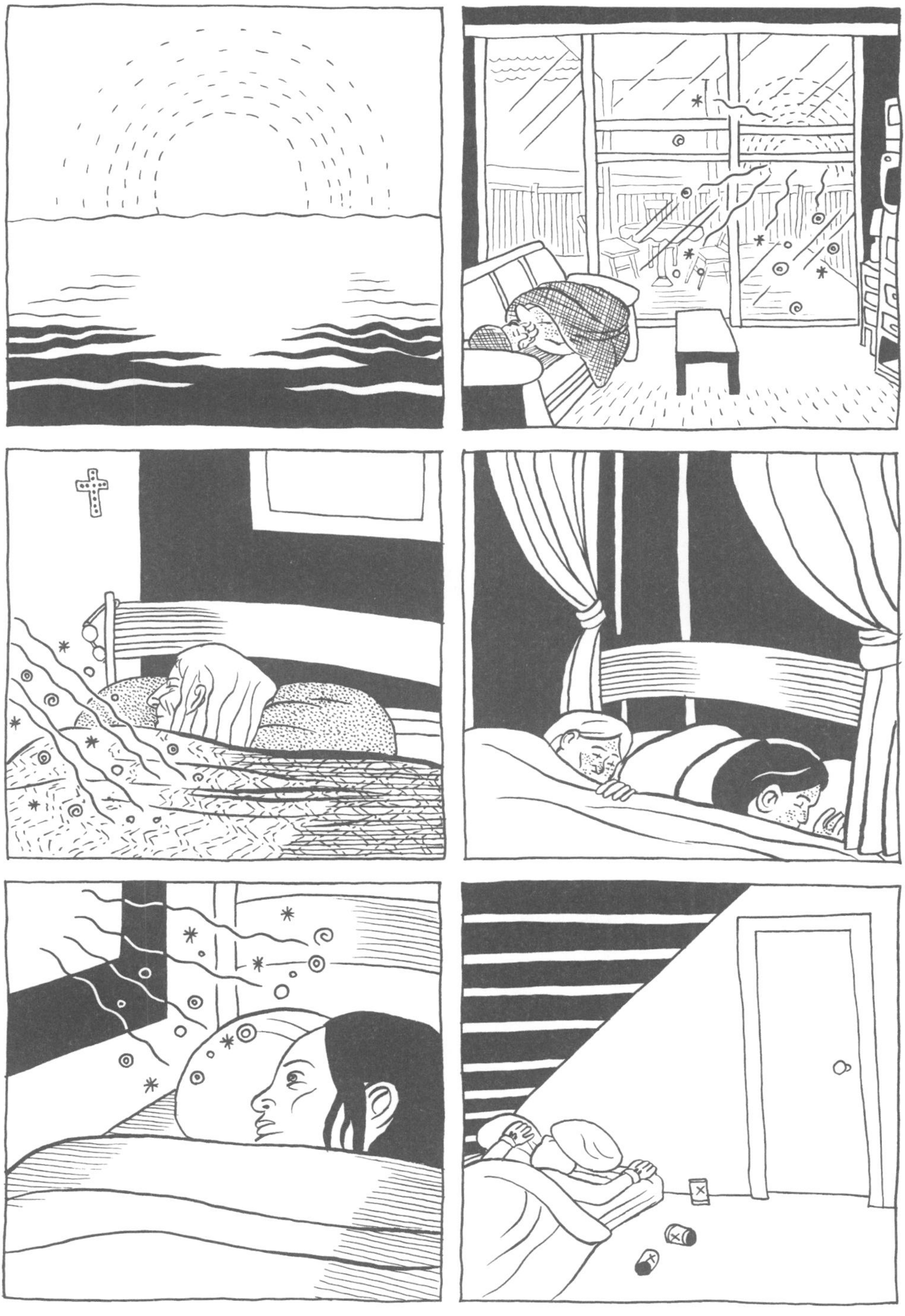

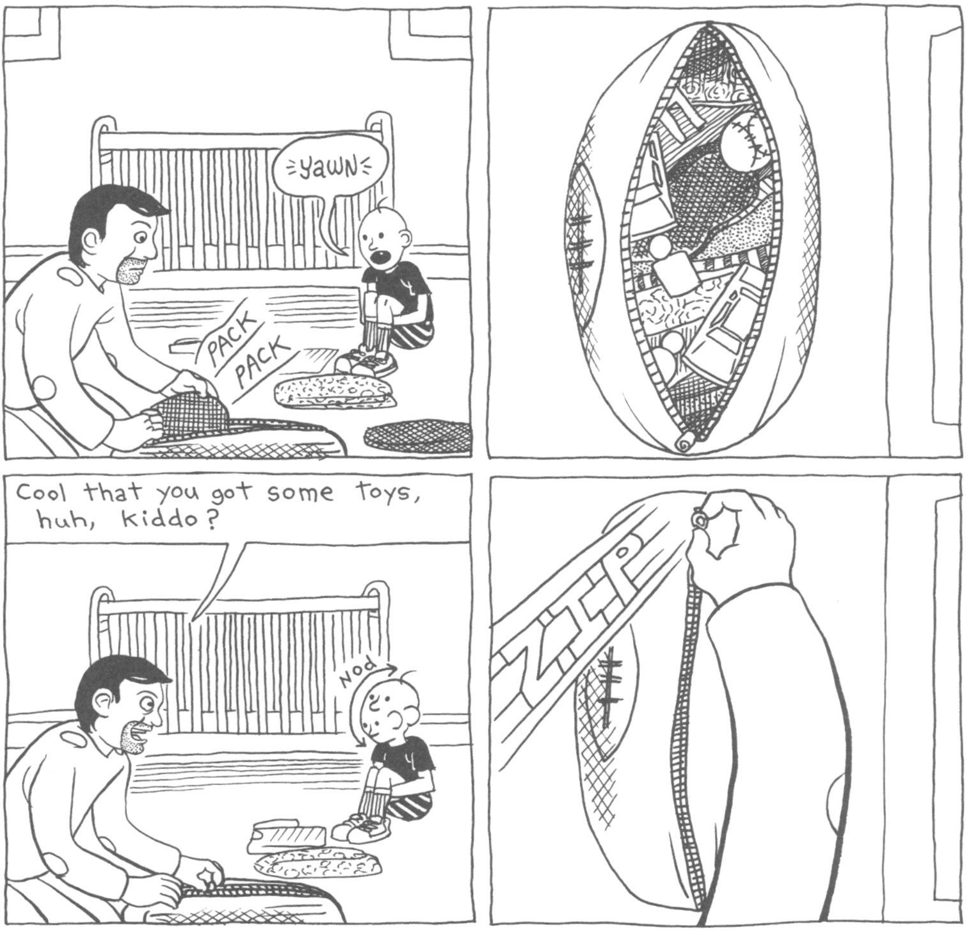
YAWN
PACK
PACK
Cool that you got some toys, huh, kiddo?
Nod
ZIP

Is there anything you want us to fit into the car? Maggie can mail other things.
Maybe something fragile you don't want to risk mailing.
Yes.

It's a model light house. My father made it. He was heavily into making model trains and villages. It's very old and extremely delicate.
When he passed away we auctioned off most of his miniatures, but I wanted to keep this light house—as a symbol of him watching over me, you know?
He spent most of his life in his studio basement, carefully painting a two-inch-tall "stop" sign or arranging microscopic shop window displays. Sort of a recluse.
wow.

KRIP
DROP
SMASH
FUCK!
OMIGOD! OMIGOD!
I'M SO SORRY!
I'M SO SORRY!

oh SHIT, oh SHIT
Don't worry about it.
It was bound to break eventually.
What's done is done. No point in being upset about it.
uh...
Right.

TWIX
MARS
TIC TAC
SHUT

fold
Please don't EVER wear that.
ha.
I'm so glad to finally leave.
Really?

YEAH. Did you actually have fun here?!
Well, maybe not "FUN." Not like circus fun.
But it was nice to see the two living together for the last time. Nice for me.

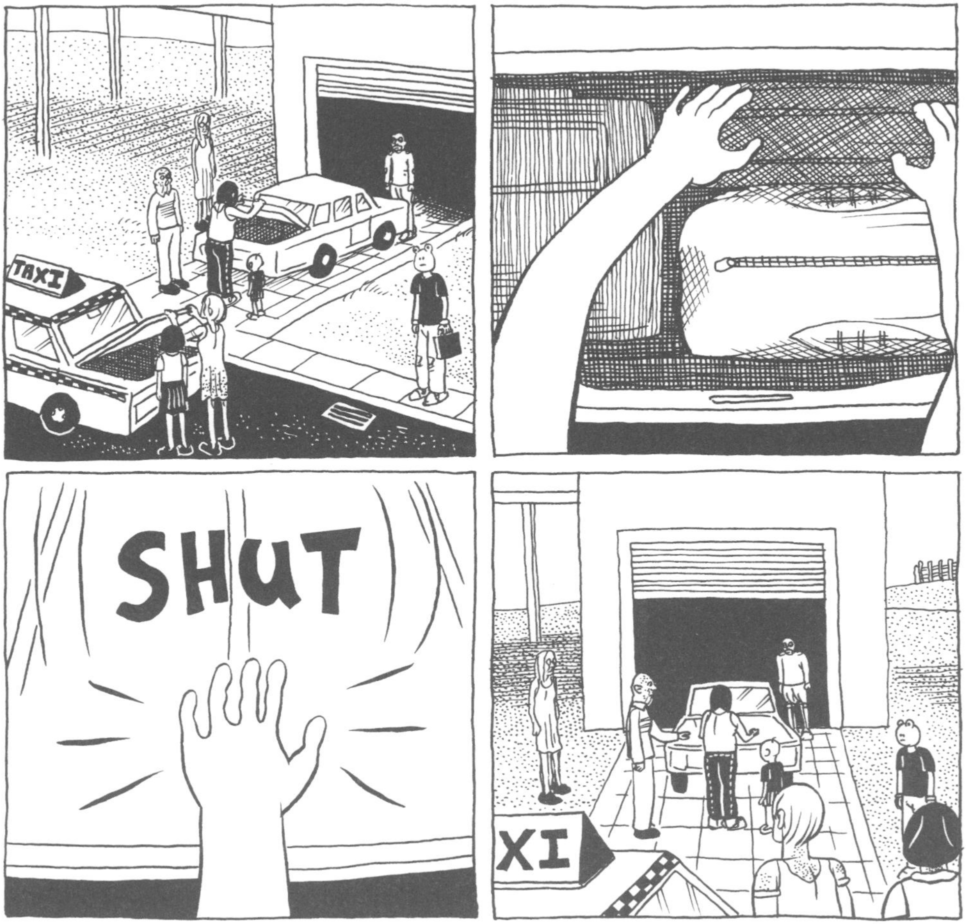

TAXI
SHUT
XI

I'll write you if you write me back.
Okay.
Promise?
Promise.
A "PINKY SWEAR."
She said she'd come.
She said she'd be here.

She couldn't get off work or something, Peter. Don't worry about it. It doesn't mean anything.
SHRUG
Yeah. You're probably right.
I just wanted to see her one last time- before I left.
I had a good time hanging out with you, Grammy.
RUB
I love you, Jill. Take care.

Goodbye, Mom.
Bye, Claire. Visit me anytime.
Wish we'd chilled more, Chill Jill.
'Sokay. I know you got your lady friend. I understand.

You know what a "fist pound" is?
I'm NOT retarded.
That's what everyone keeps telling me.
ha.
Goodbye, Sis. I love you.
HUG
I love you too, Dennis.

Goodbye, Peter.
HUG
←HIT
←HIT
We're brothers, Petey. Forever.
It's true.
RUB

Bye-Bye, Alex.
PAT
PAT
Ha.
Can you say "Goodbye."
Good bai.

wave
Ha.
Bye, Aki.
Bye.

See you later, Aki. I think you're the coolest.
Bye, sweetie.
Alex is second coolest.

I love you, Peter.
Love you, too.

Bye, Uncle Dennis.
ha.
Bye, Jill.
wave
I love you, Mom.

Bye, Dad.
Bye, Peter.
SHAKE
SHAKE

Goodbye, Dad. I love you.
I love you. Thanks for taking care of me yesterday.
No problem.

Say "Bye, Grammy"
Bai GRAAAAMMEEE

Ha Ha Ha Ha Ha.

Goodbye, Aki. Stay strong.
HUG
You too, Maggie.

HUG

I'm really going to miss you.
I'm going to miss you too.

No, you don't understand, I'm going to miss you so much.
I'm going to MISS you LIKE CRAZY.
SWIPE

I'm GOING to miss you MORE.
SNIf

I-
SHAKEY
SHAKEY
I'm going to miss you so much.

SHAKEY
WIPE
I'm really going to miss you.

WIPE
Yeah.

Good bye.

Goodbye.

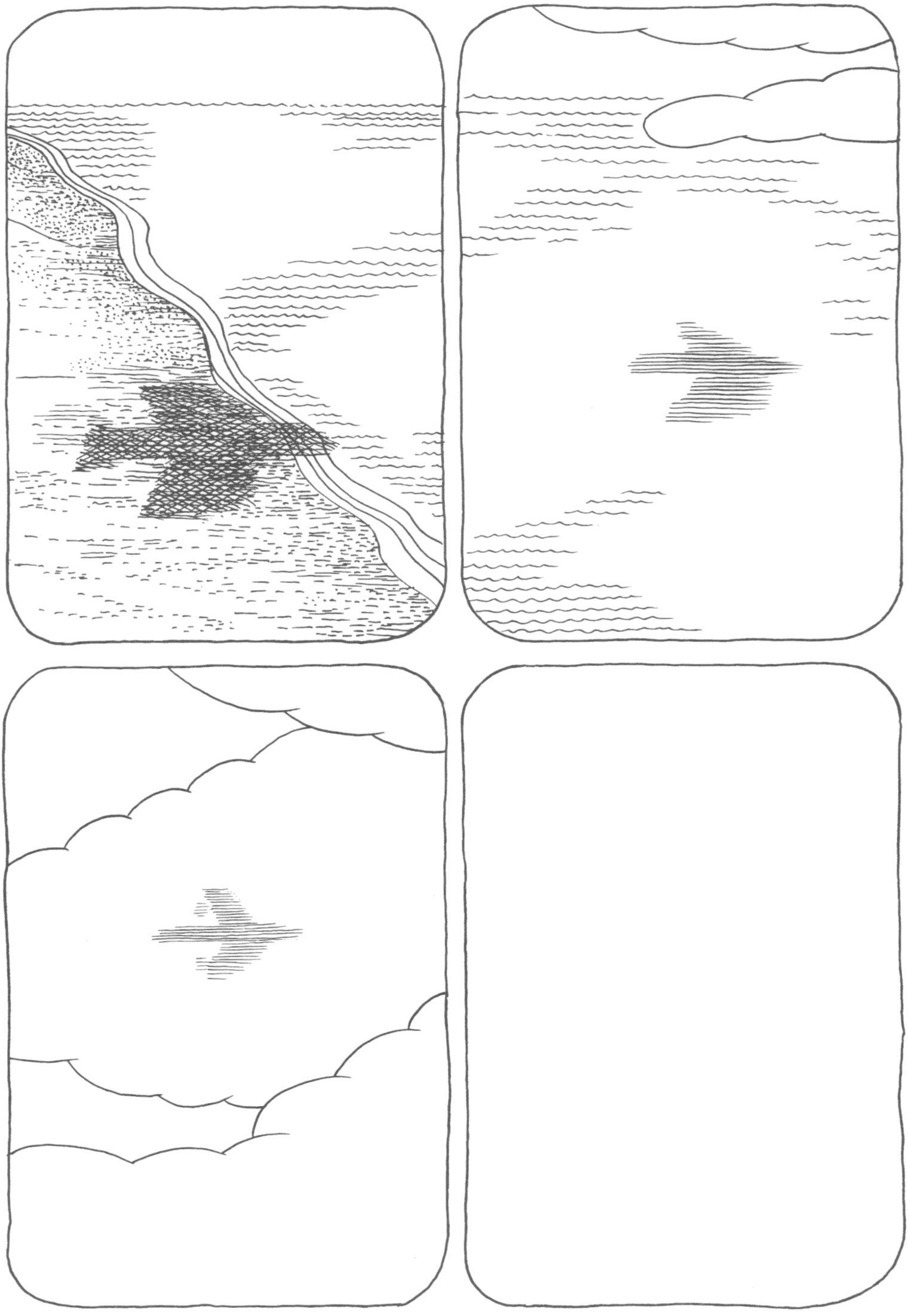

The End

DEDICATED TO:

AND:

THANKS TO:

ALSO: TEAM FANTAGRAPHICS

VISIT: WWW.DASHSHAW.COM FOR MORE COMICS.